9

4750

Nation, ideas, identities.

PRICE: $32.95 (3559/ex)

NATION, IDEAS, IDENTITIES

Essays In Honour of Ramsay Cook

Edited by Michael D. Behiels
and Marcel Martel

OXFORD
UNIVERSITY PRESS

Ramsay Cook with his family, University of Ottawa,
October, 1992.

OXFORD
UNIVERSITY PRESS

70 Wynford Drive, Don Mills, Ontario M3C 1J9
www.oupcan.com

Oxford University Press is a department of the University of Oxford.
It furthers the University's objective of excellence in research, scholarship,
and education by publishing worldwide in

Oxford New York

Athens Auckland Bangkok Bogotá Buenos Aires Calcutta
Cape Town Chennai Dar es Salaam Delhi Florence Hong Kong Istanbul
Karachi Kuala Lumpur Madrid Melbourne Mexico City Mumbai
Nairobi Paris São Paulo Singapore Taipei Tokyo Toronto Warsaw

with associated companies in Berlin Ibadan

Oxford is a trade mark of Oxford University Press
in the UK and in certain other countries

Published in Canada
by Oxford University Press

Canadian Cataloguing in Publication Data

Main entry under title:

Nation, ideas, identities: essays in honour of Ramsay Cook

ISBN 0-19-541463-2 (bound)   ISBN 0-19-541461-6 (pbk.)

1. Canada – History.   I. Cook, Ramsay, 1931– .
II. Behiels, Michael D. (Michael Derek), 1946– .   III. Martel, Marcel, 1965– .

FC51.N37 2000   971   C99-932955-3
F1008.N37 2000

Cover & text design: Tearney McMurtry

1 2 3 4 - 03 02 01 00
This book is printed on permanent (acid-free) paper ∞.
Printed in Canada

Table of Contents

Introduction

> A nation is, in many ways, a product of its ideology. Ideas provide necessary forces in the making of civilizations and express that complex of motives within which a people live, think, and move.[1]

Canada emerged as a mature nation-state, both domestically and internationally, during and especially after the Second World War. At home, as prosperity returned and grim memories of the Great Depression began to fade, a new, as yet largely undefined sense of Canadian identity sought outlets to express itself at all levels of Canadian society. Abroad, the Fascists had been defeated, but the democratic nation-states of the West were still threatened by regimes based on the ideology of communist totalitarianism. In the context of the Cold War and the threat of nuclear annihilation, television and the nascent global village, and rapidly expanding economic ties with the ebullient new superpower of the United States, French- and English-speaking Canadians alike became preoccupied with the survival of their respective cultures, institutions, and ways of life.[2] For the first time in over two decades, Canadians had the luxury of focusing on matters of the mind. What ideas, concepts, values, perceptions, institutions distinguished Canadians from Americans? What innovative perspectives could Canadians offer an increasingly polarized, disoriented, and fragmented world community?

It was in that era of a revitalized Canadian nationalism and internationalism that a young man from Saskatchewan, Ramsay Cook, began his doctoral studies at the University of Toronto, having completed a BA at the University of Manitoba in 1954 and an MA at Queen's University in 1956 (his MA thesis, under the direction of Arthur Lower, was entitled 'Canadian Liberalism in Wartime: A Study of the Defence of Canada Regulations and Some Canadian Attitudes to Civil Liberties in Wartime, 1939–1945'). By then, Canadian historians were turning away from the economic determinism that had characterized the work of Harold Innis, Vernon Fowke, John Dales, and Arthur Lower in their studies on furs, fish, timber, wheat, minerals, hydroelectric power, and railroads.[3]

At the heart of Cook's career would be a preoccupation with the life of the mind: with ideas and ideologies and their impact, for good or ill, on Canadian society. In the 1950s, however, Canadian intellectual history was still in its infancy—unlike its American counterpart, which had gained momentum in the 1930s and by the 1950s was truly beginning to blossom. As had been the case south of the border, interest in Canadian intellectual history emerged simultaneously with a renewed focus on biography among professional Canadian historians, notably Donald Creighton, Maurice Careless, and Elizabeth Wallace. In the words of the American historiographer John Higham, intellectual history and biography 'seemed to delimit the sway of impersonal forces in history. Each opened a dimension for reasserting the capacity of men to choose their destiny.'[4] Human agency, ideas, and ideologies re-emerged as major preoccupations of Canadian historians.

The terrain of the history of ideas was wide open for cultivation. A new generation of Canadian historians beginning with S.F. Wise and Carl Berger ploughed the initial furrows, the first revealing the conservatism and anti-Americanism inherent in Anglo-Protestant political thought in Upper Canada, the second demonstrating how and why British Canadian nationalism during the Laurier and Borden eras represented far more than a pale replica of British imperialism.[5] Ramsay Cook made his first contribution to the development of intellectual/political history with his 1963 book *The Politics of John W. Dafoe and the Free Press,* based on his doctoral dissertation (1960). Focusing not on a traditional politician but on a prairie journalist who, as editor of the *Winnipeg Free Press* from 1901 to 1944, played a highly influential role in Canadian intellectual life, this first book pointed to the dual interest in ideas and the process of nation-building that would characterize Cook's entire career. He followed up this ground-breaking work with two very popular collections of essays analyzing the nationalisms of French- and English-speaking Canada and demonstrating how, why, and in whose interests they fuelled one another. *Canada and the French-Canadian Question* (1966) and *The Maple Leaf Forever: Essays on Nationalism and Politics in Canada* (1971) emerged in the context of Canada's centenary celebrations, Quebec's Not-So-Quiet Revolution, and the arrival of the brash upstart Pierre Elliott Trudeau as prime minister in 1968.

Yet at the same time Cook realized that, as he wrote in 1967, 'the overriding emphasis on nation and national unity has obscured the ways in which Canada is divided into section, class and ethnic group. . . . Our history has been very much the history of the "ruling classes", while labour history has been almost totally ignored. . . . As for ethnic history, it is in its infancy in Canada.'[6] Urging historians to adopt a more pluralistic perspective, he pointed to a new trend in historiography, both in Canada and in the United States. Whereas an earlier generation of American and Canadian historians—the 'myth and symbol' school[7]—had focused on the building of national character and national consensus, in the late 1960s aspiring historians of the baby-boom generation began to abandon that integrative model of national history in favour of a pluralist paradigm reflecting the increasingly fragmented and individualistic nature of their society. The central features of this paradigm shift were, according to Berger, 'a sudden acceleration of research and publication, broadening of the scope and subject matter of history, and destruction of interpretations that had once given meaning to Canadian experience as a whole.'[8]

By the early 1970s, the focus of a new generation of historians of Canada had become intensely particular: studies of local communities, specific social groups and movements committed to advancing specific, often conflicting causes and ways of life, and to promoting competing conceptions of social, economic, political institutions. There was a sense that every identifiable group in society had to appropriate a small part of the past and reinterpret it for themselves. 'What pluralist historians pursued', according to John Higham, 'was not locality for its own sake but rather an authentic social bond, grounded in concrete shared experience. Wherever they found such communities, whatever their shape or size, books sprang up.'[9]

Initially, this turning away from the more traditional intellectual history, centred on big ideas and issues and their integrative force in society, to a more narrow focus was perceived by its practitioners as a liberation: 'the liberation of a new, multitudinous generation from the familiar questions posed by a national synthesis; the liberation, finally, of every special field from any agenda other than its own.'[10] As this community-centred approach brought the fabric of local history—what Cook described in 1967 as Canada's 'limited identities'[11]—to life, our understanding of Canada's historical experience became immeasurably more rich and complex. But there was a cost, for our understanding also became increasingly fragmented and contradictory.

What no one, either in Canada or in the United States, foresaw was the inability of the ever-expanding 'limited identities' approach to present a picture of the nation as a whole.[12] In the 1980s and 1990s, as Canada faced a series of constitutional, political, and economic crises, some pointed to the absence of a consensual national history as part of the reason for the lack of political consensus. Growing numbers of politicians, journalists, educators, and historians have perceived a crisis in Canadian historiography and called for a new integrative synthesis of our national experience.[13] Many other historians, however, do not agree. Given the intensely complex and pluralistic nature of Canada, past and present, they do not consider it necessary—or indeed possible—to construct a traditional consensual national history. In their view, if there is a genuine crisis at all, historians did not create it: they merely reflect a larger problem.[14] Only one thing is certain. This lively debate has not only illuminated several important issues, but renewed interest in Canadian history and its role in society, especially among the general public.

On a sunny and exceptionally warm weekend in October 1997, more than a hundred people met at the University of Ottawa to pay tribute to Ramsay Cook. Friends, colleagues, and former students, they had come from across Canada and beyond to celebrate the career of a distinguished scholar on his retirement from York University, and to wish him well as he embarked on a new phase of his life and work.

For 36 years, as professor of Canadian history first at the University of Toronto and then at York, Ramsay Cook motivated countless students to take up the study of Canada. As a visiting professor at universities in the United States, the former Soviet Union, Japan, India, Austria, and China, he extolled the rewards of

Canadian studies. Indeed, he was one of the best-known ambassadors for Canada in all its diversity, and in both of its official languages.

The author of some fifteen books and editor of eleven, he has also published more than sixty articles in refereed and non-refereed journals. He was editor of the *Canadian Historical Review* from 1963 to 1968 and served as the executive editor of the Canadian Centenary Series between 1983 and 1988. In addition, since 1989 he has been co-editor, first with Jean Hamelin and more recently with Réal Bélanger of Université Laval, of the indispensable *Dictionary of Canadian Biography*. Over the years his accomplishments have been acknowledged with many awards, among them the Order of Canada, the Royal Society of Canada's Tyrrell Medal, the Governor General's Literary Award for Non-Fiction (for *The Regenerators: Social Criticism in Late Victorian English Canada*, his seminal study of Canada's social gospellers), and, twice, the President's Medal of the University of Western Ontario for best scholarly article. The recipient of honorary doctorates from the universities of Ottawa and Windsor, he has been named to Japan's Order of the Sacred Treasure, and most recently, was appointed a member of the York University Founders Society.

In 1969, when Cook joined York's fledgling graduate history program, he could hardly imagine the impact that his work with doctoral students—thirty-seven in all—would have on Canadian historiography and the historical profession in Canada. As a doctoral supervisor, he encouraged his students to take the study of ideas and ideologies seriously and to apply their energies in new fields of research. Some have tackled the study of ideas directly, focusing on individuals, specific groups or movements in Canadian society. Other have explored the role of ideas within and between the multiple areas of social history: labour, religion, education, women, and the family.

As part of the Ottawa tribute, twenty-one of Cook's former doctoral students presented papers—fifteen of which were revised for this volume—reflecting his scholarly interests over four decades. Indeed, these essays bear witness to both the continuity and the change that Canadian historiography has undergone since the 1960s. The continuity can be found in the centrality of ideas and ideologies to human discourse and interaction—a theme that underlies, to a lesser or greater degree, all of them. The change is evident in their authors' focus on specific communities and movements, and their concern with identity.

This collection reflects the democratization and maturation that have taken place in the Canadian society as well as in Canadian historiography. The five broad areas in which the essays are grouped represent five of Cook's own primary interests: ideas, culture, nationalism, women's history, and Native issues. Readers seeking a single theme to the papers, beyond their broad focus on ideas, ideologies, communities, and identities, will be sorely disappointed. On the other hand, we hope that most will see these essays as affirmations of where Canadian historiography now stands. Most will also, we believe, find that the broad scope of the collection constitutes a powerful illustration of Cook's wide-ranging scholarly interests, and of his belief that historians should be as much generalists as specialists.

With one exception, these papers are not directly concerned with Cook himself. When, eventually, a detailed study of Canadian historiography for the post-1960s era is undertaken, no doubt Cook's contribution will be central to it. In the interim, these essays tell us much about Ramsay Cook, not only by the way they mirror his scholarly preoccupation with the centrality of ideas and ideologies but by the ways they go beyond it. His firm belief in well-founded and well-argued ideas permeates the work of his students. It has enabled nearly all of them to avoid the problematic forms of relativism and excessive factionalism that have come to dominate much of postmodernist historiography.[15]

This collection begins with four essays about ideas and the individuals—intellectual entrepreneurs, in a sense—who promoted them in the public domain. First, Brian Fraser examines the work and thought of James A. Macdonald, the Presbyterian minister who was editor of the Toronto *Globe* from 1903 to 1915. As such, Macdonald was exceptionally well situated to propagate the progressive values of evangelicalism—a subject central to Cook's *The Regenerators*. In that book, Cook argued that the Protestant leaders of Macdonald's era who, like him, promoted 'social regeneration' unwittingly contributed to the secularization of religion and society through their emphasis on building the City of God on Earth. By contrast, according to Fraser, Macdonald and the theologians he helped to popularize did not dilute their theological message; rather, they remained convinced that societal reform began and ended with individual reform.

Next, Michiel Horn addresses an issue of particular significance for university professors: academic freedom. His paper—drawn from his recent book on the same subject[16]—traces the evolution of that principle and its application in Canada's English-speaking universities from 1919 to 1964. Initially, the task of formulating and (reluctantly) applying policies regarding academic freedom fell to senior university administrators. Even in the early 1950s, the issue was of little concern for the newly formed Canadian Association of University Teachers. In 1958, however, the dismissal of Harry Crowe from United College brought the question of academic freedom to the fore.

The third paper in this section sheds new light on the political economist and cultural historian Harold Innis. Douglas Francis argues that there is a single leitmotif linking Innis's wide-ranging scholarly interests, from the cod fisheries of the Grand Banks to the North American fur trade, from the building of the transcontinental Canadian Pacific Railroad to the way communications media have shaped the ideas and values underpinning Western civilization. This theme is power: how it has been obtained, how it has been used, and how it has shifted within and between nation-states, empires, and civilizations. In effect, Francis suggests, in his focus on the mechanics of power Innis was a precursor of Michel Foucault.

Finally, Patrice Dutil takes as his subject Ramsay Cook himself and his role as a public intellectual in the 1960s. In that period, when Cook was just beginning his career at the University of Toronto, Diefenbaker and Pearson were sparring in the

House of Commons over bilingualism, health and social policy, Canadian-American relations, and disarmament, not to mention a new Canadian flag, and in Quebec the francophone members of the political class were beginning to demand more power for the province, couched in terms of 'special' or 'associate state' status. Cook was an astute observer and acerbic commentator on all these developments, especially those occurring in Quebec. From the very outset, Cook criticized all 'special' status constitutional options as mere way stations to independence, as ambiguous concepts serving the interests primarily of Quebec's new francophone middle class.[17]

On these topics and many others, Cook wrote commentaries for *The Globe and Mail* and *Le Devoir* and journals such as *The Canadian Forum* and *Queen's Quarterly*. His goal, as Dutil describes it, was to counter the simplistic rhetoric of politicians with rational discussion based on sound principles and empirical evidence, and to rouse Canada's lethargic, relatively immature political, intellectual, and journalistic communities to a serious rethinking of the country's problems. Cook's hopes for a higher level of public discourse were elevated in 1968, when a brilliant francophone intellectual named Trudeau agreed to run for the Liberal leadership, and they rose again a few months later, when Trudeau became prime minister. At that point Cook cut back on his extra-academic activities, moving to York University and devoting most of his energies to teaching and historical research and writing. Thereafter he would make only occasional forays into the public domain. Although Dutil concludes that Cook was one of Canada's last public intellectuals, the prominent roles played by several of his students in the constitutional debates of the 1980s and 1990s suggest that the breed may not be extinct after all.

Around the time that he was first venturing into public affairs, in the early 1960s, Cook 'awaken[ed] to the emotions that paint on canvas stirred in me'.[18] Beginning, 'rather timidly', to explore the Toronto galleries, he discovered the poignant and spiritually uplifting work of William Kurelek, in which he recognized his own prairie roots. Later he would write a number of articles on Canadian art and artists, including Cornelius Krieghoff and the Group of Seven, as well as introductions to books on Kurelek and Tim Zuck.[19] His fascination with Canadian art led Cook to reflect on the importance of culture in nation-building, especially the development of national identity. As he wrote in 1974: 'The evolution of Canadian landscape painting, and particularly its culmination in the work of the Group of Seven . . . may be seen as part of a lengthy process whereby Canada has increasingly become a North-American nation'.[20]

Part Two presents four essays exploring specific manifestations of culture in Canada. First, Norman Knowles examines the influence of evangelical Protestantism on working-class life, culture, and activism in the mining communities of the Crowsnest Pass in the early years of the twentieth century. Focusing on the efforts of the clergy to reform and Canadianize their rough-and-tumble flocks, and the responses they received, he suggests that the relations between the largely middle-class clergy, the workers themselves, and their organizations were more complex than most historians, either of the church or of labour, have thought.

Next, Peter Rider traces the history of a controversial aspect of traditional Newfoundland culture and its place in Newfoundlanders' collective identity. For more than a century participation in the annual seal hunt was crucial to the island's fragile economy, and the valiant image of the swiler was a fundamental part of its popular culture. Since the 1960s, however, the anti-sealing movement has drawn worldwide attention to the cruelty of the hunt, while technological advances have reduced considerably the challenges faced by sealers. As a result, Rider suggests, seals themselves are in far less danger of extinction than are the hunt and the heroic identity associated with it.

Mass communications have played a central role in the consolidation of the nation-state. What newspapers were for the nineteenth century, radio was for the first half of the twentieth. As part of her research into the beginnings of Canada's public broadcasting system, Mary Vipond explores the radio listeners of the early 1930s—who they were and how they responded to the programming provided by the private commercial broadcasters—through an imaginative reading of two magazines aimed at Canadian radio listeners. At the same time she reveals how the broadcasters used those magazines to construct the kind of audience they wanted: one wary of the state-funded model of public broadcasting.

The final essay in this section addresses the transformation of museums and art galleries into sites where issues of major social, political, and moral significance are contested. In her examination of five major Canadian art exhibitions, from the 1920s to the 1990s, Ann Davis argues that the curators of such institutions can no longer be seen as objective, politically neutral purveyors of 'pure', 'discovered' knowledge. Just as the modern nation-state has been transformed—some would say undermined—by the emergence of multiple identities reflecting a wide range of new societal cleavages, so the traditional operations of the museum are being forced to give way to a more democratic and interactive process in which artists and the viewing public together create meaning.

Part Three focuses on a subject that has been of central concern to Ramsay Cook from the beginning of his career. Caught up in the turbulent politics of the Diefenbaker and Pearson era, he worked to bridge the gap between French and English Canada that became increasingly apparent with Quebec's 'Quiet Revolution' of the 1960s. Cook's answer to the question 'What does Quebec want?' was based on his study of the historical development of French Canada, particularly the majority francophone community of Quebec. Believing that 'the difficulties between French- and English-speaking Canadians would be less bewildering if each partner knew a little more of the other's history',[21] he explored the historical relationship between the two communities in his books *Canada and the French Canadian Question* (1966), *Le sphinx parle français: Un Canadien anglais s'interroge sur le problème québécois* (1966), and *The Maple Leaf Forever: Essays on Nationalism and Politics in Canada* (1971). Although he did not expect historical understanding to solve anything, he was reasonably assured that with it 'the problems would be more easily identified.'[22] At the heart of Canada's difficulties, he came to believe, were two fundamental issues: the survival of national communities in a homogenizing, globalizing world, and the search for greater equality between minority and majority communities.

In Cook's view, the most powerful ideological force shaping and reshaping Canada has been—and remains—nationalism. As he put it in 1966, 'we have had too much, not too little, nationalism'; in fact, 'our various nationalisms are the chief threat to the peace and survival of Canada.'[23] This is not to say that all forms of nationalism are inherently wrong. Rather, as Cook demonstrated in his 1986 essay collection *Canada, Quebec and the Uses of Nationalism*, it is the use and abuse of nationalism by political, military, economic, cultural, and intellectual leaders that underlie many of the problems facing all modern, pluralistic nation-states.

The first contribution in this section is a provocative essay by Phyllis Senese in which she invites readers to reconsider the widely accepted distinction between 'good' civic nationalism and 'bad' ethnic nationalism. Not only have both ideologies been disruptive and divisive for Canada, she argues, but both are rooted in the same racist impulse to exclude 'the Other'. Senese concludes her scathing critique of nationalism, in all its forms, by urging us to imagine what Canada might have become without it. Yet nationalism is inherent in all societies. The question historians must ask and answer is who controls and uses it, and in whose interests.

Among the interests that nationalism generally does not further are those of minority groups. In Canada, a painful illustration is the socio-economic, cultural, linguistic, and political situation of French Canadians outside Quebec before 1982. In 1978 Cook wrote the introduction to *The Heirs of Lord Durham: The Francophones Outside Quebec Speak Out: Manifesto of a Vanishing People*—the English version of a book originally published as *Les Héritiers de Lord Durham*. Reminding readers of the long history of British-Canadian efforts to impose Durham's policy of assimilation on French-speaking minorities outside Quebec, Cook pleaded in favour of tolerance, understanding, and respect for minority rights: 'If Canada is ever to become a place where French and English Canadians can live in full harmony, recognizing the validity of each other's culture, then Lord Durham will have to become a genuinely historical figure.'[24]

Years earlier, in his essay collection *Canada and the French-Canadian Question*, Cook had suggested several ways of promoting that harmony. Among them was the proposal that the right to education in the language of their parents, whether French or English, be guaranteed to children throughout the country. Such a policy, he believed, would indicate to French Canadians that English-speakers appreciated the importance and the value of the French language and culture, and enable them to live anywhere in Canada without foregoing a French-language education for their children.[25]

Minority-language and education rights were finally entrenched in the 1982

Charter of Rights and Freedoms. Ironically, however, even as English-speaking Canadians were gradually coming to understand and accept the principles of offi-cial bilingualism, Québécois neo-nationalists were rejecting the 'two nations' view of Canada in favour of a new political and territorial model consisting of two asso-ciated nation-states, Quebec and Canada. Marcel Martel's essay traces the process whereby these neo-nationalist (and, eventually, independentist) intellectuals worked to legitimize their new model in the minds of Québécois—a process that included the abandonment of francophone minorities elsewhere in Canada. Pointing to the high assimilation rates in those communities as evidence that they were doomed to disappear, the new Quebec nationalists argued that the only hope of survival for the French language and culture lay in the emerging nation-state of Quebec.

Part Four reflects the transformation in historical writing that began in the mid-1960s. Perhaps the most vivid example of this transformation was the rapid expan-sion of women's history, which started with a re-evaluation of the first-wave women's movement that had led to the granting of universal suffrage at the end of the First World War and then quickly branched off into a vast array of fields.[26] Indeed, in the 1970s an observant Cook remarked that the '"new feminism" has had at least one important result for students of Canadian history: it has revived inter-est in the history of Canadian women.'[27] The two papers in this section illustrate the continuing development of women's history. Cook's appeal for more attention to both labour and women's history is reflected in the work of Gail Cuthbert Brandt, who combines the two in her study of female workers in the Quebec textile industry in the late nineteenth and early twentieth centuries. At that time factory owners, labour leaders, and social commentators alike generally perceived women as a cheap, sober, and docile source of industrial labour that was resistant to union organization—a perception that many historians have used to explain the relative absence of labour militancy among female workers. Brandt challenges this view. Analyzing the attitudes, behaviour, family situations, and work contexts of Quebec textile workers, she finds a lively culture of 'passive resistance' in which young female workers exercised considerable agency, if not in the same manner or for the same reasons that male workers engaged in militant job action.

In the following paper, Ruth Compton Brouwer analyzes the professional rela-tionship between two women, one Korean and one Canadian. Soon after the end of the Second World War, Dr Florence Murray, a medical missionary, was invited by Helen Kim, the president of Ewha Womans University in Seoul, to assist in the establishment of a medical training program there. But Murray's association with Ewha was short-lived. Whereas an orthodox postcolonial interpretation of this episode would focus on the familiar themes of racism and resistance, Brouwer's analysis suggests that the clash between Murray and Kim had more to do with the two women's conflicting priorities.

The collection concludes with three papers on a topic that has captured Ramsay Cook's interest in recent years: Native issues. Although his scholarly interest in this area is relatively new, its origins reflect a life-long passion: for natural history and, especially, bird-watching. Invited to give the seventh Robarts Lecture at York University in October 1992, Cook confessed that his research on the natural history of early Canada began with his ambition 'to compile an historical bird watcher's guide, a chronology of the discovery of the birds of Canada'. That ambition was dashed when he learned that such a study had already been published by W.F. Ganong in 1910.[28] Nevertheless, his efforts to rediscover the rich diversity of the pre-contact environment led him to examine the evidence provided by the Europeans who came to North America in the sixteenth and seventeenth centuries, a project that he found required 'filtering the story through the cultural lenses that [Europeans] wore'.[29]

Similar filtering is reflected in J.A. Brandão's study of how four important nineteenth-century French-Canadian historians described and explained the relations between the settlers of New France and the Iroquois in the seventeenth century. The interpretations of these men differed significantly from those of Francis Parkman, the American historian whose 'beaver wars' theory has long been the dominant influence in English-language studies of this period. Ironically, more recent generations of francophone historians have also come to favour Parkman's views over those of the nineteenth-century French Canadians. The explanation for this shift, Brandão maintains, resides in the ideological, sociological, and political transformation of Quebec after 1940.

In the following paper, James Pitsula breaks new ground by analyzing the voting behaviour of Saskatchewan's Native people after they were granted the right to vote in provincial elections in 1960. Moving beyond the conventional focus on turnout rates, he examines voting patterns and their relationship to the policies of the parties vying for Indian votes. Pitsula's innovative extension of political history to Saskatchewan's rapidly expanding and urbanizing Indian communities will undoubtedly encourage more attention to this important aspect of Canadian politics.

The concluding essay, by Michael Behiels, traces the dispute over the competing ideologies of feminism, liberalism, and Aboriginal nationalism that divided Native communities during the decade following the adoption of the Charter of Rights and Freedoms. On one side was the Native Women's Association of Canada, which combined an Aboriginal feminism based on traditional culture with a contemporary Charter rights philosophy. On the other was an organization that the NWAC saw as male-dominated: the Assembly of First Nations, which promoted an increasingly militant collectivist pan-Canadian Aboriginal nationalism. Convinced that Aboriginal self-government must be achieved simultaneously with gender rights or not at all, the NWAC's leaders campaigned vigorously against the Aboriginal constitutional package—granting Aboriginal collective rights priority over Charter rights—that the AFN had succeeded in embedding within the Charlottetown Consensus Report. Since the Charlottetown agreement was defeated in the national referendum of October 1992, the NWAC has continued its struggle to ensure that Aboriginal women's rights are protected within any new treaties and self-government agreements. As Behiels points out, however, the arguments of the Aboriginal nationalists are powerful, and the NWAC has not yet succeeded in undermining them.

Appendix A presents a selected bibliography of Ramsay Cook's scholarly work. This list includes books, edited collections, and scholarly articles in books and periodicals. (Although, as Dutil's article makes clear, Cook did not limit his writing to academic circles—he published letters to the editor, opinion pieces, and a great many essays in newspapers, most often the *Globe and Mail* and *Le Devoir*, as well as journals such as *The Canadian Forum* and the *Queen's Quarterly*—readers will have to ferret these out on their own, since no list is currently available.) Appendix B lists the Ph.D. theses that Cook supervised, and Appendix C presents the contributors to this volume.

Many people have contributed to the development of this book. First, the co-editors wish to thank all those whose participation turned the Ottawa tribute into a truly warm and memorable occasion. We are especially indebted to Molly Ungar, one of Cook's last two doctoral students, for her organizing skills and especially for the excellent commemorative programme that she prepared. We also extend our thanks to the Governor General, His Excellency Roméo LeBlanc; Marcel Hamelin, Rector of the University of Ottawa; Marc Lalonde, a longtime friend of Cook's; and professors Kazuo Kimura, Blair Neatby, Viv Nelles, Jack Saywell, and for their very kind words in Ramsay Cook's honour.

Above all, we wish to express our gratitude to the contributors without whom this book would not exist. We greatly appreciate their patience and cooperation in the revision process. The final product is a reflection of their dedication to the muse of history. We also wish to express our sincere thanks and gratitude to David Staines and Robert Major, Dean and Associate Dean (Research) of the Faculty of Arts of the University of Ottawa, who assisted in the financing of the conference as well as the publication of this volume. We commend Oxford University Press, especially its College Editor, Ric Kitowski, for undertaking the publication of this tribute—a rare event these days in Canadian academic publishing. All royalties produced by sales of the book will go to the Ramsay Cook Scholarship Fund at York University. We are grateful to the staff at Oxford University Press, in particular Phyllis Wilson and Laura Macleod, for their patience, cooperation, and support in bringing this project to fruition. Finally, we would like to thank Sally Livingston, our copy-editor, for her help in coordinating the style of all the contributors and for her queries, which helped to clarify issues that we historians often take for granted. Any and all flaws that remain are the responsibility of the contributors and co-editors. We hope that readers enjoy these essays in honour of one of Canada's most important historians of the post-war era.

MICHAEL D. BEHIELS AND MARCEL MARTEL

NOTES

1. Russel B. Nye, *This Almost Chosen People: Essays in the History of American Ideas* (Toronto, 1966), ix.

2. Paul Litt, *The Muses, the Masses, and the Massey Commission* (Toronto, 1992).

3. See Carl Berger, *The Writing of Canadian History: Aspects of English-Canadian Historical Writing since 1900*, 2nd edn (Toronto, 1986). Berger nevertheless notes that a keen interest in Marxist oriented political economy emerged in the 1960s; see 272, 319.

4. John Higham, *History: Professional Scholarship in America*, updated paperback edition (Baltimore and London, 1989), 205.

5. Doug Owram, 'Writing About Ideas', in *Writing About Canada: A Handbook for Modern Canadian History*, ed. John Shultz (Toronto, 1990), 56–9.

6. Ramsay Cook, 'Canadian Historical Writing', in *Scholarship in Canada 1967: Achievement and Outlook*, ed. R.H. Hubbard (Toronto, 1968), 80.

7. Owram, 'Writing About Ideas', 51.

8. Berger, *The Writing of Canadian History*, 259.

9. Higham, *History*, 263.

10. Ibid., 242.

11. Cook, 'Canadian Historical Writing'. J.M.S. Careless popularized the term with his article '"Limited Identities" in Canada', *Canadian Historical Review* L (March 1969), 1–10.

12. Higham's revealing chapter on this paradigm shift is entitled 'A Time of Troubles', *History*, 235–64.

13. The most articulate expression of this crisis in Canadian historiography and the historical profession can be found in J.L. Granatstein's *Who Killed Canadian History?* (Toronto, 1998). Emeritus professor of history at York University, Granatstein is currently Director of the Canadian War Museum.

14. For a lengthy critique of Granatstein's argument see Brian McKillop, 'Who Killed Canadian History? A View from the Trenches', *Canadian Historical Review* 80, 2 (June 1999), 269–99.

15. For a detailed analysis of the re-emergence of various forms of relativism in the last third of the twentieth century, consult Peter Novick's *That Noble Dream: The "Objectivity Question" and the American Historical Profession* (Cambridge, 1988).

16. Michiel Horn, *Academic Freedom in Canada: A History* (Toronto, 1999).

17. His most recent critique of these ambiguous concepts can be found in 'Civic Nations and Distinct Societies', in Cook, *Canada, Quebec and the Uses of Nationalism*, 2nd edition revised (Toronto, 1995), 237–46.

18. Cook, 'Introduction' to Brian Dedora, *With WK in the Workshop: A Memoir of William Kurelek* (Stratford, Ont., 1989), 9.

19. Cook, 'The Outsider as Insider: Cornelius Krieghoff's Art of Describing', in *Krieghoff: Images of Canada*, ed. Dennis Reid (Vancouver, 1999); Cook, *Tim Zuck: Paintings and Drawings* (Canmore, Alta, 1997).

20. Cook, 'Landscape Painting and National Sentiment in Canada', *Historical Reflections/Réflexions historiques* 1, 2 (Winter/Hiver 1974), 282.

21. Cook, *Canada and the French-Canadian Question* (Toronto, 1966), 1.

22. Ibid.

23. Ibid., 4.

24. 'Introduction', La Fédération des Francophones hors Québec/The Federation of Francophones outside Quebec, *The Heirs of Lord Durham: The Francophones outside Quebec Speak Out: Manifesto of a Vanishing People* (Don Mills, Ont., 1978), 15.

25. Cook, *Canada and the French-Canadian Question*, 3.

26. Veronica Strong-Boag, 'Writing About Women', in *Writing About Canada*; see also Deborah Gorham's chapter on the birth of women's history in English-Canadian history departments in *Creating Historical Memory: English-Canadian Women and the Work of History*, ed. Beverly Boutilier and Alison Prentice (Vancouver, 1997).

27. Cook, 'Introduction' to *The Woman Suffrage Movement in Canada*, by Catherine L. Cleverdon (Toronto, 2nd edn 1974 [1950]), ix.

28. Cook, *1492 and All That: Making a Garden out of a Wilderness* (North York, Ont., 1993), 9–19; William Francis Ganong, 'The Identity of Plants and Animals mentioned by the Early Voyagers to Eastern Canada and Newfoundland' (Ottawa, 1910).

29. Cook, introduction to *The Voyages of Jacques Cartier* (Toronto, 1993), xv.

IDEAS

James A. Macdonald and the Theology of the Regenerators, 1890-1914

BRIAN J. FRASER

No clergyman of his generation in Canada had regular access to a larger audience than the Presbyterian James A. Macdonald. The reasons are clear. Macdonald was the only clergyman in Canada who controlled a major daily newspaper: the most powerful agency of public opinion formation in the country.[1] Robert Jaffray appointed Macdonald managing editor of the Toronto *Globe* in 1903. Macdonald held the position until 1915, when a furore in the Toronto press over his continuing support for the liberal pacifist movement[2] in the United States, and growing tensions over his absentee style of management, led to his resignation. The absenteeism—'days, and sometimes weeks' according to his obituary in *The Globe*[3]—can be traced to Macdonald's use of another major vehicle for public opinion formation in the early twentieth century: the public speaker's podium. He was a popular orator, especially in demand by Christian men's organizations in Canada and the United States. The *Outlook*, a religious journal founded by the American Social Gospel advocate Lyman Abbott, stated that Macdonald 'met more people, appeared on more public platforms, and spoke before larger audiences outside his country than any other Canadian of his day'.[4]

Macdonald's contemporaries confirmed his influence as a writer and speaker. W.T. Ellis, an American journalist and missions promoter, observed that he had built a reputation for honesty and fearlessness as an editor because of the libel suits brought against him by 'politicians of the old school'.[5] Robert Falconer, whom Macdonald had been instrumental in bringing to the University of Toronto as president in 1906,[6] found his writing 'arresting' and noted that Macdonald 'thought in brilliant imagery and his Celtic fire shone out whenever he was stirred, which made his utterance very powerful'.[7] Alfred Gandier, principal of Knox College in Toronto, equated Macdonald's oratory with that of Gladstone and Lloyd George.[8] Adam Shortt, professor of political science at Queen's, attributed his strengths to 'the wide range of his sympathies, his clear and rapid appreciation of ultimate issues and the things that count, his enthusiasm for the great objects of human interest and the inspiration of great movements'. He was a strong personality and inspiring voice, Shortt concluded, advocating 'spiritual, social, and political integrity and progress'.[9]

Through the two agencies of mass communication in the early twentieth century—press and podium—Macdonald propagated a particular Christian world view shaped by the interaction between his vision for the new Canadian nation and the progressive orthodoxy of a particular school of Scottish Presbyterian theologians in the late nineteenth century. This essay comprises two parts. First, it sketches Macdonald's formation as a public figure in the late nineteenth century, his understanding of his calling, and his theological world view—all crucial elements in shaping his 'determining personality'.[10] Second, it outlines Macdonald's understanding of theological anthropology—his view of Christian character and citizenship—and sets it in the context of the current debates among Canadian historians on Christianity and secularity in Victorian Canada. In so doing, it pursues a line of inquiry suggested by the Canadian historian Robert Choquette in a recent *festschrift* for the American Martin E. Marty: 'now that the theories and findings of the social sciences (of cultural anthropology and social history in particular) have found their way into the . . . historiography of Canadian religion, perhaps it is time for the historians of Canadian religion to become literate in theology.'[11]

I MACDONALD'S FORMATION, SELF-UNDERSTANDING, AND WORLD VIEW

Several influences had conspired to shape James A. Macondald's sense of vocation by the time he assumed editorial control of *The Globe* in 1903. He was raised in a Highland Scots Free Church community in East Williams in southwestern Ontario that was uncompromising in its loyalty to the principles of God's sovereignty and humanity's moral obligations. He was educated in university and theological college by a generation of teachers, among whom George Paxton Young and William Caven were the most influential, who encouraged a greater independence of mind and a broader conceptualization of Christian faith and discipleship than had their predecessors. From the late 1880s throughout the 1890s, while editing the *Knox College Monthly*, ministering in St Thomas, Ontario, and editing the monthly *Westminster* and the weekly *Presbyterian*, Macdonald immersed himself in the writings of a new generation of Scottish theologians who sought to reformulate the faith and reform the church in ways they thought would ensure the continuing influence of Christianity in the modern world, especially in the urban centres where new sources of social power were concentrated.[12] He also followed, with admiring interest, the 'new journalism' of W.T. Stead in the *Pall Mall Gazette* and the *Review of Reviews*.[13] Macdonald emerged from these formative years with a view of himself as a prophet of providential progress.[14]

In Macdonald, Robert Jaffray hired someone whose record in journalism and public affairs suggested that he would exercise a judicious partisanship, assessing the policies and activities of the Liberal Party on the basis of its own best ideals. Macdonald's Liberal loyalties and ideals were fashioned initially by George Brown's *Globe*, along with stories of the battles for personal and political integrity waged by Highland ancestors who served as models of 'intelligence and moral character and personal power'.[15] His understanding of the ideals for which Liberalism should stand was further shaped by William Caven, Principal of Knox College during Macdonald's years there as a student, editor, and librarian. Caven was a close friend and sometime adviser to Ontario Premier Oliver Mowat. All three—Caven, Mowat, and Macdonald—belonged to the same congregation in Toronto, St James Square Presbyterian Church. As Macdonald remembered Caven's ideals, they consisted of dedication to responsible government, protection of civil liberties and ecclesiastical equality, insistence on the ethical element in politics, business, and professional life, and resistance to 'all artificial barriers placed in the way of world-wide trade'.[16] A purified or 'new' Liberalism became for Macdonald the best political means available for Christianizing civilization.[17]

Jaffray also found in Macdonald an aggressive and successful entrepreneur in the field of journalism and publishing. Macdonald had built the student journal at Toronto's Knox College into a major religious monthly during the 1880s and had consolidated a number of Presbyterian newspapers in Ontario into a major national religious weekly and monthly during the 1890s. In addition, he was a major figure in the Westminster Company, which published not only the weekly and monthly papers but also novels by such popular writers as Ralph Connor (the Revd C.W. Gordon), Marian Keith (Mary Esther MacGregor), and the Revd Robert E. Knowles, as well as popular devotional and religious books by prominent Canadian Christian scholars.[18]

In all these respects Macdonald seemed ideally suited to carry on the tradition established by Canadian editors and publishers in the late nineteenth century, in which the daily press served as 'a social authority' advocating the moral values of the urban middle classes.[19] In the early issues of *The Westminster*, the monthly religious journal that Macdonald founded in 1896, he paid particular attention to the growing influence of the press in Canadian society. 'The morality of a whole generation,' wrote Macdonald in his second issue, 'is, to a large degree, in the keeping of those who make the literature that enters the home.'[20] In the same issue he published an article by James S. Brierley, then president of the Canadian Press Association, in which Brierley described his vision for Canadian journalism: if 'the thoroughness and trustworthiness of the journalism of the British Isles' and 'the enterprise and brightness of that of the States' were to be grafted onto Canadian newspapers that remained deeply rooted in their own national life, then Canadian journalism would become a 'synonym throughout the world for courage, independence, and public spirit'.[21] As he left the Westminster Company for *The Globe*, Macdonald assured his readers that he was resolved 'to yield neither to the practical selfishness of the few, nor to the loud-voiced clamor of the many, but to stand steadfastly for those things which to me seem first and best in the life of Canada'.[22]

Macdonald's views on what seemed 'first and best' for Canada were very much in keeping with those held by the leading representatives of the Protestant urban middle classes of his day. As an editor through his editorials, articles, book reviews, and choice of feature writers, and as an orator through his sermons and speeches, often given to crowds of several thousand and later widely circulated in books, he sought to defend and propagate the progressive vision of Christian culture that dominated the Anglo-American Protestant world view of his generation.[23] He had no aspirations to be an original thinker. His goal was to promulgate what he considered the best of the progressive Christian thought of his generation in as persuasive and influential a manner as he could, and to the widest possible audience.

The construction of Canadian citizenship that emerged from Macdonald's Christian theology and world view was based on the core conviction that all things were created by and belonged to God. This conviction expressed itself in two foundational attitudes: first, an unshakeable confidence that God exercised providential control over the evolution of civilization; and second, a persistent conviction that human beings were duty-bound to obey the Christian command of love and measure up to the Christian standard of service. God's love and humanity's service were the two great principles that guided the progress of civilization. The more conscious humanity became of God's love in the life, death, and resurrection of Jesus Christ, and the more faithfully it followed Christ's example of service, the more surely civilization would evolve according to the divine purposes. In this progressive narrative, God was gradually guiding the world towards a future in which the best of what humans had accomplished would be blended together into 'the dream of the ages . . . a kingdom in which they are greatest who serve and they are kingliest who love'.[24] This vision would be accomplished through the infusion of the mind and spirit of Jesus Christ into every dimension of human life. Macdonald's vocation, the determining passion of his character, was to persuade the Canadian people, and especially those flowers of Canadian manhood who held positions of power and influence in the country, to live lives of love and service.

II MACDONALD'S CONSTRUCTION OF CHRISTIAN CHARACTER AND CITIZENSHIP

In a speech in 1909, Macdonald summarized his strategy for the social regeneration of Canada. The setting was Toronto's Massey Hall, filled with 3,500 members of Ontario's Protestant social, political, and business élites. The occasion was Macdonald's address to Canada's Missionary Congress, a men's conference organized by the Canadian Council of the Laymen's Missionary Movement.[25] The president of the Congress and the Council was Newton W. Rowell, leader of the Liberal Party in Ontario and a close friend of Macdonald's. Speaking on 'The Christianization of Our Civilization', Macdonald insisted that there was only one way to infuse 'the life and spirit and motive of Jesus' into our civilization:

> It is the positive way. It is the vita way. Men who themselves are thrilled by the Christ-life and inspired by the Christ-spirit and constrained by the Christ-motive must go into the social life and into the business life and into the political life, and into all other avenues of thought and life, and there live out the Christ-idea. . . .

What would happen if the four thousand men of this Congress went back to the offices, and shops, and market-places, and pulpits of Canada charged with love as the motive of their lives and with a passion for service to others as the inspiration of their ambition? What would happen? There would be something doing for Canada. Changed men would change conditions for themselves and for others.[26]

Behind the apparent naïveté of Macdonald's rhetoric lay a theological anthropology that commanded the loyalty of many of the best Christian minds in the Anglo-American world of the late nineteenth and early twentieth centuries.

Macdonald's theology, as it emerged from the theological controversies he followed with such keen interest in the 1880s and 1890s, belonged to the movement known among his contemporaries as 'Back to Christ'. Scottish theologian William Morgan, professor of systematic theology and apologetics at Queen's Theological College in Kingston from 1912 until 1928, described its nature and significance in James Hastings' *Dictionary of Christ and the Gospels*, a widely used reference work published simultaneously in Great Britain and the United States in 1908. Morgan considered the development of the movement to be 'the most important theological event' of the last half of the nineteenth century.[27] As he described it, this school of theology placed its primary emphasis on the Christ of history rather than the Christ of dogma. Attention shifted from the speculative constructions of doctrines and creeds to the concrete realities and example of the historical person Jesus the Christ.

Morgan attributed the movement to three chief causes. The first was the application of historical criticism to the Gospel narratives, which reconstructed the contemporary background, gave people a better understanding of Christ's teachings, and enabled people to see the man and his work in their human context. The second cause was a growing dissatisfaction with the traditional statements of Christianity. Scholars sought to go behind the creeds and rediscover the source of their religion in relationships rather than ideas. Older formulations of the faith were seen to have been grounded in ideas originating in Hellenistic philosophy or Roman legal theory. The modern mind called for an interpretation of religion that paid primary attention to relationships, ethics, and psychology. The third cause was a new sense of the importance of great personalities as factors in historical change and progress. The shift away from the 'exaggerated intellectualism' that had previously dominated theology was due, in Morgan's analysis, to German Romanticism as spread in the writings of Carlyle, Emerson, and Goethe.

Modern theologians, in Morgan's analysis, recognized more and more

. . . that the elevation and enrichment of man's spiritual life have been effected far less by the movements and instincts of the mass, or by the introduction and development of ideas, than by the appearance on the stage of history of great creative personalities. Such personalities are fountains of life for many succeeding generations. In no province is their importance so marked as in that of religion. And Christ is the supreme personality. It was the impression produced by His personality, even more than the new ideas he taught, that created the Christian Church.[28]

Of the movement's three wings, Macdonald identified with the one that departed least from traditional orthodoxy.[29] Morgan described it as 'Christo-centric':

> For Christo-centric as for traditional theology, the elements of cardinal importance in Christ's consciousness and history are the miraculous elements. The facts that give to His inner life its character are His moral perfection and consciousness of sinlessness, His assertion of a unique knowledge of God, and of a Sonship different in kind from that possible to His disciples, His assertion of His Messiahship and pre-existence, His demand for absolute devotion to His Person, His claim to a superhuman authority in forgiving sins and dealing with OT institutions and laws, His claim to be the Saviour of the world, the arbiter of human destiny, the final Judge. Similarly His outer life receives its character from the Virgin-birth, the Miracles (interpreted in the strict sense), and, above all, from the bodily resurrection. The historical Christ is the transcendent and miraculous Christ, the Christ who was conscious of a superhuman dignity, and who was declared by the resurrection from the dead to be the Son of God with power (Rom. 1:4).[30]

In this school of thought, Christ's work and self-consciousness as recorded in the Gospel narratives constitute the historical facts underlying Christian doctrines. At the same time, its chief advocates, identified by Morgan as A.M. Fairbairn, James Denney, and David Forrest, insisted that the traditional orthodox doctrines remained crucial for Christian discipleship, since they served to explain and interpret the historical facts as God intended them to be understood. Interestingly, both Denney and Forrest were offered chairs at Knox College in Toronto in the early 1900s.[31]

Macdonald found such Christo-centrism best represented in Canada by T. B. Kilpatrick, professor of systematic theology at Knox College between 1905 and 1925, when he entered the United Church of Canada and moved to Emmanuel College. While teaching in Winnipeg, Kilpatrick was brought to Toronto by Knox College in the fall of 1900 to deliver a series of lectures on the person of Christ at the University of Toronto. Macdonald wrote a long feature on the event for *The Presbyterian*. Kilpatrick, he reported, found more in the life of Jesus than the average representative of the 'Back to Christ' school because, as a philosopher, he was 'not content merely with the facts, but considers also the implications of those facts, and those implications must ultimately rest . . . in a Being who stood in an absolutely unique relation to God'. Although Kilpatrick advocated traditional orthodoxy, he based it 'not on an irrelevant philosophy, but upon a critical examination of the documents themselves, and filled the somewhat arid wastes of an older speculation with the ethical richness of the newer view'. The creeds were seen to be the 'providentially guided and legitimate outcome' of Jesus' life and teachings rather than the product of a misguided metaphysic. Macdonald assessed the lectures as 'conservative in the noblest sense, conserving all that is best in the old and the new'. Kilpatrick, he concluded, had a masterly grasp of the topic and presented his insights with moral earnestness and a devout and reverent spirit.[32]

The most extensive exposition of Kilpatrick's theological anthropology in relation to the person and work of Christ is found in two articles he wrote for Hastings' *Dictionary of Christ and the Gospels*, one on the character of Christ and the other on the incarnation.[33] He insisted that the traditional theological affirmations about Christ were essential to a full understanding of the ethical example Christ presented, and that both doctrine and ethics had to be seen as grounded in a relationship with him:

> If the Divinity of Christ is not to be a dead dogma, soon to be abandoned by the minds which it perplexes and the religious instincts which it depresses; if it is to be a living conviction, sustaining faith and unifying thought, it must not be treated as though it hung, gaunt and naked, in a metaphysical vacuum; it must be regarded and expounded in its organic connexion with the character of which it is the necessary presupposition, and from which it derives its intellectual cogency.[34]

Christ's character, as portrayed by Kilpatrick, was marked by obedience and trust in his love for God and lowliness, considerateness, compassion, and forgiveness in his love for humans. The key virtues Kilpatrick identified in Christ were faithfulness, courage, patience, calmness, and self-sacrifice. Kilpatrick was convinced that such a portrait of Christ was the answer to his generation's religious and spiritual searching to satisfy 'the age-long need of the human spirit for personal union with God'.[35]

The most concise manifesto of Macdonald's own construction of Christian character and citizenship, and the theological anthropology that shaped it, can be found in the first issue of the monthly *Westminster*, the paper for the home he launched in June 1896. Canada's greatest need, in Macdonald's view, was for statesmen in every walk of life with the strength, integrity, and sincerity of personal character to gain others' trust in the fight against the forces conspiring to destroy the home, and thus the country: ignorance, worldliness, and vice.[36] Macdonald set out to regenerate Canada by confronting these sources of personal and social decay with the answers provided by 'the Man of Nazareth'. Ignorance was to be 'beat back . . . by the positiveness of truth', worldliness to be 'overcome . . . by the better life of the spirit', and vice to be 'cast out . . . by the expulsive power of holiness'.[37] Macdonald was confident that earnest effort, inspired and infused by Christian faith, could 'make life upon earth a diviner thing'. Yet his Christian faith retained its theological rigour. 'No false liberalism must be allowed to loosen our hold on the great Christian verities. No shallow rhetoric must move us away from faith in the Almighty Saviour. Standing true to the doctrine of the Cross, we open our eyes to the new light that breaks on the vision of those who believe in a living Christ.'[38]

Macdonald found the liberalism of the American social gospellers Charles Sheldon and Lyman Abbott unacceptable, especially in their rejection of Paul's emphasis on the cross. He considered the theological reformulations of James Denney and P.T. Forsyth, with their emphasis on the gravity of sin and the objective reality of the Atonement, far more convincing. For Macdonald, Christ's propitiation for sin on the cross, as taught by Paul, was the core of the Gospel's regenerating power in both personal and social life. 'Back to Christ' for Macdonald meant 'Back to Calvary'.[39]

Macdonald believed that Canada was experiencing a return of confidence in the late 1890s. The 'substantial harmony' achieved under the new Laurier government provided the foundation upon which Canada could now begin to fulfil the destiny marked out for it by the God of the nations. 'To do something to bring one's country up to a higher plane among the nations of the world, to make one's countrymen honourable and clean in public service as well as in private life, to help forward the day of "better manners, purer laws", is not only the truest service the patriot can render, but makes for the answering of the prayer: "Thy kingdom come"'.[40]

Such patriotism and devotion required citizens and leaders with the spirit of the Old Testament prophets. The church's leaders had to become pioneers of Canada's providential progress for the sake of the world's regeneration. The prophetic Christian must remain true to the message of Christ that no matter of human interest lay outside the purview of God's concern and therefore of the Christian faith. There was no real distinction, in Macdonald's mind, between the sacred and the secular. He called Christians to active social engagement in 'every question that has a bearing on morality or religion, every question of which right or wrong may be predicated, every question making appeal in its settlement to conscience, honour, and the sense of right'.[41]

For Macdonald, it was one's state of mind and spirit that determined one's life, and those who provided reading material for Canadians were pivotal in shaping personal and social character. In introducing the new paper's book review section, he recalled the English poet Robert Southey's advice on assessing the value of reading material. If it induced dangerous thinking; made one impatient under the control of others; encouraged one to relax in that self-control without which both the laws of God and humanity indicate that there can be no virtue, and consequently no happiness; reduced admiration and reverence for the good; lessened love for others and country; appealed to evil propensities, such as pride, vanity, or selfishness; defiled the imagination; or disturbed the God-given sense of right and wrong, then 'Christ-like men' should have nothing to do with it: they would certainly not find Macdonald reviewing such literature in the columns of *The Westminster*.[42]

Like most men of his generation, Macdonald believed that women had a different, though equally important, role to play in the advance of Christian civilization. His social construction of the distinctions between men and women was heavily influenced by his assumptions about the role played by home and family in social progress. He frequently expressed concern about the increasing numbers of women seeking to go into business and professional life at the expense of their families. The proper place for women to exercise their faith, self-sacrifice, reverence, and humility was in the home, where they might nurture the strength, steadiness, and endurance of the nation.[43] It was the social responsibility of men to take the virtues of Christian character they had learned in the private sphere of the home into the public realms of business, politics, religion, and social reform.

CONCLUSION

There is nothing particularly original in Macdonald's construction of Canadian manhood. Its roots lay in the code of evangelical manliness that permeated the bourgeois Victorian culture in which he was raised. Self-control, hard work, and independence were combined with compassion, self-sacrifice, and social obligation to construct an ideal of manhood that emphasized usefulness to society.[44] Nevertheless, Macdonald's vigorous defence and propagation of this code, through the influential means of communication he used so effectively, raises questions about one of the assumptions commonly held among such scholars of manliness as David Newsome. In his 1961 book *Godliness and Good Learning*, Newsome identified a shift in Victorian ideals of manliness from the earlier evangelical ideals of earnestness, selflessness, and integrity to later ideals of stoicism, hardiness, and endurance. This shift, in Newsome's view, created an ethos of 'neo-Spartan' and 'social Darwinian' virility in the late Victorian era.[45]

Macdonald's theological anthropology, however, was rooted in the new interpretation of the great Christian verities and values found among the younger generation of Scottish Protestant theologians in the 1880s and 1890s. The prime exemplar of evangelical manliness among this group, in Macdonald's judgement, was Henry Drummond, a professor of natural theology at Free Church College, Glasgow, who was a close colleague of the evangelist Dwight L. Moody in work among university men. For many among Macdonald's generation of church leaders, Drummond provided a credible answer to Darwin's theories by arguing that the underlying principle of evolution was not the survival of the fittest, but rather maternal self-sacrifice for the well-being of future generations.[46] Macdonald, along with many others of his generation, consciously resisted the shift to the harsher and more combative ideal of manhood described by Newsome. Instead they advocated what we might call a 'social Drummondism' as the primary means of providential progress.

Macdonald's significance lay in the central role he played in relaying these views to a mass North American audience. His position at *The Globe* ensured that his construction of Christian character and citizenship would be featured in the editorials and reporting of one of Canada's leading dailies. His prominence as an orator, especially among Christian men's organizations in the early twentieth century, ensured a certain level of personal contact and influence with significant numbers in the English-speaking North Atlantic triangle. The publication of those addresses in printed form spread his views even more widely.

Many questions remain to be addressed. What was the impact of Macdonald's views? Further assessment is required of his influence in the various circles of public life in which he was active, especially with the respect to the use these groups sought to make of the mass media.

A more thorough study of Macdonald's life will also contribute to our understanding of the process of secularization in Canada. His insistence on the centrality of the cross, together with the emphasis that he and Kilpatrick put on maintaining the historical, ethical, and metaphysical dimensions of Christology, raise questions about whether they really belong among the group that Ramsay Cook has identified as Christian collaborators with secularization. In his latest reiteration of the secularization thesis, in a review of Nancy Christie and Michael Gauvreau's *A Full-Orbed Christianity*, Cook maintains that one of the touchstones of serious Protestant theology is the centrality of the cross. Cook, and David Marshall after him, find this theme missing or significantly weakened in the theology of Protestant leaders and clergy in late-Victorian English Canada. In Macdonald and the theologians he popularized, however, this was clearly not the case. Their importance among the Protestant regenerators of the early twentieth century points to the need, readily acknowledged by Cook himself, for further examination of some of the theological assumptions and historical generalizations on which the secularization thesis rests.[47]

Macdonald was convinced that he stood at the beginning of an era in which the promise of providential progress would be realized through social agencies whose evolution had been guided by the hand of God and whose effectiveness had been proven. In retrospect, we know he stood at the end of the reign of Victorian Protestant bourgeois idealism. The First World War, with its devastating impact on those ideals, broke Macdonald in mind, spirit, and body. In his declining years, between his departure from *The Globe* in 1915 and his death in 1923, he witnessed the spread at once of disillusionment with the ideals of character and citizenship he had promoted and of distrust in the agencies upon which he and many of his contemporaries had built their vision of providential progress. It was a sad conclusion to a noble life.

NOTES

1. While little attention has been paid to the significance of the development of the Christian press in Canada, major studies have dealt with the phenomenon in the United States. See Nathan O. Hatch, *The Democratization of American Christianity* (New Haven, 1989) and David P. Nord, *The Evangelical Origins of Mass Media in America, 1815–1835* (Columbia, SC, 1984). For surveys and analyses of the development of the popular press in Canada, see Douglas Fetherling, *The Rise of the Canadian Newspaper* (Toronto, 1990) and Paul Rutherford, *A Victorian Authority: The Daily Press in Late Nineteenth-Century Canada* (Toronto, 1982).

2. On Macdonald's place in this movement, see Thomas P. Socknat, *Witness Against War: Pacifism in Canada, 1900–1945* (Toronto, 1987), 39–40, 45–46, and Donald M.

Page, 'Canada as the Exponent of North American Idealism', *American Review of Canadian Studies* 3, 2 (Autumn 1973), 33–5.

3. *Globe* (15 May 1923).

4. Cited in Brian J. Fraser, 'The Pursuit of Providential Progress: The Journalism and Oratory of James A. Macdonald', in *Studies in Canadian Evangelical Renewal: Essays in Honour of Ian S. Rennie*, ed. Kevin Quast and John Vissers (Toronto, 1996), 156.

5. W.T. Ellis, 'Macdonald: Citizen of the World', *Presbyterian* (4 Sept. 1913).

6. James G. Greenlee, *Sir Robert Falconer: A Biography* (Toronto, 1988), 115–18.

7. Quoted in *Globe* (15 May 1923).

8. Quoted in ibid.

9. Adam Shortt, 'A Personality in Journalism', *Canadian Magazine* 29, 6 (October 1907), 524.

10. The phrase comes from Wallace Stevens and is quoted in Leon Edel, *Writing Lives: Principia Biographica* (New York, 1984), 17.

11. Robert Choquette, 'Christ and Culture during "Canada's Century"', in *New Dimensions in American Religious History: Essays in Honor of Martin E. Marty*, ed. Jay P. Dolan and James P. Wind (Grand Rapids, 1993), 102.

12. For greater detail on Macdonald's formation, see Fraser, 'Pursuit of Providential Progress', 156–9.

13. For Macdonald's friendship with and assessment of W. T. Stead, see James A. Macdonald, 'William T. Stead and his Peace Message', *World Peace Foundation Pamphlet Series* 6, 3 (July 1912), 1–14.

14. For Macdonald's understanding of the role of the prophet, see Fraser, 'Pursuit of Providential Progress', 156–7.

15. James A. Macdonald, *What a Newspaper Man Saw in Britain* (Toronto, 1909), 18. This pamphlet is a good example of Macdonald's rhetorical use of his Highland heritage.

16. James A. Macdonald, 'A Biographical Sketch', in William Caven, *Christ's Teaching Concerning the Last Things and Other Papers* (Toronto, 1908), xxiv–xxv.

17. Augustus Bridle, *Sons of Canada: Short Studies of Characteristic Canadians* (Toronto, 1916), 278.

18. For an analysis of the development of the popular Christian press and publishing in the Anglo-American world, see Leonard Sweet, 'Communication and Change in American Religious History: A Historiographical Probe', in *Communication and Change in American Religious History* (Grand Rapids, 1993), 1–90.

19. Rutherford, *A Victorian Authority*, 230–3.

20. *Westminster* 1, 2 (July 1896), 56.

21. Ibid., 67.

22. *Presbyterian* (10 Jan. 1903).

23. My own understanding of the Presbyterian interpretation of this culture can be traced in the previously cited works dealing with Macdonald as well as Brian J. Fraser, *Church, College, and Clergy: A History of Theological Education at Knox College, Toronto, 1844–1994* (Montreal and Kingston, 1995), 91–139, and 'Christianizing the Social Order: T.B. Kilpatrick's Theological Vision of the United Church of Canada',

Toronto Journal of Theology 12, 2 (Fall 1996), 189–200.

24. James A. Macdonald, 'The Relation of the Church to the Social and Industrial Situation', *Pre-Assembly Congress of the Presbyterian Church in Canada* (Toronto, 1913), 214.

25. The ideals and goals of the Laymen's Missionary Movement can be found throughout the addresses at the congress. See especially S. B. Capen, 'The Significance of the Laymen's Missionary Movement', *Canada's Missionary Congress* (Toronto, 1909), 126–33.

26. James A. Macdonald, 'The Christianization of Our Civilization', *Canada's Missionary Congress*, 119.

27. William Morgan, 'Back to Christ', *A Dictionary of Christ and the Gospels*, James Hastings, ed. (New York, 1908), 161.

28. Morgan, 'Back to Christ', 163.

29. Ibid., 164–7. The second wing of the movement, associated with Unitarian thinkers, emphasized the religion of Christ, and the third wing, identified with Ritschl, focused on the ethical example of the life of Christ.

30. Ibid., 164.

31. Fraser, *Church, College, and Clergy*, 103, 126.

32. *Presbyterian* (17 Nov. 1900).

33. T.B. Kilpatrick, 'Character of Christ', and 'Incarnation', in Hastings, ed., *Dictionary of Christ*, 281–97 and 796–813.

34. Kilpatrick, 'Character of Christ', 282.

35. Kilpatrick, 'Incarnation', 813.

36. *Westminster* 1, 1 (June 1896), 6.

37. Ibid., 5.

38. Ibid.

39. *Westminster* (9 Nov. 1901). See also Macdonald's report on an address by D. E. Forrest at Knox College the next week in *Westminster* (16 Nov. 1901).

40. *Westminster* (6 Nov. 1897).

41. *Westminster* 1, 1 (June 1896), 6.

42. Ibid., 36.

43. Brian J. Fraser, *The Social Uplifters: Presbyterian Progressives and the Social Gospel in Canada, 1875–1915* (Waterloo, 1988), 101–2.

44. The manual of male self-help that earned Macdonald's most enthusiastic praise in the pages of the *Westminster* was Newell Dwight Hillis, *A Man's Value to Society: Studies in Self-Culture and Character* (New York, 1896). See *Westminster* 2, 1 (January 1897), 38, and 2, 2 (February 1897), 84. Hillis was minister of Central Church in Chicago.

45. David Newsome, *Godliness and Good Learning: Four Studies on a Victorian Ideal* (London, 1961). For a review of recent literature on nineteenth-century constructions of manliness, see John Tosh, 'What Should Historians do with Masculinity? Reflections on Nineteenth-century Britain', *History Workshop Journal* 38 (1994), 179–202.

46. For Macdonald's assessment of Drummond's significance, see *Westminster* 2, 4 (April 1897), 170–2. Some scholars have dismissed Drummond as a 'crank' and his views as 'bizarre'. See, for example, Boyd Hilton, *The Age of Atonement: The Influence of Evangelicalism and Social and Economic Thought, 1785–1865* (Oxford, 1988), 303, 331–2. A more thorough and perceptive analysis of his views and impact, however, is found in James R. Moore, 'Evangelicals and Evolution: Henry Drummond, Herbert Spencer, and the Naturalisation of the Spiritual World', *Scottish Journal of Theology* 38, 3 (September 1985), 383–417.

47. See Ramsay Cook, 'Salvation, Sociology and Secularism', *Literary Review of Canada* 6, 1 (1997), 10–12. For a review of the issues and literature in the secularization debate in Canadian history, see John G. Stackhouse, 'Who is to Say? Defining and Discerning Secularization in Canadian Christianity', Brian Clarke, 'Secularizing the Faith: A Comment', and David B. Marshall, ' "Temples of an Incrusted Faith" ': An Inquiry into the Question of Secularization From Within', in *Papers 1994*, Canadian Society of Church History, 193–221.

The Concept of Academic Freedom in English Canada, 1919–1964

Michiel Horn

Academic freedom is a slippery concept. This is particularly the case in Canada, where the concept has three separate though not unrelated origins. One is the nineteenth-century German idea of *Lehrfreiheit*, the freedom of scholars to teach and carry out research, as it was adapted in the American research university. The second is the British principle and practice of academic free speech. The third is the notion that professors are not simply the employees of lay boards—that they *are* the university, either by themselves or in conjunction with administrators, students, even alumni. My purpose in this paper is to trace briefly the development of the concept of academic freedom in this country from the Great War to the mid-1960s.

In 1915, when the founders of the American Association of University Professors (AAUP) published their statement on academic freedom and academic tenure, they focused on the rights and freedoms of professors as teachers and scholars. Their rights as citizens did not fit easily into a model of academic freedom in which the idea of communities of competence was central. Although professors were supposed to be able to express themselves freely on matters in which they were professionally competent, their freedom of expression on other matters was problematic. Should professors be able to claim the protection afforded by the concept of academic freedom when speaking about subjects outside their areas of competence?

The AAUP maintained that it was inappropriate to use academic sanctions in dealing with the behaviour of professors as citizens. At the same time the association urged responsibility on professors and enjoined them not in any way to link their personal opinions to their institutions.

The British position was more permissive. Well into the twentieth century, the cult of research did not have the following in British universities that it did in Germany and the research universities of the United States. If research loomed less large in Britain, though, a tradition of political outspokenness and involvement existed that must have struck German and even some American academics as unusual.[1] Probably this was a function of the high degree of security enjoyed by academics in Britain, where life tenure (during good behaviour) was common.

Canadians who had studied in Britain, along with British academic emigrants to Canada, were in the forefront of those who asserted the right of professors to state their opinions freely.

They did so as individuals, for in Canada no organization analogous to the AAUP took form until 1951. When, in 1916, the University of Toronto's James Mavor aroused the wrath of Premier William Hearst with a well-publicized attack on the forerunner of Ontario Hydro, he had no organization to turn to for defence. (Fortunately for him, he did have powerful friends, among them the chairman of the board of governors, Sir Edmund Walker.) Asked by President Sir Robert Falconer to respond to Hearst's complaints, Mavor defended both his own free-dom of expression and the university as a place of liberty: 'A University is funda-mentally a group of scholars who meet for free discussion. If the Members of the University are to be subjected to the dictation of the Government as to what they may or may not discuss, the University may as well at once strike its name from the roll of Universities.'[2]

This was not a public statement. In fact, although during the early decades of this century a few Canadian academics defended academic freedom and professo-rial free speech, they usually did so in private. The task of explicating academic freedom in public fell to the executive heads of institutions.

The first effort of this kind was made by Principal Bruce Taylor of Queen's University. In an address to the graduating class of the University of Manitoba in May 1919, he discussed the effects of financial dependence on Canada's universi-ties. Predicting that the state would take an ever-increasing part in financing higher education, he asked whether this entitled it 'to control the type of teaching in the University[.] Will the administration of a University . . . depend upon the whims of the Legislature? Will men of independence accept positions when the tenure may be insecure?' What if 'large interests' hinted to a government 'that the removal of a certain professor might be advisable, that his maintenance is closing the money bags. . . ?' Would pressure be applied on the university? If so, how would it react?

Although Taylor was alert to the need for autonomy, the freedom he valued was that of professors to teach and publish as they pleased. He feared the caution that would ensue if administrators discouraged the expression of 'inconvenient and original' ideas in order to please those who provided the money. 'It is the business of the University teacher to stimulate thought and set forth . . . the new point of view. . . . Far better the crank with brains than the unexceptionable nobody.'

Taylor set limits to freedom. The need to live within a community and to 'play fair' with students meant that professors could not do or say whatever they wanted. They had to use common sense. All the same, the university's main task was 'not to give instruction but to awaken and to inspire. A University is not a superior kind of technical school; it is not in the first place a device for preparing a man to make a living. It is a challenge to the mind.'[3]

Taylor's silence about the direct threat that individual benefactors might pose in a private university is surprising, for in 1917–18 he had faced down an attempt by a few wealthy men to dislodge the political scientist O.D. Skelton for his opposition to conscription for overseas military service. It was left to another president to discuss the threat posed to academic freedom by powerful private interests.

Speaking at the spring convocation of his own institution in June 1919, E.E. Braithwaite of Western University in London, Ont., stated that wealthy men had put 'undue pressure' on professors in the United States, and that similar pressure was not unknown in Canada. This undermined 'the spirit of independence in . . . which alone the best work can be accomplished'. Scientists should not be judged by the financial benefit of their research to the college or the community, he continued; teachers should not be judged by the number of students their courses attracted. And 'if the Professor of Political Economy must make his conclusions conform to the ideas of the capitalists who may occupy a seat on his governing board, the usefulness of the institution is seriously impaired.'

Braithwaite was for free inquiry and discussion. Governing boards should remember that 'it is the faculty that make the institution, and not the trustees.' The worth of an educational institution had nothing to do with the latter body. But he saw problems with faculty self-government. Many professors shirked their duty to think independently and to challenge their students to do likewise, and would not oppose infringements of academic freedom if those who applied pressure were powerful enough. 'We must retain the ideal freedom to think independently,' he concluded, sounding less than sanguine.[4]

Taylor and Braithwaite presided over small, private institutions. By contrast, Sir Robert Falconer was the leading figure in Canadian higher education. More than the addresses of the others, moreover, his speech on academic freedom was shaped by local circumstances. Among them were Premier Hearst's reaction to James Mavor's articles and, more recently, evidence that the government led by Premier E.C. Drury did not appreciate what the 1906 University Act had accomplished in freeing the institution from political interference. As well, a wealthy member of Toronto's board of governors, Reuben Wells Leonard, had been questioning whether the political economist Robert M. MacIver should be teaching at the university.[5]

Speaking on 14 February 1922, Falconer began by praising 'the freedom which gives its distinction to the ancient English academic life'. Academic freedom, he said, 'is best understood as a phase of the general course of people's development in liberty of thought'. The nineteenth century had been one of bitter scientific, religious, and social controversy, and universities had become 'centres of fierce discussion'. The new knowledge had triumphed, however, and with it academic freedom. Universities, Falconer said, existed for teaching 'ascertained knowledge and truth', for training professionals, and for the investigation and extension of new truth. Freedom to investigate and evaluate new truth was of the essence.

The academic freedom enjoyed by professors was 'one of the most sacred privileges of a university', whose stature could be measured by the degree of security its staff enjoyed in their work. However, professors should not be merely destructive of old truth; they should also be constructive, providing information 'which will be intelligible to [students] and will equip them to fulfil their duties as citizens and as searchers for the truth'.

Academic freedom also brought restraints. The professor was 'the servant of the nation' in matters of the intellect. Like a judge or a civil servant, he was not free to do as ordinary citizens might. It was 'expedient that a professor in a State University should take no active share in party-politics'. Any discussion of 'burning political questions' might harm his institution: 'a government might well without giving any reason easily show its displeasure in such a way as to affect adversely the fortunes of the institution and the financial position of many guiltless and wiser colleagues.'

Finally, Falconer discussed the role of governing boards. One of their duties was to secure 'the best possible persons available for the professorial office'. The views of such people might differ from those held by the governors, but the latter were unwise either to challenge a professor's competence or to deny 'that there is a place in the University for his type of thought'. It was better 'to tolerate an erratic or even provocative teacher' than to disturb the normal functioning of the university.[6]

During the next few decades, other executive heads occasionally addressed the issue of academic freedom, usually in the course of an annual report. Even those who headed the private universities sometimes echoed the message of prudence that Falconer had delivered. If a professor ventured into the larger world, Principal W.H. Fyfe of Queen's wrote in his *Report* for 1933–4, 'it behoves him to remember what astonishing weight that world attaches to a professorial pronouncement.' Caution was required. 'A University teacher should certainly be clever; he needs also to be wise; and of the factors of wisdom not the least are self-restraint and kindliness and patience.'[7]

In his report for 1934–5, the University of Toronto's President H.J. Cody stated that the professor enjoyed 'a full measure of academic freedom' but owed a duty to the university 'to use that freedom with wisdom and good taste': specifically, 'to approach his work not as a propagandist or partisan, but as a seeker for the whole truth, with open mind, fair judgment, and regard for all the facts'.[8] As well, because the public often assumed that statements by faculty members implicated the university, they should realize that the legal right to express their personal or professional views did not imply a moral right to do so. The argument, not surprisingly, resembled Falconer's in 1922.

In spite of several controversies over issues of academic freedom in the early 1930s, interest in the subject was not overwhelming. When the president of Dalhousie University, Carleton Stanley, tried in 1937 to organize a session on academic freedom at the annual meeting of the National Conference of Canadian Universities, he was unable to find anyone to address the issue. In the end, Stanley himself said a few words in his presidential address: in the light of recent events in Europe, notably in Nazi Germany, an interest in academic freedom was 'nothing but the instinct for self-preservation. No freedom, no university.' [9]

Within a year of the outbreak of war three universities witnessed attacks on academic free speech. Two speeches—at McGill in November 1939 by the historian E.R. Adair, and at the University of Toronto in August 1940 by the historian Frank Underhill (delivered at Lake Couchiching)—raised the question whether professors had the right to address issue of current political interest if what they said offended influential elements in the community. [10] At the University of Alberta in April 1940, the biochemist George Hunter made some classroom comments that an RCMP informer described as 'anti-Christian and pro-Marxism'. [11] This matter was handled quietly, with Hunter undertaking to break the habit of using his last lecture of term to link his subject to the larger world. The Adair and Underhill cases were highly public, but did not lead to any statement on academic freedom in wartime.

McGill's Principal Cyril James drafted some remarks on the subject for his 1942–3 annual report. It was 'vitally important,' he wrote, to maintain 'academic freedom of speech' while recognizing that the federal government had restricted the limits of legality for the duration of the war. As well, 'all things that are lawful are not expedient': faculty should 'use wisdom and judgment above average'. To express 'mere hypotheses' or opinions that disturbed public morale was 'highly undesirable'. [12] On reflection, however, he decided not to discuss the topic.

Various Canadians referred to the principle of academic freedom during the 1940s, but exactly what they meant by it was rarely clear. In the two best-known academic-freedom controversies of the decade, Underhill's near-dismissal in 1941 and George Hunter's dismissal in 1949, Presidents H.J. Cody (in Underhill's case) and Robert Newton (in Hunter's) stated that academic freedom was not at issue. [13]

One might have expected the Canadian Association of University Teachers (CAUT), which took shape in 1950–1, to express itself on academic freedom, but in its early years the organization generally limited itself to the bread-and-butter issues of salaries and benefits, especially pensions. Brecht said it well, if cynically: 'Erst kommt das Fressen, dann komt die Moral' (first grub, then ethics.) Only in June 1958 did the national council of the CAUT decide to ask a committee to draft a statement on academic freedom and tenure.

This decision reflected in part a wish to expand the role of professors in university governance, and in part an awareness that trouble was brewing at Ramsay Cook's undergraduate institution, United College. The dismissal of the historian Harry Crowe in the summer of 1958 was not a classic academic-freedom case. At issue were the contents of a private letter and the relationship between employer and employee. That academic freedom nevertheless came to be seen as central to the Crowe affair was due largely to the report written by the University of Saskatchewan political economist Vernon C. Fowke and the University of Toronto law professor Bora Laskin.

Fowke and Laskin held that Crowe, in protesting against an invasion of his privacy—i.e., Principal Wilfred Lockhart's photocopying of a private letter that had been illegally misdirected—was 'neither intemperate nor vigorous beyond the point of reasonable firmness'. In the board's use of his protests to justify his dismissal Fowke and Laskin saw an attack on academic freedom. But they were even more concerned about the dignity and autonomy of the professoriate. Faculty at United, and not there alone, were expected to defer to the authority of executive heads and lay boards. In challenging this expectation, Fowke and signalled a major change in the self-perception of the professoriate. Commenting on the photocopying of Crowe's letter, they wrote: 'Canadian scholars are not commonly or properly held in such low esteem that they must abstain from protest in such circumstances.'[14]

The attitude to which Fowke and Laskin objected was well stated by T.B. McDormand, executive vice-president of Acadia University. Crowe, he wrote, 'was dismissed not in violation of the principle of academic freedom, but in recognition of the principle that individuals . . . are responsible for what they do, what they write, and what they are. Irresponsibility in these fundamental matters disqualifies any man for the privilege of exercising academic freedom. . . .' Who was to judge what constituted responsible behaviour? The answer was the governing board, which had 'a right to determine what kind of people shall be on its faculty, and what kind of behaviour shall be considered unacceptable in the light of standards which the college prizes and seeks to maintain'. Denial of this right 'could lead by a short route to social anarchy and a chaotic fragmentation of society as we know it'.[15]

McDormand's views about board rights were well founded in law, but whether those rights were appropriate was coming into question. By 1958 a growing number of Canadian professors were asking why members of boards, who did none of the institution's essential work and often seemed to lack sympathy for it, should have the power to dispose of their careers. Fowke and Laskin took a logical leap in linking this issue to the idea of academic freedom. That senior academics from one end of Canada to the other welcomed their report implied a rocky future for McDormand's college.

The Crowe affair stimulated the CAUT to give academic freedom increased attention. The June 1958 national council meeting authorized the executive to solicit a statement on academic freedom and tenure. Headed by the psychologist Gordon H. Turner, a committee of the University of Western Ontario Faculty Association took charge of the project. In the fall of 1958 this committee drafted a statement on academic freedom and tenure that closely resembled the document on which it was based, the 1940 statement jointly issued by the AAUP and the Association of American Colleges.[16]

Perhaps somewhat troubled that their report was based exclusively on one foreign source, the committee thought it 'desirable that a survey of Canadian universities be made in order to discover what principles and practices concerning academic freedom and tenure are currently being followed'.[17] The CAUT council asked Turner and his colleagues to carry out this survey and report in June 1959.

At that time, the Turner committee reported that 'Canadian university teachers feel that there is virtually no restriction on their freedom to conduct and to publish the results of research of their own choosing, or on their freedom to conduct their classes as they see fit.' Many lacked confidence, though, 'that they could make utterances unpopular with their administrative officers and governing boards without fear of incurring discrimination or censure'.[18] Believing that their original report answered such concerns, the Turner committee recommended that the CAUT adopt it.

CAUT council delegates divided on the merits of adopting a statement of principles and practices. Some delegates argued that the document should 'define as precisely as possible the conditions which CAUT considers to be acceptable guarantees of freedom and security'; others believed that 'no statement of principles at all should be adopted,' because once rights were codified, both sides would try 'to sail close to the wind'. The middle position was that 'precise definitions and detailed descriptions . . . should be avoided, [but] a very general statement would be of value.' The middle position carried the day. The council voted by a large majority to delete sections dealing with the freedom of professors as researchers, teachers, and citizens, the making of appointments, the probationary period before the granting of tenure, and dismissal for cause.[19]

Adopted in their final form in 1960, the CAUT's 'Principles of Academic Freedom and Tenure' stated that universities existed 'for the common good and the common good depends upon the free search for truth and its free exposition'. Essential to these was freedom in teaching, research, and speculation. 'Academic freedom carries with it responsibilities as well as rights,' though what these were the document did not say. Tenure was justified as a means of safeguarding academic freedom and providing professors with economic security, such freedom and security being necessary conditions if universities were to succeed in meeting their obligations to students and to society.[20]

Not everyone was happy with this document. Turner was highly critical of its lack of detail; a committee of the UBC Faculty Association commented that it contained 'little of substance'.[21] Nevertheless, the CAUT would be satisfied with this brief statement for years to come.

This did not mean that the idea of academic freedom once again receded from academic consciousness. The Academic Freedom and Tenure Committee that the CAUT council established in 1959 was not, at first, a notably active group, and in the early 1960s issues of academic governance loomed larger than those of academic freedom. That professors nevertheless linked the two emerges clearly from A Place of Liberty, a book of essays on the government of Canadian universities edited by George Whalley of Queen's University and published in 1964.

Frank Underhill, whose academic freedom had been threatened more than once from the 1920s into the early 1940s, wrote the book's essay on the subject. He distilled the experience of five decades of university life in assessing the place of the scholar in Canada. Using A Man for All Seasons (1960), Robert Bolt's play about

Sir Thomas More, as his point of reference, Underhill cited its theme: 'How can a man of penetrating intellect and clear faith maintain his personal integrity in an age of revolutionary change in which all the pressures from government, from his friends and from the public, are to adjust himself, to conform to whatever ortho-doxy is proclaimed by the established authorities?'[22]

Bolt's Common Man avoided making trouble, or at least unexpected kinds of trouble; the committed university teacher could not help doing so. '[He] is up against the Common Man. Directly or indirectly, he is requiring the Common Man and his children to stretch their imaginations, to refine their sensibilities, to discipline their intellects to a degree that they are apt to find uncomfortable and disturbing.'

Why should professors be allowed to do things that the people who pay for their services do not want done? Underhill quoted from the article on academic free-dom that Arthur O. Lovejoy, first secretary of the AAUP, had contributed to the *Encyclopedia of the Social Sciences*. The paradox inherent in academic freedom was 'that those who buy a certain service may not prescribe the nature of the service to be rendered'. Why was this so? 'There are certain professional functions generally recognised to be indispensable in the life of a civilized community which cannot be performed if the specific manner of their performance is dictated by those who pay for them, and . . . the profession of the scholar and teacher in higher institu-tions of learning is one of these. . . .' Lovejoy, Underhill said, claimed for professors the role of a collective Socrates.

The historian did not remind his readers of the fate of Socrates. Instead he wrote about the gulf that existed in North America between the high standards of university life and the 'collective mediocrity' of a society shaped by plutocracy and egalitarian democracy. 'Academic freedom will only be securely established through the growth in the community at large of a genuine belief in the supreme value of intellectual activity.' Since this belief could be damned as 'elitist', it was unlikely to triumph anytime soon.

'Academic freedom,' Underhill continued, 'is the collective freedom of a profes-sion and the individual freedom of the members of that profession.' But it was not absolute: freedom entailed responsibility. The CAUT would be more persuasive if it were seen to worry less about salaries and benefits and more about professional standards: 'Members of the public learn from their sons and daughters at the university more than we suspect about how much dead wood is scattered among the academic departments.'

If academics were in need of self-criticism, they also needed to forge alliances with others who sought freedom of expression. 'In the meantime, the university today is being subjected to fresh pressures from outside which raise problems of academic freedom in new forms.' The demand for higher education created pres-sures to drop standards; growing enrolment led universities to rely on govern-ments whose objectives differed from those of scholars. Because its services were so essential to the powerful, moreover, 'the contemporary university tends to be absorbed into the Establishment, and the . . . administrative bureaucracy, which expands in accordance with Parkinson's Law,[23] tends to become more and more Establishment-minded.' These pressures, more than McCarthyite attacks, would threaten academic freedom in the future. Underhill did not presume to specify a defence: 'The price of liberty is, however, the same in universities as elsewhere.'

Underhill's cautionary note was embedded in a book whose mood was generally upbeat. More than thirty years later, his warnings seem more realistic than the dominant optimism that otherwise pervades *A Place of Liberty*. In 1964, however, nourished by an unprecedented flow of money into the universities and assisted by a shortage of qualified academics, changes were taking place that advanced the position of the professoriate and the cause of academic freedom. To most professors in the mid-1960s, among them the young Ramsay Cook, the future looked bright.

NOTES

1. See A.H. Halsey and M.A. Trow, *The British Academics* (Cambridge, Mass., 1971), 117; Conrad Russell, *Academic Freedom* (London, 1993), 43–4.

2. University of Toronto Archives, President's Office (Falconer), A67-0007/43, James Mavor to Sir Robert Falconer, 9 Nov. 1916.

3. R. Bruce Taylor, 'Academic Freedom', *Queen's Quarterly* 27, 1 (Summer 1919), passim.

4. E.E. Braithwaite, 'Academic Freedom', *Globe* (4 June 1919).

5. James G. Greenlee, *Sir Robert Falconer* (Toronto, 1988), 257–64, 278.

6. Sir Robert Falconer, *Academic Freedom* (Toronto, 1922), passim.

7. Quoted in A.B. McKillop, *Matters of Mind: The University in Ontario, 1791–1951* (Toronto, 1994), 644.

8. University of Toronto, *President's Report 1934–35* (Toronto, 1936), 23.

9. Dalhousie University Archives, President's Office, Correspondence, MS 1-3-A398, vol. 14, NCCU 1936–9, Carleton Stanley, address to NCCU, 31 May 1937.

10. On Adair see Michiel Horn, 'The Mildew of Discretion: Academic Freedom and Self-Censorship', *Dalhousie Review* 72, 4 (Winter 1992–3), 449–50; on Underhill see R. Douglas Francis, *Frank H. Underhill: Intellectual Provocateur* (Toronto, 1986), 114–15.

11. University of Alberta Archives, RG 19, Personnel files, 73–112, George Hunter Personal, 'Re: Prof. G. HUNTER, University of Alberta, Edmonton, Alta', 12 Apr. 1940.

12. McGill University Archives, RG2, Principal's Office, c.85/2202, 'Academic Freedom of Speech' [1943].

13. Michiel Horn, 'Academic Freedom and the Dismissal of George Hunter', *Dalhousie Review* 69, 3 (Fall 1989).

14. 'Report of the Investigation by the Committee of the Canadian Association of University Teachers into the Dismissal of Professor H.S. Crowe by United College, Winnipeg, Manitoba', *CAUT Bulletin* 7, 3 (January 1959), 49.

15. T.B. McDormand, 'Time Bomb to Destroy Freedom', *United Church Observer* (1 Oct. 1959).

16. National Archives of Canada, CAUT Papers, vol. 123, Interim Report of the Ad Hoc Committee on Academic Freedom and Tenure of the Faculty Association, University of Western Ontario, 10 Nov. 1958.

17. Ibid.

18. CAUT Papers, vol. 1, Ad Hoc Committee on Academic Freedom and Tenure, Report to the Executive Council, May 1959, 2–3.

19. CAUT Papers, vol. 73, Minutes, National Council, 14–15 Nov. 1959, Summary of discussion on Report of ad hoc Committee on Academic Freedom and Tenure.

20. CAUT Papers, vol. 161, Principles of Academic Freedom and Tenure (As revised and adopted by Council, June 1960).

21. CAUT Papers, vol. 1, Turner to Reid, 14 Dec. 1959 and 4 May 1960; vol. 126, Turner to Professors Dansereau, Graham, Milner, Read, and Smith, 16 May 1960, copy; University of British Columbia Archives, President's Office, microfilm reel 229, Faculty Association, Report of the Personnel Services Committee. . . , 14 Mar. 1960.

22. Frank H. Underhill, 'The Scholar: Man Thinking', in *A Place of Liberty: Essays on the Government of Canadian Universities*, ed. George Whalley (Toronto and Vancouver, 1964), 61. Unless otherwise noted, all quotations in the next few paragraphs are from this source.

23. Parkinson's Law—'work expands so as to fill the time available for its completion'— grew out of the historian C. Northcote Parkinson's analysis of staffing in the British Admiralty and Colonial Office during the first half of the century. This led him to claim, only partly in jest, that the annual rate of growth in the size of a bureaucracy would 'invariably prove to be between 5.17 per cent and 6.56 percent, irrespective of any variation in the amount of work (if any) to be done'; *Parkinson's Law and other Studies in Administration* (Boston, 1957), 12.

The Anatomy of Power

A Theme in the Writings of Harold Innis

R. Douglas Francis

Since his death in 1952, Harold Innis has been the subject of considerable study. Economists, historians, geographers, and communication theorists have all claimed him as one of their own, and then proceeded to examine some aspect of his thought from their own disciplinary perspectives.[1] In doing so, they have focused on one avenue of his thought, often to the exclusion of others, with the result that Innis appears fragmented in his thinking. A few Innisian scholars have looked at certain topics that appear at various times in some of his writings, such as the role of the university, but have failed to show how such topics give continuity to his thinking. To date, no one has attempted to discover any overriding themes running like leitmotifs throughout all of Innis's major works—from his first major publication, *A History of the Canadian Pacific Railway* (1923), through his economic 'staples' studies, to his later communication studies—that might show how all these studies are connected and reveal the continuity of his thought.

This paper explores one such theme in Innis's writings: the anatomy of power. Throughout his life, Innis was fascinated by what constituted power; what forces or relationships, technological or human, created power; who held power and who didn't, and why; how those in positions of power obtained and maintained their power base, and then were eventually supplanted by new power élites—what might be called the ebb and flow of power; the factors that caused old power structures to fall and new ones to arise within nation states, empires, and civilizations. The theme of power reveals a continuity and unity in Innis's thought, and in particular explains the important shift in his research interests in the early 1940s, when he abandoned his economic staple studies within the Canadian context in favour of communication studies within the context of the rise and fall of civilizations of the West, from Mesopotamia in the seventh century BC through to and including Europe and the United States in his own time. This paper will examine the power theme as it enabled Innis to explain the unique evolution of Canada as a nation on the North American continent, the dominance of the British Empire within Western civilization, and ultimately the rise and fall of that civilization. It will attempt to explain why Innis was so interested in power, and to show how that interest was in keeping with the intellectual currents of his time.

I

From an early age, Harold Innis saw power as a major factor in world politics. When, as a university student, he decided to join the army and go to war, he did so not for the reasons that most young men gave at the time—because others were joining, for glory, or because he felt compelled to fight for God, King, and Country—but because Germany had abused its power. In a letter home, explaining his decision to sign up, the young Innis wrote: 'Germany started in this war by breaking a treaty, by breaking her sealed word. Not only did she do that but she trampled over a helpless people with no warning and with no excuse. If any nation and if any person can break their word with no notice, whatever, then, is the world coming to.'[2]

Power was clearly a major theme in Innis's Ph.D. dissertation, completed at the University of Chicago and subsequently published as *A History of the Canadian Pacific Railway* (1923). Given the upsurge of Canadian nationalism immediately following the First World War, when Innis completed the study, it would have been natural for him to have seen the railroad as a noble national project, tying the country together and giving it a sense of identity and purpose. Yet he chose instead to examine its role in the matrices of power within Canada, the British Empire, and Western civilization in the late nineteenth century.[3] In essence, Innis argued that the importance of the CPR lay in the role it played in extending the sphere of influence and therefore the power of Western civilization—represented by central Canada within British North America and by the British Empire within the international context—beyond the river valleys of British North America to incorporate regions previously inaccessible, particularly the western interior. In this way the CPR enabled Canada, as a British colony, to secure control and power over the North West before the Americans were able to do so, and enabled Britain, as a major world power, to maintain a foothold in North America, and to link its vast empire together by means of an extensive communication and transportation network.

Innis viewed the building of the CPR and its role in the acquisition of the North West as the Canadian version of an imperial power struggle. It was a deliberate means by which central Canada came to dominate the hinterland of the west. And within central Canada, it was the Upper Canadian settlers who predominated. Their 'individualistic and aggressive nature' forced the new nation of Canada to expand too far too fast after 1867, before it was adequately prepared economically and financially to do so, and pitted region against region, or centre against margins, resulting in western discontent. In 1923 Innis did not foresee how this power relationship would change in the near future, despite the emergence of agrarian protest in the post-war era in the form of the Progressive movement. As he concluded in his study:

On the whole, important as the [Progressive] movement in western Canada must become for the future development of the country, the dominance of eastern

Canada over western Canada seems likely to persist. Western Canada has paid for the development of Canadian nationality, and it would appear that it must continue to pay. The acquisitiveness of eastern Canada shows little sign of abatement.[4]

Thus Innis saw the railroad, the ribbon of steel, as the power link—the life blood—in the dynamic relationship between centre and margin. Within the national power structure, it bound the country together under the aegis of central Canada at the expense of the hinterland regions of the west and the east; within the context of Western civilization, the railroad was part of a vast transportation network that tied the British Empire together under British dominance at the expense of colonial hinterlands such as Canada.

What enabled the railroad to command such influence was the fact that it represented the latest and the greatest of Western technology: already, at this early stage in his thinking, Innis had come to realize that technology was power. Whoever controlled the most advanced form of technology held the superior power. In the nineteenth century, railroads were the most advanced form of technology, and Britain was the most advanced railroad nation in the world. In fact, that was the reason for Britain's position at the centre of Western civilization in the late nineteenth century. The CPR's role was to ensure Britain's continued control over British North America even after its colonies there had united in nationhood. Innis made the importance of the CPR as a source of technological power in British North America quite clear:

> The history of the Canadian Pacific Railroad is primarily the history of the spread of western civilization over the northern half of the North American continent. The addition of technical equipment described as physical property of the Canadian Pacific Railway Company was a cause and an effect of the strength and character of that civilization. The construction of the road was the result of the direction of energy to the conquest of geographic barriers. The effects of the road were measured to some extent by the changes in the strength and character of that civilization in the period following its construction.[5]

In seeing technology as power, Innis went beyond the obvious association of technology with machinery and industrialism as sources of that power to argue that technology really represented a mind set or *mentalité* within Western civilization that put power front and centre in its thinking. What is striking about his study of the CPR is the absence of discussion either of machinery or of the railroad as a form of industrialism. Instead he emphasized the political and economic factors behind the decision to build a transcontinental railroad, dwelt in detail on the construction of the main line and the addition of spur lines, and cited statistics on passenger traffic, earnings from operations, expenses, capital, and profits. The implication was that these decisions and actions reflected a way of thinking that was 'technological', that enabled those in positions of power to maintain their power. That technological mentality measured everything in quantitative, mechanical, and mathematical terms—as profits, material values, and, most important, power—rather than human and spiritual terms. It was this 'technological mentality' that made Western civilization dominant, that gave Britain the commanding position within that civilization, and that kept Canada tied to the British Empire, and through it to Western civilization.

Such an awareness of technology as power was in keeping with the perspective of the post-1918 era.[6] The Great War, the most technologically advanced war of all time, revealed the destructive uses to which the power of technology could be put, and thus for the first time raised serious doubts about the implications of technology for civilization. The negative potential of technology came to be associated with Germany's cold, calculating abuse of the power of technology in the war. In this respect, the young Innis's condemnation of the Germans for their abuse of power was very much in keeping with the attitude of the times.

At the same time, Canadian intellectuals, like their counterparts in other Western countries, could not overlook the fact that Germany was part of Western civilization—if not its epitome. The Great War, then, was a power struggle within Western civilization, a struggle in which technology would determine which European nation—Britain or Germany—would hold the centre of power. Thus in seeing the Canadian Pacific Railroad as part of Britain's technological might, a means by which Britain extended and maintained its imperial dominance over the northern half of the North American continent, Innis was contributing to the post-war debate over the future of Western civilization: tracing the role that the technology of railroads had played in British supremacy in the nineteenth century, and by implication questioning the role that technology would play in the European power struggle in the twentieth century.

II

Having completed his study of the CPR, Innis became interested in discovering the roots of European dominance over the northern half of North America. He found it in the early fur trade and cod fisheries.[7] The staple trade not only secured first French and then British imperial control, but also established the dynamics for later American imperial dominance over Canada. As well, it established a pattern of governmental rule that determined the nature and jurisdiction of the newly created federal power when Canada became a nation in 1867. In addition, the staple trade shaped the dynamics of power between the centre, which invariably resided outside the country, and the margins represented by British North America. As Innis noted in his conclusion to the *Fur Trade in Canada* (1930): 'The economic history of Canada has been dominated by the discrepancy between the centre and the margin of western civilization. . . . Agriculture, industry, transportation, trade, finance, and governmental activities tend to become subordinate to the production of the staple for a more highly specialized manufacturing community.'[8]

Again, Innis found the source of power in technology. In the case of the fur trade, it was the superior technology of the Old World that enabled Europe to dominate over the North American hinterland. While he acknowledged the importance of the indigenous peoples of North America in enabling the early European traders and settlers to survive in the harsh climate and unfamiliar terrain of the New World, he admitted that Native cultures ultimately succumbed to the European culture because of the latter's technological superiority:

> The history of the fur trade is the history of contact between two civilizations, the European and the North American, with especial reference to the northern portion of the continent. The limited cultural background of the North American hunting peoples provided an insatiable demand for the products of the more elaborate cultural development of Europeans. The supply of European goods, the product of a more advanced and specialized technology, enabled the Indians to gain a livelihood more easily—to obtain their supply of food, as in the case of the moose, more quickly, and to hunt the beaver more effectively. . . . [But] the new technology with its radical innovations brought about such a rapid shift in the prevailing Indian culture as to lead to wholesale destruction of the peoples concerned by warfare and disease.[9]

Innis was clearly using the term 'technology' to refer to much more than iron knives, guns, and kettles. As in his study of the CPR, Innis saw the 'technical equipment' as part of a cultural matrix that put power front and centre in the European value system. Innis saw technology as a means of domination, of controlling others. In the case of the fur trade, technology had given Europeans the upper hand over the Native people, thus enabling the dynamics of centre and margin within Western civilization to work to the advantage of Europe. And when industrial technology developed in North America, it first emerged as a powerful force in the United States. Again Canada was left on the economic margin—only now it was dependent on the American, as opposed to European, imperial centre.

By the time Innis had completed his staple studies (circa 1940) he had clearly come to see Canada's marginal position in relation to the centres of power in Europe and the United States as disadvantageous, making the country dependent on external metropolitan centres, creating an economy of vulnerability, and fostering artificial growth through major government subsidies to private industries and a National Policy of high tariffs that shielded Canadian industries from international competition. Such an economy perpetuated the country's colonial position—to quote Innis's famous aphorism, 'Canada went from colony to nation to colony.' Technology as power had ensured that the centre of economic dominance would remain outside Canada's borders, leaving the country on the margin and thus powerless in the face of forces outside its control.

III

Analysts of Innis's thought have noted that it underwent a significant change around the time of the Second World War. Following his economic staples studies within a Canadian historical context he embarked on a cultural study of what Marshall McLuhan perceptively described as 'staples of the mind'[10]: the technologies of communications (stylus, papyrus, parchment, stone, clay tablets, paper, printing press) that in Innis's view had shaped the thought patterns of civilizations. This study led him to examine all the major civilizations of the West, from Mesopotamia up to and including Western Europe and the United States. While this new focus appeared to represent an abandonment of the work on Canada that he had pursued in the inter-war years, in fact it did not. His comment on Edward Gibbon's monumental *Decline and Fall of the Roman Empire*, namely that it was more a study of Gibbon's native Britain in the nineteenth century than it was of Rome, was equally true of Innis's own communication studies of ancient civilizations.[11] They had more to say about the decline of Western civilization in the twentieth century, and with Canada's role as a nation on the margin of that civilization, than they did about the past. In particular, his communication studies continued to explore the theme of power that had dominated his staple studies—only now the dominant source of power was the technology of communication.

There have been many explanations for Innis's dramatic shift in research focus. One of the most important, clearly, was the impact of the Second World War. The Great War had wounded Innis both physically and, more important, psychologically. For one thing, the war had made him more rebellious, leading him to question and challenge those in positions of power. When Innis's colleague Frank H. Underhill was threatened with dismissal from the University of Toronto in 1940–1 for challenging the views of those in political and academic authority, Innis defended him even though he disagreed with his views. His explanation of Underhill's rebelliousness revealed as much about Innis as Underhill. 'It is possibly necessary to remember,' Innis wrote to President Cody of the University of Toronto at the height of the Underhill controversy, 'that any returned man who has faced the continued dangers of modern warfare has a point of view fundamentally different from anyone who has not. Again and again have we told each other or repeated to ourselves, nothing can hurt us after this. The psychic perils of civilization mean nothing to us.'[12] That 'point of view' was one of rebelliousness against authority. Innis made the same point in a slightly different way when, in the midst of the Second World War, he recalled his permanent aversion to the bureaucrats he saw as self-important servants of distant power:

> After eight months of the mud and lice and rats of France in which much of the time was spent cursing government officials in Ottawa, I have without doubt developed an abnormal slant. I have never had the slightest interest since that time in people who were helping in the war with a job in Ottawa or London. The contrast between their methods of living and France made it simply impossible for me to regard them as having anything to do with the war and I continue to look upon them with contempt.[13]

Underhill challenged figures of authority directly and publicly; Innis challenged them indirectly and less conspicuously, but with no less animus. His approach was to study the source of power in societies and civilizations of the past so as to have a better understanding of the present.

Power is an underlying theme in Innis's essay collection *Political Economy in the Modern State* (1946), published in the immediate aftermath of the Second World War. That the war loomed large in Innis's mind was evident in his Preface to the book. Like the Great War, twenty-five years earlier, what the Second World War symbolized for Innis was a power struggle within Western civilization. The difference lay in the nature and extent of that struggle. In the Great War, the struggle had taken place on the battlefields of Europe by means of physical force; in the Second World War, by contrast, the site of the struggle was the mind of the general populace, and the means was the power of communication technology. As Innis perceptively noted:

> The first essential task [of peace] is to see and to break through the chains of modern civilization which have been created by modern science. Freedom of the press and freedom of speech have been possible largely because they have permitted the production of words on an unprecedented scale and have made them powerless. Oral and printed words have been harnessed to the enormous demands of modern industrialism and in advertising have been made to find new markets for goods. Each new invention which enhances their power in that direction weakens their power in other directions. It is worth noting that large majorities in political elections accompanied the spread of the newspaper on a large scale in England after the sixties in the last century, and the spread of the radio on this continent. Swings in public opinion are most violent with new inventions in communication, and independent thought is more difficult to sustain. It is scarcely necessary to add, that words have carried a heavy additional load in the prosecution of the war and have been subjected to unusual strains.[14]

Further on in his Preface Innis noted how the demands of war had increased the demand for centralization of political power, which he saw as a danger. In one typically cryptic comment, he linked centralization to morality and then to power: 'Extensive government expenditure and intervention and large scale undertakings have raised the fundamental problems of morality. A friend in power is a friend lost. A decline in morality has followed war and the growth of hierarchies in church, state, and private enterprise. *Power is poison.*' What made power 'poisonous', Innis maintained, was its destructive effect on freedom of thought. 'Improvements in communication have weakened the possibility of sustained thought when it has become most necessary. Civilization has been compelled to resort to reliance on force as a result of the impact of technology on communication.'[15] Here was the nucleus of Innis's interest in the technologies of communication, from ancient Mesopotamia to the present: a desire to understand the sources of power within those civilizations, the sources of challenge to that power structure, and the role of communication technology in the rise and fall of civilizations. At the roots of his new research was the old theme of power—now, however, he was seeking to understand the anatomy of power not in the economic relationship of empire and colonies but in the cultural relations between the centres and margins of civilizations based on the impact of communication technology. In particular, Innis was convinced that the centre of Western civilization in the mid-twentieth century, the United States, was in crisis, challenged by a new source of creativity and power on the margin.

Innis was looking for a pattern, or at least a convincing explanation, for the current decline of the West in the historical study of earlier civilizations. He found that pattern in the role played by the dominant medium of communication within a civilization in shaping its social structure and cultural values: with the establishment of a 'monopoly of knowledge', any new creative thinking that might have allowed the civilization to flourish and continue to grow was stifled. Each form of communication technology was oriented towards either time or space—in Innis's terminology, 'time-biased' or 'space-biased'. Communication media that were durable and difficult to transport, such as stone, clay, or parchment, were time-biased, whereas those that were light and easy to transport over long distances, such as paper and papyrus, were space-biased.[16]

By 'bias' Innis meant much more than a simple preference for one type of technology or the other. He argued that civilizations oriented towards time or space created a dominant paradigm of thought—a monopoly of knowledge—that in most cases prevented counter-values or alternative social structures from emerging. As well, the principal medium of communication favoured one particular group within that civilization—the group that controlled the technology of communication—which maintained its power by preventing the emergence of any alternative communication technology that could threaten it. The oral tradition, for example, enabled the Spartan oligarchy to prevail; writing on papyrus benefited the Roman imperial bureaucracy; parchment allowed the medieval clergy and the Roman Catholic Church to monopolize knowledge in the Middle Ages; by contrast, Gutenberg's mechanical print fostered the vernacular and allowed the monarchs of nation states to consolidate their power and, through the merchant class, create vast empires.[17] The modern newspaper, a hybrid of the printed word and electronic media, particularly the telegraph, came under the control of the press lords, who in turn were pressured by charismatic political leaders and totalitarian rulers to print what they dictated.

The monopoly of knowledge enabled a civilization to maintain itself and even to achieve temporary cultural greatness, but it also led to the inevitable demise of that civilization, since it did not allow for the rise of the new ideas required for renewed growth. In essence, the civilization went into a comatose state where no rejuvenating new thought or spiritual growth could occur. At this point the civilization was open to challenge from societies on its margin that were beyond the influence of those in positions of power within the civilization. It was here, on the margin, that new technologies of communication emerged, capable of surpassing and supplanting the dominant medium of communication.

While Innis was fascinated with those who held power and the means they used to do so, he was equally interested in understanding those who challenged authority: where they came from; how they undermined the monopoly of knowledge, causing the civilization to collapse; and the means they used to establish themselves in power. Innis took a Darwinian view of the evolution of civilizations, seeing those in authority as constantly struggling to maintain their power while marginal societies outside the pale of power constantly worked to supplant them and the civilization that they represented.

In Innis's view, the truly creative thinking and the indomitable human spirit always emerged on the margins of civilization. He was just beginning to explore the material conditions and values in the marginal societies that fostered creativity and vitality as his life came to an end. As Robert Cox notes, Innis wanted to understand 'the technologies of intellectual and moral struggles'.[18] Innis discovered that these marginal societies shared a profound belief in freedom. Innis observed, in Robin Neill's words, that 'where there is liberty there is creativity; and the absence of liberty is not so much a consequence of force as of the intellectual and moral assumptions inherent in the bias of communication.'[19] Freedom flourished in a state of anomie and instability; it required conflicting ideas and open-ended debate. Power—the antithesis of liberty—required stability, security, and tyranny of thought.

Innis realized, however, that the decline of civilizations was not simply a matter of power versus freedom. Rather, he discovered a paradox: cultural creativity reached its peak in those civilizations where the power dynamics were in a state of equilibrium, not where there was an absence or weakness of power. Ironically, however, it was when a monopoly of power and the resulting stability had allowed cultural creativity to reach its height that the civilization began to decline as a result of the very power structure that had enabled it to thrive. Innis attributed the flowering of culture in fifth-century Greece to a balance between the forces of the oral and the written traditions within Athenian society, and a brief period of peace and stability among the Greek city states. The Byzantine empire reached its peak of cultural creativity because the power of the ruling élite maintained a balance between church and state, and deterred any external attacks. The tremendous creativity of the Renaissance era was due in large part to the balance of power among the emerging nation states of Europe. Yet each of these peak periods of creativity was invariably followed by a period of decline—the point when Minerva's owl took flight to a new centre of cultural creativity—because power stifled freedom and therefore the creativity essential for a civilization to sustain itself. The civilization was left vulnerable to challenges from marginal societies where new and superior technologies of communication had developed, capable of supplanting the existing dominant medium of communication and the power élite that controlled it. Thus power and creativity, authority and freedom, stood at opposite ends of the value spectrum, paralleling the centre and the margin—the sources of power and creativity respectively. Given the power of communication technologies to create a monopoly of knowledge at the centre of civilization, opposition to that monopoly would inevitably arise, it seemed to Innis, from marginal societies that initially valued freedom over power.

In the mid-twentieth century, Innis believed that Minerva's owl was once again taking flight from the centre of Western civilization in the United States. By the end of his life in 1952, he had grown cynical with regard to a civilization that had waged two wars of unparalleled destruction and was threatening to begin a third with the discovery of the atomic bomb, that had initiated a worldwide depression and that accepted, in its societies, extremes of wealth and poverty. He criticized the universities and the churches—the two institutions that should be the upholders of freedom against authority and power structures—for their failure to offer new ideas and to question the dominant paradigms of thought within the modern West.[20] Clearly, mechanized print, along with the new electronic communication technology of the telegraph and the radio (the latter Innis saw as accentuating and extending the space-bias and therefore the monopoly of mechanized print), had an iron-clad hold on Western thinking, reducing rationalism to its lowest common denominator as popular thought based on blind emotionalism.

Did he see any hope for the future? The lessons of history taught that the only hope lay in a challenge to America's imperial dominance at the centre of Western civilization from a society on the margin. Marginal forces were both internal and external. They were the new creative ideas in the minds of those individuals who were not duped or mesmerized by the prevailing ideology or dominant paradigms—those creative individuals whose spirit could not be crushed. Such human spirits, however, had to be nurtured in the bosom of a society and culture that respected and fostered creativity. Innis was too much of a realist, and materialist, to believe that new ideas developed and creative individuals emerged in a vacuum. They required a society that was not part of the existing matrix of power, not at the imperial centre. Such a society also needed to have a healthy balance of cultural values associated with time and space—what might be described as conservative and liberal values. (In Innis's view, time-biased values were traditional, hierarchical and moral (qualities of conservation), while space-biased values emphasized the present and the future, the technical, and the secular (qualities of liberalism).)

Innis believed that Canada was such a creative society. Its entire history, from the time of European exploration and settlement, had been one of marginality within Western civilization under first the French empire, then the British empire, and, more recently, the American. During the period when Europe was the centre of Western civilization, Canada was able to remain on the margin, and therefore beyond the direct dominance of imperial power, thanks to simple distance and the physical barrier of the Atlantic Ocean. Canada was not so fortunate, however, when the centre of power shifted from Europe to the United States in the twentieth century. There could be no illusion of Canadian independence from American political, economic, and cultural control. Nevertheless, through a long tradition of anti-Americanism, an association and identification with Britain offsetting the American influence, and a political ideology that incorporated both conservative and liberal values—in other words, both time-biased and space-biased values—Canada had created a society and culture different from those of the United States.

In his last publication, *The Strategy of Culture* (1952), Innis set out his concern for Canadian creativity and survival in the face of American imperial power. He also offered his belief that Canada, a country on the margin of power, had something positive to contribute to the modern world:

> The dangers to national existence warrant an energetic programme to offset them. In the new technological developments Canadians can escape American influence in communication media other that those affected by appeals to the 'freedom of the press'. The Canadian Press has emphasized Canadian news but American influence is powerful. In the radio, on the other hand, the Canadian government in the Canadian Broadcasting Corporation has undertaken an active role in offsetting the influence of American broadcasters. It may be hoped that its role will be more active in television. The Film Board has been set up and designed to weaken the pressure of American films. The appointment and the report of the Royal Commission on National Developments in the Arts and Sciences imply a determination to strengthen our position. . . .
>
> We are fighting for our lives. The pernicious influence of American advertising reflected especially in the periodical press and the powerful persistent impact of commercialism have been evident in all the ramifications of Canadian life. The jackals of communication systems are constantly on the alert to destroy every vestige of sentiment towards Great Britain, holding it of no advantage if it threatens the omnipotence of American commercialism. This is to strike at the heart of cultural life in Canada. The pride taken in improving our status in the British Commonwealth of Nations has made it difficult for us to realize that our status on the North American continent is on the verge of disappearing. Continentalism assisted in the achievement of autonomy, and has consequently become more dangerous. We can only survive by taking persistent action at strategic points against American imperialism in all its attractive guises.[21]

IV

What accounts for Innis's fascination with power? I would trace it to Innis's belief that he was on the margin of power, always looking in, so to speak, at those who held it. This was true in his personal as well as his academic life. At first glance, this statement might appear absurd. Few Canadian intellectuals have received the honours and recognition within their lifetime that Innis received. Elected president of the Royal Society of Canada, he was awarded its coveted Tyrrell Medal in recognition of his outstanding contribution to scholarship; he was the only Canadian to be chosen president of the American Economic Association; and in 1948 he was invited to give the distinguished Beit Lectures on imperial economic history at Oxford University, subsequently published as *Empire and Communications* (1950)—to name only a few of the honours and awards he received.[22]

Even so, Innis believed himself to be on the margin of power. As a farm boy, he never felt at ease in an urban setting; later as an academic, he was never comfortable with the urban power élite. As an undergraduate, coming from a poor family, he believed that he did not have the opportunities or influence that students of middle- and upper-class backgrounds enjoyed; as a graduate student at the University of Chicago, he rejected the idea of working on a dissertation topic in American, European, or international economics, as most students were doing, choosing instead to focus on Canada, a nation itself on the margin of power. In the First World War, he joined the Canadian army at a time when many university-educated Canadians were joining the more prestigious British army. He was wounded at Vimy Ridge and discharged from the army before he could distinguish himself in battle. In his subsequent academic career, he chose research topics outside the intellectual mainstream; he preferred the role of critic to that of advocate; and his writings attracted limited interest at the time of publication. He died prematurely, with no following to continue his life work. The fact that power eluded him might account for his fascination with those who did hold it, and with the role that power played in history.

In terms of intellectual context, power was much on the minds of the generation of academics writing, as Innis did, in the aftermath of the First World War, throughout the Great Depression, and in the shadow of the Second World War and the atomic bomb; for them, power politics appeared to be the dominant force in the world. The inter-war years witnessed a reaction to the optimism, sentimentalism, and romanticism of the Victorian age. Certainly the Great War brought the issue of power to the fore, making a mockery of the liberal beliefs in rationality and progress towards ultimate peace in the world. A generation earlier, Sigmund Freud had 'discovered' the irrational side of human nature. In the 1920s, idealism was giving way to realism in literature and philosophy as the urge to power underlying human actions was exposed. It was an age of debunking, of pointing out that human beings were not so noble and idealistic as some had believed them to be.

In his own writings in the inter-war years, Innis reacted against the romantic and sentimental nineteenth-century conception of history in which 'great and noble men' were depicted as the moral leaders of society; instead, he looked for the impersonal economic forces, the subconscious cultural hegemony, and the naked play of power that constituted the dynamics of history. He came to see the struggle for power as the most convincing explanation for, and hence the underlying theme in, the history of the Canadian nation state, in the dynamics of imperial and colonial relations, and in the rise and fall of civilizations.

Innis's study of the anatomy of power parallels Northrop Frye's anatomy of criticism and George P. Grant's work on the anatomy of technology.[23] All three of these important mid-twentieth-century Canadian intellectuals had at least one thing in common: a desire to get at the essence of modern thought by linking it to one central concept or theme that appeared to underlie that thought and give it form and meaning—a thread or bloodline running through the entire body of scholarship. Each of the three thinkers explored the ramifications of his central theme: Innis, the role of power in shaping societies, nations, empire, and civilizations through technology; Frye, the significance of biblical patterns in the structure of modern literature; Grant, the impact of technology on modern morals and values. In each case, that theme became their holy grail, the hidden text for which they searched in their quest for meaning in the modern world. While none found Truth, all three brought new and deeper understanding to modern thought.

The theme of power itself is very modern. Innis's fascination with power reflects Michel Foucault's writings on the subject in *Power/Knowledge* and elsewhere. Like Innis, Foucault reacted to historians' emphasis on abstract and noble concepts— for example, 'the will to knowledge'—arguing that such ideals blind historians to the reality of power throughout history. 'The history which bears and determines us,' he argued, 'has the form of a war rather than that of a language: relations of power, not relations of meaning.' In *Power/Knowledge*, he went on to explain how historians of the past tended to skirt the issue of power rather than address it directly:

> The way power was exercised—concretely and in detail—with its specificity, its techniques and tactics, was something that no one attempted to ascertain; they contented themselves with denouncing it in a polemical and global fashion as it existed among the 'others', in the adversary camp. Where Soviet socialist power was in question, its opponents called it totalitarianism; power in western capitalism was denounced by the Marxists as class domination; but the mechanics of power in themselves were never analyzed.[24]

In his fascination with power, Innis showed how modern his thinking was, offering insights that would be pursued by a later generation of historians. Here, ironically, Innis has enjoyed a power and influence that eluded him in his lifetime.

NOTES

I wish to express my thanks to Bill Westfall of Atkinson College, York University, who read an earlier draft of this paper and made valuable suggestions for change. I alone am responsible for any limitations that remain.

1. On Harold Innis as an economist, see Mel Watkins, 'The Staple Theory Revisited', and Ian Parker, 'Innis, Marx, and the Economics of Communication: A Theoretical Aspect of Political Economy', in *Culture, Communication and Dependency: The Tradition of H.A. Innis*, ed. William H. Melody et al. (Norwood, NJ, 1981), 53–72 and 127–44 respectively; and Robin Neill, *A New Theory of Value: The Canadian*

Economics of H.A. Innis (Toronto, 1972). On Innis's contribution to geography, see 'Focus: A Geographical Appreciation of Harold A. Innis', *Canadian Geographer* 32, 1 (1988), 63–9. On Innis as a historian, see Carl Berger, *The Writing of Canadian History* (Toronto, 1976), 85–111; William Westfall, 'The Ambivalent Verdict: Harold Innis and Canadian History', in *Culture, Communication and Dependency*, 37–52; and Frank Abbott, 'Harold Innis—Nationalist Historian', *Queen's Quarterly*, 101, 1 (Spring 1994), 92–102. On Innis and communication studies, see Paul Heyer and David Cowley, 'Introduction to Harold A. Innis', *The Bias of Communication*, reprint with a new introduction (Toronto, 1991), ix–xxviii; J. Carey, *Communication as Culture* (Boston, 1989); and D. Czitrom, *Media and the American Mind* (Chapel Hill, 1987).

2. Quoted in William Christian, *Harold Innis as Economist and Moralist* (Guelph, 1981), 2.

3. For a discussion of the importance of nationalism in the writing of Canadian history in the 1920s, see Ramsay Cook, '*La Survivance* English-Canadian Style', in his *The Maple Leaf Forever: Essays on Nationalism and Politics in Canada* (Toronto, 1971), 141–65.

4. Harold A. Innis, *A History of the Canadian Pacific Railway* (Toronto, 1923), 294.

5. Ibid., 284.

6. For a good discussion of the First World War as a technological war, see Modris Ekstein, *Rites of Spring: The Great War and the Birth of the Modern Age* (Boston, 1989).

7. Innis discusses the fur trade in *The Fur Trade in Canada* (Toronto, 1930), and the fish trade in *The Cod Fisheries: The History of an International Economy* (Toronto, 1940). For reasons of space, I have discussed the theme of power in his study of the fur trade only, although it is also present in his study of the cod fisheries.

8. *The Fur Trade in Canada*, 385.

9. Ibid., 388.

10. Marshall McLuhan, 'The Later Innis', *Queen's Quarterly* 60 (1953).

11. The idea is presented in Neill's *A New Theory of Value*, 16–17.

12. R. Douglas Francis, *Frank H. Underhill: Intellectual Provocateur* (Toronto, 1986), 123.

13. Quoted in Berger, *The Writing of Canadian History*, 104.

14. Harold A. Innis, *Political Economy in the Modern State* (Toronto, 1946), vii–viii.

15. Ibid., xiii–xiv.

16. The best analysis of Innis's theories on communication media is still James W. Carey, 'Harold Adams Innis and Marshall McLuhan', *Antioch Review* 27 (Spring 1967), 5–39.

17. See Harold A. Innis, *Empire and Communications* (Oxford, 1950), and *The Bias of Communication* (Toronto, 1951), especially 'Minerva's Owl'.

18. Robert W. Cox, 'Civilizations: Encounters and Transformations', *Studies in Political Economy* 47 (Summer 1995), 20–6.

19. Neill, *A New Theory of Value*, 101.

20. See, for example, H.A. Innis, 'Discussion in the Social Sciences', *Dalhousie Review* 15 (1936), 401–13; 'The University in the Modern Tradition', in *Political Economy in the Modern State*, 71–82; 'Adult Education and the Universities,' in *The Bias of Communication*, 203–13; and 'The Church in Canada,' in *Time for Healing: Twenty-Second Annual Report of the Board of Evangelism and Social Services* (Toronto, 1947), 47–54.

21. Harold A. Innis, *The Strategy of Culture* (Toronto, 1952), 19–20.

22. There is no full-scale biography of Innis. For a biographical sketch, see Donald G. Creighton, *Harold Adams Innis: Portrait of a Scholar* (Toronto, 1957); Carl Berger, 'Harold Innis: The Search for Limits', in *The Writing of Canadian History*, 85–111; and for a personal reminiscence, Eric A. Havelock, *Harold A. Innis: A Memoir* (Toronto, 1982).

23. Northrop Frye, *Anatomy of Criticism: Four Essays* (Princeton, 1957); George Grant, *Technology and Empire: Perspectives on North America* (Toronto, 1969).

24. Michel Foucault, *Power/Knowledge: Selected Interviews and Other Writings, 1972–1977*, ed. Colin Gordon (Brighton, 1980), 114, 115–16.

Ramsay Cook's Quest for an Intellectual 'Phoenix', 1960–1968

PATRICE A. DUTIL

> 'It is perhaps old-fashioned to appeal to rational,
> pragmatic approaches to our problems
> in this age of ideology.'[1]
>
> —Ramsay Cook, 1966

In the fall of 1960 Daniel Bell published *The End of Ideology*, a seminal work in which he argued that the ideologies that had marked the Western world since the French Revolution were spent. If the book reflected its author's despair at the quality of politics in the 1950s, it also suggested hope. The end of ideology could be a positive development, Bell contended, for without the raging passions necessarily associated with rigid thought systems, many conflicts—even war itself—could be eliminated. Out of the ashes of ideology would rise reason, logic, intelligence.

Ramsay Cook's reaction to the politics of the 1950s could not have been more different from Bell's. Barely 30 years old but already a wise historian at the University of Toronto, Cook shared Bell's wish for an end to ideology. The problem was that in Canada, contrary to Bell's view, ideology seemed to be thriving: for Cook, it was as much a contemporary problem as a historical one. Cook, like Bell, addressed the issue on both fronts. On the historical plane, Cook applied himself to understanding manifestations of ideology and intelligence in the past and drawing the distinction between the two. Also like Bell, during the 1960s Cook assumed the role of a commentator in the media, where he campaigned publicly for an end to ideology and what Bell called its 'terrible simplifiers'. Later in the decade Cook's campaign against ideology and anti-intellectualism would find an ally in Pierre Elliott Trudeau, whose constitutional and socio-economic policies corresponded to a considerable degree with what Cook had called for in his eight years of contributions to many of English Canada's daily newspapers, *The Canadian Forum*, *Le Devoir*,[2] and CBC radio and television.

The life of intellectuals fascinated Cook. As a graduate student, he analyzed the work of a thinker who might have been quoted now and then in the family home in Manitoba: John W. Dafoe, the editor of the *Winnipeg Free Press*. Admiring Dafoe because 'he lived by his mind and his pen',[3] the young Cook used Dafoe's life as a window through which he could study events from the Manitoba Schools question to the Second World War. To examine such events through the eyes of a journalist rather than a politician represented an interesting departure in Canadian historiography. 'Dafoe was a man whose emotions always required intellectual expression,' Cook wrote. 'Therefore much of his writing was devoted to explaining his views on the nature of his country and its place in the world.'[4] In her review of the book that emerged from the doctoral thesis, Margaret Prang appreciated this milestone in Canadian intellectual history: Cook's *Dafoe* told 'us more about Dafoe than we know about any other Canadian political mind of this century'.[5]

Dafoe's energy and originality seemed to highlight the intellectual failures of Canadian society in the 1960s. Through Dafoe Cook saw an era that, despite its many errors and tragedies, appeared to offer hope for clarity, consistency, and progress; by contrast, Cook's own Canada seemed to have regressed.[6] Ramsay Cook took up the cranky typewriter that would become his trademark and embarked on a career that made him, like his hero Dafoe, a rare thing indeed in Canada: a public intellectual.[7] As such, Cook was critical of a political and intellectual culture that discouraged originality. Believing that the country's political and intellectual shortcomings were related, he set out to expose those responsible on the public stage.

In 1994, in *Images of the Intellectual*, Edward Said wrote that 'One task of the intellectual is the effort to break down the stereotypes and reductive categories that are so limiting to human thought and communication,'[8] and argued that 'the intellectual appeals to (rather than excoriates) as wide as possible a public, who is his or her natural constituency.' Like Said, Cook believed that the problem lay not with the society at large but rather with the 'insiders, experts, coteries, professionals' who made public policy and helped to shape public opinion. 'Intellectuals,' according to Said, 'should be the ones to question patriotic nationalism, corporate thinking, and a sense of class, racial or gender privilege.'[9] This is precisely what Cook did in reaching for a broader audience, in attempting to slip the bonds of his profession, and in applying the wisdom of his discipline to the problems of the day.[10]

Cook launched his career as a commentator at *The Canadian Forum* in October 1960 with a post-mortem of a recent conference of the British Labour Party, in which he wrote that the 'intellectual vigour' of that party 'might turn Canadian radicals green with envy'. A year later, in October 1961, he joined the journal's editorial board along with Kildare Dobbs. Founded in 1920, the *Forum* had provided an independent voice for the left throughout the 1940s and 1950s, when it published much of Frank Underhill's trenchant commentary. When Cook joined it, the magazine regularly featured articles by Frank Scott and Eugene Forsey, as well as more nationalist economists such as Abraham Rotstein and Mel Watkins.

In Cook's grim diagnosis, Canada was in crisis. Together, the politics of the 1950s, the prosperity of that decade, and the Cold War had 'blind[ed] Canadians to the very existence of their difficulties'. 'We were living,' he wrote, 'beyond our

means,' at a time when it was incumbent on us to examine the new forces struc-
turing global politics and economics.[11]

In that article, published in 1962, Cook boldly voiced the question that seemed
to move him the most: 'Have Canadian public leaders and Canadians in general
stopped thinking?'[12] He was concerned with the declining quality of public debate,
and had seen signs of an alarming exhaustion of ideas in the seductive but shallow
presidential campaign of John F. Kennedy in 1959. 'His persistent repetition of the
phrase about America moving forward seemed in danger of reducing a public
philosophy to a cliché by the last days,'[13] Cook observed, regretting the absence of
the more intellectually rigorous Adlai Stevenson. Kennedy might have fired imaginations in 'the less intellectual sectors of the electorate', but Cook suspected that
the American president's public philosophy was far less profound than his ambition for power. Remembering Arthur Schlesinger's consoling remark that
Kennedy's liberalism was more 'an intellectual commitment' than a 'visceral reaction', Cook concluded hopefully—Kennedy 'fits well into the tradition of successful American progressivism in the twentieth century'—and even saw in his victory
hope for better things in Canada: 'Dare one add that the lesson that a liberal party
can win elections in times of prosperity should not be lost on Canadian radicals?'

In Cook's view, the need for debate among English Canada's cultural and intellectual élite was urgent, especially on the Quebec question. As he observed in 1963,
the history of Quebec had taken a radical new course, and it was wishful thinking
to believe that the regime as it had existed before 1960 could be rehabilitated.
'French-Canadian nationalism is much more powerful, much more deeply rooted
in the masses and much more creative and positive than it has ever been before,'
he wrote. 'As a creative force it should be welcomed, not derided or feared by
English Canadians. . . . It is just as dangerous to sit back and await a complete
formulation of demands by Quebec itself.'

Cook presented his recommendations for research and policy:

> The task before English Canadians who desire to prevent their country from laps-
> ing into chaos is to break silence. First we must try to understand what is taking
> place in Quebec, and why it is taking place. Second we must try to respond posi-
> tively by attempting to formulate for ourselves what we believe to be the reasons for
> the present 'passive resistance' of French Canadians toward Confederation. Having
> done this, we must then—and this is more important—begin to think about what
> we are willing and able to do to redress the legitimate grievances of French Canada.
> There are a number of questions which we must seriously ask ourselves. Are we in
> the English-speaking provinces willing to reconsider our past, deplorable attitude
> to public support for the kind of schools that would satisfy the cultural aspirations
> of French Canadians outside Quebec? Are we ready to reconsider our attitude to the
> status of the French language in the legislatures, law courts and publicly-owned
> corporations in English Canada? Are we willing to alter practices respecting the
> French language in business and commercial activities? Are we willing to make an

effort to provide the means for increased bilingualism among at least the better educated groups in English Canada? Are we willing to explore even the possibility that our federal system may require some radical modification to meet the changed circumstances of the 1960s?

Any hope for progress depended on the articulation of new ideas. 'Right now the first necessary step is for English Canada to break silence and admit that the problem does not rest only with Quebec, or only with the federal government, but with all Canadians,' Cook argued. 'To refuse to make this admission is to deny, implicitly, the existence of Canada as a community.'[14]

The fact that English Canada did not respond to this call for new ideas reflected a political and intellectual problem that Cook called 'Diefenbakerism'.

DIEFENBAKERISM

For Cook, one of the most odious dimensions of Diefenbakerism was its particular brand of nationalism. Noting that Diefenbaker's rise to power had fuelled an upsurge in Canadian nationalism, he argued that 'many Canadians, inebriated by Mr. Diefenbaker's particular brand of national joy juice, failed to realize that behind glib promises to restore national sovereignty and independence, lay an intellectual vacuum.'[15] Cook observed that the new Canadian nationality of Macdonald and Cartier had been transformed into something that was not true to Canada. Since their time 'Canadian politicians and intellectuals . . . have found nationalist appeals easier or more profitable than the hard intellectual labour involved in maintaining the distinction between nationalism and the nation-state.'[16] Writing in *Le Devoir*, Cook explained that there existed an inherent antagonism between nationalism and progressive ideas. 'Diefenbakerism illustrates the dangers of appealing to nationalism in politics,' he wrote. 'Politicians use it as a weapon to appeal to people's emotions, instead of offering carefully designed policies.'[17]

The rebirth of nationalism was hardly exclusive to Canada; many nations were struggling to shake off colonialism. In Canada, however, what Cook called an 'Alice in Wonderland reality' existed, and it could only be explained by 'the abysmal failure of our political leaders and advisers to come to grips with Canadian problems as they exist in the 1960s'. Perhaps, Cook suggested, this could be attributed to habits of mind developed during the Mackenzie King era. Now public opinion polls, not leadership, seemed to drive politics. 'Canada,' Cook declared in 1962, 'is a sick country.'[18]

Diefenbaker's 'platitudinous political rhetoric' magnified the worst aspects of Canadian politics. Lamenting the 'windy rhetoric, impossible promises and double-think' engaged in by all the country's political parties, he contended that the modern political circus presented a serious threat to Canada's political culture. Before the 1963 election, in an article entitled 'Wanted: A Phoenix', he asked: 'Can our politicians recover from the Diefenbaker disease in time to give the country a serious campaign?'[19]

The Liberal, New Democratic, and Social Credit parties did not escape Cook's wrath. 'Are the other parties as intellectually bankrupt as the government?'[20] he asked as he noted that all parties had to come to terms with their collective failures in finding a national consensus. Worse, the abandonment of intellectual leadership and the pursuit of short-term popularity were having an effect on the electorate. Cook argued that a greater malaise was affecting Canadians—a malaise that ran deeper than a declining dollar, falling foreign investments, cold war politics, or Quebec's place in Confederation. Instead, Cook wanted his politicians to answer a deeper question: 'how can Canada be restored and continued as a viable political community?'[21] He did not limit his campaign for a more sophisticated, more intellectual politics to the print media. 'Do you think,' he asked J.B. McGeachy of the *Financial Post* before a national audience on CBC television, 'that there are any clear issues which will be placed before the country?' The answer, on the cold February night in 1963 when Diefenbaker's minority government was defeated, was a resounding 'no'.[22]

In Cook's opinion, the Liberals under Lester B. Pearson had refused to follow the path of intellectual renewal taken by some of their liberal cousins in the United Kingdom and the United States, and the Nobel laureate Pearson was nothing more than a Mackenzie King 'with a dash of Water Gordon'.[23] In a blistering article published as the Liberals assumed the mantle of minority government in 1963, Cook quoted Mrs Marion Pearson, who had told the *Toronto Star* that her husband was 'an intellectual. His powers of concentration are enormous. Hockey and other sports of TV can absorb him completely.'

The Liberals had squandered their time in opposition: 'The great tragedy of Canadian liberalism,' Cook wrote,

is that Mr. Pearson and his party had five years to work out a new and imaginative plan for Canada. And they failed. Even the much acclaimed and declaimed Kingston Conference of intellectuals (including a poet) produced nothing (except a poem by George Johnson for the *Forum*). The real trouble is that too many people, dazzled by Mr. Diefenbaker's (and Mr. Kennedy's) triumphs as a super leader, have accepted the all-too-easy explanation that the Conservative failure was a Diefenbaker failure. So the tribal cry goes up for a new leader. . . . Leadership alone is no answer—and that is fortunate for the Liberals, since Mr. Pearson has failed to fill even the role of an adman's Caesar. What is needed are new ideas—and here again it is doubtful if Mr. Pearson can fill the bill.[24]

For Cook, the cult of 'the chief' and the battles for the better brand of nationalism could only do further harm to Canada's fragile political culture. Even more discouraging than the failures of leadership, however, was the apparently widespread refusal to engage in the hard intellectual work required to address the problems of foreign policy, the role of the state, and relations between English and French in Canada. Although he hoped that Pearson's new Liberal government might attempt to come to terms with the new realities, he feared that 'the current composition of his party, and that party's past history, should not leave the articulate sections of the community in a state of euphoria.'[25] Observing, in January 1964, that 'the Liberals have quickly proven as short of ideas as their predecessors,' Cook was particularly critical of the prime minister. Although Pearson appeared to recognize some aspects of Confederation's problems, he seemed 'unable, perhaps unwilling' to explain them to the people.[26]

Cook was equally frustrated with the recently formed New Democratic Party. As a founding member in 1961, he had hoped that the NDP would 'increase the content of Canadian political debates'; yet he also feared that an obsession with short-term tactics and electoral strategies would distract it from its mission.[27] The NDP had to play an 'intellectual' role in politics: 'One of the major functions of third parties in Canada has always been to introduce imaginative ideas into our political life when the old parties seem bankrupt in the face of new problems.' However, he also cautioned that in so doing it must be careful to 'distinguish between constructive and destructive proposals'.[28]

In particular, Cook had wanted the new party to rethink the orthodoxies of its predecessor, the CCF, as it headed for its founding convention in the summer of 1961. He took issue with Kenneth McNaught, who in the March 1961 issue of the *Forum* had cautioned that the NDP should not lose sight of its origins. Cook countered that the NDP should not make a fetish of the past, and that indulgence in 'excessive ancestor worship' could only hamper the growth of a new radicalism. He reminded his readers that among the 'many excellent qualities' of the CCF's first leader, J.S. Woodsworth, the foremost, 'next to his moral courage, was his insistence that solutions to social and economic problems arose out of careful study of existing conditions'.[29]

In fact, Cook resigned from the editorial board of the *Canadian Forum* in 1964 over a dispute that was tearing the party between militant CCFers and the emerging generation of New Democrats. In the July 1964 issue of the *Forum*, Edith Fowke had written an article about the Exchange Conference held in May 1964 to explore how Liberals and New Democrats might share ideas. Fowke, a traditional CCFer, described at length the earlier history of the Woodsworth Memorial Foundation (which had sponsored the effort) and implied that the Exchange was merely another ill-fated attempt by the 'new' Democrats to generate new ideas. Cook had been one of the original directors of the Exchange Conference but had quit it in December 1963 to protest the interference of politicians. He responded to Fowke's article with an angry public letter, and ended his formal relationship with the *Forum*. In his view, Fowke had demonstrated 'a totally irresponsible attitude toward the efforts that are being made at present to give some intellectual substance to public debate in this country'.[30]

He had originally hoped for great things for the NDP in Quebec. It was 'the only serious minority party, one that could almost certainly benefit from the public's discontent with the old parties'.[31] But his hopes soon chilled as the NDP's evolving positions on the Quebec question increasingly alienated him. In particular, he disagreed with the NDP's support for the idea of a special status for Quebec with respect to its language, culture, and traditions. Cook considered the term 'special status' a reckless use of language: 'Intellectual clarity, not obfuscation should be the goal of the NDP in all matters,' he told party members in 1966, especially 'in a matter so technical, so important, and so explosive as a discussion of the constitution and of French-English relations'. Not only was the distinction meaningless, but in supporting it the NDP was 'confused and contradictory', for it threatened to undermine the party's broader dedication to building a country greater than the sum of its parts. Cook's split from the NDP on the Quebec issue proved irreconcilable. He resigned from the party in 1967.

INTELLECTUALS IN QUEBEC

Cook had concluded his biography of Dafoe by admitting that his subject had not been infallible, particularly in his disregard of French Canada.[32] He would not make the same mistake. Indeed, Quebec in the late 1950s and early 1960s offered inspiring examples of intellectuals in action. Cook's achievement in this regard was significant. Almost alone, he sought to shed light on Quebec realities that were threatening to uproot Confederation, but that were almost completely ignored by the media, the politicians, and the people of English Canada—as he put it, 'it is in English Canada, not in Quebec, that the issues need explaining.' His diagnosis of the problems separating Quebec and the rest of Canada was linked to the political problems of the leading parties: 'Both the Liberal and the NDP leaders have shown an intelligent sympathy for the new aspirations of Quebec, but both have almost completely failed to bring the matter to the attention of English Canada.'[33]

The only English-Canadian thinker to whom Cook referred as an 'intellectual' was George Grant. In French Canada, by contrast, a number of figures qualified for this description. The ideal, of course, was André Laurendeau, who never had 'the "pure" intellectual's disdain for politics and politicians'.[34] But there were others, including Henri Bourassa,[35] George Lapalme (Quebec Liberal leader in the 1950s),[36] René Lévesque,[37] and Pierre Trudeau,[38] whom Cook would later describe as an 'intellectual *coureur de bois*' and a 'democratic intellectual'.[39] Though highly critical of *Le Devoir*'s Claude Ryan, Cook admitted that 'No one in Canada in the last three years had done more . . . in attempting to keep our constitutional debate reasonable and specific.'[40]

Ideas were at work in Quebec. The provincial election of 1962 seemed to represent the triumph of intellect and democracy that Cook wanted to see in the rest of Canada, and he was harshly critical of the CBC for not covering it.[41] 'Clearly elections can be won by intelligence, hard work, and perhaps above all a compellingly conceived and explained programme,' he wrote in the *Canadian Forum*. 'This is the most fundamental lesson of the Quebec election. René Lévesque with his blackboard and chalk playing the role of public educator should be held up before all our image-conscious, poll-taking politicians.'[42]

Cook considered the Quebec nationality 'problem' to be of an intellectual and cultural nature rather than a constitutional one. In what might be considered the classic intellectual's fashion, Cook called for more study, more talk, more evidence. The creation of the Bilingualism and Biculturalism Commission raised his hopes for an honest and frank dialogue[43] and even prompted him to say kind words about Lester Pearson. But even then he was cautious. In his review of the Commission's first Report he criticized the lack of historical perspective in the Laurendeau-Dunton text. 'That a serious crisis exists is not in doubt,' he wrote in *Le Devoir.* 'But as a historian I fear that the . . . commission's members may have become carried away by an obsessive concern with the present.'[44]

If Cook demanded more intelligence from English Canada, he made the same demand of Quebec politicians of all stripes. Although he criticized the *Financial Post* in 1964 for asking Quebeckers to explain more clearly 'what they want', the following year Cook took up the same cry himself.[45] The idea of a more 'coopera-tive federalism' in which provinces might have the right to opt out of federal programs and receive compensation drew his fire. 'It seems,' he declared, 'that the time has come for proponents of cooperative federalism to define their criteria and precise long-term objectives, so that public opinion can make an informed judge-ment on the value and implications of their conception of federalism. Then, after careful consideration, the latter will be either accepted or rejected.'[46] He would make the same argument in English: 'At present the "associate state" plan gives every appearance of being the product of fuzzy thinking. Intellectually and practically, it lacks the logic of either our present federal system or outright separation.'[47]

The Fulton-Favreau formula for amending the Constitution was criticized for the same reasons. Cook argued that constitutional changes were so complex and technical that it would be dangerous to approach them with haste and emotion. He expected that the passions awakened by this issue would hurt the country far more than modification of the Constitution would help it, and concluded that the time had not come for such an idea.[48] 'It is possible that the Fulton-Favreau formula does not meet our present needs, but this must be demonstrated on the basis of facts, not prejudices,' he wrote later.[49] When Claude Ryan expressed his support for some sort of constitutionally recognized status for Quebec, Cook immediately rejected the proposal.[50] Not surprisingly, the separatist argument struck Cook as something akin to Diefenbakerism: 'Like ideologues of every type, separatists offer a simplistic explanation of political problems and pat, almost magical solutions that are the concoctions of closed minds that refuse to be confused by facts.'[51]

The solution for Cook, in part, was a better politics and a more ambitious sense of democratic culture. With five political parties, Canada still needed a political team that could simultaneously understand the aspirations of Quebec and accept the legitimate concerns of the West and the Maritimes. 'The moment a single party finds an answer to this problem, there will no longer be any need to talk about a crisis in the federation.'[52] It would take a while to find that party, but the steps taken by Pearson suggested that the Liberals (especially after a potential 'phoenix' named Pierre Trudeau was appointed Minister of Justice) might offer the right solutions after all. Not surprisingly—given that he himself made the same argument—she was instrumental in having the *Canadian Forum* publish the translated manifesto of those Quebec intellectuals (among them Trudeau) whose 'Appeal for Realism in Politics' had been published by *Cité libre*. Calling for the political class to be more precise 'in our analysis of situations, more intellectually honest in debate and more realistic in decision', it declared that 'We must descend from the euphoria of all-embracing ideologies and come to grips with actual problems.'[53]

Of the many forward-thinking Quebec intellectuals who seemed capable of assuming leadership, none was better suited than Trudeau. 'Whereas the leaders of the previous decade had pat policies for every problem, and solutions for none, Mr. Trudeau admitted that he simply did not have answers to every single difficulty of the post-industrial society,' Cook would write in his post-mortem of the 1968 election. 'The best he could do was to insist that past answers be reappraised, and to indicate that he had approaches to these problems which were new. This attitude of tentativeness and frankness conformed well to the mood of the country, skeptical of the easy answers of traditional politicians.'[54] What made Trudeau different, according to Cook (who joined the Liberal Party in 1968 to support his leadership bid) 'was a quality that had become almost extinct in our public life: his refusal to engage in the windy circumlocutions that had come more and more to characterize our great debate.'[55] At last an intellectual phoenix had risen from the ashes of Diefenbakerism.

Both personally and intellectually, 1968 was a turning point for Cook. In the spring of that year his good friend André Laurendeau died; he helped the Trudeau leadership campaign; and he ended his five-year editorship of the *Canadian Historical Review*. That fall he left Canada to take up a visiting professorship at Harvard University. After his return a year later, Cook's presence in the mass media was less obvious. There were many occasional pieces, of course, but he did not sustain another collaboration with a particular journal. The 1968 election represented something of an intellectual victory; a shining example that ideas could overcome mere sympathies. Perhaps now was the time to lay down some arms and focus on more academic pursuits. Cook did not renew his membership in the Liberal party after that year.

Conclusion

It is hardly surprising that Ramsay Cook responded to events in the 1960s by publicly calling for a more reasoned, intellectual approach. Among the issues that concerned him, the rise of nationalism was particularly troubling for two reasons. The first was obvious: the politicians were appealing to nationalism because they were either unwilling or unable to generate the new ideas required to redefine Canada at a time when many in Quebec were concluding it had no identity worthy of adherence. But the second reason ran far deeper. As he began his academic career, Cook diagnosed a fundamental problem with the intellectual class in Canada: unresponsive to new trends, it also appeared insensitive to what was worth preserving about the Canadian tradition. Above all, it seemed unwilling to come out into the light of the broader society and to use its influence among all political parties.

Nowhere was the 'cult of mediocrity, Cancult', and leftist 'radical chic' that irritated Cook more noticeable than in the media. The profession of journalism 'has not lacked honoured names in Canadian history', Cook wrote in 1963.[56] As a virtual member of the media, however, he grew as demanding of journalists as he was of politicians. He would vent his frustration in an article published in *Saturday Night* in 1980: 'it is difficult to think of a country where the standards of daily political journalism are so mediocre as in Canada, especially English-speaking Canada.'[57]

In 1964 Cook outlined his hopes for the intellectual community. He argued that if what Canada needed was a new 'National Policy' to meet the challenges of the 1960s, it should not count on politicians to design it. Cook hoped that the 'intellectual community' might offer new insights and solutions, but saw 'no sign of any vigorous stirring' there. Many people, he wrote, 'want to know how an English-Canadian version of the Quiet Revolution could be stimulated. There is, of course, no easy answer. But it is at least legitimate to wonder if our intellectuals, busy filling the learned journals, the literary magazines and our newspapers' "midcult" entertainment pages, have even bothered to ask themselves the question.'[58]

In 1960 Daniel Bell had written that 'a repudiation of ideology, to be meaningful, must mean not only a criticism of the utopian order but of existing society as well.'[59] Cook echoed Bell's demands. If he asked for rigour from politicians, he demanded it of journalists and intellectuals. Convinced that reasoned thinking—ideas—would elevate social and political goals as well as the democratic will, he hoped that the politicians would respond. There is no doubt that Cook's presence in the press and on television during the 1960s affected a particular generation of young journalists. His analysis of Quebec's place in Canada, his critique of nationalism, his conservatism in constitutional matters, his understanding of Canada's particularity and of its history generally seemed impartial and relatively free of ideology at a time when new brands of intellectuals—the technical specialists at one end of the spectrum and the ideologues at the other—were emerging. Drawing on his own experience in NDP politics, his work as a scholar, even his work as an editor of the *Canadian Historical Review* from 1963 to 1968, he knew that the problems he encountered often reflected a broader malaise. As he wrote on leaving the CHR in June 1968, the journal itself 'suffers the same structural and psychological difficulties as beset Canada'.[60]

In 1989, Russell Jacoby provoked an interesting controversy with his book *The Last Intellectuals*. Harshly critical of intellectuals in the 1980s, he was careful to specify that his thesis applied to Canada as well as the United States. Cook's observations in the press regarding Canadian intellectual life in the 1960s suggest that he had come to the same conclusion twenty years earlier. Sadly, Cook won for himself something he ardently did not wish: a place in Canada's history as one of its last public intellectuals.

Notes

1. Ramsay Cook, *Canada and the French-Canadian Question* (Toronto, 1966), 5.

2. Cook reminisced about his experience with *Le Devoir* in 'Le Devoir, Year 85', *Literary Review of Canada* (June 1995).

3. Cook, *The Politics of John W. Dafoe and the Free Press* (Toronto, 1963), viii.

4. Ibid., 288.

5. *Canadian Forum* (September 1963).

6. A similar theme was raised by the historian Richard Hofstadter, *Anti-Intellectualism in American Life* (New York, 1962).

7. The best definition is the simplest, and is offered by Russell Jacoby: 'A public intellectual' is 'an incorrigibly independent soul answering to no one. The definition must include a commitment not simply to a professional or private domain but to a public world—and a public language, the vernacular'; see *The Last Intellectuals: American Culture in the Age of Academe* (New York, 1987), 235. The literature on 'public intellectuals' as a sociological phenomenon is sparse. Edward W. Said's work is an impassioned summary of the role of the intellectual by a political *engagé*; see *Images of the Intellectual* (New York, 1994). Since the 1950s, many have lamented the passing of the independent thinker and the increasing 'institutionalization' and 'professionalization' of intellectuals by universities. The net effect has been an abandonment of discourse with the broader public. See Hofstadter, *Anti-Intellectualism*, Thomas Molnar, *The Decline of the Intellectual* (New York, 1961), Paul Johnson, *Intellectuals* (London, 1988). Other interesting treatments of the relationship between intellectuals and public life can be found in Tony Judt, *Past Imperfect: French Intellectuals, 1944–1956* (Berkeley, 1992); Régis Debray, *Le Pouvoir intellectuel en France* (Paris, 1979) and *Le scribe* (Paris, 1980); and Edward Shils, *The Intellectuals and the Powers & Other Essays* (Chicago, 1972). See also William M. Banks, *Black Intellectuals: Race and Responsibility in American Life* (New York, 1996); Norman Podhoretz, *Ex-Friends: Falling out with Allen Ginsberg, Lionel and Diana Trilling, Lillian Hellman, Hannah Arendt and Norman Mailer* (New York, 1999); and Hilton Kramer, *The Twilight of the Intellectuals* (New York, 1999). There is no equivalent study in Canada.

8. Said, *Images of the Intellectual*, xi.

9. Ibid., xiii.

10. The best example of this dimension of Cook's work falls outside the parameters of this study. It was 'The Craft of History', a CBC television series that featured interviews with Donald Creighton, Michel Brunet, Arthur Lower, and W.L. Morton; a transcript was later published.

11. 'Lewis Carroll's Canada', *Canadian Forum* (August 1962).

12. Ibid.

13. 'The American Election: A Victory over "Creeping Mediocrity"', n.d., York University, Fonds Ramsay Cook (FRC), 15/356.

14. 'A Time to Break Silence', *Canadian Forum* (July 1963).

15. 'A New Awakening', *Canadian Forum* (June 1964).

16. *The Maple Leaf Forever: Essays on Nationalism in Canada* (Toronto, 1971), 6.

17. 'Le diefenbakerisme illustre les dangers de l'appel au nationalisme en politique. Le politicien se sert de cette arme pour faire appel aux émotions des gens au lieu d'offrir des politiques prudemment conçues'; 'Du "Goldwaterisme" au "Diefenbakerisme"', *Le Devoir* (13 Nov. 1964).

18. Ramsay Cook, 'Lewis Carroll's Canada', *Canadian Forum* (August 1962).

19. 'Wanted: A Phoenix', *Canadian Forum* (March 1963).

20. 'Election miasma', FRC, 16/381.

21. 'Lewis Carroll's Canada'.

22. See Robert Fulford, *Crisis at the Victory Burlesk* (Toronto, 1968), 51.

23. 'Not Left, Not Right, But Forward', *Canadian Forum* (February 1972).

24. 'A New Liberal Government?' *Canadian Forum* (May 1963).

25. Ibid.

26. 'The New Year and the Old Order', *Canadian Forum* (January 1964).

27. 'Lewis Carroll's Canada'.

28. 'Crisis in the NDP', *Canadian Forum* (August 1963).

29. 'The Old Man, The Old Manifesto, The Old Party', *Canadian Forum* (May 1961).

30. Letter to the editor, *Canadian Forum* (August 1964).

31. 'Le seul parti minoritaire sérieux, un parti qui pourrait presque sûrement bénéficier de la désaffection envers les vieux partis. Le régime risque de souffrir de l'impuissance des grands partis'; *Le Devoir* (9 Jan. 1965).

32. . . . 'he ignored it'; *Politics of J.W. Dafoe and the Free Press*, 294.

33. 'Wanted: A Phoenix', *Canadian Forum* (March 1963).

34. 'André Laurendeau: A Hard Man to Follow', *Saturday Night* (February 1974).

35. *Canada and the French-Canadian Question*, 105.

36. Ibid., 9.

37. Ibid., 15.

38. *The Maple Leaf Forever*, 26.

39. Ibid., 39, 45.

40. 'Analysing the options for Canada', *Montreal Star* (28 Oct. 1967).

41. 'Elections Are Not Won By Prayers', *Canadian Forum* (December 1962).

42. Ibid.

43. 'Une Commission pas comme les autres', *Le Devoir* (5 March 1965).

44. 'Je ne veux pas mettre en doute l'existence d'une crise sérieuse. Mais, en ma qualité d'historien, j'ai peur que les membres de la commission d'enquête . . . n'aient été emportés par un souci trop obsédant du présent'; ibid.

45. At this point, I must take issue with Guy Laforest's interpretation of Cook's thinking in his *Trudeau et la fin d'un rêve canadien* (Québec, 1992). Claiming that in 1967 Cook 'sang the praises' of the dualist ('two nations') concept of Canada, Laforest maintains that Cook symbolizes an anti-Quebec shift among English-Canadian intellectuals in the late 1980s (p. 24). In fact, Cook clearly condemned the idea of dualism, and has been remarkably consistent in his views.

46. 'Le temps parait venu pour les tenants du fédéralisme coopératif de définir des critères et des objectifs précis à long terme de sorte que l'opinion publique puisse juger en connaissance de cause de la valeur et des implications de leur conception du fédéralisme. Celui-ci dès lors sera rejeté ou accepté après mûr examen'; 'Fédéralisme coopératif et droit d'option', *Le Devoir* (10 April 1965).

47. *Canada and the French-Canadian Question*, 78.

48. 'Le débat sur la constitution est inopportun et mal engagé', *Le Devoir* (6 April 1965).

49. 'La formule Fulton-Favreau n'est peut-être pas adaptée à nos besoins actuels, mais la démonstration doit reposer sur des faits, non sur des préjugés'; 'Peut-on parler de camisole de force?', *Le Devoir* (15 March 1965).

50. 'Un régime particulier pour le Québec?' *Le Devoir* (5 Dec. 1964). Cook never changed his mind in this regard. He was categorically against the conclusions of the Pépin-Robarts commission. 'Special status is not an idea but a nostrum,' he said. See 'Why it won't Work,' n.d., FRC, 16/401. Not surprisingly, Cook was one of the earliest critics of the Meech Lake Accord in 1987.

51. *Canada and the French-Canadian Question*, 68

52. 'La crise du parti conservateur', *Le Devoir* (15 Feb. 1965).

53. *Canadian Forum* (May 1964).

54. 'Never so much promised to so many', *Montreal Star* (18 Jan. 1969).

55. *Maple Leaf Forever*, 27.

56. *Politics of John W. Dafoe*, ix.

57. 'How the Tories Self-Destructed', *Saturday Night* (1980); see also 'The Standard Stanfield: A Humble Tortoise', *Canadian Forum* (October 1973).

58. 'The New Year and the Old Order', *Canadian Forum* (January 1964).

59. *The End of Ideology*, 16.

60. 'Goodbye to all That', *Canadian Historical Review* XLIX, 3 (September 1968).

PART TWO

CULTURE

Christ in the Crowsnest

*Religion and the Anglo-Protestant Working Class
in the Crowsnest Pass, 1898–1918*

NORMAN KNOWLES

In 1909 the Superintendent of the Methodist Church in Canada, S.D. Chown, asserted that 'the Crow's Nest Pass is of prime strategic religious importance for the whole of Canada.' For Chown, the Crowsnest Pass embodied many of the concerns and challenges confronting Canada's Protestant churches at the turn of the century: 'drink and crime abound, revolutionary doctrines are being propagated, and foreigners are crowding in who have not the first idea as to how to begin to live according to Canadian ideals.'[1] Concern with the spread of vice, growing working-class discontent, and the challenge posed by immigration to Anglo-Canadian hegemony resulted in a tremendous increase in home mission work in frontier communities such as those of the Crowsnest Pass in the late nineteenth and early twentieth centuries. Church leaders insisted that unless an effort was made to save the worker and to firmly plant the Gospel on the frontier, the social and moral future of the nation would be imperilled.[2] While the imperatives underlying home mission work have been well documented, very little attention has been given either to the ways in which home missions were carried out at the local level or to their reception by the missionized. Using local newspapers, denominational records, congregational registers, and family histories, this paper explores the different roles that religion played in the mining communities of the Crowsnest Pass between 1898 and 1914. The focus is on the strategies employed by Protestant churches to appeal to the miners and labourers of the region, and the responses of workers to these ministrations.

While several generations of British and American historians have demonstrated the important relationship between religious ideas, forms, and experiences and the development of the working class, the roles played by religion in shaping working-class life, culture, and protest has been largely ignored by Canada's historians.[3] Preoccupied with the messengers and the message rather than popular belief and practice, Canadian religious history has been dominated by clergy-centred histories of religious thought and reform and an ongoing debate over the nature and impact of secularization.[4] Canada's labour historians have been equally negligent in their lack of attention to working-class religiosity. In the past, many studies of the working class tended to view religion simply as a mechanism of social control or as a source of fragmentation that prevented the development of a unified class consciousness.[5] Although Bryan Palmer and Gregory Kealey, in their important studies of Hamilton, Toronto, and the Knights of Labor, acknowledged that religion may have helped to shape working-class culture, they did not explore this possibility in any depth or detail.[6] Several recent works, however, have begun to redress this oversight. In her study of class and gender in the small towns of late nineteenth-century Ontario, Lynne Marks demonstrates that religion continued to be an important influence in many working-class homes despite the alienation of male youth from the churches. Further evidence that religion occupied a vital place in the lives of many working people is provided by Nancy Christie, Michael Gauvreau, and Eric Crouse in their examinations of urban revivalism.[7] Such works suggest both the serious need to explore the relationship between religion and the working class in Canada further and the potential insights such analysis might produce. One area yet to be examined is the role of religion in the lives of workers located in resource-based frontier communities. This case study of religion in the coal-mining towns of the Crowsnest Pass marks an initial attempt to fill that void.

With the completion of the railway in 1898, the Crowsnest Pass region of southeastern British Columbia and southwestern Alberta began to experience rapid economic development. Much of this growth resulted from the exploitation of the area's rich coal deposits. In 1898 the Crow's Nest Pass Coal Company began mining operations at Coal Creek, near Fernie, to supply the smelters of the BC interior and the American northwest. The American-owned company later established mines in Michel (1899), Morrisey (1902), and Corbin (1908). The Pacific Coal Company, a subsidiary of the Canadian Pacific Railway, opened a mine at Hosmer in 1908. A variety of companies developed mines on the Alberta side of the pass in Bellevue, Lille, Blairmore, Coleman, and Hillcrest between 1900 and 1910.[8] With the opening of the mines, thousands of speculators, entrepreneurs, workers, and immigrants flocked to the Crowsnest, hoping to cash in on the region's economic expansion. Missionaries soon followed. In 1897 the Revd T. Oswald and divinity student D.L. Oliver began preaching in the coal camps around Fernie and conducting worship in the homes of Presbyterian miners and merchants from Nova Scotia and Ontario. The following year, the Revd Alexander Dunn began construction of a Presbyterian church in Fernie. The Methodists planted a mission at Fernie under the direction of the Revd R.F. Stillman at the same time and erected a church in 1900. An Anglican presence was established in 1898 when the Revd W.H. Hedley began holding services in the bank building. These early missions served as bases for work in the surrounding mine sites. During the summer months, student missionaries ministered to the miners at Michel, Natal, Corbin, Morrisey, and Hosmer before churches could be established in the camps on lands leased from the Crow's Nest Pass Coal Co. A Protestant presence was quickly established in the new mining towns on the Alberta side of the Pass as well.

A student missionary, D.A. Stewart, began work for the Presbyterians at Frank and Blairmore in 1901, and the Methodists sent another student missionary the following year. Scarce resources, together with a desire to avoid competition and duplication of efforts, resulted in an agreement between Methodists and Presbyterians to divide the Alberta section of the Pass between them. The Methodists took charge of Frank, Bellevue, Hillcrest, and Lille; the Presbyterians of Coleman and Blairmore. In 1903 a Church of England clergyman, the Revd F.G. Richard, started work in Frank and Blairmore. The following year the Revd R.A. Robinson established a parish in Coleman. A Baptist mission was organized at Frank in 1905 by the layman F.M. Pinkney. A second mission opened in Blairmore in 1908. The lack of clergy and resources, a transient population, the instability of the coal industry, and frequent labour disputes made mission work in the Crowsnest difficult. Despite these challenges, the churches became important institutions within their communities.[9]

The establishment of missions and churches in the predominantly working-class mining and logging camps of western Canada has often been interpreted as an attempt to transplant the small-town, middle-class values of eastern Canada to the frontier and to impose religion upon an indifferent, if not hostile, population.[10] This interpretation ignores the fact that religion was an important part of the 'cultural baggage' of many immigrant workers: many of the miners in the Crowsnest came from Wales, England, Scotland, and eastern Canada and brought with them a commitment to evangelical Protestantism as well as a tradition of labour protest and organization.[11] The close relationship between these two traditions is evident in the life of F.H. Sherman, the president of District 18 of the United Mine Workers of America. Born in Gloucestershire in 1869, Sherman worked as coal miner in Wales before immigrating to North America in 1898. A devout Methodist as a young man, he became a lay preacher and seriously considered studying for the ministry. During his early years as a labour leader in the Crowsnest, Sherman actively supported local churches in their assault against the region's saloons and brothels. His religious sympathies were reflected in the *District Ledger*, the official organ of District 18, which regularly reported on local church affairs, carried a Sunday School column, and ran editorials on religious issues. In later years Sherman became a committed socialist, often attacking the church and dismissing the clergy as 'apologists and defenders of capitalism'. Yet his radicalism continued to be shaped and informed by Christian precepts. For Sherman, capitalism was 'contrary to every principle that Christ has ever taught'. Socialism and the creation of a cooperative commonwealth, he argued, were at the heart of the Gospel.[12]

Sherman was not unique. Many miners, British- or Canadian-born, carried a strong Protestant faith with them to the Crowsnest and became active members of local churches. Bill Chappell was typical of many in the British contingent. Born in Nottingham in 1883, he arrived in the Crowsnest in 1902, where he worked as a labourer at West Canadian Collieries mine at Lille and became a founding member of both the Methodist church at Bellevue and District 18 of the United Mine Workers. Ed Christie had a similar story. Christie was born in 1866 in Hawthorne, Durham, where he worked in the coal mines and served as a Methodist lay preacher before immigrating to Canada and settling in Calgary in 1907. In 1910 he moved his family to Bellevue, where he found work in the mine. Christie became an active member of the local Methodist congregation, serving as Sunday School superintendent, lay preacher, and member of the church's board of management.[13] The active involvement of such individuals belies the assertion that the churches of the Pass were almost entirely made up of 'relatively prosperous middle class congregations'.[14] In fact, workers played a prominent role in the establishment churches: they constituted a sizeable presence in most congregations, and were well represented on church vestries and boards during these early years.[15]

Churches performed a number of important functions within the Anglo-Protestant working class of the Crowsnest Pass. Significant centres of community life, they provided places for people to meet and offered a wide range of social activities, from dances and dinners to plays and entertainments, in addition to lectures and courses. Churches were also centres of support and assistance for workers, who in times of need often looked to the clergy and their fellow parishioners for help. At the same time, as the ethnic composition of the Crowsnest became more diverse, churches became important proclamations of ethnic identity. For Welsh, Scottish, English, and Anglo-Canadian miners, affiliation with a Protestant church served as a significant declaration of their position and status, differentiating them from the mostly Catholic labourers from southern and eastern Europe who performed much of the unskilled work in the Pass.

The close relationship between religious identity and social status contributed to the rise of nativist feeling among a large segment of the Anglo-Protestant working class in the Crowsnest. Protestant preachers and labour leaders frequently voiced anti-Catholic and anti-immigrant sentiments. The Revd D. Holford of Fernie's Baptist church denounced the pernicious effects of 'the Slavs and Dagos' and their 'superstitions' on the local labour market. The labour press often complained about the influence that priests exercised over immigrant workers and attacked the Roman Catholic church as 'corrupt' and 'dictatorial'. Nevertheless, Protestant churches attempted to reach out to the non-British 'aliens in their midst' in an effort to 'Canadianize' them.[16] An important part of both individual and group identity, religion also offered hope and a sense of coherence in a chaotic and hostile world. Even people who were not particularly religious found it necessary to maintain some church affiliation, if only to sanctify life's rites of passage—birth, marriage, and death. An examination of parish and congregational registers confirms the importance of religion in the lives of working people. Members of the working class accounted for a sizeable majority of all the baptisms, marriages, and burials conducted in Crowsnest churches.[17] Christenings, weddings, and funerals placed the church at the heart both of workers' family and community celebrations and of their efforts to bear the setbacks and tragedies of life.

Thus workers made full use of the spiritual, social, and cultural services provided by the churches. Yet relatively few of them became full church members. This has often been interpreted as an indication that workers lacked strong religious convictions or that the churches had little impact on their lives. It should be remembered, however, that the working-class population in the Pass was highly transient. Hence many people left their congregations before satisfying the requirements for full church membership. 'During my stay in Fernie,' D.L. Gordon of Knox Presbyterian church recalled, 'the personnel of the congregation rapidly changed. It was like preaching to a procession. A year after I went to Fernie more than half of those who had signed my call were gone.'[18] Formal church membership, moreover, is not an adequate measure of working-class religiosity. To fully appreciate the role of religion in workers' lives we need to look at the wider framework of working-class life and culture. Churches were social institutions that provided opportunities for involvement and participation in many ways beyond formal membership and regular attendance at Sunday worship.

As a transient population, subject to frequent lay-offs because of poor market conditions and occasional strikes, workers often lacked the resources to support a pastor and to build and maintain a church on their own. Hence the establishment of churches in the Crowsnest often depended on the cooperation of the various mining companies. This was especially the case in the mining towns around Fernie, where much of the land was owned by the Crow's Nest Pass Coal Co. The latter encouraged mission work and the establishment of churches in these towns by providing buildings for church services. Seeing institutional religion as a stabilizing force that could be used to maintain social order and inhibit the development of class consciousness among its workers, the company hoped that such paternalist support would instil loyalty towards it among congregations and clergy alike. The Crow's Nest Pass Coal Co. did not favour any particular denomination: it supported not only Protestant—Presbyterian, Methodist, Anglican, and Baptist—but Roman Catholic missions and churches as well. This policy did not reflect any impartial ecumenism: rather, it was part of a larger divide-and-conquer policy intended to inhibit worker unity. The company adopted a number of strategies to exercise control over clergy and churches. For many years it refused to lease or sell land to the churches, insisting that services be held in its own buildings. D.L. Gordon recalled that at Coal Creek 'we tried to secure land for a church building, but the Coal Co. gave us no encouragement.' Instead the company built a community hall that would be available for religious services. 'If only they could keep us in this building', Gordon complained, 'they could the more easily control our activities.'[19] Mindful of its public image, the company eventually yielded to growing pressure from denominational authorities and agreed to lease land to the churches. But in many cases it continued to exercise control by issuing leases that contained a restrictive clause stipulating that the property was 'to be used for church purposes only'.[20] Such provisions were intended to prevent churches from allowing their premises to be used for union purposes or to promote social or political causes that the company opposed. At the same time the company attempted to secure clergy support for its policies and interests through financial contributions and the presence of its own officials on church boards and vestries.[21]

Despite their dependence on the coal companies, many Crowsnest clergy attempted to assert their autonomy and establish close relationships with the workers who filled their churches.[22] One of the most vocal supporters of the miners was the first pastor of the Fernie Baptist church, the Revd D. Holford. Shortly after his arrival in Fernie, Holford preached a sermon on 'The Solution to the Labor Problem' in which he endorsed the need for unions and attacked the coal company. 'One of the most signal and unquestionable characteristics of the present day,' Holford asserted,

> is the struggle of labour against capital—of the weak against the strong—of the undisciplined many against the organized few. A struggle of those who would enjoy the fruits of their labor with those who would enjoy the fruits of the labor of others. A struggle between money and the masses; between those who create wealth and those made wealthy by partial legislation.[23]

Holford's outspoken defence of labour and his public criticism of the coal company earned him the admiration and respect of many working people. When he left Fernie, he was presented with a resolution of appreciation by the Gladstone local of the Western Federation of Miners that hailed him as 'a champion of right and justice and a friend of the wage earning classes'.[24] Holford's pronouncements also made him many enemies within the Crow's Nest Pass Coal Co. After only two years in Fernie he was forced to relinquish his charge, ostensibly for health reasons. The Presbyterian D.L. Gordon frequently 'crossed swords' with company officials as well. In an address to the General Assembly of his church he observed that 'great companies like the Crow's Nest Pass Coal Company practically own the towns and woe be to the miner or missionary who resists the power of the company.'[25]

The foremost concern of Crowsnest clergy was not the labour question, however; it was the proliferation of licensed taverns, illegal 'blind pigs' and whisky dives, gambling dens and brothels in the region.[26] Deanery councils, presbyteries and ministerial associations passed numerous resolutions on temperance, prostitution, and Sabbath observance; many sermons were preached on the evils of alcohol and the 'social vice'; and Moral Reform leagues were organized throughout the Pass.[27] These endeavours have often been interpreted as efforts by the middle class to exert social control over workers. The clergy were not alone in promoting such causes, however: many Anglo-Protestant workers and their unions were equally strong critics of alcohol and moral vice. Moreover, much of the opposition to the churches' moral reform agenda came not from labour but from middle-class merchants and hotel proprietors who profited from the dark side of life in the Crowsnest. In 1900, for instance, D.L. Gordon began a campaign against the granting of new liquor licences in Fernie and called on the police to crack down on prostitution. This assault on the 'corrupting influence' of alcohol and the 'social evil' resulted in a bitter exchange with local hotel keepers. Offended by the suggestion that their establishments were 'dens of iniquity', the latter advised Gordon to confine his public remarks to 'spiritual matters'. While local business interests attacked Gordon, his efforts were supported by members of the local miners' union.[28] The shared concerns of clergy and many workers in the Crowsnest suggests that historians who argue that the working class and the middle class had different views on alcohol, sexual mores, and work habits need to re-examine their assumptions about working-class culture and middle-class social control.

Although many workers supported the churches in their fight against the speakeasies and brothels, they did not share the clergy's concern about Sabbath observance. Crowsnest clergy frequently decried the desecration of the Sabbath by people who worked, conducted business, or enjoyed leisure activities on the Lord's day.[29] This latter point was of particular annoyance to many workers. The District Ledger denounced the 'righteous wrath' of one 'aristocratic bible-thumper' who would deny workers 'the opportunity of the temporary respite from unceasing toil to enjoy a game of football' on a Sunday afternoon; it also predicted 'a lively scrap' if the 'reverend gentleman continues on this warpath'.[30] The clergy's concern about Sabbath desecration reflected a larger problem of church attendance and membership. Although there was a significant working-class presence in the Protestant congregations of the Crowsnest, large numbers of workers did not attend Sunday services on a regular basis. Fewer still became communicants or, as we have seen, full church members. D.L. Gordon complained that many residents of Fernie 'neither come to church themselves nor send their children to Sabbath school. And yet those same parents are anxious to have their children baptized into the Christian church.'[31] T.M. Murray of the Institutional church in Coleman observed that there was a general 'indifference, carelessness and inattention' to spiritual matters; 'people dislike responsibilities and obligations and shun actual membership.'[32]

The problem of working-class attendance and membership became the subject of considerable discussion and debate within the churches. In 1905 the synod of the Diocese of Kootenay established a committee on workers' alienation from the church.[33] In its presentation to synod the following year, the committee reported that the 'working man criticizes the church adversely' because he believes it is controlled and dominated by 'those who maintain the present social order' and consequently takes 'a one-sided and bourgeois view in the great labor troubles and social problems of the day'. The committee also observed that many workers in the diocese had socialist sympathies, but noted that their socialism was 'Christian in sentiment and ethics'. 'The Socialistic working man criticises the church,' the committee explained, 'because he maintains that she has stultified herself and failed to properly expound Christianity by allowing herself to be dominated by a social system which he claims to be in opposition to our Lord's own teaching, and with which he is in opposition.' The committee recommended that the church take immediate steps to include working people in its parish and diocesan councils and commit itself 'to the happiness and well-being of humanity without fear or favour from any class or system'.[34]

The perception that the church was not sympathetic to the interests of labour was not the only factor affecting working-class involvement in church life. An informal survey by a correspondent for the Fernie *Free Press* discovered a wide range of reasons for not attending church. The paper reported that many people avoided church because 'they are not welcomed into the church as an institution except on conditions that cannot be accepted.' One man responded, 'I do not go to church because I cannot become a member and I feel out of place. I do not feel that I am on the same footing as those who are members. I do not believe some things that church members must profess to believe and I feel that I would be sailing under false colors if I were a regular attendant at the services in any church.' Others reported that they did not attend because of 'social distinctions': 'I have no clothes' was a common explanation. Many replied that 'too much importance is attached to forms and confessions of faith.' One working man responded that he avoided church 'not because I am not in sympathy with the work that the church purports to do, but because I cannot attend a service without feeling that I have been witness of or participated in a lot of sham and hypocrisy'. Another commented that he would attend services 'when the parsons and church members can show me that they are living any better than many of us who do not go to church'. 'Instead of bread,' the correspondent concluded, the church 'offered fossils—or confectionery.'[35] If working-class people were to be drawn back to the churches, a concerted effort had to be made to present Christianity in meaningful and relevant ways.

The churches adopted a variety of strategies to attract workers. Reading and recreation rooms, gymnasiums and meeting halls were added to many church buildings.[36] The aim was to make the church the centre of community life and provide an alternative to the tavern and the gambling den. Efforts to present workers with a practical Protestantism that stressed personal piety and public virtue over denominational creeds and abstract theology led to the creation of union and Institutional churches in several communities. In 1905, Coleman's Presbyterians and Methodists joined together to form the first Institutional church in the Crowsnest. T.M. Murray, the church's first minister, preached a message of personal regeneration and social activism that was characteristic of the period's social Christianity. Murray's church organized a Temperance and Moral Reform League, a Helping Hand Brotherhood, and a boys' club; hosted public debates on topics such as prohibition and socialism; and offered English classes to immigrants.[37] Many clergy also preached a 'robust' and 'virile' Gospel that they hoped would appeal to the young men who dominated the work force. Proponents of this 'muscular Christianity' sought to dispel the image of religion as weak or effeminate by showing that 'the ideal Christian life and the ideal manly life are one and the same.'[38] Revival services were another important strategy employed by the churches of the Pass to increase attendance and membership. Such services were common throughout North America in the first two decades of the twentieth century, when many believed that a return to old-time revivalism was essential if the churches were to win back the working class. Learned exegesis on scripture and doctrine, these people argued, should be replaced by straightforward and practical preaching delivered in the common language of the people. Advocates of the new revivalism called for an end to narrow denominationalism and theological formalism in favour of a more inclusive appeal to ordinary people.[39] In the fall of 1908, the celebrated American evangelist Billy Sunday held a revival in Spokane, Washington. Inspired by the reports of his success, the Kootenay Presbytery resolved to organize a revival of its own 'to promote a deepening of religious interest throughout the entire district'. Local Presbyterians appealed to the General Assembly's committee on Evangelism and Moral Reform for assistance.[40] Concerned about the Pass's reputation for vice and labour radicalism, the committee responded enthusiastically and readily secured financial backing from central Canadian businessmen and church leaders.[41] Significantly, labour also heartily endorsed the campaign. The miners' newspaper, the *District Ledger*, proclaimed that the organizers had 'the co-operation of all people in Fernie and district . . . interested in the best interests of the people and the community'.[42] Although the Presbyterians took the lead in organizing the campaign, other local churches were invited to participate. Stressing that the aim of the campaign was 'absolutely undenominational', organizers promised that all churches would benefit from the awakening of religious spirit in the region. Planning committees met throughout the winter to make preparations, and a team of evangelists associated with the well-known American revivalists J. Wilbur Chapman and Charles M. Alexander were engaged to carry out the campaign simultaneously in towns throughout the region during April and May 1909. Arrangements were made to visit as many homes as possible before the campaign's launch. Special invitations were sent to individual miners and labourers as well as unions and other working-class organizations. Dozens of volunteers from local churches were mobilized as greeters, ushers, and counsellors, and a mass choir was formed to sing at each of the meetings. A special train was scheduled to carry people from throughout the Pass to the nightly meetings held in Fernie. Those unable to attend the meetings would be able to read about them in *The King's Business*, a daily newspaper to be published by the organizing committee throughout the campaign. The months of careful planning and preparation led many to predict that 'tangible results will accrue to the community in the changing of many lives and a deepening interest in the things of God.'[43] When, two days before the start of the campaign, Frank Sherman called a strike against many of the coal operators in the Pass, organizers worried that a prolonged labour dispute would disrupt all their well-laid plans.[44] But their fears proved unfounded.

The much anticipated campaign began on Sunday 4 April when over a thousand people jammed into Bruce's Hall in Fernie. Despite the strike, the revival meetings attracted large audiences throughout the Pass. At the end of the first week, the Fernie *District Ledger* reported that 'the seating capacity of the hall is taxed to its utmost' and that 'already marked results have attended the labours of the workers.' The revival attracted similar crowds elsewhere in the Crowsnest. The Coleman *Miner* observed that 'the work of inspiring the Christians, converting the sinners and redeeming the wanderers is scoring a big success in Coleman.'[45] Although special meetings were held for women and children and for business-men, the evangelists focused their attention on the workers of the Pass.

Most of the revival meetings were held in halls and hotel parlours, rather than churches, in the hope that such settings would be less threatening to the unchurched workers and backsliders that organizers hoped to attract. Speaking in the vernacular of the working man, the evangelists preached 'a manly, common-sense religion' with 'simplicity and power'. Communicating a basic message of repentance and forgiveness, preachers sought to inspire a personal confession of Christ that would lead to personal regeneration and active church membership.[46] To bridge the gap between themselves and their working-class audiences, evange-lists presented themselves as common men and often shared their own life stories. In a sermon preached in Coleman, for instance, Fred W. Davis recounted his upbringing in a humble but religious home and the sacrifices his parents had made to send him to college. Like the prodigal son, however, he had turned his back on his family; expelled from college in disgrace, he had succumbed to the temptations of alcohol and descended into a life of 'crime and debauchery', meet-ing his 'Waterloo' only when he was nearly killed in a barroom brawl in Butte, Montana. At that moment, he said, 'I recognized the evil course that my life had taken and resolved to turn my life around and return to Christ.' Assuring his audi-ence that God's forgiveness was waiting for them as well 'despite the errors of their ways', no matter how far they had 'descended into depravity and hopelessness', Davis concluded by contrasting the 'frustrations and afflictions' of his earlier life with the 'peace of mind and spirit' he enjoyed after accepting Christ.[47]

Although such stories resonated with the experience of many ordinary people and proved effective in communicating the need for conversion, evangelists first had to overcome the 'suspicion and hostility' that many workers had towards the church. Careful not to comment directly on the issues involved in the current strike, preachers nonetheless made a point of expressing sympathy with the plight of working people and identifying themselves as friends of the working man. One preacher, for example, decried the 'industrialists' obsession with profit', insisted that workers 'deserved to enjoy the fruits of their labour', and called for 'reconcili-ation' between the classes on the basis of 'equality, justice and Christian love'.[48]

How successful such appeals were is difficult to gauge. Stories of individual conversions and the restoration of backsliders filled the reports of the evangelists who participated in the campaign. As it ended, the *Western Methodist Recorder* proclaimed that all the meetings had been 'wonderfully well attended', and predicted a great spiritual 'uplift' and 'awakening of the public conscience' throughout the Pass.[49] The large crowds that attended the meetings certainly attest to the continuing importance of evangelical Protestantism within the popular culture of a large segment of the working class. However, for the clergy who had hoped the campaign would increase church membership, revive church attendance, and strengthen the cause of social and moral reform, the results were decidedly mixed. Several churches in the Crowsnest did experience significant growth in membership. Fernie's Methodist congregation, for example, increased by over 30 per cent between 1898 and 1918, and the church roll at Knox Presbyterian more than doubled. The gains made by other churches were less impressive, but almost all congregations in the region reported new members in the wake of the campaign. Yet these increases did not translate into increased attendance at Sunday services.[50] The popularity of the 1909 revival meetings suggests that they appealed to the working class in a way that regular Sunday services did not, but much more needs to be known about piety among working people before any final conclusions can be drawn. In any case, it should be stressed that attendance figures ultimately tell us little about the true depth of religious feeling. As for alcohol use and vice, it was reported that taverns experienced a decline in business during the campaign, but there is no evidence that the revival had a lasting impact.[51] Despite these mixed results, annual revival meetings became a regular part of life for most congregations in the Crowsnest Pass. This development reflected both the continuing appeal of such events for working people and the constant need of congregations to renew their memberships because of the highly transient nature of the population and the economic instability of the coal industry.

The simultaneous occurrence of both a strike and a major evangelistic campaign provides a powerful demonstration of the degree to which religion and labour activism existed side by side in the Crowsnest. Church and labour leaders alike invoked Christ's example in calling for social regeneration; they shared the same moral fervour and expressed the same millennial expectations of a coming Kingdom of God.[52] For labour radicals, socialism was to be the vehicle through which that kingdom would be brought into being. Crowsnest socialists insisted that 'socialism' contained 'the essence of Christianity' and 'should come through the church'.[53] Many Crowsnest clergy were sympathetic to the socialists' call for justice, cooperation, and social reform. They were uncomfortable, though, with socialism's materialistic understanding of society and emphasis on class conflict. For them, the key to solving the social and economic problems of the age was social harmony based on Christian values.[54] More significant than these differences, however, was the degree to which church and labour leaders shared a common language. Labour leaders and the labour press were just as likely to invoke scripture and Christian values as the local clergy. Music, moreover, was an important part of both religious and labour gatherings. The tunes of familiar hymns were used to carry the message of brotherhood and solidarity at the heart of the union gospel.[55] Emotional public exhortations designed to awaken and stir the people to action and participation were staples of both religious and labour events, and expressed a shared belief in the perfectibility of man. Both church and union preached a message of hope for a promised land free of want and oppression. These similarities suggest that ideas, beliefs, and practices of a religious nature were more widespread among the working class than is often thought.

Conclusion

Evangelical Protestantism was a significant part of the cultural baggage of many Anglo-Celtic immigrants who worked in the mines of the Crowsnest. The establishment of churches thus became a priority for these workers. British- and Canadian-born workers accounted for most of the founding members of the Protestant churches in the Pass. For these workers, church affiliation was an important declaration of ethnic identity and status. Although the working-class presence on church boards and vestries declined over the years, the churches were never the middle-class institutions they are often assumed to have been. Nor were they simply vehicles of corporate or middle-class social control. Congregations resisted the efforts of the coal companies to control their churches. Contrary to popular belief, the churches' support of moral reform causes was not in conflict with working-class values; concerns about alcohol, crime, and prostitution were not by any means limited to the middle class.

The pervasive influence of Christianity within the labour movement is evident in its ongoing debate over socialism. Labour radicals appropriated and reinterpreted Christian teaching to defend their policies and platforms to their fellow workers and the general public. The fact that many workers did not attend services on a regular basis does not necessarily mean that religion was unimportant in their lives. Together, the continuing use of church for baptisms, marriages, and burials and the large crowds attracted to revival meetings demonstrate the vitality of religious convictions within the popular culture of the working class. The success of Institutional and union churches in the Crowsnest suggests that workers eschewed doctrinal and denominational loyalties in favour of a pragmatic and practical Protestantism that stressed the importance of cooperation and mutual support—values that were shared by the labour movement. Historians of both church and labour need to re-examine their assumptions about worker alienation and indifference to religion in late nineteenth- and early twentieth-century Canada, and explore more fully the different ways in which popular religious sentiments shaped working-class lives and attitudes.

Notes

1. *Christian Guardian* (24 March 1909), 12; T.B. Kilpatrick and J.G. Shearer, *The Kootenay Campaign April and May 1909* (Toronto, 1909), 3–5.
2. For examples of this concern see *Christian Guardian* (22 Feb. 1888, 4 Dec. 1889); *The Presbyterian Review* (20 Jan. 1898); *The Methodist Magazine and Review* (July 1901), 49–58; (Dec. 1902), 565–6; (Jan. 1903), 13–20; (Dec. 1906), 512–17; 'The Working Man and His Problems', *The Canadian Church Congress and Other Proceedings at Halifax, Windsor and Annapolis Royal N.S.* (Halifax, 1910), 146–55; *Social Service Congress,*

Ottawa, 1914: Report of Addresses and Proceedings (Toronto, 1914). On the growing concern within Canada's Protestant churches regarding the religious condition of the working class, see Richard Allen, *The Social Passion: Religion and Reform in Canada, 1914–28* (Toronto, 1971); S.D. Clark, *Church and Sect in Canada* (Toronto, 1948); Stewart Crysdale, *The Industrial Struggle and Protestant Ethics in Canada: A Study of Changing Power Structures and Christian Social Ethics* (Toronto, 1961).

3. British studies include Logie Barrow, *Independent Spirits: Spiritualism and English Plebians, 1850–1910* (New York, 1986); Robert Colls, *The Colliers Rant: Song and Culture in the Industrial Village* (Cambridge, 1977); Thomas Lacqueur, *Religion and Respectability: Sunday Schools and Working Class Culture, 1780–1850* (Oxford, 1976); Robert Moore, *Pitmen, Preachers and Politics: The Effects of Methodism and the English Mining Community* (Cambridge, 1974); E.P. Thompson, *The Making of the English Working Class* (Harmondsworth, 1963) and Deborah Valenz, *Prophetic Sons and Daughters: Female Preaching and Popular Religion in Industrial England* (Princeton, 1985). American studies include Ken Fones-Wolf, *Trade Union Gospel: Christianity and Labour in Industrial Philadelphia, 1865–1915* (Philadelphia, 1989); Herbert Gutman, *Work, Culture and Society in Industrializing America: Essays in American Working Class and Social History* (New York, 1976) and Bruce Laurie, *Working People of Philadelphia, 1800–1850* (Philadelphia, 1980).

4. See, for example, Ramsay Cook, *The Regenerators: Social Criticism in Late Victorian English Canada* (Toronto: 1985); Brian Fraser, *The Social Uplifters: Presbyterian Progressives and the Social Gospel in Canada, 1875–1915* (Waterloo, 1988); Michael Gauvreau, *The Evangelical Century: College and Creed in English Canada from the Great Revival to the Great Depression* (Montreal, 1991), and David Marshall, *Secularizing the Faith: Canada's Protestant Clergy and the Crisis of Belief, 1850–1940* (Toronto, 1992).

5. On religious and ethnic divisions within the Canadian working class, see Michael S. Cross, *The Workingman in the Nineteenth Century* (Toronto, 1974) and Donald Avery, *'Dangerous Foreigners': European Immigrant Workers and Labour Radicalism in Canada, 1896–1932* (Toronto, 1979).

6. Bryan Palmer, *A Culture in Conflict: Skilled Workers and Industrial Capitalism in Hamilton, Ontario, 1860–1914* (Toronto, 1979); Gregory Kealey, *Toronto Workers Respond to Industrial Capitalism, 1867–1892* (Toronto, 1980); Bryan Palmer and Gregory Kealey, *Dreaming of What Might Be: The Knights of Labor in Ontario, 1880–1900* (Toronto, 1982).

7. Lynne Marks, *Revival and Roller Rinks: Religion, Leisure and Identity in Late-Nineteenth-Century Small Town Ontario* (Toronto, 1996); Nancy Christie and Michael Gauvreau, "The World of the Common Man is Filled with Religious Fervor": The Labouring People of Winnipeg and the Persistence of Revivalism, 1914–1925', in *Aspects of Canadian Evangelicalism*, ed. George Rawlyk (Montreal and Kingston, 1997); Eric Crouse, 'American Revivalists, the Press and Popular Religion in Canada, 1884–1914', Ph.D. diss., Queen's University, 1996.

8. On the development of the coal industry in the Crowsnest Pass see *Crowsnest and its People* (Coleman, 1979); William Cousins, *A History of the Crow's Nest Pass* (Calgary, 1981); Charles Allen Seager, 'A Proletariat in Wild Rose Country: The Alberta Coal Miners, 1905–1945', Ph.D. diss., York University, 1981.

9. On the history of Crowsnest missions and churches see *Crowsnest and its People*, 285–310; Diocese of Kootenay Archives [DKA], Parish Files, Christ Church Fernie and St Paul's Michel; Elsie G. Turnbull, *Church in the Kootenay: The Story of the United Church of Canada in Kootenay Presbytery* (Trail, 1965); United Church Alberta and North West Conference Archives, Rev. John M. Fawcett, 'A History of St. Paul's Church, Coleman, Alberta' and Alex Tiberg, 'Blairmore United Church'.

10. Clark, *Church and Sect*; W.E. Mann, *Sect, Cult and Church in Alberta* (Toronto, 1955).

11. British- and Canadian-born workers dominated the work force in the Crowsnest during the early years. They were eventually outnumbered by workers from central and eastern Europe, but as late as 1921 a third of all coal company employees were of Anglo-Celtic background (Seager, 'Proletariat in Wild Rose Country', 82). On the role of religion in the lives of British miners see Colls, *The Colliers Rant*, and Moore, *Pitmen, Preachers and Politics*.

12. Allen Seager, 'Frank Sherman', *Dictionary of Canadian Biography* XIII (Toronto, 1994), 950–2; Coleman *Miner* (8 Oct. 1909). On Sherman's criticism of the church see Lethbridge *Herald*, 8 Feb. 1909 and Fernie *District Ledger* (20 Feb. 1909).

13. *Crowsnest and its People*, 461–2, 464. Also see the family histories of Edgar Ash, James Fairhurst, Thomas Flynn, William Gate, the Goodwin family, Frank George Graham, Albert Halworth, Thomas Marshall Hamilton, the Hibbert family, David Telfer Hutton, the Kerr family of Passburg, Thomas Kidd, Elias Sutherland, Alex May, Robert McDicken, Evan Morgan, Fred Padgett, John Albert Price, Thomas Price, and Michael Robinson in the same volume.

14. Seager, 'Proletariat in Wild Rose Country', 104.

15. Between 1905 and 1920, 34.1% of all vestry members for Christ Church Fernie and 47.5% of the congregational board members of Coleman's Institutional Church were drawn from the ranks of miners and skilled workers.

16. Fernie *Free Press* (23 Nov. 1900); Fernie *District Ledger* (26 Aug. 1911). Also see Fernie *District Ledger* (9 March 1912, 15 June 1912), and *Western Clarion* (26 April 1913). On missions to non-British immigrants see Lethbridge *Herald* (8 Feb. 1909), and Blairmore *Enterprise* (22 May 1914).

17. An analysis of the parish registers for Christ Church, Fernie, reveals that workers accounted for 65.5% of baptisms, 31.9% of confirmations, 63% of marriages, and 68.9% of burials performed in the parish. Workers accounted for 64.7% of baptisms and 80% of marriages at St Paul's mission, Michel, and 77% of baptisms at Coleman's Institutional Church.

18. United Church British Columbia Conference Archives (UCBCC), Kootenay Presbytery-Fernie, Rev. D.L. Gordon to Rev. John C. Goodfellow, 28 Aug. 1934.

19. UCBCC, Gordon to Goodfellow, 28 Aug. 1934.

20. DKA, Parish Files-St Paul's, Michel.

21. In 1899, for example, the President of the Crow's Nest Pass Coal Co. donated $500 for the construction of a Presbyterian church in Fernie and $50 to furnish the parsonage. For church complaints about their dependence on the coal companies see UCBCC, Kootenay Presbytery, Minutes, 4 June 1902; West Kootenay Ministerial Association, Minutes, 5 April 1900.

22. *District Ledger* (14 Sept. 1907); Blairmore *Enterprise* (6 March 1916).

23. Fernie *Free Press* (21 Sept. 1900).

24. Fernie *Free Press* (11 Oct. 1902).

25. Fernie *Free Press* (10 June 1904).

26. Sermons on such themes were often printed in the local press. See, for example, D.L. Gordon, 'Our Lord's First Sabbath in Capernaum', Fernie *Free Press* (20 July 1900), and T.M. Murray, 'Am I My Brother's Keeper', Coleman *Bulletin* (11 Feb. 1915).

27. UCBCC, Kootenay Presbytery, Minutes, 14 Sept., 1905, 8 Sept., 1909, and West Kootenay Ministerial Association, Minutes, Oct. 1902, Sept. 1910.

28. See the letters and editorials in the Fernie *Free Press* of 23 Nov. 1900, 30 Nov. 1900, and 7 Dec. 1900.

29. Fernie *Free Press* (20 July 1900, 9 Nov. 1901).

30. Frank *Vindicator* (7 June 1912); Fernie *District Ledger* (15 June 1912).

31. Fernie *Free Press* (20 July 1900).

32. Coleman *Bulletin* (23 July 1909).

33. *Journal of the Sixth Session of the Synod of the Diocese of Kootenay, June 7th and 8th, 1905*, 17.

34. *Journal of the Seventh Session of the Synod of the Diocese of Kootenay, June 6th and 7th, 1906*, 91–3.

35. Fernie *Free Press* (30 Dec. 1910).

36. See Fernie *District Ledger* (6 Aug. 1910); Fernie *Free Press* (16 June 1905); *Western Methodist Recorder* (Oct. 1909).

37. On the activities of Coleman's Institutional church see Coleman *Miner* (19 June, 27 Nov. 1908; 30 April, 10 Dec., 31 Dec. 1909; 11 Feb. 1915; 18 Jan., 28 June 1918).

38. 'The Young Man's Problem', *Methodist Magazine and Review* (Oct. 1905), 311. On muscular Christianity see Susan Curtis, 'The Son of Man and God the Father: The Social Gospel and Victorian Masculinity' in *Meanings for Manhood: Constructions of Masculinity in Victorian America*, ed. Mark C. Carnes and Clyde Griffen (Chicago, 1990), 79–84; David Francis Howell, 'The Social Gospel in Canadian Protestantism: Implications for Sport', Ph.D. diss., University of Alberta, 1980; Norman Vance, *The Sinews of the Spirit: The Ideal of Christian Manliness in Victorian Literature and Religious Thought* (Cambridge, 1985).

39. On revivals see Christie and Gauvreau, 'The World of the Common Man'; Crouse, 'American Revivalists, the Press and Popular Religion'; Darrell Robertson, *The Chicago Revival, 1876: Society and Revivalism in a Nineteenth-century City* (Metuchen, NJ, 1989).

40. UCBCC, Kootenay Presbytery, Minutes, 10 Jan. 1909. On the Spokane revival see Dale E. Soden, 'Billy Sunday in Spokane: Revivalism and Social Control', *Pacific Northwest Quarterly* 79, 1 (Jan. 1988), 10–17.

41. Lethbridge *Herald* (20 Feb. 1909).

42. Fernie *District Ledger* (4 April 1909).

43. Fernie *Free Press* (2 April 1909); *The Kootenay Campaign*, 4–13.

44. On the 1909 strike see Seager, 'Proletariat in Wild Rose Country', 237–42. On the orga-
    nizers' concerns about the strike see UCBCC, Knox Presbyterian Church Fernie, Board
    Minutes, 2 April 1909.

45. Fernie *District Ledger* (10 April 1909); Coleman *Miner* (16 April 1909).

46. *The Kootenay Campaign*, 8–10.

47. *The King's Business* (15 April 1909); Coleman *Miner* (16 April 1909).

48. *The Kootenay Campaign*, 16; *The King's Business* (9 April 1909).

49. *Western Methodist Recorder* (May 1909), 23; *The Kootenay Campaign*, 24–9.

50. Membership in Fernie's Methodist and Presbyterian churches increased from 65 to
    95 and 49 to 100 respectively. Data on church membership can be found in the annu-
    al reports published by the Methodist Conference and the General Assembly of the
    Presbyterian Church in Canada. Congregation service registers provide a record of
    weekly attendance. The registers for Fernie's Anglican and Methodist churches indi-
    cate little change in attendance at Sunday service.

51. *Western Methodist Recorder* (May 1909), 23.

52. On the millennial expectations of labour see Carlos Schwantes, 'The Churches of the
    Disinherited: The Culture of Radicalism on the North Pacific Industrial Frontier',
    Pacific Historian 25, 4 (Winter 1981), 55–6. On the churches and the establishment of
    the kingdom see Phillips, *A Kingdom on Earth*.

53. Fernie *Free Press* (29 Nov., 6 Dec., 12 Dec. 1902); *District Ledger* (2 March 1912).

54. See, for example, UCBCC, A.N. Sandon, 'A Sermon on the Labor Situation' and 'The
    Church and the Workingman' in Sandon Scrapbook.

55. Clark Halker, 'Jesus was a Carpenter: Labor Song Poets, Labor Protest and True
    Religion in Gilded Age America', *Labor History* 32, 2 (Spring 1991), 273–89.

Swiling and Newfoundland's Identity

Peter E. Rider

The annual seal hunt off Canada's east coast differs from most other marine hunts. Here it is the exploiters of the resource that are threatened with extinction while the resource itself thrives. The seal hunt enjoys little public sympathy and uncertain political support. Seals are widely believed to be endangered, despite official studies documenting stable numbers and anecdotal stories of seals ravaging what remains of the groundfish stocks. Swilers are routinely vilified as thugs mercilessly butchering helpless animals for small personal gain. Critics advocate bans both on the hunt and on the sale of seal products. In vain swilers and their supporters plead that the hunt is a traditional activity for rural folk who badly need supplementary income.

The seal hunt reaches back to early human settlement on Newfoundland. Archaeological evidence establishes the presence of seal hunters 9,000 years ago.[1] The French undertook sealing commercially in the late seventeenth century, and by 1720 were sending 500 tons of seal oil annually to France.[2] Later, the English gained control of the hunt and moved its focus to harbours in Bonavista Bay and, in time, Notre Dame Bay and Labrador. For resident fishermen the land-based seal hunt provided precious food at the end of a long winter.[3]

Eventually, the commercial potential of seal oil prompted ships' masters to leave crewmen behind to await the arrival of harp seals the following spring. Profits were sufficient to encourage the establishment of permanent communities. The land-based hunt was later extended into the bays by fishermen who shot seals from small boats. A new phase opened in 1793 when a St John's merchant sent two schooners to search for seals on the whelping ice farther offshore.[4] The venture was successful, and about 1,600 seal pelts were brought in. Six years later, approximately 120,000 pelts were landed in St John's and Conception Bay—an exceptional total when compared with the results of land-based hunting. A swiler working on the ice floes could harvest five times as many seals as a landsman.[5]

Ready markets for seal oil and skins in Great Britain and southern Europe ensured a rapid expansion of the industry.[6] Between 1825 and 1860 the annual catch exceeded 500,000 pelts eleven times; the high point was reached in 1832, when 744,000 pelts were landed.[7] Scholars who have documented the magnitude of the hunt conclude its economic value was critical for settlements that were barely sustainable on the basis of the cod fishery alone.[8] More than a seasonal source of income, the hunt became by the mid-nineteenth century an essential feature of Newfoundland's economy. Indeed, Shannon Ryan asserts that 'the study of the Newfoundland seal fishery to 1914 is, to a great extent, the study of the colony itself in the nineteenth century.'[9]

Seal hunting made a deep impression on the collective psyche of Newfoundlanders. There was pride that Newfoundland had developed a substantial oil industry based on seals; moreover, sealskin products were prestigious exports. The industry also created spinoff activities, principally shipbuilding. In the mid-nineteenth century Newfoundlanders put the famous steam-powered reinforced wooden ships known as 'wooden walls' into service, allowing the hunt to penetrate farther into the ice fields. These were supplanted after 1906 by steel-hulled icebreakers. Experience gained in ice navigation made Newfoundlanders valuable for expeditions into polar regions. A few, like Captain Robert Abram (Bob) Bartlett, achieved international renown, but his skills were shared to some extent by all ice-hunters.

Surprisingly, the seal hunt failed to provide Newfoundlanders with the kind of collective symbolic icon that, say, the beaver-fur trade did for Canadians. The artifact collection of the Newfoundland Museum provides only a few examples of either commercially available or home-crafted objects on which seal motifs are used as ornamentation. For such purposes the cod was favoured, and the caribou, not the seal, was the animal chosen for public statuary and official badges. Neither the appealing but passive harp seal nor the ugly and ornery hood represented qualities desirable in a people. If it is true, as Shannon Ryan contends, that 'by 1914, the "Newfoundland" identity was, in large part, the result of the seal fishery,' it is for reasons beyond the hunt itself.[10]

Indeed, the rich and varied folklore that grew up around sealing focused not on the hunt but on the swilers. In song, story, and ritual, the annual adventure on the ice floes was celebrated for what it demonstrated about the people involved.[11] While there are many images, they fall into three basic categories documenting mental and physical competence, love of family, and a harsh environment.

Sealing captains were frequently cited as examples of the first set of traits. The obituaries of these 'vikings' typically praised their skills not only as navigators but as hunters: Hon. Edward White was 'one of the most successful seal hunters the colony ever produced'; Arthur Jackson was 'a great navigator and seal-killer'.[12] The most successful 'viking' of all was Abram Kean (1855–1945), a self-made man who went to the ice for 67 years and credited himself with taking more than a million pelts.[13] A Conservative politician and minister in the government of Sir James Winter, he was both feared and admired. He tended to steal pelts marked with flags from other ships and was infamously implicated in two of Newfoundland's worst sealing disasters, but he received an Order of the British Empire and the respect of the community. Brave and highly competitive, 'the Old Man' was able to sense the whereabouts of the main seal herds, reach them with his vessel, and get his crew 'into the fat'. *The Newfoundland Quarterly* reported in 1913 that Kean had accounted for 569,718 kills since assuming his first command in 1889, and noted that his record was 'one that he [had] great cause to feel proud of as well as the whole country'.[14]

Individual crewmen were also celebrated. After recounting the bravery of Master Watch Tim Curtis of Carbonear, the St John's *Evening Telegram* proclaimed: 'Think over it readers! Could any, but a Newfoundlander be the hero of such an act?'[15] On another occasion a poem in the same newspaper described swilers stranded on the ice:

We marvel at their courage,
And bravery on the floe;
Trying to help a weaker brother
As they struggle onward go.[16]

'Acts of gallantry,' the paper asserted, 'are not uncommon things in Newfoundland . . . and many a courageous act had been done without word of it penetrating beyond the settlement near which it happened.'[17]

The requirements for crewmen serving on the sealing vessels were basic: a willingness to endure a hostile environment, cramped living conditions, and hard labour, and a kit consisting of a gaff, a sculping knife, a tow or hauling rope, and occasionally snow goggles and a compass.[18] No special clothing was worn except, perhaps, for sealskin leggings and boots known as 'skinny woppers'. Strength and agility were essential. On leaving their ship, the men had to cross treacherous ice patches, sometimes jagged and sometimes broken by water, to reach the seal herds. Where open water was found, the swilers had to jump from ice pan to ice pan. 'Copying', as this was called, took skill and experience. Gaffs were used for balance and often, when someone fell into the water, for rescue.

Killing took place on the ice, and the animals were usually sculped on the spot.[19] The pelts were either piled on the ice for future pickup ('panned') or towed back to the ship immediately following the slaughter. Once aboard the vessel, pelts were stowed below in pounds which were located in the same area where the crew had their bunks. As the holds filled with pelts and fat, the men were displaced, eventually being forced to sleep on top of the slimy, stinking cargo. Fat and blood got everywhere: on the men, on the decks, in the drinking water. Despite these hardships, a diet consisting of sea biscuits and tea,[20] and the danger of drowning or— if caught on the ice in a storm—freezing to death, the competition for berths was brisk. For many young men from the bays of Newfoundland, the first voyage to the ice was a rite of passage,[21] but they would continue to repeat the experience until age or mishap made further trips impossible.

The swilers' willingness to endure such hardships year after year can be explained partly by the poverty of the outports. The food, inadequate as it may seem, was at times an incentive. A chance to supplement a meagre income was often irresistible, even though the returns for the individual swiler were frequently low.[22] Captain Bob Bartlett noted that after two or even three months of 'hard sealing life', a fisherman might return 'with total earnings of as low as $15!'[23] George Tuff survived the *Greenland* disaster of 1898 in which 48 men stranded on the ice froze to death and the 1914 *Newfoundland* disaster in which 78 died. He remarked later in life that sealers were 'all insane men'. 'There was only one sane man on board and that's the captain. He gets paid for the job.'[24] Those who returned safely from a successful voyage, however, gained cash—a precious commodity for a fisherman.

For some, the simple prospect of purposeful activity was enticing. On board the sealing ships, the swilers shared a sense of camaraderie, adventure, and friendly competition, together with dedication to a common purpose.[25] And the slaughter itself could be thrilling. William Coaker, union leader and powerful advocate of fishermen's rights, ventured to the ice in 1914 to observe the hunt first-hand. He joined a watch from the *Nascopie* in one slaughter and, despite personal scruples and the prey's pitiable cries, managed to kill and sculp nine whitecoats 'like a real man'.[26]

The hardiness of Newfoundland swilers was recognized by outsiders. A Scottish surgeon on the *Aurora*, after reflecting on the nature of Newfoundland sealers in a not entirely favourable fashion, commented on the hard life they led—although they were 'brought up to it' and 'that no doubt tooke the edge off'.[27] Soon after steamships based in Dundee, Scotland, began sailing to Newfoundland, local men displaced Shetland Islanders as their crews.[28] American filmmaker Varick Frissell was so impressed with 'the hardships and dangers of these Vikings of the North' whom 'he came to love and admire'[29] that he chose to record them in *The Great Arctic Seal Hunt* and *The Viking*. Ironically, Frissell died while shooting additional footage for *The Viking* when the vessel of the same name, on which he was a passenger, exploded and sank. In response to this disaster the *Halifax Chronicle* commented, under the heading 'Iron Men': 'Not for glory, nor for great material reward do those hardy seal hunters man the sealing steamers. It is a question of livelihood, and duty; and the heroism which they display is strikingly indicative of their courage and fidelity.'[30]

The swilers' commitment to home and hearth is reflected in an old ditty: 'Greenspond is a lovely place / And so is Pilcher's Island / Mother will have a new dress / When father comes home from swilin'.'[31] Various stories tell of the spiritual connections between swilers and those left behind at home.[32] Familial loyalty was noted by *The Newfoundland Quarterly* as a quality of Abram Kean, who looked after the widows and children of his three brothers as well as his own family and 'never wavered in his fidelity and love of those he had promised to cherish and support'.[33] More generally, the hunt sustained the whole community. Merchants regarded the conclusion of the hunt as the beginning of another business year and an occasion for renewed hope. Citizens of St John's, as elsewhere on the island, celebrated with a feast of fresh seal flippers.

The setting of the seal hunt was extremely harsh. Beautiful days with calm breezes and mild temperatures could be rapidly supplanted by freezing winds, blinding snow, stormy seas, and suffocating ice that crushed the sides of trapped ships. To manoeuvre their vessels, the men occasionally had to chop or blast them free or haul them forward through the ice. Individual stories of danger and anxiety were told by the seal hunters themselves and recorded in journals kept by observers.[34] Recurring disasters were constant reminders of the power and menace of the sea and were occasions of public grief. Grotesque images of men frozen in postures of death evoked both dread and respect for the elements. Yet, concluded one editorialist, 'is there not indeed reason for pride in the fact that such disasters have not deterred others from carrying on?'[35]

Cumulatively, the cost of carrying on was onerous. 'The Sea is made of mothers' tears' was a common proverb in Newfoundland. Ballads celebrated the yearnings of those touched by disaster.[36] Captain Bob Bartlett told the sad tale of a young mother of five whose husband perished in the 1914 *Southern Cross* disaster; his attempt to earn $25 or $50 with which to buy flour, medicine, and tools proved disastrous.[37] Another observer noted that, faced with the loss of their menfolk, the widows and orphans of seal hunters could only 'shriek their curses' and endure 'miseries that cannot be compensated'.[38]

From these portraits of skill, loyalty, and endurance a heroic identity emerges. This vision of Newfoundlanders does not derive from swiling alone: the seal hunt was part of a greater struggle with the sea and was only one facet, albeit an important one, of the fishing colony's experience. Nor is this kind of valiant image unique. Similar images were constructed around western cowboys and the lumberjacks of the Ottawa and St John River valleys. Only in Newfoundland, however, did seal hunting become so economically and culturally significant. Moreover, Newfoundlanders took pride in their identification with the seal hunt.

Even so, one aspect of the hunt was rarely stressed: its butchery. Joseph Jukes, who observed hunts in 1839 and 1840, described standing 'more than knee deep in warm seal skins, all blood and fat'.[39] 'The hunting spirit,' he concluded, 'makes every man an animal of prey. . . .'[40] A later witness described 'the moans of the young seals', 'the agonies of the mothers', and 'the ice strewn with skinned carcuses . . . almost quivering with life'.[41] When in 1889 the wife of Sir Henry Blake, the former Governor of Newfoundland, published a diatribe against the seal hunt entitled 'Seals and Savages', she brought the issue of cruelty to animals to the attention of the general public.[42] Her negative characterization of Newfoundlanders, based on conditions that had existed at least fifty years previously, provoked considerable indignation in the colony. Still, few denied the bloody nature of the hunt. Even 40 years later, in a review of *The Viking* written at the time of the film's release, R. Pollett commented that 'details of the merciless killing and sculping of helpless seals are omitted.'[43]

Scenes of the carnage on the ice, however, eventually gained a wide audience when the French-language network of the Canadian Broadcasting Corporation aired the documentary *Les Phoques de la Banquise* in 1964. Ironically, the film depicted the land-based hunt off the Magdalen Islands and had nothing to do with Newfoundland. Indeed, Newfoundlanders' participation in the hunt had diminished since the 1930s because of dwindling markets in the Depression, the Second World War, and prolonged low seal prices after 1938. Only four Newfoundland-based vessels went to the hunt in 1932 and only one in 1943. Nova Scotians, Americans, and Norwegians partially filled the gap in the 1930s. Although Newfoundland's commercial interest in the hunt revived slightly after the war, by the mid-1950s there were more vessels from Nova Scotia than Newfoundland participating in it, and by the 1960s Norwegian sealing ships outnumbered the entire Canadian fleet.[44]

Overall, the intensity of the hunt had increased by mid-century, with the result that the stocks of harp seals in particular were becoming threatened. The Canadian government responded to this situation in 1964 by placing quotas on the numbers of harp seal pups taken in the Gulf of St Lawrence, creating a system of licences and permits and developing regulations requiring the use of clubs, of a specified size, rather than gaffs. In 1970, a ban was placed on the taking of harp pups. Quotas were imposed on the whole hunt in 1972, and the ship-based hunt was banned in the Gulf. (The entire offshore hunt was ended in 1987.) Although the seal herds were gradually restored to health, the hunt remained immersed in controversy.[45]

Conservationists, who had become concerned about dwindling resource stocks in the 1950s and 1960s, turned their attention instead to the apparent cruelty of the hunt. Peter Lust, a journalist for the *Montreal Star*, wrote a column in April 1964, entitled 'Murder Island', which was widely reprinted and led him to write his book *The Last Seal Pup*, published in 1967. Brian Davies, a former official of the New Brunswick Society for the Prevention of Cruelty to Animals who had made a documentary film on sealing, *The Seals of the Ice Pans*, organized the International Fund for Animal Welfare in 1969 to battle the hunt. The environmentalist group Greenpeace also joined the fray, and by the early 1970s a broadly based international campaign against the seal hunt was being mobilized. Protests were mounted in the United States and Europe, fed in part by egregious publicity stunts involving visits to the ice by American children (1971), airline stewardesses (1976), Yvette Mimieux and Brigitte Bardot (1977), and US Congressmen (1978).[46]

Ominously, the attacks were directed as much against the swilers as the hunt itself. 'I think [sealing] brutalizes a man,' remarked Brian Davies; 'it makes him something different perhaps to you and I.'[47] Paul Watson of the Sea Shepherd Conservation Society wrote from his jail cell in Orsainville, where he was imprisoned for his anti-sealing activities, 'Our energies will be directed at the boycott of fish products from Newfoundland and towards discouraging tourism to Newfoundland.'[48] The community as well as the hunt was under attack. Newfoundlanders' reaction was widespread and profound.

Responses to the anti-sealing agitation quickly emerged, some taking the form of works of literature and graphic art. While each of these efforts to situate the issue within a thoughtful context had its own points to make, most reaffirmed the heroic qualities traditionally associated with swilers. If the critics could appreciate the traits that in the past had lent dignity and honour to the Newfoundland identity, so the thinking ran, current antagonisms might be abated. Several important works produced during the early years of the anti-sealing campaign illustrate the point.

One of these was a powerful account of the 1914 *Newfoundland* disaster written by Cassie Brown and published in 1972. Entitled *Death on the Ice*, the book is a blow-by-blow account of the loss of 78 of the ship's crew during a violent storm. Beginning on 30 March and lasting two days, the blizzard trapped some 120 men in the open. Brown, writing with the aid of official documents, contemporary accounts, and the recollections of eyewitnesses, describes telling examples of courage, loyalty, love, and bravery on the part of the stranded men. In the death of Edward Tippett, frozen rigid as he embraced two of his sons (a third would also die in the storm), and in the struggle of Cecil Mouland to survive and return to marry his sweetheart, Jessie, we see images of profound humanity. It was the weather and ice conditions—not the swilers—that were brutal and merciless. Even the government, the merchant houses, and individual ships' masters displayed variously arrogance, greed, and irresponsibility. Page by page, however, the merits of ordinary swilers are confirmed.

The following year, artist David Blackwood published a portfolio of prints and drawings depicting outport life in pre-Confederation Newfoundland.[49] Although the illustrations were accompanied by a sympathetic text by Farley Mowat, they needed no written support to convey their meaning. Gaunt figures in fishing boats protected by a soaring white dove, an anxious old woman peering seaward from her window, and long lines of stooped men bracing themselves against the wind blowing across the ice floes testify to the vulnerability of seal hunters confronting the elements. Lined, stoic faces and the tortured shapes of freezing swilers fighting off death suggest the strength of character demanded by the hunt. Those who perished were memorialized in one print by a corpse lying in a submerged coffin, lit by a kerosene lamp, while in the distance a snug harbour and its quiet houses suggest an eternal attachment to hearth and home. Another print foretold the consequences of failing to wrest a living from the sea: glimpsed through a broken window pane, a line of stooped figures trails off to the horizon and some unknown destination.

A second artist updated the images to refer to the modern sealing industry. In March and April 1974, at the height of the anti-sealing protests, George Noseworthy created a series of 38 paintings. Swilers are depicted as reluctant and, in 'A Hard Way to Make a Living', exhausted by their task. Danger persists even in modern times: 'For Want of a Gaff', a swiler sinks from sight beneath an ice floe while his mates disappear far in the distance. Unlike Blackwood, however, Noseworthy depicts the hunt itself, including the clubbing of seals and the futile efforts of whitecoats to hide behind pinnacles of ice. As an explanation for the hunt, the artist offers 'The Longing', in which a line of figures emerge from an ice-

bound ship and cross jagged ice to a sturdy house encircled by gardens with children playing in the yard. In the foreground, a baby seal snuggles into the ice. Once
again we see the seal hunter's perseverance in the face of danger, as well as his love
of home and family, but we also glimpse his prey.

In 1978 the Mummers Troupe in St John's produced a play entitled 'They Club
Seals, Don't They?', a forceful depiction of the sealing debate from the swiler's
perspective.[50] In it a fisherman named George Bugden and his wife Maggie
confront characters symbolizing various elements in the contemporary sealing
controversy. Animal-rights advocates endow seals with human qualities and vilify
the swilers; scientists debate the size of the seal herds; a Toronto housewife frets
about the morality of wearing a fur coat while ignoring the implications of her
leather shoes; and a reporter from the *Ottawa Citizen* badgers George for an
admission that he kills seals because he hates them.

Maggie reveals the anguish of a child who had been promised an abundance of
apples by her father upon his return from the floes. She watched him 'an' d'udders
walkin' down da road. . . . Dat . . . was da last I seen of my father.'[51] George, for his
part, remains true to his way of life and still hopes to make a living from the fishery 'if dey'd just leave us alone for a while. . . .'[52] Throughout the play the admirable
qualities of mental and physical competence, love of family, and heroic endurance
mock the charges of brutality laid by scornful urban outsiders. While empathy is
expressed by another primary-resource worker—Stan, a logger from British
Columbia—salvation lies in the swiler's own conviction that justice is ultimately
on his side. Criticism of the seal hunt is just one more adversity to confront.

For some Newfoundlanders, particularly among the educated urban middle
class, the seal hunt helped to sustain a distinct identity. The province had been in
Confederation less than twenty years when the anti-sealing controversy emerged.
Many adjustments were painful as federal authority encroached on home-grown
ways of doing things. Memories of the debates over Newfoundland's future were
still fresh in many minds, and the sense of loss of autonomy was acute for some.
In defending the hunt, the middle class reflected both urban angst about cultural
identity and a North America-wide wave of nostalgia for rural life[53] that expressed
itself in a yearning to return to nature and a more focused interest in folk songs,
arts, and crafts. By supporting an economic activity important to rural
Newfoundlanders, urban activists also placed themselves at the head of a united
society. Meanwhile, in the outports of the province, a swiler was still accorded
respect as 'a special kind of person' and honoured for his 'adherence to heritage,
stoic endurance, hardiness, the ability to provide'.[54] Different needs thus promoted
a common urge to repel, in the words of Art Scammell, 'pampered city slickers'
from away.[55]

Such reactions resonated among the public at large even though only a minority
of Newfoundlanders were involved with the hunt. Some, like Albert J. March of
Stephenville and Madeline Pitts of Dunville (Placentia Bay), wrote poems defending
seal hunting even though they did not know anyone who actually went to the ice.

March began his work after reading *Death on the Ice* because he 'felt sorry for seal hunters'.[56] Of course not all were so removed from the issue. Bella Hodge from St Anthony recalled the time her father got lost on the ice: a rescue team found him 'frozen like a chunk of ice' and it took Mrs Hodges' grandmother and other women all night to revive him. Those were the people on whose behalf the *Evening Telegram*[57] spoke when it asked in a rhetorical flourish, 'Tell me, Miss Bardot, do you recall at lamplight melting ice with your breath from the kitchen window?' 'Yes, ten tiny faces peeping through, looking, waiting anxiously for a dad long overdue from the seal hunt, risking his life . . . for barely enough money to buy molasses and tea.'

The protesters, on the other hand, were depicted as lacking credibility. Their compassion for seals was dismissed as a superficial attachment to a cuddly image. If seals had the faces of pigs, ran one line of argument, outsiders would favour them less. Protesters 'never saw a seal in their life except a tame one', one swiler remarked. 'If they seen a good dog hood they'd never stop running.' At times opponents of the hunt were even represented as perverting the wholesome values embodied by the sealers. Swilers might kill animals to make a living but—unlike some immoral outsiders—they did not kill their own unborn children.[58] Arguments like this point to the core of a dispute that pitted rural folk and rural sensibilities against urbanized adversaries with a different value system. In the

The controversy over the seal hunt is now an annual media event in which both sides struggle to win public support. For some animal-rights organizations, the issue also offers opportunities for fundraising. (Courtesy of Kevin Tobin, St John's Telegram.)

clash between the two, the determination to defend a traditional lifestyle was backed by the fear that the battle might be lost, with grave consequences. 'We will not let anybody . . . destroy our traditional values,' declared the *Evening Telegram*; 'we're fighting for our very survival in Newfoundland.'[59]

Although that struggle continues to the present, the sealers appear to be losing ground. The boycott invoked by the European Union has undercut markets for seal pelts, and anti-sealing campaigners have become permanent fixtures at the annual hunt, which is now subject to increasingly stringent controls. Yet, threatened as the hunt itself may be, its role as an integral part of the Newfoundland identity is even more in doubt.

However justified it may be on economic and cultural grounds, the killing of seals is clearly gruesome to watch, and it cannot be concealed from the probing cameras of environmental activists. The seals are too appealing and the hunt's economic advantages too indistinct for seal hunters to win approval from many urban Canadians, some even in Newfoundland.[60] Above all, critical parts of the old heroic image are now lacking. The environment may be just as hostile as ever, but landsmen working close to shore, with modern clothing, transportation, and equipment, now appear less vulnerable to it than in the past. They are required to be less physically adept than their fathers and grandfathers who ventured onto the ice fields, and the risks appear less onerous. The seal hunt thus contributes little to a positive image of Newfoundlanders, and much that is negative.

If icons of identity are to endure they must be useful. When they cease to uplift and energize their owners, they will be swept from the family altar to make way for new ones. The seal hunter as the archetype of the heroic Newfoundlander is sharing a fate common to many icons of the past. At one time the trapper, the lumberjack, and the cowboy also enjoyed legendary status. Each was assigned qualities deemed to represent the finest traits of his compatriots. As Canadians have moved away from direct association with the land and the need to wrest a living from nature, they have developed new measures of accomplishment. Some of the new heroes may represent different qualities; others, like athletes and astronauts, may simply be new embodiments of old traits. Few, though, demarcate an identity as clearly as the Newfoundland swiler once did.

NOTES

The author wishes to acknowledge and thank two summer employees, Jo-Anne Brownlee and Eric Charlebois, for their research assistance. 'Swiling', 'swaling', and 'swoiling' are all variants of 'sealing'; G.M. Story, W.J. Kirwin, and J.D.A. Widdowson, eds., *Dictionary of Newfoundland English* (Toronto, 1982), 455.

1. James E. Candow, *Of Men and Seals: A History of the Newfoundland Seal Hunt* (Ottawa, 1989), 19–22.

2. David M. Lavigne and Kit M. Kovacs, *Harps and Hoods: Ice-breeding Seals of the Northwest Atlantic* (Waterloo, 1988), 103.

3. A good fictional portrayal can be found in Bernice Morgan, *Random Passage* (St John's, 1992), 39–41, 100–8.

4. Shannon Ryan, 'Newfoundland: Fishery to Canadian Province', in Boyde Beck, Greg Marquis, Joan M. Payzant, and Shannon Ryan, *Atlantic Canada: At the Dawn of a New Nation* (Burlington, 1990), 25.

5. Shannon Ryan, *The Ice Hunters: A History of Newfoundland Sealing to 1914* (St John's, 1994), 55.

6. Chesley W. Sanger, 'Newfoundland Seal Fishery', in 'The Dundee-St. John's Connection: Nineteenth Century Interlinkages Between Scottish Arctic Whaling and the Newfoundland Seal Fishery', *Newfoundland Studies* 4, 1 (1988), 6.

7. W.D. Bowen, 'The Harp Seal', *Underwater World* (Ottawa, 1991), 5.

8. C. Grant Head, Rosemary E. Ommer, and Patricia A. Thornton, 'Canadian Fisheries, 1850–1900', Plate 37 in R. Louis Gentilcore, ed., *Historical Atlas of Canada*, vol. II (Toronto, 1993).

9. Ryan, *The Ice Hunters*, xviii.

10. Ibid., 396.

11. See John Feltham, *Sealing Steamers* (St John's, 1995); Gerald S. Doyle, *Old-Time Songs and Poetry of Newfoundland* (St John's, 1927, 1955); Shannon Ryan and Larry Small, *Haulin' Rope & Gaff* (St John's, 1978).

12. Ryan, *The Ice Hunters*, 380–3; *Evening Telegram* (21 April 1931), 14.

13. Hon. Captain A. Kean, OBE, 'The Seal Fishery for 1934', reprinted in *Newfoundland Quarterly 75th Anniversary Special Edition*, ed. Harry A. Cuff and Cyril F. Poole (St John's, 1976), 142.

14. 'Newfoundland's Most Successful Seal-Killer', reprinted in *Newfoundland Quarterly 75th Anniversary Special Edition*, 91.

15. Quoted in Ryan, *The Ice Hunters*, 376.

16. S. Pike, 'The Viking Disaster', *Evening Telegram* (23 March 1931).

17. Editorial, *Evening Telegram* (25 Mar. 1931), 6.

18. The 1893 diary of James Allan of the *Aurora*, National Archives of Canada, MG 30, B 134; Captain Robert A. Bartlett, 'The Sealing Saga of Newfoundland', *National Geographic* LVI, 1 (July 1929), 123–5.

19. 'Sculping' involved separating the skin, with the fat attached, from the seal, leaving only the body flesh (of which there was very little on young seals) and bones. The whole process could take 40 to 60 seconds, and a good hand could kill and sculp 120 seals in a day, given the opportunity; Bartlett, 'Sealing Saga', 125.

20. Food quality improved over time; D.M. Lindsay, *A Voyage to the Arctic in the Whaler Aurora* (Boston, 1911), 41–2; Bartlett, 'Sealing Saga', 122–3.

21. 'There are few young men in the colony who have not been on the "ice" and an expedition is looked upon as a test of manhood'; Report of the Newfoundland House of Assembly, 23rd session, app. 516, 19 May 1913.

22. Ronald Rompkey, 'Philip Henry Gosse's account of his years in Newfoundland, 1827–35', *Newfoundland Studies* 6, 2 (1990), 226–7; and Bartlett, 'Sealing Saga', 95–101, 130.

23. Captain Robert A. Bartlett, *The Log of Bob Bartlett: The True Story of Forty Years of Seafaring and Exploration* (New York, 1928), 8–10.

24. George Tuff, letter to the editor, *Evening Telegram* (7 March 1931), 5.

25. Briton Cooper Busch, *The War Against the Seals* (Kingston and Montreal, 1985), 75.

26. Cassie Brown with Harold Horwood, *Death on the Ice: The Great Newfoundland Sealing Disaster of 1914* (Toronto, 1972), 29–33.

27. James Allan's diary, National Archives of Canada, MG 30, B 134, 47.

28. Chesley W. Sanger, 'The Dundee-St. John's Connection . . .', 1–21.

29. Report by Henry I. Sargent, a friend of Frissell, in *Evening Telegram* (14 Aug. 1931), 15.

30. *Evening Telegram* (26 March 1931), 6.

31. *Evening Telegram* (2 March 1997), 11.

32. Alice Lannon and Mike McCarthy, *Ghost Stories from Newfoundland Folklore* (St John's, 1995), 46–50.

33. 'Newfoundland's Most Successful Seal-Killer', 90.

34. Sir M.G. Winter, 'Trip to the Seal Fishery', *Newfoundland Quarterly* LXXV, 2 (Fall 1979), 21–7; A.E. Rutherford, 'Newfoundland Log Book', *Newfoundland Quarterly* LXVII, 1 (Christmas 1968), 21–6.

35. Editorial, *Evening Telegram* (24 March 1931), 6.

36. For example, Kenneth Peacock, comp. and ed., *Songs of the Newfoundland Outports*, vol. 1 (Ottawa, 1965), 903–4.

37. Bartlett, *The Log of Bob Bartlett*', 8–10; T.B. Rogers, 'The Last Voyage of the Southern Cross', *Newfoundland Quarterly* LXXVI, 3 (Fall 1980), 21–30.

38. Philip Tocque, *Newfoundland: As it was and as it is in 1877* (Toronto, 1878), 306.

39. J.B. Jukes, *Excursions in and about Newfoundland during the years 1839 and 1840* (London, 1842), 276, 290.

40. Ibid., 291.

41. 'Newfoundland', *Blackwoods Magazine* CXIV (1873), quoted in Ryan, *The Ice Hunters*, 390.

42. This article was published in *Nineteenth Century*, a widely circulated British magazine; it is quoted in Ryan, *The Ice Hunters*, 390–1.

43. *Evening Telegram* (30 June 1931), 6.

44. Candow, *Of Men and Seals*, 110.

45. The Convention on International Trade in Endangered Species ruled in April 1983 that neither harp nor hood seals were threatened.

46. Cynthia Lamson, *'Bloody Decks and a Bumper Crop': The Rhetoric of Sealing Counter-Protest*, Social and Economic Studies No. 24 (St John's, 1979), 91–4.

47. Testimony before the House of Commons Standing Committee on Fisheries and Forestry, 15 April 1969, quoted in ibid., 92.

48. Guy David Wright, *Sons and Seals: A Voyage to the Ice*, Social and Economic Studies No. 29 (St John's, 1984), 116–17.

49. Farley Mowat, *Wake of the Great Sealers*, prints and drawings by David Blackwood (Toronto, 1973).

50. Helen Peters, *Stars in the Morning Sky* (St John's, 1996), 2–47.

51. Ibid., 13.

52. Ibid., 46.

53. James Overton, 'Living Patriotism: Songs, Politics and Resources in Newfoundland', *Canadian Review of Studies in Nationalism* XII, 2 (Fall 1985), 239–57.

54. Wright, *Sons and Seals*, 97–8.

55. Art Scammell, 'A Sealer's Song (1977)', quoted in Overton, 'Living Patriotism', 247.

56. Quotes from Lamson, '*Bloody Decks and a Bumper Crop*', 83, 13, 14, 19.

57. *Evening Telegram* (25 March 1977), 6.

58. Ibid., 41.

59. Ibid., 18, and Patrick O'Flaherty, 'Killing Ground', *Weekend Magazine* (31 March 1979), 22–4. He saw the perpetuation of a seal hunt as the *sine qua non* of a distinct Newfoundland character.

60. A letter to the *Evening Telegram* (29 Feb. 1996, 4) suggests the kinds of doubts that tend to arise in the face of persistent criticism from outside. Ken Hannaford wrote, 'Newfoundland is steeped in such cruelty from the extinction of the Newfoundland wolf to the clubbing of the last Great Auk. It is time to remove this ridiculous and barbaric behaviour from our culture and stop denying its existence.'

Desperately Seeking the Audience for Early Canadian Radio

Mary Vipond

One of the most challenging aspects of studying the history of Canadian radio, especially in its earliest years, is the lack of source material relating to its essence: programs and audiences. A mass medium is not only an economic enterprise but also a cultural site, a place where meaning is made. Yet most of the books written on Canadian radio history have focused on other matters: academic works on policies and structures, non-academic works on people and pictures. Both have virtually ignored the cultural dimension of the history of Canadian radio. This silence is hardly surprising; very little material has survived on which an analysis of the cultural aspects of early radio might be based. Almost no recordings of Canadian programs from the pre-CBC era remain, and only a few scripts. Ratings services to conduct listener-preference surveys did not exist in Canada before the 1940s, and what studies advertisers conducted have long since been discarded.

Radio historians must therefore invent new ways to uncover the programs and audiences of the past. Imagination and creativity are required, as well as tools not always familiar to historians—but avoidance of the issue is no longer possible. Some way must be found to understand the cultural impact of the historical experience of radio listening.

In my view, three general strategies should be undertaken simultaneously. First, if we lack the statistical information to answer with any accuracy such conventional questions as 'who listened?' and 'to what programs?' we must ask different ones—questions of interpretation and meaning rather than of statistical probability or demographic classification.

Second, we must attempt, through close reading and sensitivity to context and interconnections, to squeeze every possible meaning out of the scattered remnants that do survive. These sources include program listings, some scripts and tapes, a few unscientific listener surveys of particular locales, carefully structured interviews, and written texts such as listeners' letters and broadcasters' musings.[1]

Finally, historians must become familiar with recent theory and research in the fields of mass communications and cultural studies. While these works focus mainly on television in the contemporary period, they nevertheless suggest many issues and avenues that may inform a more historical study.[2] Ultimately, however, the task of uncovering the radio experience of the past also requires acceptance of Clifford Geertz's dictum that 'it is not necessary to know everything in order to understand something.'[3]

The goal of this paper is to demonstrate what early radio magazines can reveal about the characteristics and expectations of listeners in the early 1930s.[4] It is part of a larger project tracing the cultural history of the Canadian Radio Broadcasting Commission (CRBC), the predecessor of the CBC, in the early 1930s. That study focuses on how public broadcasting was created, constructed, and defined, and particularly on how the CRBC constituted itself as 'different' from the commercial broadcasting that had dominated North America since the early 1920s.

Like other early radio material, fan magazines are rare. So far, short runs of only two such publications that overlap—barely—the CRBC period have been located. But a close reading of their texts has been most rewarding. At the first level, of course, they provide much information about the programs and performers of the era. That was why people bought them—to get the background, pictures, and detailed program listings that are also naturally useful to the historian. At another level, however, these magazines are of interest because they did not just talk *about* radio performers: they also talked *to* radio listeners. Not only did they respond to the interests of radio fans; more important, they moulded those fans by the way they portrayed the role and practice of being a radio listener. Ien Ang argues throughout her influential book *Desperately Seeking the Audience* (whose title has been borrowed and altered here) that the 'audience' is socially constructed by the discourses of broadcasters.[5] But broadcasting does not exist in a vacuum. Other social and cultural agents and texts shaped the radio listening audiences of the early 1930s as well, among them radio magazines.

These magazines must be understood as cultural and commercial products themselves. They were primarily concerned with their own economic viability; at least some of their contents were not so much commentaries on radio or radio fans as they were attempts to attract readers. The editors and columnists of the radio magazines bore something of the same relationship to the radio industry as their counterparts in the daily press did to the political system. They were of it but not in it; the relationship was symbiotic but premised on the pretence of objectivity. Although they proclaimed that they provided a 'link' between broadcasters and fans, and that they were leaders 'in securing for listeners the service which they desire and have a right to expect', in fact radio magazines did not tell broadcasters what listeners wanted, but the reverse: they told fans how to listen.[6]

Canadian Radio Guide, subtitled *The National Weekly of Programs and Personalities*, was published in Toronto from December 1931 to February 1933. It was a subsidiary to *Radio Guide*, a successful Chicago-based journal, and at least eighty per cent of its content was American. The editor was Frank Armstrong, a former singer, stage manager, and programmer originally from the Maritimes who had lived a number of years in New York and Los Angeles.[7] The magazine provided program listings for the week, gossip about radio stars (mainly but not exclusively American), and pictures. There was virtually no editorial or critical content; the two columnists simply provided brief snippets of news and gossip.

Radio Weekly was a Maclean Publishing Company paper. Its subtitle was Canada's National Radio Weekly, although in truth it covered little more than southern Ontario and English Montreal. The fact that it too failed, after less than a year of publication (May 1932 to March 1933) and despite desperate attempts to broaden its appeal, indicates the difficulty such magazines faced in Depression-era Canada. The problems of Radio Weekly were doubtless exacerbated by the expense involved in employing a number of Canadian correspondents and editors. Most notably, the magazine featured weekly columns by Raymond Mullens, formerly a music reporter with the Chicago Tribune and radio columnist for Saturday Night, and probably the only serious radio critic in Canada at the time.[8] Thus although Radio Weekly had its share of program listings, press-agent puffery, and American network gossip, it made a much greater effort than Canadian Radio Guide to report and comment critically on Canadian radio.

Despite these differences, the two magazines presented their readers with a similar normative view of the world of radio. This view rested on three main assumptions: that radio existed primarily for the entertainment of a wide variety of listeners with different tastes; that it was run by private enterprises seeking profit, was financed by advertising, and was therefore 'free' to the audience; and that it produced stars who were idolized by fans.

As to an alternative vision of radio—specifically public broadcasting—the two magazines differed in their approach. Canadian Radio Guide did not condemn public broadcasters like the BBC or the CRBC: it marginalized them by simply ignoring their existence. Radio Weekly, on the other hand, acknowledged the introduction of public broadcasting and the creation of the CRBC, but was almost entirely negative about the new option. Until the last month of its existence the magazine's editorials consistently opposed the new Commission, mainly on the grounds that a bureaucratic body was incapable of assessing or responding to the needs and tastes of listeners.[9] The Weekly also criticized both the BBC and the Australian Broadcasting Commission (ABC), primarily because they had set themselves up as 'master[s] of . . . the air' when the real masters should be the listeners.[10] Thus both magazines positioned themselves as champions of ordinary listeners and at the same time reinforced the message that public broadcasting was not only authoritarian and anti-listener but alien—the 'other'. What was 'normal' for Canadian radio listeners, according to both, was the American system of privately owned, commercial, popular, entertaining radio, for Canadians closely resembled Americans in their 'speech, thought and behaviour'.[11] Many readers also seem to have shared this position, such as the fan who wrote to Radio Weekly in mid-1932: 'Let us have North American broadcasting for North American people.'[12]

The mainstay of the two magazines was gossip about the lives of radio performers, virtually all the product of press agents' releases. Their principal fare comprised brief biographies of radio personalities, information about their private lives and work practices, and insights into their quirks and foibles.[13] The magazines were also filled with pictures of the star performers, for of course one of their main services was to 'put the face to the voice' for radio listeners. The pictures seem to have been very important to readers; young women wrote in to the editors to describe their radio-celebrity scrapbooks and share their hobby with others.[14] Most of the photos were relatively conventional head-and-shoulders studio portraits or action scenes featuring the star before the microphone, on the golf course, relaxing at home with her children, and so on, although leggy beauties in bathing suits also seem to have been *de rigueur*. Thus for the most part the magazines emphasized the ordinary, 'everyday' personalities of the radio performers.[15] Together, the gossip and pictures helped to make these celebrities more interesting, more human, more *known* to radio listeners, presenting them as the kind of people one would be happy to have visiting in one's home every evening.

Despite this image of 'everydayness', another prominent theme in both *Canadian Radio Guide* and *Radio Weekly* was the Horatio Alger 'rags to riches' story. Countless articles focused on how the stars had got where they were, and a surprising number (in the context of the Depression) on how much money they now made.[16] Publication of their large salaries made the stars enviable; however, it also distanced them. The magazines, perhaps because of their largely American material, and because Hollywood and the US radio networks were already acting in symbiosis by the 1930s, presented radio stars who shared many of the glamorous characteristics of Hollywood idols.[17] Thus a mixed message was sent: while radio performers led everyday lives that made them seem ordinary and human, at the same time they were also celebrities—rich, famous, and clearly residents of another world.

Both magazines consistently, indeed aggressively, maintained that the sole purpose of radio was entertainment and diversion: 'Radio Means Relaxation,' they constantly proclaimed.[18] Even *Radio Weekly*, the more serious of the two, argued that faking a sports broadcast in order to heighten the excitement was quite legitimate, and maintained that even informational programs like news and talks must be judged largely by how well they entertained. As the editor of the journal put it early in 1933:

> Radio entertainment is entertainment or it is nothing. . . . The radio set is a thing of the home. It is a guest. Friends and guests don't talk in ponderous sentences; their conversation is, or ought to be, colloquial, racy with idiom and thoroughly friendly.[19]

Moreover, *Radio Weekly* criticized Canadian broadcasting on precisely these grounds: Canadian performers were as able as any in the United States, it asserted, but they lacked the 'light touch' and polish necessary to fulfil radio's incessant demand for diverting material.[20]

The second important message sent by these magazines to radio listeners was that they, the listeners, had the power to select from the wide range of available programs the ones that best suited their own individual inclinations. Stories and articles highlighted the diverse (and sometimes peculiar) program preferences of listeners.[21] An editorial in *Radio Weekly* made the point this way:

> An immensely learned university professor recently was arrested for speeding. He offered the magistrate the excuse that he was trying to get home in time to hear Amos 'n' Andy. One of the stalwart lads who helps to put this publication into type confessed that if Sir James Jeans or his colleague Eddington would talk every night he would go without his supper rather than miss the address.
>
> Sunday school superintendents have been known—when the doors are locked— to tune in on 'hotcha' and 'torch' singers. Professors of English feel lost without their nightly dose of detective drama. In other words, no one knows what the other fellow likes.[22]

Articles, editorials, and columns also emphasized the huge repertoires of the performers and the vast music libraries of the networks—all prepared to cater to the infinite diversity of listener tastes.[23]

Similarly, the great majority of the letters to the editors concerned program preferences. 'May I say a word about Don Romanelli. His orchestra is the best in my opinion,' one correspondent wrote. 'May I shout from the house-tops that I am a Billy Bissett fan?' asked another.[24] Rarely was justification or explanation offered; these were statements of personal and private taste, not measures of quality but expressions of appreciation for the vast array of possibilities that radio presented. Program preferences were also a means of self-definition; listeners shaped their identities around the entertainers they preferred. Such identities were individual and private, based on membership not in an external group or community but in the radio-created community of, say, Billy Bissett fans—a subset of that equally artificial community the radio audience.[25]

No doubt one reason the magazines emphasized the importance of choice and selection was that this was precisely what made them necessary. Almost invariably, ads for the magazines proclaimed that only they provided listeners with the knowledge required to select the programs they preferred.[26] Yet despite telling listeners that each one of them was an individual with particular interests, the magazines also framed them as part of a single whole—the mass audience. What really determined radio fare was popularity: many articles were devoted to reports of formal and informal surveys listing the best-liked performers and programs. Implicitly or explicitly, listeners were encouraged at once to be tolerant of other people's choices and to climb on the bandwagon.[27] Thus a tension existed between the notion of the diversity of individual tastes and the economic imperative, in a commercially financed system, to cater to the preferences of the largest number of listeners; but this tension was never addressed openly, and it was never resolved.

Ien Ang argues in *Desperately Seeking the Audience* that broadcasters' biggest challenge has been the constant need to re-attract and reconstruct their audiences. One solution to that problem has been the endlessly reiterated claim of novelty. The radio magazines of the 1930s did their part. They reminded their readers time and again that broadcasters were always on the lookout for the new and different. As an article in *Canadian Radio Guide* put it: 'There is always something new on radio. It may be a sponsor, or a program, an artist or a new type of entertainment. New radio personalities are constantly being brought to the microphone, and as a result, radio's listeners are never allowed to grow weary.'[28] But a fundamental ambivalence resulted: while the current status quo was presented as complete and satisfying, at the same time novelty, progress, and change were lauded. The normative world of radio was one that celebrated change—but only within very narrow margins.

As already mentioned, readers of these magazines were repeatedly told that they were the 'masters of the air', that they were in the driver's seat. Program directors, they were often reminded, spent all their waking hours seeking the satisfaction of those mysterious beings 'Mr. and Mrs. Average Listener'.[29] All broadcasters, it seemed, cared for nothing in life but to fulfil the desires of the restless, insatiable, discriminating, and demanding 'listening public'.

These messages also conveyed the flattering assumption that radio listeners were progressive, up-to-date, and modern. And the best and the brightest of radio listeners were those who read radio magazines, for they were the most involved in the radio world; they knew its inner secrets, they appreciated its inside jokes. The magazines fostered this impression through frequent articles explaining the behind-the-scenes practices of the broadcasting business: how sound effects were created, how mikes were placed, how engineers fed networks.[30] Similarly, and perhaps surprisingly, the magazines often printed unkind comments about sponsors, particularly deriding advertisers who insisted that they wanted to design their own programs.[31] The message was clear: the radio specialists—the broadcasters and listeners—knew what was best, not outsiders such as sponsors or, of course, governments.

Another way of framing a community of insiders was by means of frequent jokes or asides targeting people who did not listen to the radio or who failed to 'get' it. Sometimes these unregenerate individuals were portrayed simply as naive and old-fashioned. For example, one anecdote described an encounter between the popular singing trio the Boswell Sisters and an elderly woman in their home town of New Orleans when they returned to visit after six years of singing on NBC. 'Oh,' the 'dear old soul' gushed: 'I remember you. Do you still sing?'[32] The story was designed to elicit a knowing chuckle and a feeling of self-satisfied superiority in the reader. Other articles poked fun at ignorant listeners who were fooled into thinking that sound effects were real, or at the naive and pathetic love-starved fans who showered their idols with gifts and letters.[33] By implicit contrast, radio magazine readers were thus told that they were the experts on radio. They gained self-definition and a sense of belonging from that expertise. They were a part of the 'shared world' of broadcasting.[34]

Despite the stress on the tastes and knowledge of regular listeners, however, the role defined for them was essentially a passive one. There would always be something that satisfied everyone—the industry would see to that. There was no need for listeners to rouse themselves, beyond turning the dial and occasionally responding to polls that classified them and their tastes. North American broadcasting as it existed was fundamentally sound, and any small imperfections would be remedied by the evolution of the system through natural competition.

One group of non-listeners was nevertheless perplexing for the radio magazines. These were the snobs, the 'highbrows' who considered radio's offerings, especially crooners and jazz, vulgar and mediocre.[35] Against these types the magazines seemed to feel somewhat defensive. *Canadian Radio Guide* handled this problem the same way it handled the issue of public broadcasting: by ignoring it. Articles about classical music programs, conductors, and performers appeared, but they almost never addressed questions of tradition, status, or class with respect to this highbrow fare. By avoiding debate about concepts of cultural hierarchy, the magazine relayed the message that radio provided for all tastes, and that the liking for high culture was just another idiosyncrasy, not related to any external value system. It was also made quite clear that minority opinions like these could not expect to receive much attention on radio.[36]

Radio Weekly presents a more complex case, for it did address issues of quality and hierarchy regularly and explicitly.[37] In fact, the first few numbers of the magazine carried a series entitled 'A Lowbrow Writes on Music', in which the columnist explained to readers what they should listen for in classical music, namely tune, rhythm, and harmony. The burden of his argument was that 'classic' music could be enjoyed by all, not just 'arty' people who looked down their noses at 'you and I'. The really great music, he insisted, 'has only lived because it has been enjoyed by us lowbrows'.[38] We see here, then, another mixed message: listeners were encouraged to be knowledgeable about music, including classical music (and part of that knowledge could be gained by reading *Radio Weekly*), but at the same time their own ordinary, everyday feelings and opinions were endorsed and ratified.

Thus although *Radio Weekly* paid more attention than *Canadian Radio Guide* to a scale of cultural values, it did not support that notion. Rather, it attempted to blur the distinctions between 'high' and 'low'. It did so on one hand by suggesting that classical music was now, by the miracle of the airwaves, accessible to everyone and, on the other hand, by highlighting the musical talent, classical training, constant practising, and diverse repertoire of popular performers like dance bands.[39] *Radio Weekly* thus accepted that it had a duty to improve the knowledge of its readers and to help them to appreciate quality, but it also insisted that nothing must be shoved down their throats: the listeners must remain in control.

I have argued thus far that the radio magazines presented a normative model of private commercial radio to their readers—radio that was implicitly defined as popular, entertaining, and capable of responding to the needs of all North Americans. As far as one can tell, most readers seemed to agree with this representation. The majority of letters to the editor talked about radio the same way, emphasizing personalities, tastes for different programs, popular fads, and so on. In only one area did the readers seem to offer some resistance to the magazines' discourse: this was the area of national identity. A significant number of correspondents, many of whom signed their letters with names like 'Patriotic' or 'A Canadian', criticized the magazines for not carrying more information about 'our own Canadian artists', who were 'as good as any others'.[40]

Two comments may be made about this phenomenon. The first is that these letter-writers did not endorse the creation of a Canadian public network; all they asked was encouragement for Canadian performers, and none made any link between the two issues. They were calling for more coverage of Canadian artists not because those artists offered something of national cultural significance, but because they deserved equal career opportunities. Nevertheless, the explicit expression of patriotism does suggest that these correspondents felt that they shared a community with Canadian radio artists, as of course did their decision to subscribe to a *Canadian* radio magazine. Second, these letters were really critical not so much of radio fare itself as of the magazines' coverage of broadcasting. Similar criticisms were made, for example, about their tendency to ignore amateur performers and smaller stations, both more typical of local communities than of large cities.[41]

From time to time the editors defended themselves against these complaints, on the legitimate grounds that they could not publish what they did not know about.[42] The structural flaw lay in the fact that Canadian stations and performers lacked the constant promotion provided for their American counterparts by press agents and flacks. Without widespread and costly publicity, Canadian artists and programs by definition were less well known and less popular, and therefore fell off the air.[43]

The long-term effect of highlighting American programs and personalities was to establish the American model as the norm, and in this the radio magazines, even the ostensibly Canadian ones, played a central role. Nonetheless, the consciousness of at least some readers that there was a distinction between Canadian and American radio, and between network and local stations, does suggest that a nascent site of resistance existed.[44] Unfortunately, *Canadian Radio Guide* and *Radio Weekly*, which provided at least some coverage of the Canadian component of North America's private broadcasting system, were not financially stable enough to survive beyond 1933. Central Canadian radio fans were then left to read wholly American magazines, which provided *no* publicity for the products of Canadian broadcasting, private or public, large or small.

Both *Canadian Radio Guide* and *Radio Weekly* went out of business before the CRBC began a full broadcasting schedule, so they do not reveal any explicit reaction to it. Nevertheless, they suggest the environment of expectations that surrounded the CRBC at the time of its formation. Most important, they defined a world in which public broadcasting in any form was alien and abnormal. *Canadian Radio Guide* silenced discussion of the public broadcasting alternative by virtually never mentioning it. While *Radio Weekly* did occasionally discuss the CRBC, BBC, and ABC, it was only to marginalize them through constant reminders that these regimes did not care about their listeners—the very listeners celebrated by the magazines as the 'masters' in the customary, normal, world of radio. The few readers who objected to this portrayal placed their loyalty with local community stations, not with the prospect of a government-owned national network. Thus was created the CRBC's greatest dilemma: how, in such a context, to achieve credibility with listeners while at the same time beginning to present an alternative vision of how broadcasters might relate to their audiences.

NOTES

1. For a study of two such surveys, see Mary Vipond, 'London Listens: The Popularity of Radio in the Depression', *Ontario History* 88, 1 (1996), 47–63.

2. Useful recent collections on audience research include Ellen Seiter et al., eds, *Remote Control: Television, Audiences, and Cultural Power* (London and New York, 1989); Jon Cruz and Justin Lewis, eds, *Viewing, Reading, Listening: Audiences and Cultural Reception* (Boulder, Col., 1994); and James Hay et al., eds, *The Audience and Its Landscape* (Boulder, Col., 1996).

3. Clifford Geertz, *The Interpretation of Cultures* (New York, 1973), 20.

4. This study owes much to the model provided by Lesley Johnson in *The Unseen Voice: A Cultural Study of Early Australian Radio* (London, 1988).

5. Ang also believes, however, that there is an 'actual' audience, which she argues we must continue to seek using ethnographic methods; Ien Ang, *Desperately Seeking the Audience* (London and New York, 1990), 13.

6. Statement of purpose from the first issue of *Radio Weekly* (hereafter *RW*) (28 May 1932), 3.

7. Douglas Maclennan, 'Maritime Diversions', *RW* (4 Feb. 1933), 15.

8. Editorial, 'Purpose and Policy', *RW* (21 Jan. 1933), 4.

9. Editorial, *RW* (28 May 1932), 6; editorial, 'B.B.C. Blunder Shows Canada Error of Monopoly', *RW* (9 July 1932), 12.

10. 'National Radio for Australia', *RW* (28 May 1932), 5; Editorial, 'Scotsman Complains B.B.C. Gives Poor Service', *RW* (4 June 1932), 6; editorial, 'B.B.C. Asks Correspondents to Prepay Answers', *RW* (18 June 1932), 9; Raymond Mullens, 'As I Was Just Saying . . .', *RW* (19 Nov. 1932), 4.

11. Editorial, *RW* (16 July 1932), 9.

12. Letter to editor from M. Alexander, *RW* (2 July 1932), 14; see also letter to editor from 'A Radio Guide Booster', *Canadian Radio Guide* (hereafter *CRG*) (12 Nov. 1932), 13.

13. For example, see 'Radio People Do Everything on Week Ends', *RW* (18 June 1932), 11.

14. Letter to editor from 'Harriet', *CRG* (13 Oct. 1932), 13; see also letter to editor from 'An Ardent Reader', *CRG* (29 Oct. 1932), 13.

15. Johnson, *The Unseen Voice*, 82–100.

16. See, for example, 'Rich Little Orphan Annie', *CRG* (8 Oct. 1932), 9; 'Lucre Lures Lombardos', *CRG* (9 July 1932), 1.

17. See, for example, 'Wanted—Radio's Garbo', *CRG* (16 July 1932), 2.

18. Raymond Mullens, 'As I Was Just Saying . . .', *RW* (18 Feb. 1933), 4.

19. Editorial, 'Heaviness on the Air', *RW* (11 March 1933), 4; see also editorial, 'Less Classroom', *RW* (1 Oct. 1932), 4.

20. Editorial, 'May We Hint, Mr. Charlesworth?', *RW* (5 Nov. 1932), 4.

21. For example, Raymond Mullens, 'As I Was Just Saying . . .', *RW* (15 Oct. 1932), 6; 'Art. Tracy Sorts Mail', *RW* (29 Oct. 1932), 21.

22. Editorial, 'What Do You Want?', *RW* (24 Sept. 1932), 4.

23. For example, see Mark A. Stevens, 'Ten Tons of Music', *CRG* (5 Nov. 1932), 8.

24. Letter to editor from 'Another Hamiltonian', *CRG* (22 Oct. 1932), 13; letter to editor from 'A Detroit Girl', *CRG* (26 Nov. 1932), 16.

25. Johnson, *The Unseen Voice*, 29.

26. Advertisement, *RW* (11 June 1932), 7; see also editorial, 'To Twirlers and Sqawkers [*sic*]', *RW* (17 Sept. 1932), 15.

27. For example, Porthos, 'Reviewing Radio', *CRG* (18 June 1932), 3; Raymond Mullens, 'As I Was Just Saying . . .', *RW* (18 Feb. 1933), 4.

28. 'All-Star Revue', *CRG* (22 Oct. 1932), 2.

29. The term was used in *RW* (5 Nov. 1932), 21.

30. See, for example, Montreal Mike, 'Air Lines', *RW* (4 June 1932), 2; Ellen Evelyn Mackie, 'Radio's Trick Bag', *RW* (7 Jan. 1933), 7; 'Sign Language of the Studio', *CRG* (19 Dec. 1931), 5.

31. See 'The Walls Have Ears', *CRG* (8 Oct. 1932), 2; Raymond Mullens, 'As I Was Just Saying . . .', *RW* (10 Dec. 1932), 4.

32. Porthos, 'Reviewing Radio', *CRG* (5 Nov. 1932), 3.

33. See, for example, 'Tried to Buy Tin Can Dog', *RW* (28 May 1932), 10; 'Love-Starved Fans!', *CRG* (27 Aug. 1932), 1.

34. Johnson, *The Unseen Voice*, 123.

35. All discussions of issues of cultural hierarchy focused on music programming.

36. Porthos, 'Reviewing Radio', *CRG* (14 May 1932), 3.

37. See, for example, Raymond Mullens, 'Jazz Music', *RW* (31 Dec. 1932), 17; Raymond Mullens, 'Are Highbrows to Blame for Avalanche of Jazz', *RW* (7 Jan. 1933), 17; The Dictaphone, 'What Music Does the Public Want', *RW* (11 Feb. 1933), 8.

38. Michael Sinclair, 'A Lowbrow Writes on Music', *RW* (11 June 1932), 3.

39. 'Can Modern Dance Bands Do Classics', *RW* (11 June 1932), 7; 'Charles Dornberger is Just a Good Guy', *RW* (18 June 1932), 11.

40. Letters to editor from 'Patriotic' and 'O.K.', *CRG* (8 Oct. 1932), 13; letter to editor from Margaret MacFadyen, *CRG* (22 Oct. 1932), 13.

41. Letter to editor from 'Not Satisfied', *CRG* (1 Oct. 1932), 13.

42. Raymond Mullens, 'As I Was Just Saying . . .', *RW* (5 Nov. 1932), 4.

43. Raymond Mullens came close to making this point in one column, but drew back and concluded with criticisms of the BBC; Mullens, 'As I Was Just Saying . . . ', *RW* (19 Nov. 1932), 4.
44. My thanks to commentator Brian McKillop for reminding me of this point.

Much Ado About Something

A Brief Study of the History of Canadian Art Exhibitions

ANN DAVIS

According to the conventional wisdom, art museums are neutral institutions that disseminate discovered knowledge. In Canada the public art gallery or art museum has usually presented itself as neutral and impersonal, a conduit for the transmission of a body of knowledge that is universal, timeless, and homogeneous. The implication is that there are worldwide, consistent values through which all works of fine art can be judged and understood.

This wisdom is now being directly challenged. Over the last few decades art galleries and museums have been accused of being racist, sexist, élitist, largely Eurocentric instruments of capitalist exploitation, among other sins. Stephen E. Weil, the past deputy director of the Hirshhorn Museum and Sculpture Garden at the Smithsonian Institution and a widely published critic of the art museum, explains that the latter 'is not now nor has ever been the neutral and disinterested institution it claims to be. Notwithstanding its claims to be pure, autonomous, and beyond worldly things, it cannot be otherwise than deeply coloured by its social, economic, and political setting.'[1] Marcia Tucker of the New Museum in New York agrees. What museums 'purport to disseminate', she writes, 'is not neutral; knowledge is not discovered, but is socially produced and reflective of the power relations of the society within which it is situated.'[2] Duncan Cameron, the widely published Canadian museologist and Director Emeritus of the Glenbow Museum in Calgary, has expanded on this idea with respect to the definition of a museum as an institution that 'researches, communicates and exhibits':

> for 'researches' read identifies, classifies and labels; for 'exhibits' read contextualizes; and for 'communicates' read pronounces. This is the ritual of naming. As the priest is the gatekeeper of the temple, granting admission to the faith by baptism, so the curator is the gatekeeper of the museum, granting an object admission to the institution's very specific reality by naming, by labeling, by imposing a construct specific to the museum's perceptions of reality, mythology or even ideas of absolute truth.[3]

From the University of Ottawa Edwina Taborsky concurs, arguing that the image of the museum as a neutral, objective purveyor of truths could be supported only if conjoined with an assumption of divine revelation.[4] Michael Ames, the recently retired and highly respected Director of the Museum of Anthropology at the University of British Columbia, explained in 1992 that museums

> frequently serve as playing fields upon which the major social, political, and moral issues of the day are contested. Not only are the definitions of truth and beauty subject to debate, as one might expect, but so are other thorny issues, such as what constitutes public taste and who has the right to determine it, what kind of knowledge is deemed to be useful—indeed, even what constitutes proper knowledge, and who has the right to control its production and dissemination.[5]

Power relations, divine or otherwise, are ubiquitous. It is those power relations in Canadian art galleries that I would like to explore. I will begin by trying to parse the values attributed to art museums. Then I will look at five major twentieth-century Canadian art exhibitions to see how they express those values and demonstrate power relations.

What is the purpose of an art museum? Is it to disseminate scientific knowledge? What does the audience want? Stephen Weil has perceptively analyzed the historical intellectual foundations of the American art museum. These, I suggest, apply equally well in Canada, and to a considerable degree they extend to the present day. Weil sees four historic fundamentals:

1. 'the idea that visual artists were people of a special, privileged, and elevated kind';
2. 'the idea that the works of art that these artists created were objects of a singular or even, at their best, inherently spiritual significance';
3. 'the idea that those who . . . were best able to understand and appreciate these works of art—connoisseurs, collectors and ultimately, curators—were also people of a special, privileged, and elevated kind'; and
4. 'the idea that the accumulation and display of these works of art in an art museum must of necessity constitute a public good of an all but religious dimension'.[6]

The romantic, privileged point of view underlying these ideas is still widely held. In 1964 and 1965, the eminent French sociologist Pierre Bourdieu conducted a series of surveys among museum visitors in Europe. His findings supported his theory that art museums, along with universities and a broad range of other cultural institutions, contribute to what he called 'the consecration of the social order'.[7] This is done by replicating anew, with each generation, the sense of distinction between the few who are perceived to be cultivated and the many who are perceived to lack cultivation. In short, Bourdieu's findings support Weil's historical premise and suggest that the purpose of museums may be to establish and maintain the distinction between the élite and the hoi polloi. Art museums, according to Bourdieu, function principally to reproduce the existing class structure. They do so by organizing occasions around which notions such as taste, sensibility, and aesthetic discernment can be determined. The difference in status that Bourdieu perceives between classes of viewers may be equated to the difference in power between those who dominate society and those over whom they exercise control. But for museum workers who question or reject Bourdieu's theory, there is worse to come. Bourdieu concluded that cultural manifestations, such as art museums, theatres, and universities, may not have *any* fundamental value in and of themselves. Whatever value objects classified as works of art have may be wholly arbitrary—a value constructed and imputed, not inherent and discovered. Supporting this possibility, the literary critic Fredric Jameson called this aspect of Bourdieu's thesis an 'implacable assault on the very rationalizations and self-justifications of culture itself'.[8]

I would like now to examine Weil's theory with respect to five specific Canadian art exhibitions. Each of these shows specifically set out to question established notions of taste, sensibility, and aesthetic discernment. Each was innovative in intent, controversial in result, and seminal in influence. Each changed the way art exhibitions are organized and viewed. Two of the shows dealt with issues of landscape and Canadian identity; two addressed Aboriginal issues; and one looked at colonialism. Together they span seventy-six years, from 1920 to 1996. Each exhibition was intended to suggest to the viewers new political and social and aesthetic considerations. What their organizers discovered, often to their surprise, was that the museums themselves became the playing fields on which social, political, or moral issues were contested.

The 1920 exhibition was the first Group of Seven show held in what was then the Art Gallery of Toronto. In a number of respects this exhibition reflected elements in Weil's argument. One is that the curating—in Duncan Cameron's terms, 'naming'—was done not by a gallery professional, a curator, but by the artists themselves. The members of the Group of Seven chose which of their own works they wanted to show and then, without consulting any other authority, hung them. The catalogue, written by the artists, contextualized and gave meaning to the exhibition. This sort of control on the part of artists, not unusual at the time, certainly gave them great power and special status, although it was soon to be challenged by the growing body of professional curators.

The catalogue made it clear where the power lay: the artists were special and so was their art. Proclaiming that they 'held a like vision concerning Art in Canada', they contended that 'an Art must grow and flower in the land before the country will be a real home for its people.' The Group of Seven also defined the range of reactions they expected their work to provoke: ridicule, abuse or indifference; refusal to recognize a non-commercial and native product; skepticism because of lack of history on the part of the group; and, finally, for 'a very small group of intelligent individuals'—that special, privileged group who understood that 'the greatness of a nation depends on "[i]ts Words, its Deeds, and its Art"'—welcome and support. Finally, irrefutably, the Seven announced that the display of their work was a public good: 'they do most emphatically hold that their work is signif-icant and of real value to the country.'[9]

The next show I want to consider is the *Exhibition of Canadian West Coast Art: Native and Modern*, jointly organized by the National Gallery of Canada and the National Museum. It was hung in the National Gallery, the east wing of the Victoria Memorial Building, in December 1927 and subsequently travelled to Toronto and Montreal. This show is usually remembered for giving eastern Canadians their first look at the work of Emily Carr. Another very important feature of this exhibition, however, was that it marked the first time a Canadian art gallery displayed Native cultural materials.[10] In the introduction to the catalogue, Eric Brown, the Gallery's director and the curator of the show, explained its purpose: 'to mingle for the first time the art work of the Canadian West Coast tribes with that of our more sophis-ticated artists in an endeavour to analyze their relationships to one another, if such exists, and particularly to enable this primitive and interesting art to take a definite place as one of the most valuable of Canada's artistic productions.'[11] Brown recog-nized the novelty of his approach: 'this will be the first time such an exhibition has been held that has been artistic first and ethnological second.'[12] Certainly Brown wanted to validate Native art as a distinctly Canadian art form.

The hanging of the show seems to have supported this goal. Native and non-Native works were intermingled, with balance, symmetry and rhythm providing

Exhibition of Canadian West Coast Art: Native and Modern, 1927. (Courtesy of National Gallery of Canada.)

the dominant visual matrix. The Native works were grouped not according to cultural areas, as would have been the case in an ethnographic display, but so that connections and comparisons could be made with non-Native pieces. However, the way the works were obtained, the curatorial selection and naming, belied the putative equality between Native and non-Native artists. The Native pieces were all borrowed from museum collections, while the non-Native works were borrowed directly from living artists. This had two effects: first, it rendered anonymous the Native creators, for their works were labelled simply by reference to cultural group and function—Chilkat robes and headdresses—rather than by creator; and second, it tended to reinforce the contemporary notions that the Indians were (inevitably) disappearing, that their art traditions were dead and dying, and that there were no contemporary Indian artists worth showing.

This ground-breaking, if prejudiced, show illustrates some of the problems that Weil associates with the romantic attribution of special power to art, artists, and art patrons. Deeply concerned for the very survival of art museums, Weil wonders not only about those who are hostile to such institutions and the romantic notion of power but, equally if not more important, about those who are indifferent. Are art museums relevant? If they are to survive, how should they change? Michael Ames contends that museums must be 'moral educators'.[13] Duncan Cameron maintains that museums must undertake a 'social re-definition'.[14] Stephen Weil proposes four new considerations:

1. 'the art museum should serve as a site of open discourse, a discourse that must extend beyond the museum's traditional subject matter of art and artists to a consideration of the museum itself';
2. 'there must be a rebalancing of the relative emphasis that the museum gives to the aesthetic and other-than-aesthetic aspects of the objects displayed';
3. 'the range of objects displayed ought to be expanded beyond objects considered meritorious to include works of lesser merit or even objects whose interest may be other than purely aesthetic'; and
4. 'the traditional concept of the art museum as a temple in which to celebrate the human genius of a few must be expanded into a view of a place in which to celebrate the human accomplishments of the many'.[15]

My own thinking is that relevance is especially important. Nor do I fully support Weil's desire to de-emphasize aesthetic quality, because I think it is aesthetic quality that distinguishes art museums from other kinds. In general, however, Weil's, Cameron's, and Ames's suggestions together point to a new direction for art museums. How can these suggestions be put into effect? The two exhibitions we have examined so far seem to support Weil's analysis of power. Three comparatively recent exhibitions show Canadian museums struggling to be more inclusive, to adopt a broader focus, and to be more relevant. The results have not always been the ones anticipated or desired.

Perhaps the first Canadian exhibition that attempted this new breadth was the 1988 show *The Spirit Sings*, organized for the winter Olympics in Calgary by the Glenbow Museum. The purpose of this exhibition, according to the museum's director at the time, was 'to enhance awareness of the rich cultural and artistic traditions of Canada's aboriginal peoples'.[16] More specifically, the artifacts exhibited would illustrate three themes: 'the diversity of cultures among Canada's native peoples; the commonality of a world-view among those diverse cultures, based on the quintessential necessity of harmony between man and nature; and the continuity and resilience of native culture in spite of overwhelming European influence, oppression, and suppression.'[17] The exhibition concentrated on the early contact period of Canadian history. Compiled of materials currently housed in museums all over the world, many of which had not been seen in Canada since their removal, the show was to have been a model of revisionism, a non-racist celebration redressing years of discrimination against First Nations creators. A major sponsor, Shell, pledged $1.1 million towards the costs of mounting this extravaganza and the Olympic Organizing Committee endorsed the project, pledging $600,000. In terms of Weil's proposals, the Glenbow was doing all the right things: being a site for open discourse; introducing relatively non-aesthetic materials; enlarging the range of objects; and expanding the celebration of human genius to a hitherto neglected section of the population.

But trouble soon emerged on two fronts. First, the Lubicon people of southern Alberta, angry that their land-claims dispute with the federal and provincial governments was going nowhere, decided to use the show politically. Mounting a

Lucibon Lake Cree protesting The Spirit Sings *outside the Glenbow Museum, Calgary, Alberta, 1988. (Glenbow photographer, Jim Shipley. Courtesy of Glenbow Museum, P3543-G-33A-34.)*

boycott and a worldwide propaganda campaign, they persuaded some two dozen institutions and governments to refuse to lend material to the show.[18] The Lubicon Lake Cree Band were also disturbed that Shell Canada, which they claimed was actively involved in destroying their economy and way of life, was sponsoring the exhibition. The same criticism was levelled against the whole of Canada's white élitist society. One commentator castigated the Glenbow for showing 'debris we robbed from the cultural traditions we first demolished', and suggested that to mount such an exhibition was parallel to the Berlin Olympics putting on a show of Jewish religious objects.[19] Another problem was the conjunction of past and present. Some critics, both Native and non-Native, felt the Glenbow was perpetuating a 'Golden Age' myth of Native people by glorifying the past while neglecting the present. Bruce Trigger, the honorary curator of the McCord Museum, saw this show as an example of Canadian museums' neglect of moral and political concerns.[20] There were also issues of authority of interpretation. The Mohawks of Kahnawake felt it inappropriate for the Glenbow to display an Iroquois False Face mask on the grounds that such masks have healing powers, are sacred, and should be seen only by those deemed appropriate by the medicine society. On the land-claims issue the Glenbow was powerless: the matter was entirely out of its purview. However, the museum contested the Mohawks' injunction because the False Face mask, owned by the Royal Ontario Museum since the 1920s, had already been displayed in a major show,[21] in 1969, without protest. Initially the Mohawks won an injunction to have the mask removed, but this was overturned and the mask was put back into the show. *The Spirit Sings* went ahead, though not without pickets and disruption.

Overall, the exhibition provoked serious consideration of the questions surrounding the use of sacred objects, sponsorship, Native consultation and control in the presentation of Native history,[22] and the imposition of the 'art' category on non-Western cultures.[23] *The Spirit Sings* was a striking illustration of Ames's 'playing fields' thesis: external matters have become central to the museum, whether the institution wants it or not.

A number of the same issues were raised in the Royal Ontario Museum's 1989 exhibition *Into the Heart of Africa*. Like the Glenbow, the ROM set out, in good faith, to provide a forum for debate, to challenge or expose racism, and to use selection criteria that went beyond the aesthetic. In addition the institution sought to make itself more transparent, to expose the collecting practices behind many of its acquisitions in the late nineteenth and early twentieth centuries. Drawn from the museum's own distinguished collection of African artifacts, *Into the Heart of Africa* focused on 'the dark continent' as seen through the eyes of Canadian missionaries and soldiers in the late nineteenth century. To help organize the show, the curator, Jeanne Cannizzo, enlisted a committee of Africans to advise her on all aspects of the process. In label material, Cannizzo went out of her way to point up the narrowness of the white Canadian concept of Africa and the richness of the culture that the colonialists most often missed. She did this with an irony that struck some as heavy-handed. The curator's purpose and the visitors' readings did not always mesh.

The Royal Ontario Museum was quite unprepared for the reaction to the show. Some members of the public, notably among Toronto's Black community, were intensely hostile. They charged the museum with racism, with supporting colonialism and stereotyping African culture. They picketed the show and demanded changes in the exhibition. The Coalition for the Truth about Africa, an umbrella organization representing about twenty groups composed mostly of students, held regular demonstrations outside the museum. They said that the exhibition, which included such insensitive materials as photographs of missionaries teaching Black Africans to do their laundry, was offensive and should be dismantled. Because of the controversy, the Vancouver Museum and the Museum of Civilization in Hull cancelled bookings for the show. For Cannizzo the story did not end there. Hired to teach an African anthropology course for the University of Toronto in the fall of 1990, she was harassed and heckled by students who again accused her of racism. She took sick leave and later left the country permanently.

Ironically, both Cannizzo and the Royal Ontario Museum had set out to fight racism with *Into the Heart of Africa*. As Cannizzo explained, 'the exhibition does not, as had been alleged, promote white supremacy or glorify imperialism. On the

Installation from Into the Heart of Africa, *1989. (Photo © the Royal Ontario Museum. Courtesy of the Royal Ontario Museum ROM.)*

contrary, it should help all Canadians understand the historical roots of racism.'[24] An editorial in *The Globe and Mail* described *Into the Heart of Africa* as 'a multi-layered exhibit that documented how objects from an indigenous culture are transformed into imperialist spoils of war to decorate Victorian parlors, and later end up as treasures in a museum', and went on to note that 'Ms. Cannizzo highlighted the ethnocentrism of the Canadian collectors in showing how the artifacts came together in the first place.'[25]

What went wrong with *The Spirit Sings* and *Into the Heart of Africa*? In each case the host museum seems to have addressed the issues that concerned Weil, trying to position the institution as a site of discourse and displaying a wider range of artifacts than had hitherto been the norm. Yet in each case the very people whose artifacts the museum authorities were trying to interpret, at the Glenbow the First Nations and at the ROM Black Africans, were the ones who objected to the show. Are Weil's suggestions inappropriate, at least for Canada? I think not. The real problem was that the museums started with the artifacts rather than the viewers. Weil's analysis suggests two factors that contributed to their problems. First, they did not *celebrate* accomplishments. Instead of emphasizing positive accomplishments, the ROM concentrated on the negative—the racism of white collectors—with the result that Black African accomplishments were not recognized. More subtly, to celebrate accomplishments requires a thorough understanding of their cultural and social purpose and importance. This is where the Glenbow got into trouble in its attempt to display sacred objects. The solution is to involve the group in question even more closely than the Glenbow and the ROM did—something that is time-consuming and often difficult to do. The second problematic factor in these two shows has to do with the disadvantaged groups' own perceptions of the importance or power of the museum. Both the First Nations in Calgary and the Black community in Toronto were reacting to historical and contemporary iniquities, lashing out at institutions they deemed powerful, public, and provocative and hence deserving of disruption or challenge. Museum workers, constantly questioning the validity of their work, may be able to take some sort of perverse solace in knowing that their institutions are still considered so important; then they must accept this fact as a political reality.

The last show I want to look at sheds additional light on some of the problems evident in *The Spirit Sings* and *Into the Heart of Africa*. It also resonates in an interesting and perhaps unexpected way with concerns evident in the 1920 *Group of Seven* show and the *Exhibition of Canadian West Coast Art*. This final example is the *OH! Canada* exhibition hung at the Art Gallery of Ontario in Toronto from February to May 1996. *OH! Canada* was actually two shows, or one show within another. The core exhibit was the National Gallery of Canada's celebration of the seventy-fifth anniversary of the Group of Seven, called *The Group of Seven: Art for a Nation*, created by Charles Hill. Around this exhibition the AGO built a contemporary framework consisting of 'community-based' installations and works by First Nations, Latino, African-Canadian, Chinese, and regional (Hamilton, Ont.) artists to attempt to address questions of landscape and nation from different and contemporary locations. I will look at the core exhibition and the community-based show in turn.

In his National Gallery show Hill attempted to replicate the eight major Group of Seven exhibitions held at the Art Gallery of Toronto between 1920 and 1931. In so doing Hill hoped to avoid imposing the heavy hand of curatorial authority—to avoid acting as what Cameron called the 'gatekeeper' of truth. He presented the works in context for the first time since the original exhibitions as an alternative way of working to a further understanding.[26] Furthermore, in writing the catalogue Hill tried to present the historical facts in a straightforward way, drawing on contemporary correspondence and newspaper or periodical articles to strive for transparency rather than distancing analysis, preferring that readers and viewers arrive at their own interpretations. This transparency was first evident in the selection of works for display. Unlike most art exhibitions, in which the pieces are chosen on the basis of aesthetic quality, here they were chosen on the bases of history (whether they were shown at a particular time) and availability (whether they could be identified and borrowed for this particular showing). In short, Hill was trying to replicate the process by which the artists originally selected their own works for exhibition; in this he reflected the historic idea that the artist is a special, elevated person (Weil's first point), as well as Weil's recommendation to expand the range of objects displayed beyond those simply considered aesthetically meritorious. That is, Hill combined Weil's historic fundamentals and recommendations for the future. The problem arises in the separation of the two time periods, past and present. The present-day viewer has no way of knowing how these paintings should be judged today: what is their significance now? As Matthew Bower notes, 'To so insist on the inscription of the works in a replica of their original context suggests that they are unable to go beyond it. . . . It suggests that in order to understand the works one must see them in their proper context, but this moment of preservation removes them from their present context in order to preserve their meaning.'[27]

The second part of the *OH! Canada* show tried to address the problem of present significance by framing *The Group of Seven: Art for a Nation* within the context of contemporary, culturally pluralistic creativity. The idea was that diverse artists would examine the land and nationalism from the point of view of the 1990s and thus create, both for themselves and for the audience, a dialogue with the historic material. This portion of the show included interactive educational materials such as computer terminals, a large blackboard for 'graffiti' responses, a fax machine, and a *Bravo!* TV speaker's corner, as well as the five installations by the 'community-based art groups'. The National Gallery show was hung in the Zacks Gallery of the AGO, with the community component, including interactive material, down the hall. This spatial and temporal separation was the object of considerable derision. According to Rinaldo Walcott,

> What [this] placement seems to do is to collapse the art of the 'community-based groups' into a kind of pop culture collage where those works appear to be just as

ephemeral and disposable as the rants and raves of the 'public' soap box of speaker's corner. These works, then, are the disposable scraps of little-used parts of the nation that keep returning to disturb the happy story of the Group of Seven's discovery of Canada's unique national essence in the landscape.[28]

The critic Christopher Hume, writing in *The Toronto Star*, was no less caustic, complaining bitterly that, in this show, 'art has no part to play in the creation of Canada' and that here 'the very notion of Canadian culture seems irrelevant.' Like Walcott, he was particularly critical of the technological component, concluding that 'the presence of *Bravo!* says everything you need to know about where official culture is headed in Canada.'[29] In *The Globe and Mail* John Bentley Mays was no gentler. Reversing the complaint about the positioning of the community-based material, Mays felt that the *Group of Seven* works 'had been herded out of sight into the cul-de-sac Zacks wing' and that 'the AGO has been transformed into a bright, busy midway of cultural entertainment.' He then added, contemptuously: 'There's some art stuck here and there. . . .'[30]

OH! Canada attracted almost universal criticism. On the one hand the National Gallery show was seen as a cop-out, replicating nineteenth-century romantic methods without contemporary interpretation or even contemporary validation. On the other hand, the community and interactive components added by the AGO were variously seen as perpetuating a racist, classist, and imperialist stance; as reducing the 'community' material to the level of 'rants and raves'; and as non-art. The interactive material seems to have been particularly disliked. The AGO, having addressed virtually all of Weil's recommendations for making an art museum more open and accessible, was roundly castigated for its efforts. What went wrong?

The once standard view that knowledge is objective and verifiable has been widely challenged by the notion that knowledge is socially constructed and shaped by individuals' particular interests and values. The contemporary view is that objects may hold multiple meanings, all of which, depending on context, are potentially valid. In this context the role of an exhibition is not to impose meaning on objects but to produce it—by inviting visitors to bring and contribute their own interpretations to those of the museum. Together, the museum's and the visitors' interpretations create new meanings. Exhibitions are no longer simply about institutions teaching visitors; rather, they are about visitors using exhibitions in ways that are personally significant to them. As Lisa Roberts notes, to allow for and encourage alternative ways of interpreting and experiencing works of art represents a challenge not only to the museum's power and authority over objects and their display, but also to the very basis and credibility of the knowledge that the institution presumes to possess.[31] As the five exhibitions I have discussed demonstrate, the locus of power has shifted to the visitor. Museums today must learn how to work in this new context.

The real strength of the 1920 Group of Seven show was that it dealt with the here and now; thus it was relevant and meaningful to viewers. The exhibited paintings depicted what the Seven saw when they looked at their country. The same could be said for the non-Native part of the 1927 *Exhibition of Canadian West Coast Art.* The First Nations part of that show was more problematic in retrospect, partly because the creativity it celebrated no longer existed—its makers were dead—and partly because virtually no connections were suggested between Native and non-Native creativity. This same emphasis on the historical, without sufficient links to the present, caused major problems in *The Spirit Sings, Out of the Heart of Africa,* and *OH! Canada,* despite the fact that in each case the declared purpose was to establish precisely such links. Inadvertently, these three shows appeared to support Bourdieu's thesis about the reproduction of existing class distinctions, with the concomitant negation of inherent value in works of art. Viewers belonging to the power élite were generally happy with all three, for as Cameron suggests, they want 'the comfort and safety of a known, mythic reality, for nostalgia and fantasy'.[32] Non-élite viewers, however, did not see these shows as neutral, objective purveyors of expert truth. They saw them as narrow and one-sided at best, racist and bigoted at worst. Viewers, then, were not satisfied with exhibitions that simply showed history, even revisionist history. Rather, they specifically sought relevance; they wanted exhibitions that would not simply identify political, social, and moral problems, but point to solutions. The reactions to these five shows also support Ames's notion of museums as playing fields on which contestation occurs. All five genuinely tried to provoke dialogue, and all succeeded, many far beyond the organizers expectations. Each challenged conventional notions of what should be in an art show, and each was criticized for trying to redefine art. Each invited non-élite viewers in, but each had great difficulty accommodating them. Perhaps we can learn from these magnificent failures how to recognize the political base of aesthetic discernment, cultural sensibility, and tastes, and how to deal better with issues such as Native activism and political correctness. For art museums this issue is pressing: the very survival of such institutions depends on finding more equitable ways of producing meaning.

NOTES

1. Stephen E. Weil, 'On a New Foundation', in *A Cabinet of Curiosities: Inquiries in Museums and Their Prospects* (Washington and London, 1995), 101. Some of the problems I discuss are analyzed in *Naming a Practice: Curatorial Strategies for the Future,* ed. Peter White (Banff, 1996) 23.

2. Marcia Tucker, "Who's on First?" Issues of Cultural Equality in Today's Museums', in *Different Voices,* ed. Michaelyn Mitchell, (New York, 1992), 13.

3. Duncan F. Cameron, 'Getting Out of Our Skin: Museums and a New Identity', MUSE 10, 2 and 3 (Summer/Fall, 1992), 9; see also Duncan Cameron, 'Values in Conflict and Social Re-definition', MUSE 8, 3 (Autumn 1990), 14–16.

4. Edwina Taborsky, 'The Discursive Object', in *Objects of Knowledge,* ed. Susan Pearce (London, 1990), 50–77.

5. Michael M. Ames, *Cannibal Tours and Glass Boxes: The Anthropology of Museums* (Vancouver, 1992), 152.

6. Weil, 'On a New Foundation', 84–5.

7. Pierre Bourdieu, Alain Darbel, and Dominique Schnapper, *Love of Art: European Art Museums and Their Public* (Paris, 1969), trans. Caroline Beattie and Nick Merriman (California, 1991), 112.

8. Fredric Jameson, 'Hans Haacke and the Cultural Logic of Postmodernism', in *Hans Haacke: Unfinished Business*, ed. Brian Wallis (Cambridge, Mass., 1986), 44.

9. Catalogue, 1920, Art Gallery of Ontario. For the religious nature of this fervour see A. Davis, *The Logic of Ecstasy: Canadian Mystical Painting 1920–1949* (Toronto, 1992).

10. Diana Nemiroff, 'Modernism, Nationalism and Beyond: A Critical History of Exhibitions of First Nations Art', in *Thinking about Exhibitions*, ed. Ressa Greenberg, Bruce W. Ferguson, and Sandy Nairne (London and New York, 1996), 415.

11. Eric Brown, 'Introduction' in *Exhibition of Canadian West Coast Art: Native and Modern* (Ottawa, 1927), 2. On the question of primitivism see, for example, Susan Hiller, ed., *The Myth of Primitivism: Perspectives on Art* (London and New York, 1991).

12. Eric Brown, letter to J. Murray Gibbon, Canadian Pacific Railways, Montreal, 10 Oct. 1927, National Gallery of Canada Archives.

13. Michael Ames, 'Daring to be Different: An Alternative', MUSE 6, 1 (Spring 1988), 41.

14. Duncan Cameron, 'Values in Conflict and Social Re-definition', MUSE 8, 3 (Autumn 1990), 15.

15. Weil, 'On a New Foundation', 108.

16. Cameron, 'Values in Conflict', 15.

17. *The Spirit Sings: Artistic Traditions of Canada's First Peoples* (Toronto, 1978), preface, np.

18. There is some dispute as to how many institutions actually participated in the boycott. See Lis S. Stainforth, 'Did the Spirit Sing?: An Historical Perspective on Canadian Exhibitions of The Other', MA thesis, Carleton University, 1990.

19. Ibid., 127.

20. Ibid., 128.

21. *Masterpieces of Indian and Eskimo Art from Canada.*

22. For a sensitive, passionate view see Gerald McMaster, 'Problems of Representation: Our Home, BUT the Natives' Land', MUSE VIII, 3 (Autumn) 1990, 35–8.

23. 'Art categorization' is a vast and complicated topic. A balanced approach is taken by Ruth B. Phillips, in 'Indian Art: Where do you put it?', MUSE VI, 3 (Autumn 1988), 64–7. See also James Clifford, *The Predicament of Culture* (Cambridge, Mass. and London, 1988).

24. *Toronto Star* (5 June 1989).

25. *Globe and Mail* (19 Oct. 1990).

26. Charlie Hill to Ann Davis, 3 Dec. 1997.

27. Matthew Brower, 'Framed by History', *Journal of Canadian Studies* 31, 2 (Summer 1996), 179. Lynda Jessup, in 'Art for a Nation?' *Fuse* 19, 4 (Summer 1996), 11–14, also complains about Hill's narrow reading of the Group of Seven; she would have pre-

ferred the Group's activities to have been set in the larger historical context offered by the international art scene.

28. Rinaldo Walcott, 'Lament for a Nation: The Racial Geography of "The OH! Canada Project"', *Fuse* 19, 4 (Summer 1996), 15.

29. Christopher Hume, 'Group Therapy in Art', *Toronto Star* (14 Feb. 1996), D1. For a further, and earlier, discussion of art as therapy see Adam Gopnik, 'The Death of an Audience', *The New Yorker* LXVIII, 33 (5 Oct. 1993), 141–6.

30. John Bentley Mays, 'Uh-OH! Canada', *Globe and Mail* (17 Feb. 1996), C1.

31. Lisa C. Roberts, *From Knowledge to Narrative: Educators and the Changing Museum* (Washington and London, 1997), 8.

32. Cameron, 'Getting Out of Our Skin', 8.

PART THREE

NATIONALISM AND THE CANADIAN QUESTION

Weeds in the Garden of Civic Nationalism

Phyllis M. Senese

The ideology of nationalism has been an agent of social and political discord in Canada ever since its arrival in the early nineteenth century. Its effects are still evident in the strains that competing visions of nationalism create in Canadian life almost daily.[1]

In recent years, especially in English-speaking Canada, it has become common to identify two kinds of nationalism in this country, mirroring the asymmetrical 'two nations' model of Confederation: a civic nationalism of shared political institutions and progressive social values in English-speaking Canada, contrasted with an ethnic nationalism of a common language and culture and exaggerated homogeneity in Quebec. This is a false dichotomy.

Civic nationalism is, in my view, little more than a rhetorical device obscuring in a cloak of respectability and presumed moral superiority what is nothing more than nineteenth-century nationalism. Bluntly, it is a formula designed—in response to the renewed and reinvigorated movement for national self-determination that has been entrenching itself in Quebec for more than thirty years—to persuade the peoples of what is called English-speaking Canada that their nationalism is open, virtuous, free from ethnic posturing, and altruistic (good), in contrast to the inward-looking, reactionary, ethnic, selfish (bad) nationalism of Quebec. Those who make this distinction—who think of Canada as being torn apart by ethnic nationalism and/or held together by civic nationalism—fail not only to recognize civic nationalism for the false front it is; they also fail to give full consideration to nationalism as an ideology. In essence, civic nationalism is simply the same old lament: if only 'they' would be more like 'us', all 'our' problems would disappear.[2] In trying to unravel a complex problem, let us begin at the beginning, with nationalism.

What keeps nationalism alive? Why, at the end of the twentieth century, when it was supposed to have disappeared as a relic of a troubled past, does nationalism flourish everywhere? Why does a preoccupation with 'blood and belonging'[3] still consume so much human energy and generate so much passion? Why have Canadians become 'addicted to ideologies'?[4]

Nationalism is an ideology. It claims to know when a nation exists, who belongs to it and who does not, and why. It advocates the creation of an independent state as a nation's natural right, a precondition for realization of its fullest potential. Nationalism invents a group of people who recognize in each other a shared community of culture, history, and future expectations.[5] Moreover, in Elie Kedourie's words, 'it pretends to supply a criterion for the determination of the unit of population proper to enjoy government exclusively on its own.'[6] With utter certainty, nationalists claim special knowledge of the nation and its people: their unique origins, glorious triumphs, singular sorrows; the threats that imperil the nation; how to mould the nation and its people to assume their rightful destiny. But things have never been that simple, because humans have not obligingly distributed themselves geographically so as to achieve the perfect correlation between territoriality and a specific people (ethnicity) that is increasingly taken to be the mark of a nationality. Nor have human populations remained ethnically pure. Over time, by choice, by chance, by force, populations have intermingled continuously to produce a multiplicity of groups of mixed origins who do not observe any rules of geographic precision. In short, there are no pure nations, no neat geographical boundaries. 'Nationalism requires too much belief in what is patently not so.'[7] Any nation that proposes to create an independent political state to fulfil itself will contain minority populations of numerous kinds. In the end, like other ideologies, nationalism has become a way for powerful élites, powerful classes, to restructure politics for their own ends. And the style of politics that nationalism invokes '[runs] to extremes. It represent[s] politics as a fight for principles, not the endless composition of claims in conflict.'[8]

Thus nationalism is a far more dangerous set of ideas than we generally acknowledge. Nationalists everywhere, always, insist that their nationalism is based on a set of self-affirming principles, and that it is not directed against any other nation. Yet somehow neither proposition turns out to be entirely true. This is so because nationalism rests, at base, on a foundation of opposition and exclusion. In Kedourie's formulation of nationalist rhetoric, 'humanity is divided into nations' and 'nations are known by certain characteristics which can be ascertained.'[9] And Benedict Anderson has observed that a nation is 'an imagined community—and imagined as both inherently limited and sovereign'.[10] Nationalism, notwithstanding its protestations of simple self-affirmation, always needs one essential ingredient to stimulate and sustain national solidarity: a threat. At some point every nationalism seeks out an Other—an enemy—on which to focus attention.

Belonging to a nation has no particular meaning unless it is exclusive: some people must be excluded, and that exclusion requires a reason. The prerequisites for belonging can be extremely precise or purposefully vague: all that matters is that belonging must be capable of being compared to not belonging. Nationalism A is compelled to insist that it is better than—superior to, more authentic than— nationalism B; otherwise there is no point in espousing nationalism. In its exclusivity, its anxiety about security, its belief that differences contaminate and destroy national cohesion, its rejection of the Other, nationalism is always about being afraid. Consider how nationalism appeals to the dark side of human nature; how it brings out the worst, not the best, human impulses; and, especially, the extent to which it provides ideological camouflage for racism.

Racism in a formal sense—defined as a series of theories about human origins that divided humanity into biological categories of distinct species and sub-species, and insisted that physical attributes and moral qualities were biologically linked, creating superior and inferior species—was an invention of the late eighteenth and early nineteenth centuries. By the time of Darwin's *On the Origin of Species* and Spencer's popularization of the 'survival of the fittest' notion, this set of theories was popularly accepted under the guise of 'scientific racism'. But such theories about 'races' of humans merely provided a new conceptual language for the age-old effort to manage the observable differences between and among groups of people. What preceded these biological theories of 'race' was a much longer and deeper cultural tradition of aggression and hostility in accounting for human differentiation. Simply put, racism is the preoccupation over time with the observation, categorization, representation, valorization, and ranking of *perceived* human differences—differences consisting of largely false assumptions and assertions that can be manipulated to create stereotypes upon which—against which—action has to be taken. This pattern has been a basic feature of the intellectual landscape of Western culture at least since the time of the Greeks. Although it was not until the nineteenth century that biological, 'scientific' explanations for human diversity became available, the fear of indelible, dangerous group characteristics, embodied in some imagined Other, had existed for millennia. This fear is racism.

Among the many Greek contributions to Western civilization was a preoccupation with drawing boundaries to contain 'contending opposites'.[11] It has bequeathed to us a way of comprehending the world through polarized dualities: good/evil, white/black, young/old, male/female, civilized/barbarian, us/them. Greek thinkers grappled with the realization that while human beings in all their variety shared a common nature as humans, individuals could be seen as belonging to different groups. Undercutting any sense of common humanity sharing a common destiny was a 'fear of diversity—a fear that differences bring on chaos and thus demands that the world be put into an orderly pattern'.[12] Some 2,500 years later, Western society still thinks in dualistic terms, and has found few ways of successfully harmonizing unity and diversity. '[T]he one idea that has scarcely varied is that there is an "us" and a "them", each quite settled, clear, unassailably self-evident.'[13]

Western culture has shown a consistent pattern of hostile response to differences—every kind of difference. Initially, an attempt would be made, by a variety of means, to persuade those who differed in some vital aspect from a given dominant community to change, to conform, to convert, to recant—to abandon their differentness in order to belong. A significant element in the demand for change was the idea that differentness posed a danger of some kind to the dominant community. Moreover, those who refused to transform themselves demonstrated their inherent unfitness to belong by that very act of defiance. Of course, transformation was never really sufficient. The convert was always suspect, never quite legitimate. When persuasion failed, repression followed. And when repression did not obliterate differences, the next step was demonization—and, finally, extermination. The history of antisemitism, a species of racism, demonstrates the point. The road to Auschwitz has a long history in Western culture. The Jews were not, however, the only people to face this kind of onslaught.

Until relatively recent times, at least in most places in the West, the excluded, the Other, was demonized: linked—literally, not just metaphorically—to Satan. While the religious need to personify evil, so deeply embedded in the fabric of Christianity, may no longer be the norm in most of Western society, a secular version is still widespread. Deviance from a given norm was taken as evidence of satanic liaison; frequently, in medieval as well as modern times, the Other was also described as a disease, a plague to be eradicated. The notion that identifiable groups of people are not just different but an infection to be purged is easily recognizable in the contemporary practice of 'ethnic cleansing'. The insistence on seeing those who differed from the norm as members of a separate species, as a source of inherent, permanent infection, was a precursor of the biological determinism that took hold in the nineteenth century. In fifteenth-century Spain, for instance, proof of 'blood purity' was required, in order to preserve Catholicism from allegedly insincere and subversive Jewish converts: belonging was explicitly linked to blood lines, genealogy, lineage. Racism, then, existed long before it acquired a 'scientific' explanation. Nor has it limited itself to distinctions based on inherited characteristics (skin pigmentation, hair type, shape of eye): it has included religious affiliation, ethnicity, gender, sexuality, and illness. In fact, there are many kinds of racism, each shaped by specific historic contexts and continuities. Racism depends on images, stereotypes and assumptions about the Other that are fluid, that move and reshape across time; Europe's Other was always 'a simultaneous reaffirmation and reconstruction of earlier representations'.[14]

Racism constitutes an ideology which insists that natural and unchanging biological features are the paramount criteria for defining specific human groups, for assessing their worth in relation to one another, and for ascribing negative qualities to, and subsequent actions against, those deemed inferior. Racism is always about exclusion. This ideology appeals to an uncritical commonsense supposition that 'race' provides the explanation of observable human differences that is required to make sense of the world and to impose order on diversity. The Other is never confined to a specific time or place: it is constantly reimagined over time as circumstances dictate. As Robert Miles puts it:

> Different racisms are . . . not necessarily independent of each other, are not continually created anew in any absolute sense. Rather, any one instance of racism will be

the product of both a reworking of at least some of the substance of earlier instances, and a creation of novel elements.[15]

The ideology of racism has been an all-purpose vehicle for expressing deep-seated fears about human differences.[16] Like nationalism, racism first invents groups of people who supposedly share distinctive commonalities and then devises criteria for inclusion and exclusion. Like nationalism, racism demands belief in imaginary creations. Like nationalism, racism claims to 'offer a semblance of order, an empowerment, or at minimum an affectation of power'.[17]

The racism woven into the fabric of Western experience was carefully packed in the cultural baggage that Europeans brought with them to the Western hemisphere. This way of looking at human differences as dangerous, to be transformed or eliminated, has deep roots in Canada. The ideology of racism mingled with, intensified, and inflamed the new ideology of nationalism as it emerged in Enlightenment Europe: first in the language of liberalism, then in the emotional absolutism of Romanticism, and finally in the false rationality of pseudo-science.

The most dangerous and least considered dimension of nationalism is its historic tendency to intersect with racism.[18] As David Theo Goldberg puts it: 'The popular Enlightenment concern with national characteristics often identified those characteristics racially. Similarly, the great nationalist drives of the late nineteenth century, as well as their imperialist counterparts, commonly invoked the banner of race as a rallying cry.'[19] What made this intersection possible was the fact that both 'nation' and 'race' are essentially empty terms—they can be continuously refilled with invented, and reinvented, notions 'explaining' human difference. When nationalism insisted that each 'nation' possessed singular identifying attributes, those same attributes also served to demarcate and separate 'races'. Nationalism and racism alike strove to define and reinforce understanding of the self and the Other, of those included and excluded, and each resorted to natural law to validate its claims. 'Scientific racism' tightened the interdependence between the two: if '"race" determined both cultural capacity and hierarchical development, . . . it therefore followed that each "nation" was the expression of a particular biological capacity'.[20] And it is this intersection of nationalism and racism that inspires my doubts about civic nationalism.

It is the attempt to disentangle nationalism from racism that has resulted in the supposed distinction between civic and ethnic nationalism, according to which racism skulks in the latter but not the former. One well-known and highly regarded proponent of this approach is Michael Ignatieff. He has written passionately about civic nationalism, which he argues 'envisages the nation as a community of equal, rights-bearing citizens, united in patriotic attachment to a shared set of political practices';[21] '. . . a nation based in citizenship rather than ethnicity'.[22] What Ignatieff writes about is the idea of nationalism refracted through liberalism. 'This idea of the nation as a progressive, universalizing force was common both to Enlightenment discourse and that of nineteenth century liberals.'[23]

Liberalism stresses individualism, universal principles applicable to all humans, reform of society through reasoned action, progress of all sorts through education and institutional improvements, and commitment to human equality. Ignatieff is convinced that *civic nationalism* reflects these liberal ideals:

> [a]ccording to the civic nationalist creed, what holds a society together is not common roots but law. By subscribing to a set of democratic procedures and values, individuals can reconcile their right to shape their own lives with their need to belong to a community. This in turn assumes that national belonging can be a form of rational attachment.[24]

Yet consideration of 'law', 'rights', and 'belonging' suggests that in fact the liberal underpinnings of civic nationalism are precisely what make it substantively no different from ethnic nationalism. Early on, the egalitarian and universalist impulses of liberalism were subverted by the realization that neither principle conformed to social reality. European societies were riddled with inequalities that liberals had no intention of eliminating, and before long 'race theory provided legitimacy for inequality.'[25] Both individual liberty and its applicability to all peoples became contingent on 'rational capacity'—the standard used to define and put a 'limit upon the natural equality of all those beings ordinarily taken to be human'.[26] Until quite recently the notion of rights and equality under the law has been shaped by the view that it included only those deemed to possess—inherently and naturally—the capacity to reason, on the assumption that only rational individuals shared common 'interests' and thus qualified for the protection of law. Liberalism, then, especially as it developed in Britain, championed liberty and property rights for some over equality of all: social realities such as class and gender were reduced to irrelevancies. In practice those who lacked property or 'interest', by virtue of their rational incapacity, were excluded from political participation, equal protection under the law, and personal liberty. In effect, in its formation and application, liberalism became tainted with racism. As Goldberg has noted: 'By working itself into the threads of liberalism's cloth just as that cloth was being woven, race and the various exclusions it licensed became naturalized in the Eurocentered vision of itself and its self-defined others, in its sense of Reason and rational direction' to become 'the racializing paradox at liberalism's heart'.[27] 'They' are not 'us'; 'they' should assimilate to become 'us'; if 'they' disappear, how would 'we' know 'we' are 'us'? As Yael Tamir has observed, 'there is a long-standing though much denied alliance between liberal and national ideas that might explain the inconsistencies pervading modern liberal theory.'[28] Contrary to the theory of liberalism, in its practice 'all men' were not equal: 'the rational, hence autonomous and equal subjects of the Enlightenment project turn out, perhaps unsurprisingly, to be exclusively white, male, European, and bourgeois.'[29]

In the Canadian experience, civic nationalism has simply been ethnic nationalism in disguise: the nationalism of nineteenth-century British liberalism, one in which, by the early nineteenth century, the ideologies of nationalism and racism had developed 'an interdependence such that the parameters of each ideology overlapped to determine the criteria for membership of the emergent state'.[30] After 1800, the steady migration from Britain to British North America of administrators, bureaucrats, businessmen, clergy, educators, farmers, half-pay officers, labourers, and tradesmen—all those displaced by deep, rapid social and economic dislocation in Britain—guaranteed the transfer of that ideological convergence to Canada. As Frantz Fanon was to observe: 'the settler makes history and is conscious of making it. And because he constantly refers to the history of his mother country, he clearly indicates that he himself is the extension of that mother country.'[31] From the early nineteenth century until very recently, Canada, outside Quebec, has been shaped by the conviction that, in Miles's words,

> the people of the Anglo-Saxon [English] 'race' had a special capacity for self-government by constitutional means, from which it was concluded that those not so biologically endowed should be excluded. Thus the idea of the Anglo-Saxon 'race' sustained a belief in a sense of superiority of both 'race' and 'nation'.[32]

Today, the appeal of civic nationalism for some Canadians lies in the mistaken belief that this form of nationalism is *only* about the political institutions, principles, and values that would best serve the interests of the citizens of an independent state containing many nationalities, many ethnicities. But *which* political institutions, principles, and values would prevail? And *who* would apply them to governance? From the days of British colonialism until long after the Second World War the answer was clear: British men would govern on the basis of British institutions, principles, and values[33]—institutions, principles, and values that had been contoured by cultural racism.

The search for an appropriate framework for civic nationalism has been driven by a narrow and selective reading of Canadian political history. In tracing the country's political evolution, many point to the winning of responsible government by Robert Baldwin and Louis-Hippolyte LaFontaine, and the crafting of Confederation under the leadership of John A. Macdonald and George-Étienne Cartier, as evidence of a unique non-ethnic nationalism at work. George Brown, whose willingness to join Macdonald and Cartier in a coalition government for the express purpose of creating a federation made it all possible, is given much less prominence. In fact, he is usually left unmentioned—as are his bigotry and the powerful economic forces he represented that played a major role in securing a new political arrangement. As a result of those omissions, the standard version of Canadian history centres on the ability of French and English politicians (no other groups need be included) to work together in nation-building, that elusive pursuit that seems to hold such promise today. It is true that Baldwin and LaFontaine found ways for Reformers on either side of the ethnic divide to join forces, but each had a different reason for pursuing responsible government. What tends to get overlooked is the extent to which their collaboration was rooted in a British *colonial* setting. Baldwin's commitment to responsible government was always tempered by a refusal to accept any reform beyond elementary local control, lest more sweeping reform threaten the monarchy; hence his displacement by radical Reformers in the 1850s. LaFontaine, for his part, saw responsible government chiefly as a means to secure *la survivance* for the Canadiens as a distinct people. All their gestures of respect and solidarity between French and English in Canada were limited by the two men's social conservatism and their profound attachment to Britain. It was the *colonial context,* together with their personalities, that made their collaboration possible, a collaboration that illustrates how colonialism manipulates nationalism to maintain the status quo.[34] They would retire from public life to watch a younger generation, representing new economic and political interests, use the themes of nationalism to create newer, nastier relations between French and English in Canada.

Macdonald and Cartier are similarly hailed for creatively linking their political fortunes in such a way as to carry on the work of Baldwin and LaFontaine. Yet they too were prisoners of their own ethnic nationalisms. Cartier continued LaFontaine's strategy of using political arrangements to protect the language, culture, and religion of the Canadiens within a British colonial framework. At every turn he praised the British connection and the importance of being a British subject. In 1865 he defended the Quebec Resolutions by connecting the survival of British power in North America to the survival of the Canadiens; it was their loyalty and steadfastness, especially against the Americans, that had made the British connection possible:

> These historical facts teach us that French Canadians and English-speaking Canadians should have for each other a mutual sympathy, having both reason to congratulate themselves that Canada is still a British Colony. . . . If we unite we can form a political nationality independent of the national origin and religion of individuals.[35]

What Cartier failed to appreciate was that the British connection and the British institutions developing in Canada were wrapped in a British ethnic nationalism. The point would be obvious when the final form of Confederation left minority rights, those of Canadien Catholics, weakly protected and vulnerable to assault outside Quebec; rights for other minorities were not even considered. Moreover, the federal system itself encouraged the continued cultivation of British and Canadien nationalisms. The splitting of jurisdictions between Ottawa and the provinces ensured that nothing like a new nationality developed; the provinces became the repositories and advocates of all the old nationalisms. Cartier's hope for a new political nationality was rarely echoed by Macdonald; more commonly he imagined post-Confederation Canada as a British, even 'Arian',[36] nation. As colonials, Macdonald and Cartier never escaped a colonial mentality. They wanted greater powers for Canada, but only within the empire; and, unhappily, they were not immune to the confluence of nationalism and racism that the empire represented.

Both the political reform and the compromise that these men achieved were certainly of consequence, but the long-term effects were limited because of the dominance of British liberal nationalism. In English-speaking Canada that nationalism blinded citizens to their colonial condition (after all, Canada was part of Britain; it just happened to be across a larger than usual body of water). In turn, colonialism created a garrison mentality in English-speaking Canada in which 'the official culture [became] more and more willed, more and more threatened by hostile forces without and by subversive forces within.'[37] It was to escape those colonial confines that Stephen Leacock would later embrace imperialism: 'I . . . am an Imperialist because I will not be a Colonial.'[38] But only a muddled notion of nationalism, infused with the racism concealed in liberalism, could claim that imperialism was an improvement on colonialism. Meanwhile, the Canadien identity was growing stronger as a result of the protections that Cartier had secured in Confederation. And it grew stronger still with the realization that outside Quebec an ethnic nationalism had come to dominate and control Canada's political, economic, and social institutions: British liberal nationalism, a nationalism that had a *particular* cultural hegemony at its core.[39] For many in English-speaking Canada, Confederation was predicated on the assumption that the new Dominion, however it might expand territorially, was and would remain British. A French component in Canada might be tolerated (never entirely accepted) on the Quebec 'reserve' but nowhere else—as the experience of Louis Riel and the Franco-Manitobans would attest.

That British-Canadian nationalism merits closer scrutiny. In fact, it was an *English*-Canadian nationalism based not just on the primacy of the English language but on an English God, history, culture, and society. The term 'British' included the Scots, Irish, and Welsh in a united front against other nationalities, but within the category 'British' existed a hierarchy in which all things English were privileged. And despite the eventual chipping away of English primacy in religion and education, the English element has remained dominant in Canadian culture (until the post-1945 onslaught of the US version), political institutions, and historical outlook until very recently. Late-nineteenth-century imperialism only underscored the ethnicity of nationalism in English-speaking Canada. This English-Canadian nationalism was the nationalism of the élites, its strength tied not to numbers but to power. What made this nationalism especially successful and long-lived was its capacity to incorporate into itself members of other ethnic communities. Through seduction and intimidation it urged them to transform themselves; it persuaded them that to become English was to become truly Canadian and hence eligible (at least theoretically) to share in the power of the state—a prospect that by the late nineteenth century included the possibility of participation in imperial grandeur on a global scale. This sort of persuasion became increasingly evident after 1885, as non-British immigration to Canada began to soar.

Immigrants were rated, officially and in popular culture, on a scale of desirability, suitability, and assimilability that, not surprisingly, reflected the racism of the late nineteenth century. In reality, the chances of admission depended on how easily and quickly an immigrant could become English.[40] After all, as the young Sandor Hunyadi put it in John Marlyn's novel *Under the Ribs of Death*:

'Pa, the only people who count are the English. Their fathers got all the best jobs. They're the only ones nobody ever calls foreigners. Nobody ever makes fun of their names or calls them "balogny-eaters," or laughs at the way they dress or talk. Nobody,' he concluded bitterly, ''cause when you're English it's the same as bein' Canadian.'[41]

Like every other nationalism, the English-Canadian variety needed an enemy to promote solidarity. From the late eighteenth century it has been 'blessed' with two; the neighbouring American republic and the French-speaking Canadiens concentrated largely in Quebec.[42] Baldwin, LaFontaine, Macdonald, and Cartier had all worked to ensure that an international boundary kept the Americans at bay, while the Canadiens (later Québécois), by virtue of Confederation, were no ordinary neighbours. Confederation may have been intended by the more fanatical among the English migrants to Canada to contain, if not smother, Quebec nationalism, but it failed to accomplish either objective. The result has been an unending dance of the two nationalisms.

The way English and Canadien nationalisms contended to define Canada after 1867 created a nationalist quagmire for non-British immigrants to the new Dominion.[43] Immigration served not just to populate the Prairies and make the National Policy work; it had the additional purpose of swamping the Canadiens through numbers. Numbers equal votes; votes equal power in Ottawa. Up to Confederation, immigration patterns suggested that the primary, if not exclusive, source of immigrants for the foreseeable future would continue to be Britain. It would have come as no surprise if Canadien nationalists were not enthusiastic about such immigrants. If that immigration pattern were sustained, there was every expectation that the rest of Canada would become a demographic replica of Ontario (perhaps a pale reflection of the Atlantic region). But—as usual—circumstances changed, and with them immigration patterns. Immigrants from eastern, central, and southern Europe, from Asia, the Caribbean, the Middle East, all learned quickly and painfully that neither 'nation' in Canada really wanted them. For the majority of non-British immigrants who established themselves outside Quebec, three conditions of settlement became obvious.

First, immigrants had to accept the all but total loss of their own ethnic identity to have any hope of being considered desirable. In order to become Canadian, they had to find a way to become English, abandoning dress, foods, music, and names that shrieked 'foreigner'—though for increasing numbers it would be impossible ever to appear English enough. Second, immigrants had to adopt the English-

Canadian nationalist definition of the nation's enemies. Finally, however, the true test of belonging was the cultivation of hostility to things French and Québécois. To become an insider required attacking the outsider; and if in some way Quebec francophones could be seen as presenting a direct threat to an immigrant community, the chances for success of an English assimilationist drive were enhanced. One need only think of Irish Catholics in Ontario or Ukrainian Catholic immigrants on the Prairies, at odds with French clergy and bishops from Quebec. Even today, recent (and not so recent) immigrants are encouraged to see recognition of a 'distinct society' in Quebec as an affront to the 'nation's heritage'. What nation? What heritage? Although the Englishness of Canada is fading now, it has not completely disappeared,[44] and nothing obvious looms on the horizon to takes its place; thus immigrants still understand that, at least for now, their acceptance as Canadians is tied to adopting the residue of English attitudes, including English-Canadian nationalism. Until demography alters the balance (as it will), inclusion will continue to depend to a high degree on appearing to be English. As many Canadians with African, Asian, Middle Eastern, or Caribbean roots find, nationalism in English-speaking Canada frequently insists that 'home' for them must be somewhere else, no matter how long they and their families have been here. For them, assimilation never means truly belonging here, at least not yet.

I once heard Pierre Berton wonder aloud how differently Canada might have turned out if non-British immigrants and the Canadiens had ever made common cause against the English. English-Canadian nationalism ensured that the price for non-British immigrants would be too high to contemplate. Assimilation into the dominant English culture demanded imitation of its anti-Quebec, anti-French attitudes and behaviour as the price of belonging. And nationalism always insists that belonging matters more than anything else.

Canadien nationalism, like its English counterpart, saw (and sometimes still sees) immigrants as unwelcome, threatening Others. Neither was ever able to choose the immigrants it wanted; each had to find ways of making do with those who came its way. As a minority in Canada, the Canadiens were insufficiently secure about their own collective future to develop subtle techniques for incorporating the Other. Heavy-handed strategies (all in the name of the national good) offered immigrants little positive inducement to side with the Canadiens in what would appear to be a losing cause. There was, too, a wall of incomprehension dividing immigrants and Canadiens, a barrier greater even than differences of language, religion, and culture. Part of the mystique about the past that every nationalism cultivates is its own litany of past sorrows, sufferings, humiliations, conquests, and bloodshed. While it was not uncommon for early Canadien nationalists to correspond with Irish or Polish nationalists, the conditions of life for French Canadians were not comparable to the real suffering experienced elsewhere. In the late nineteenth century and into the twentieth, Jews fleeing pogroms, Ukrainians escaping tsarist and later Soviet repression, Mennonites seeking sanctuary, African Americans evading lynch laws, Chinese labourers exchanging famine for hard work and a hate-filled reception, First Nations peoples surviving the exterminationist provisions of the various Indian Acts—not one of these groups recognized anything familiar in the experiences of the Canadiens.[45] This gulf separating divergent memories of experience helps to explain why, to this day, it is easy to whip up anti-Quebec, anti-French sentiments, especially in western Canada. For those whose personal and ethnic histories (not least their histories in Canada) have been brutal, Quebec and its predominantly French-speaking population look like the pampered darlings of Confederation. Nationalism always demands comparison. More than anything, though, Canadien nationalism lacked sufficient power within Canada to make a difference. True power terrifies, intimidates, subdues, manipulates, and controls; it does not merely irritate.

English-Canadian nationalism kept reinventing, reimagining, itself so that successive waves of immigrants (at least those from some parts of Europe) could be invited to play 'let's pretend'. Let's pretend that English-speaking Canada is white, Anglo-Saxon (English), Protestant—pretend even if it is not. Let's pretend that everyone, from anywhere, can join this 'nation', even when in reality they will be excluded in some fashion. Let's pretend that Ontario and Nova Scotia never legislated segregated schools to spare white children from the 'contamination' of their Black neighbours. Let's pretend that Asian immigrants, their children, and even their grandchildren were never denied full citizenship rights until 1947. Let's pretend that Jews fleeing Nazi Germany were never barred entry into Canada, or that for decades Jews were not kept out of professions, universities, social and recreational facilities. Let's pretend that the Indian Acts, land grabs, residential schools, and bureaucratically induced poverty never tore Aboriginal communities apart. Let's pretend that the Supreme Court of Canada never sanctioned racial discrimination. And there is so much more we could pretend never happened. The 'let's pretend' strategy succeeded because the game was so easy and—at least at first glance—so painless to play. Its greatest 'success' can be detected in the numbers of those of non-British ancestry who snap to an anti-Quebec stance at the drop of a 'distinct society'. They have forgotten that persecution and exclusion—the lost names, the lost languages, the lost cultures—were the price their parents, grandparents, even great-grandparents paid as the price of admission. The 'let's pretend' strategy appeared to express the power of the English, though in fact it was shaped by anxiety, by fear of rivals and of eventual decline.[46] 'Let's pretend' is the way a liberal state that 'prefer[s] birthright over choice as a criterion of membership'[47] always operates. 'Let's pretend', most dangerously for all who live in Canada, has induced historical amnesia about the undercurrents of hatred in Canada inspired by the racism that riddles every nationalism, including civic nationalism.

But times change. As the English contours and flavours of Canada continue to diminish, national identity for Canadians outside Quebec is less and less clear. Canada is officially bilingual and multicultural, but there is no consensus on what those concepts mean in practice, beyond the anger and resentment they provoke all around. In the midst of all this the idea of civic nationalism has gained a certain currency in English-speaking Canada. With no single ethnic group yet able to dominate as the English once did, civic nationalism appeals to a non-ethnic, multicultural view of society in which no ethnicity dominates, all are equal, Native people are entitled to nothing special, Quebec must be a province like all the rest, no one is entitled to a distinct society, the rights of unpopular or inconvenient claimants are limited, then . . . what?[48] Neither civic nor ethnic nationalism offers a way out of our Canadian dilemmas. Nationalism in any guise creates confusion, not clarity; anxiety, not tranquillity. Isaiah Berlin once reminded us that nationalism

> started in alliance with other forces: democracy, liberalism, socialism. But whenever they fell out among themselves, nationalism invariably won, and enslaved its rivals, and reduced them to relative impotence. German romanticism, French socialism, English liberalism, European democracy were compromised and distorted by it. They proved powerless against the torrent of nationalist pride and greed which culminated in the conflict of 1914.[49]

And nationalism's record since 1914 inspires little confidence.

Civic nationalism, finally, implies endorsement of multiculturalism and tolerance. Multiculturalism is the latest liberal attempt to deal with differences. Yet in its celebration of diversity and differences racism is not eradicated—merely shifted from the public to the private sphere. It becomes simply one more 'attempt to impute rational meaning to inequality'.[50] In fact, minorities remain at the margins. According to Goldberg: 'The more ideologically hegemonic liberal values seem and the more open to difference liberal modernity declares itself, the more dismissive of difference it becomes and the more closed it seeks to make the circle of *acceptability*.'[51] And this is the central issue: *acceptance*, not tolerance. Tolerance, often trumpeted as the highest Canadian virtue, denies the relevance of the Other; to tolerate is to endure, grudgingly, the objectionable Other as he really is—someone who needs to be made over. What the Other wants, needs, demands is to be embraced in all the dimensions of otherness, not merely tolerated.

Northrop Frye once made an observation about Canada that, for me, captures why English-speaking Canadians should be wary of civic nationalism.[52] Recounting his train journeys, as a student, from Fredericton to Toronto, he described the eagerness with which he waited for the view of Quebec City from Lévis:

> Here was one of the imaginative and emotional centres of my own country and my own people, yet a people with whom I found it difficult to identify; what was difficult being not so much language as cultural memory. But the effort of making identification was crucial: it helped me to see that a sense of unity is the opposite of uniformity. *Uniformity, where everyone 'belongs', uses the same clichés, thinks alike and behaves alike, produces a society which seems comfortable at first but is totally*

lacking in human dignity. Real unity tolerates dissent and rejoices in variety of outlook and tradition, recognizes that it is man's destiny to unite and not divide, understands that creating proletariats and scapegoats and second-class citizens is a mean and contemptible activity. Unity, so understood, is the extra dimension that raises the sense of belonging into genuine human life.[53]

Civic nationalism is still nationalism after all. To achieve the kind of Canada that would meet the aims of its proponents, nationalism needs to be edited out. The focus must be on creating political and legal institutions that could secure an ethical society entrenched not in any nationalism, or in a perpetual 'let's pretend', but in social justice. As Canada continues to change rapidly in every respect, democracy, freedom, civility, and human dignity must remain the collective goal of all who live in this country. Canada needs and deserves more debate about how to build a society that includes everyone and excludes no one on the basis of ethnicity, skin colour, beliefs, sexuality, health. If civic nationalism does not offer a solution, perhaps (and only perhaps) liberalism's original optimism about human potential might suggest directions for the future, but only after liberalism divests itself of all links to nationalism.

In the 1998 Massey Lectures Jean Vanier offered a non-nationalist perspective on how to achieve both individual freedom and a sense of belonging.[54] And recently, in the wake of the NATO entry into Kosovo, Michael Ignatieff has argued that no lasting progress towards peace can be made in that region until Serbs are willing to acknowledge and come to terms with their recent history, especially the actions of their government and military forces in Kosovo.[55] Ignatieff is right in insisting that meaningful reconciliation can begin only with an honest evaluation of what has occurred there. If Serbs and Albanians are to find any measure of reconciliation, both will need to abandon the ideology of nationalism.

Nationalism has been imagined, created, learned. Imagine what Canada might have become without it! Are we ready to risk unlearning nationalism?

NOTES

This essay is dedicated to the memory of two people: Stephanie Gilbert, who died as I was first writing it; and Pierre Savard, whose unexpected death came as I struggled with revisions. It is also my thanks to Ramsay Cook, who always encouraged me, as his student, to discover my own conclusions, even when he disagreed with them. This essay has benefited from the insightful criticisms of Xavier Gélinas, Michael Behiels, Marcel Martel, and anonymous readers, all very generous with their time.

1. Consider the furor in May 1998 when David Levine was appointed CEO of the about-to-be merged hospitals of Ottawa; see, for example, Graham Fraser, 'The David Levine Affair: Fear and Loathing in Ottawa', *Globe and Mail* (23 May 1998), D3.
2. Michael Ignatieff, *Blood and Belonging: Journeys into the New Nationalism* (Toronto,

1993), 134, slides towards this formula: '. . . and wish, suddenly, that we actually did love the same nation and not merely cohabit the same state'.

3. Ibid.

4. John Ralston Saul, *The Unconscious Civilization* (Toronto, 1995), 2.

5. See Ernest Geller, *Nations and Nationalism* (Ithaca, NY, 1983), 7, 53–8.

6. Elie Kedourie, *Nationalism* (New York, 1960), 9.

7. E.J. Hobsbawm, *Nations and Nationalism Since 1870: Programme, Myth, Reality*, 2nd edn (Cambridge, 1990), 12.

8. Kedourie, *Nationalism*, 18.

9 Ibid., 9.

10. Benedict Anderson, *Imagined Communities: Reflections on the Origin and Spread of Nationalism*, rev. edn (London, 1991), 6.

11. Arlene W. Saxonhouse, *Fear of Diversity: The Birth of Political Science in Ancient Greek Thought* (Chicago, 1992), 2.

12. Ibid., x.

13. Edward W. Said, *Culture and Imperialism* (New York, 1993), xxv.

14. Robert Miles, *Racism* (London, 1989), 25.

15. Ibid., 84.

16. Two excellent examples of work in this vein are Jeffrey Richards, *Sex, Dissidence and Damnation: Minority Groups in the Middle Ages* (London, 1994) and R.I. Moore, *The Formation of a Persecuting Society: Power and Deviance in Western Europe 950–1250* (Oxford, 1990).

17. David Theo Goldberg, *Racist Culture: Philosophy and the Politics of Meaning* (Oxford, 1993), 210.

18. Miles, *Racism*, 87–98.

19. Goldberg, *Racist Culture*, 78–9.

20. Miles, *Racism*, 89.

21. Ignatieff, *Blood and Belonging*, 3–4.

22. Ibid., 5.

23. Kenan Malik, *The Meaning of Race: Race, History and Culture in Western Society* (New York, 1996), 135.

24. Ignatieff, 4. John Ralston Saul has addressed these issues similarly in *Reflections of a Siamese Twin: Canada at the End of the Twentieth Century* (Toronto, 1997).

25. Malik, *Meaning of Race*, 100.

26. Goldberg, *Racist Culture*, 27; see also Malik, *Meaning of Race*, 55–70.

27. Goldberg, *Racist Culture*, 10.

28. Yael Tamir, *Liberal Nationalism* (Princeton, 1993), 117.

29. Malik, *Meaning of Race*, 28.

30. Miles, *Racism*, 90.

31. *The Wretched of the Earth*, cited in Said, *Culture and Imperialism*, 270.

32. Miles, *Racism*, 91.

33. See Goldberg, *Racist Culture*, 69–83.

34. For example, see David Spurr, *The Rhetoric of Empire: Colonial Discourse in Journalism, Travel Writing, and Imperial Administration* (Durham, NC, 1993).

35. J.-C. Bonenfant, 'Sir George-Étienne Cartier', *Dictionary of Canadian Biography* X, 147.

36. House of Commons, *Debates*, 30 April l883, 905; see also Carl C. Berger, 'Race and Liberty: The Historical Ideas of Sir John George Bourinot', *Historical Papers* (1965), 87–104.

37. D.G. Jones, *Butterfly on Rock: Images in Canadian Literature* (Toronto, 1970), 36. Northrop Frye first described the 'garrison mentality' in the 'Conclusion' to *Literary History of Canada*, ed. Carl Klinck (Toronto, 1967), 830. Although Frye was referring specifically to English-Canadian literature, one could make the same argument about the Québécois literary imagination and its relationship to nationalism; but that is another paper.

38. Stephen Leacock, 'Greater Canada: An Appeal', *University Magazine* (April 1907), 133.

39. See Tamir, *Liberal Nationalism*, 140–50, for a discussion of the cultural imperative of liberalism.

40. 'For a type of middle-class English gentry, the French and the Irish, the Italians, the Poles and various others could be lumped together among *the children of the devil, to be ignored or refashioned in the image of their betters*'; Jones, *Butterfly on Rock*, 36; italics added.

41. John Marlyn, *Under the Ribs of Death* (Toronto, 1964), 24. Sandor's father's retort—that 'we are all foreigners here. . . . nationality is of no consequence' (24)—reflects the dream that most immigrants had, but few realized. See also Terrence Craig, *Racial Attitudes in English-Canadian Fiction, 1905–1980* (Waterloo, 1987).

42. There were, of course, minor players in the category of 'enemy', but they were never accorded the same status as the Canadiens or Americans. The First Nations and Blacks were the two most notable. That they were both usually marginalized in nationalist squabbles accounts in no small way for their absence from the writing of Canadian history (in either official language) until relatively recently.

43. It also served as a device to derail and deny Aboriginal claims; see Goldberg, *Racist Culture*, 212.

44. Examples of this crop up from times to time: see the reaction ('We are not amused', *Globe and Mail*, 23 May 1998, D7) to the earlier suggestion by Donald B. Smith ('From Here to Heritage Day', 18 May 1998) to remove the English vestiges of the May holiday and make it more truly Canadian. For some time now, at my own university's Convocations, many First Nations students have worn their own traditional ceremonial clothing instead of replicas from British institutions, enriching and transforming the ceremonies; the sky has not yet fallen.

45. Consider the visit of Catalonia's Jordi Pujol to Quebec in July 1996, when his observations about Quebec's relative lack of real suffering generated a furor in nationalist circles.

46. For example, see Arthur Herman, *The Idea of Decline in Western History* (New York, 1997), 13–46; see also Carl Berger, *The Sense of Power: Studies in the Ideas of Canadian Imperialism 1867–1914* (Toronto, 1970), 4–11.

47. Tamir, *Liberal Nationalism*, 125; 128.

48. Positions taken by the Reform Party of Canada—attacks on the Supreme Court of Canada for extending Charter protections to homosexuals and lesbians, and calls for Parliament to legislate limits to Aboriginal land claims in the wake of the Delgamuukw decision—underscore the grim prospects that civic nationalism really offers: see 'Reform seeks curbs on judicial activism'; 'Restrict native land claims, Reform says', *Globe and Mail* (9 June 1998), A4.

49. Isaiah Berlin, *The Sense of Reality: Studies in Ideas and Their History*, ed. Henry Hardy (London, 1996), 251. Many proponents of civic nationalism look to Berlin's formulation of British liberalism to support their claims. Ian Buruma notes that for Berlin (and many other anglophiles) England was a '*fabled* land of common sense, fairness and good manners'; *Anglomania: A European Love Affair*, (New York, 1998), 275; italics added.

50. Malik, *Meaning of Race*, 170; 169–77.

51. Goldberg, *Racist Culture*, 6–7; italics added.

52. I would insist that this applies equally to nationalisms in Quebec.

53. Northrop Frye, *The Bush Garden: Essays on the Canadian Imagination* (Toronto, 1971), vi; italics added.

54. Jean Vanier, *Becoming Human* (Toronto, 1998).

55. Michael Ignatieff interviewed on *The Magazine*, CBC-TV, 16 June 1999.

'Hors du Québec, point de salut!'

Francophone Minorities and Quebec Nationalism, 1945–1969

MARCEL MARTEL

At the first Forum de concertation francophone, held in Quebec City in March 1997, the leaders of the institutional network of francophone minority communities outside Quebec regretted the virtual absence of participants from Quebec; the few Québécois who did attend were almost exclusively bureaucrats. Participants at the forum identified and even deplored the lack of understanding among Québécois of the realities faced by francophone minority communities throughout Canada. But no one seemed able to offer concrete proposals to correct this situation.

Lack of knowledge has not prevented politicians and public opinion-makers from making inflammatory judgements about the vitality of those communities. In fact, francophones outside Quebec seem to occupy a very specific place in the imagination of some Québécois nationalists: the graveyard. The few who have investigated this problem simply acknowledge that it exists. For instance, the political scientist Linda Cardinal argues that minority francophone and Acadian communities have become the subjects of a 'misérabiliste' discourse.[1] I prefer to qualify that discourse as 'funereal', for it is dominated by expressions such as 'death', 'near-the-end', and 'non-survival'.

In this funereal discourse, French Canadians inside Quebec represent life; those outside the province represent death. This ghoulish trend started in the early 1960s with the publication of Marcel Chaput's book *Why I Am a Separatist*, in which the author offered a set of explanations that have profoundly influenced the way French Canadians outside Quebec are understood and represented. Using data from the 1951 *Census of Canada*, Chaput wrote that Confederation was 'the graveyard of minorities' because of the high rate of assimilation—approaching 50 per cent—for francophones living outside Quebec.[2] In subsequent years, others became gravediggers too. In a 1968 radio interview in Ottawa, René Lévesque, then leader of the Parti québécois, was asked about the future of French Canadians outside Quebec. He answered that French-Canadian minorities were simply 'dead ducks'—a devastating appraisal that is still repeated today by some Québécois nationalists. In the same year, in his manifesto *Option Québec*, Lévesque painted a general picture of francophone minority groups as existing in an 'advanced state of cultural decomposition'.[3] Fourteen years later, in 1982, the well-known Quebec novelist Yves Beauchemin declared that francophones outside Quebec were 'still-warm corpses'.[4] The image had changed: now these people were not only threatened with extinction, they had actually died—if only recently. Other pundits and political commentators have refrained from using death metaphors, but they nonetheless come close when they argue that, outside Quebec, there is no future for the 'French fact' in Canada.[5]

This funereal discourse reveals an important and fundamental change in francophone nationalist thought. In their analysis of the developing discourse over the disappearance of the French fact outside Quebec, Lawrence Oliver and Guy Bédard argue that Québécois nationalism underwent a fundamental change that resulted in the exclusion of francophone minority groups. However, whereas they link this change to the Quiet Revolution of the 1960s,[6] I would argue that it began much earlier—in fact, soon after the Second World War. The process of rethinking nationalist thought involved a dramatic transformation of the idea of nation and national identity.[7] The new definition of the Québécois nation led directly to the diffusion of a negative discourse about francophones outside Quebec, including Acadians. In the new nationalist cosmology, francophone minorities would be radically transformed: from full-fledged members of the French-speaking community in Canada to mere examples of what the Québécois should not become.

The present survey of this shift in French-Canadian nationalist thought will start with an analysis of the evidence and data on which it is based; in particular, I will examine some of the writings of the Montreal historical school, whose members were among the first to attack what they called the 'consolatory' myths of French-Canadian nationalism, such as la survivance. In the second part I will look at the way the new thinking and the impressive body of evidence supporting it was used by the first indépendantistes to justify abandoning some segments of the French-Canadian nation. The essay concludes with an examination of some of the work on francophone minority communities done by Father Richard Arès, SJ, who, contrary to his initial intentions, actually contributed to the process of nationalist rethinking that condemned francophone minority groups to eventual disappearance, at least in the collective imagination of the Québécois nationalists and indépendantistes.

I 'THE LINGUISTIC RESISTANCE [OUTSIDE QUEBEC] DECEIVES ONLY THOSE WHO WISH TO BE DECEIVED.'[8]

This quotation reflects the tone of Michel Brunet's writings about francophone minority communities. A professor of history at the Université de Montréal, Brunet engaged in a personal crusade to eradicate the 'consolatory' myths and comfortable rationalizations spread by traditional French-Canadian nationalists. Brunet played the role of an ideological entrepreneur pursuing strategies and taking advantage of institutions such as the media, as well as organizations such as the Société Saint-

Jean Baptiste, to further the dissemination and wide acceptance of his redefinition of French-Canadian nationalism into Québécois neo-nationalism.

The new set of theories promoted by the Montreal historical school has been brilliantly analyzed by Jean Lamarre.[9] My analysis focuses specifically on three concepts popularized by Brunet, who was by far the most controversial member of that school, which also included Guy Frégault and Maurice Séguin. The first of these concepts (influenced by Séguin) was a new answer to the old question of *la survivance*: how French Canadians might guarantee the survival of their language and culture in the face of an overwhelmingly English-speaking majority. In the past, attachment to the essential components of French-Canadian identity—in particular, the Catholic Church and the French language—had been enough. For the empirically minded Brunet, however, the answer lay in the objective observation that any people could guarantee its survival if it preserved its freedom and autonomy: in other words, he framed the problem of *la survivance* as one of freedom of collective action.

Brunet's second concept was similarly empirical. Having studied the 'objective data' on francophone communities in Canada—demographic statistics and territorial analysis—he concluded that the survival of the majority French-Canadian community in Quebec was already guaranteed: any attempt to assimilate those people was doomed to fail. (His celebrated statement on the importance of the demographic factor in history was popularized in Denis Arcand's film *Le Déclin de l'empire américain*: in history, according to Brunet, all that counts is numbers.[10])

Brunet's second concept reflects the idea of historical determinism, the idea that the laws of history dictate the inevitable conditions from which no people can escape. According to Brunet, the building of a nation-state is a legitimate aspiration for a people because it is dictated by the laws of history. In his 1953 lecture 'Canadians *et Canadiens*' Brunet pointed to the centralization of legislative powers by the federal government after 1930—when it introduced unemployment insurance, the wartime tax rental agreements, and the system of universal family allowances—as an illustration of English Canada's determination to build a nation-state centred in Ottawa. To avoid falling behind the worldwide historical trend towards nation-building, and because of what was happening in Canada, francophones had an obligation to undertake a similar task, using the only state fully under their control: the Quebec state.[11]

Finally, Brunet deliberately used the objective notion of historical determinism to predict the fate of francophones living outside the national territory: since demographic factors handicapped francophone minority communities, the logical outcome was for them to be assimilated by the anglophone majority. There seemed to be no escaping the harsh judgement of history: like any other people without control of a state, French-speaking Canadians outside Quebec, including Acadians, were condemned to assimilation and, ultimately, extinction. The studies of the francophone minorities undertaken by Father Richard Arès, published in the journal *Relations* in 1954 and based on 1951 Census data, corroborated Brunet's theoretical model, confirming the trend towards assimilation and unquestionably demonstrating that it was impossible to believe in the demographic reconquest of Canada by francophones. 'Those who still dream about this possibility,' wrote Brunet, 'refuse to face reality.'[12]

These objective examinations of francophone reality provided enough new material to revise French Canadians' understanding of what it meant to be a nation. Statistics, territorial control, the laws of history, and the inevitability of assimilation together guaranteed francophones in North America that they could survive where they constituted the majority—but only there. This notion, presented as a reality that could not be questioned, was used to validate the idea that the disappearance of francophones was inevitable outside the national territory of Quebec. In their effort to promote a form of nationalism that would capture the imaginations of Quebec francophones, the Montreal historians developed an intellectual framework in which the new way of thinking and the old way were equated to life and death. In other words, cultural and linguistic death was the inescapable fate of francophones outside Quebec. Only inside Quebec—where they were in the majority and had control of a state—could francophones look forward to rebirth and life.

Much of Brunet's writing on the subject reveals a certain conflict between his pursuit of an intellectual task that was by nature neutral and 'objective', and his unwavering belief in the absolute truth of his conclusions. This conflict is especially apparent when he addresses the question of minority francophone communities. In a letter of 15 August 1956 to François-Albert Angers, director of the nationalist journal L'Action Nationale, Brunet explained his view of francophones living in the rest of the country. These groups, he wrote, 'seem to imagine that we are a minority in the province of Quebec. You would think it pained them to know we are a majority in a province where we can rely on our government,' which is capable of 'serving us as a collectivity. These poor minorities would seem to like nothing better than to see us reduced to the level of a minority.' Brunet could no longer tolerate it. 'I think it is imperative to define the real positions of French Canadians in Quebec in their relations with the minorities. They cannot go on being a dead weight for us and a pawn in the hands of English Canada.'[13]

The role played by the Montreal historians, especially Brunet, is important in understanding the process that changed perceptions of francophone minority communities. According to them, the survival of any collectivity depends primarily on its ability to exercise its freedom of collective action. Quebec francophones enjoyed this freedom; those living outside Quebec did not. In this view, assimilation was inescapable because of the inevitable law that any minority group would be absorbed by the majority. By asserting this as fact, these historians gradually marginalized French Canadians outside Quebec. Instead of condemning English Canada's treatment of those groups and seeking to assist them, as some other French-Canadian institutions did, Brunet contributed to the idea that those groups were simply doomed to disappear. This process of rethinking nationalist thought was squarely based on notions of what was normal, especially with respect to linguistic assimilation. In both their substance and their tone, those ideas promoted the acceptance of powerful assumptions that would work their way into the new nationalist discourse. The notion of the imminent disappearance of the French fact outside Quebec is perhaps the most striking of those assumptions.

II CASTING THE DIE: FRANCOPHONE MINORITY GROUPS WERE TO BE ASSIMILATED IN ANY CASE

Any study of the formation of new perspectives on old problems raises questions about the process by which the new thinking takes hold. The production of any new understanding involves a complicated set of circumstances: certain people have to formulate ideas, disseminate them, and gain support for them; to achieve a wide acceptance, ideas need to be vested with authority.[14] In this process, individuals, intellectual debates, and the reactions both of the media and of the public all play a part.

Not surprisingly, among the many groups who reacted to this reformulation of nationalist thought was the academic community. Many criticized both the ideas and the overall tone of the discourse. Léon Dion, for example, challenged some of the assumptions of the Montreal historical school. In 1961 he wrote that Séguin and his followers had changed traditional French-Canadian nationalism into an even more pessimistic form.[15] Ramsay Cook pointed out that Brunet's bleak perspective on the future of the French fact outside Quebec made him wonder if the analysis was based more on perceptions than historical evidence.[16] Nevertheless, Brunet defended his work by arguing that his historical school was neither defeatist nor pessimistic but objective and realistic.[17] Reflecting on his career, Brunet wrote that 'I hope that my life and career have made a modest contribution to that awareness without which a collectivity becomes a mere plaything of historical evolution.'[18]

Among the *indépendantiste* leaders, however, the University of Montreal historians found devoted followers. Delighted to have 'objective' support for their position, *indépendantiste* leaders helped to make public some of the historians' work. In 1962, for example, Raymond Barbeau, director of the journal *Laurentie* and founder of the organization L'Alliance Laurentienne, published the TV transcripts of Maurice Séguin. As academics, the Montreal historians were assumed to be beyond the influence of political pressures or political struggles. Most significantly, however, *indépendantiste* leaders were able to imbue both their theory and their discourse of disappearance with the aura of scientific authority. They were able to achieve this because of the general reputation attached to professional historians and the objective nature of the evidence used to justify their intellectual conclusions.[19]

From the left to the right of the political spectrum, the *indépendantistes* who emerged at the end of the 1950s agreed that francophone minority groups were condemned to disappear. Whether the reasons were political—the nature of the

Canadian federal system—or sociolinguistic, these groups had neither the ability nor the will to maintain their French language and culture.

At the beginning of the 1960s, the publication of Marcel Chaput's book *Why I Am a Separatist* created considerable controversy, in part because Chaput was well known in the institutional network that helped to create and maintain institutions essential to the vitality of the French fact. Chaput was, for a time, a leader within the Ordre de Jacques-Cartier[20] and in the fall of 1959 was involved in that organization's committee charged with studying the possible outcomes of Quebec independence. However, as G.-Raymond Laliberté's study revealed, Chaput was expelled from the Ordre. His opponents blamed him for using the organization to promote his 'heretical' ideas and to recruit new members into his *indépendantiste* movement.[21]

According to Chaput, Quebec must become an independent country if French Canadians were to put an end to their minority status in Canada. He dismissed fears about the fate of other French Canadians in the event of Quebec independence by arguing that the time had come to put an end to the illusions that had nourished the collective pan-Canadian dream.

To play down any fears about the consequences of Quebec independence for francophones outside the province, Chaput reminded his readers that these groups were to be assimilated; already, he charged, many of those still clinging to the French language could barely speak it. In any case, demographic survival was clearly impossible: 'ever since the period 1941-1951, these minorities have been giving birth to more English babies than French ones.'[22] Chaput was convinced that the trend was irreversible: 'with more and more Anglification, the day had to come when the new generation of babies was more English that French. Does this demand an explanation?'[23]

Raymond Barbeau came to similar conclusions. His reasons for supporting Quebec independence were made public in two books, the first of which, *Le Québec est-il une colonie?*, appeared in 1962. In the second, *Le Québec bientôt unilingue?* (1965), Barbeau maintained that the 1961 Census data demonstrated beyond a doubt that 'the survival of the French Fact in Canada is a myth; we can now talk only about the survival of the French Fact in Quebec, and if French unilingualism is not proclaimed the day will come when it will be possible to talk of the French Fact in Canada as a memory as in Louisiana.' And, using the death imagery that by now was increasingly used to characterize the French fact outside Quebec, he asked: 'isn't it our pressing duty to cease to be a dying minority in Canada and to become a majority of French-speaking people in Quebec?'[24]

André D'Allemagne, one of the founders of the Rassemblement pour l'Indépendance nationale, also played a part in the effort to eliminate the French minorities outside Quebec from the collective imagination of the Québécois. In *Le colonialisme au Québec*, D'Allemagne shared Brunet's view of the 'consolatory' myths propagated to conceal the true destiny of French Canadians—to be a colonized people. If the 'traditional perspective saw the French-Canadian nation as a *minority* in Canada', he wrote, 'the *indépendantistes* would make this minority a *majority* in a Quebec that henceforth they [would] consider their "only country".'[25] Although he made no specific reference to French groups outside Quebec, D'Allemagne denounced the established French-Canadian institutional network as perpetuating a 'traditional and static nationalism', and declared its campaigns to promote the French language or help minority groups to be ineffective and 'futile'.[26]

Although this survey of the literature produced by the *indépendantistes* of the early 1960s is very brief, it shows that the idea of the inevitable disappearance of the French fact outside Quebec received growing support even outside *indépendantiste* circles. The case of the historian Robert Rumilly is a good illustration. At the end of his *Histoire des Acadiens*, published in 1955, Rumilly concluded that 'an objective analysis supports neither a delirious optimism, nor a systematic pessimism.' The last sentence of his book gave no hint of the pessimism about the French fact that would influence his later writings. 'The history of the Acadian people, the virtues that everybody attributes to them, the institutional support that they have created, their consistent progress in different fields lead to, demand, one conclusion: hope.'[27]

By 1961, however, when Rumilly published *Le Problème national des Canadiens français*, his thinking on the matter had been influenced by the writings of the Montreal historical school, notably Brunet, especially with respect to the process of nation-state building and the constitution of the Canadian nation-state. Since francophones had no chance to constitute the majority in Canada, Rumilly argued, Quebec was the only nation-state that could guarantee their survival. And if Acadians became only a simple majority in the neighbouring province of New Brunswick, he saw no hope that the trend would be reversed in that province either: 'They would need, because of their state of survival and their level of national consciousness, a proportion of 70 to 75.'[28] Writing at length about francophones outside Quebec, Rumilly echoed Chaput's claims about the progress of assimilation among these groups and approvingly quoted the conclusion of Gaétan Legault's thesis: 'Nothing lets us anticipate that the assimilation rate of the French Fact outside Quebec will cease. Based on scientific data, we must consider this trend to be a progressive one.'[29]

III THE ACCIDENTAL EMBALMER: FATHER RICHARD ARÈS

The Jesuit Richard Arès, a former member of the Royal Commission on Constitutional Problems and director of the journal *Relations* between 1959 and 1969, had been preoccupied with the uncertain future of minority French groups since his years as a teacher at Saint-Boniface College in Manitoba in the early 1940s.[30] Yet, perhaps unwittingly, Arès gave even greater currency to the idea of the disappearance of francophones outside Quebec.

In 1954, in several articles published in *Relations*, Arès expressed his concerns about the future of the French fact. Drawing on the 1951 Census data, Arès wrote that except in New Brunswick assimilation rates in the Maritime provinces were increasing,[31] and he catalogued the progress of assimilation in the Prairie provinces with great sadness, concluding with a warning that some protective policies should be implemented to prevent the situation from worsening by the time of the next Census, in 1961.[32] Although the situation of Ontario's francophones was not nearly as bad as in other parts of English-speaking Canada, it remained critical.[33]

By 1963, however, Arès fully shared the pessimism about the French fact outside Quebec that pervaded Quebec intellectual circles. In an article entitled 'La grande pitié de nos minorités françaises' he attributed this pitiable situation to a political factor: Confederation. The federal regime was 'very costly for the French language: not only was the French-speaking community unable to retain its numbers, but it lost more than 400,000 among those who used to be French-speakers.'[34] Because of the decline in the number of francophones even, though to a lesser extent, in New Brunswick, Arès made a dire prediction: 'The drama of French minority groups in Canada is also one of all Confederation; the destiny of the latter is tied to that of the former. If these minorities die, nothing will be left for Confederation but to also descend into the grave.'[35]

In the same year, speaking before the General Assembly of the Association des commissaires d'écoles catholiques de langue française du Canada, Arès could barely conceal his pessimism, especially in the light of the new 1961 Census data. According to Arès, if nothing was done in the near future to help francophone minority groups, rates of linguistic assimilation would continue to climb.[36]

The Arès case is interesting not simply for the evolution of his ideas, but because of the way his writings came to be used. Arès tried to raise the alarm among federal and provincial political leaders, urging them to take action. To get their attention, he did not hesitate to link the future of Confederation itself to the fate of minority francophone communities. In describing 'the death sentence and gradual descent into the grave' of francophones outside Quebec,[37] Arès was trying to move those who refused to rethink the federal system to change their minds. According to Pierre Trépanier, Arès did not favour the formation of a Quebec nation.[38] Yet his analysis and predictions had the unintended result of serving as powerful arguments both for the members of the Montreal historical school and for the first indépendantistes, the former using Arès to legitimate their theories, the latter to justify their political program.

CONCLUSION

The intellectual 'liquidation' of French Canadians outside Quebec, who were once considered close relatives of the Québécois, began with fundamental changes in the way nationalists defined themselves and their national community. With the work of Brunet in particular, the Montreal historical school tried to break the chains of a past they rejected. To accomplish this liberation, they recast the collective identity of French Canadians by transforming the focus. No longer were they a minority community in Canada—now they were French majority in the new national territory of Quebec. This transformation led to the emergence of a Québécois identity. But it also led to the abandonment of francophones outside Quebec. The promoters of the new Quebec collective identity saw this abandonment as natural and inevitable—a simple acknowledgement of the fact that these groups were destined to be assimilated anyway: not a judgement based on a particular set of assumptions constructed by the Montreal historians themselves. According to the first *indépendantistes*, the disappearance of francophone minority communities was a direct consequence of Confederation—a political arrangement that the francophone majority in Quebec must repudiate if it was to avoid a similar destiny. Arès, for his part, helped to validate this interpretation of the Montreal school and the *indépendantistes* because his analysis illustrated the rapid advance of linguistic assimilation among francophones outside Quebec and the consequent weakening of their communities. For both the Montreal historians and the *indépendantistes*, portraying those communities as moribund helped to validate their expulsion from the emerging Québécois collective identity. To drive home their point, they emphasized the dialectic of life and death in their statements and writings on francophone minority communities, contrasting these 'dying' minorities to the Québécois francophones whose cultural vitality symbolized the promise of a future that was beyond doubt.

Over time, under the influence of a political agenda created in reaction to what Brunet and his colleagues called old myths, these views became the foundation of a new myth: the imminent disappearance of francophone minorities outside Quebec. Since the 1950s, many have announced the death of the French fact, and have never hesitated to use dramatic language to do so. The fact that the issue is still under discussion suggests a vitality that undermines the validity of this argument.

NOTES

I thank Michael Behiels, André Larose, Laurence Mussio, and the anonymous readers at Oxford University Press for their useful comments and observations.

1. Linda Cardinal, 'Identité et dialogue: l'expérience des francophonies canadienne et québécoise', in *Pour un renforcement de la solidarité entre francophones au Canada: Réflexions théoriques et analyses historique, juridique et sociopolitique* (Quebec, Conseil de la langue française, 1995), 59–80.
2. Marcel Chaput, *Why I Am a Separatist*, trans. Robert A. Taylor (Toronto, 1962), 73.
3. 'état avancé de décomposition culturelle'; René Lévesque, *Option Québec* (Montreal, 1968), 115.
4. 'les francophones hors Québec, ça me fait penser à un cadavre encore chaud'; Beauchemin quoted in Lawrence Olivier et Guy Bédard, 'Le nationalisme québécois, les Acadiens et les francophones du Canada', *Égalité, Revue acadienne d'analyse politique* 33 (1993), 81.
5. In October 1997, Gilles Duceppe, leader of the Bloc québécois, argued that it was impossible for francophone artists outside Quebec to make a living unless they moved to Quebec; *Le Devoir* (4 Oct. 1997).

6. Olivier and Bédard, 'Le nationalisme québécois . . ', 81–100.

7. See Benedict Anderson, *Imagined Communities: Reflections on the Origin and Spread of Nationalism* (London, 1983).

8. 'La résistance linguistique [hors Québec] ne trompe que ceux qui veulent bien se laisser tromper'; Brunet, 'Le nationalisme canadien-français et la politique des deux Canadas', *La présence anglaise et les Canadiens: Études sur l'histoire et la pensée des deux Canadas* (Montreal, 1958), 288.

9. Jean Lamarre, *Le devenir de la nation québécoise selon Maurice Séguin, Guy Frégault et Michel Brunet, 1944–1969* (Sillery, 1993).

10. 'En histoire c'est d'abord le nombre qui compte: premièrement, le nombre, deuxièmement, le nombre et troisièmement, encore le nombre'; Brunet, 'Les immigrants, enjeu de la lutte entre les deux collectivités fondatrices du Canada', *Québec, Canada anglais: Deux itinéraires, un affrontement* (Montreal, 1968), 211.

11. Brunet, 'Canadians et Canadiens', *Canadians et Canadiens: Études sur l'histoire et la pensée des deux Canadas* (Montreal, 1971), 17–32.

12. 'Ceux qui y rêvent toujours refusent de voir la réalité en face'; Brunet, 'Canadianisme et Canadianism', *La présence anglaise et les Canadiens*, 181.

13. 'semblent s'imaginer que nous sommes une minorité dans la province de Québec. On dirait qu'ils souffrent de nous savoir en majorité dans une province où nous pouvons compter sur un gouvernement'; . . . 'mis à notre service comme collectivité. Ces pauvres minoritaires semblent n'avoir qu'un désir: nous réduire au niveau de minorité'; 'Je crois urgent de définir les positions réelles des Canadiens français du Québec dans leurs relations avec les minorités. Celles-ci ne doivent plus être un poids mort pour nous et un gage entre les mains du Canada anglais'; quoted in Lamarre, *Le devenir . . .*, 416.

14. See Hervé Coutau-Bégarie, *Le phénomène nouvelle histoire. Grandeur et décadence de l'école des Annales*, 2nd edn (Paris, 1989); Gérard Namer, *Court traité de sociologie de la connaissance: La triple légitimation* (Paris, 1985).

15. Léon Dion, 'Pessimistic Nationalism: Its Source, Meaning, and Validity', in *French Canadian Nationalism: An Anthology*, ed. Ramsay Cook (Toronto, 1978 [1969]), 294–303.

16. Ramsay Cook, 'L'historien et le nationalisme: Le cas de Michel Brunet', *Cité libre* 15, 73 (January 1965), 5–14.

17. Michel Brunet, 'La science historique au Canada français: son évolution et ses développements actuels', *Québec. Canada anglais: Deux itinéraires, un affrontement* (Montreal, 1968), 40.

18. Michel Brunet, *Le Québec à la minute de vérité* (Montreal, 1995), xix.

19. On the role played by historians in the construction of collective memory, see Jocelyn Létourneau, 'Historiens, sociogrammes et histoire: l'interaction complexe entre mémoire collective, mémoire individuelle, passé construit et passé vécu', in *Étude de la construction de la mémoire collective des Québécois au XXe siècle: Approches multidisciplinaires* (Quebec, 1986), 106.

20. The Ordre de Jacques-Cartier was created in 1926. This secret nationalist organization was active in the defence of French-Canadian rights throughout the country. See

G.-Raymond Laliberté, *Une société secrète: l'Ordre de Jacques Cartier* (Montreal, 1983).

21. Ibid., 295.

22. Chaput, *Why I Am a Separatist*, 72.

23. Ibid., 73.

24. 'la survivance française est un mythe au Canada; on ne peut plus parler que de la survivance française au Québec, et si l'unilinguisme n'est pas décrété, un jour on ne pourra plus parler que de souvenir du français au Canada, comme en Louisiane'; 'notre devoir le plus évident n'est-il pas de cesser d'être une minorité mourante au Canada pour devenir une majorité de langue française dans le Québec?'; Raymond Barbeau, *Le Québec bientôt unilingue?* (Montreal, 1965), 116–17.

25. 'l'optique traditionnelle qui voyait dans la nation canadienne-française une *minorité* au Canada, les indépendantistes font de cette nation une *majorité* dans un Québec qu'ils considèrent désormais comme leur "seule patrie"'; André D'Allemagne, *Le colonialisme au Québec* (Montreal, 1966), 150.

26. 'un nationalisme traditionnel et statique'; 'restent sans lendemain'; ibid., 117.

27. 'l'examen objectif ne commande, ni un optimisme délirant, ni un pessimisme systématique'; 'Toute l'histoire du peuple acadien, les vertus que tous lui reconnaissent, l'encadrement qu'il s'est constitué, la régularité de ses progrès dans plusieurs domaines postulent, commandent une conclusion: *Espérance*'; Robert Rumilly, *Histoire des Acadiens*, vol. 2 (Montreal, 1955), 1030.

28. 'Il leur faudrait, dans l'état actuel de la survivance, de la conscience nationale, une proportion de 70 ou 75 pourcent'; Robert Rumilly, *Le problème national des Canadiens français* (Montreal, 1961), 86.

29. 'Rien ne laisse prévoir que l'anglicisation en dehors du Québec doit s'arrêter. Scientifiquement parlant, nous devons considérer cette courbe comme progressive'; ibid., 113.

30. Pierre Trépanier, 'Richard Arès', *Action nationale* 82, 2 (February 1992), 167–98.

31. Richard Arès, 'Positions du français aux Maritimes', *Relations* 161 (May 1954), 145.

32. Arès, 'Positions du français dans l'Ouest canadien', *Relations* 163 (July 1954), 195.

33. Arès, 'Positions du français en Ontario et au Québec', *Relations* 164 (August 1954), 220.

34. 'fort coûteuse à la langue française: non seulement cette dernière n'a pas réussi à conserver tous ses adhérents, mais elle doit encore accuser une perte de plus de 400,000 parmi ceux qui normalement auraient dû la parler'; Arès, 'La grande pitié de nos minorités françaises', *Relations* 267 (March 1963), 65.

35. 'Le drame des minorités françaises au Canada est aussi celui de toute la Confédération canadienne; le destin de celle-ci est lié au sort de celles-là. Si les premières meurent, il ne restera plus à la seconde qu'à descendre, elle aussi, dans la tombe . . .'; ibid., 68.

36. Arès, *Justice et équité pour la communauté canadienne-française* (Montreal, 1963), 12.

37. 'lente condamnation à mort et descente graduelle au tombeau'; ibid., 18.

38. Trépanier, 'Richard Arès', 191.

PART FOUR

WOMEN

The 'Problem' of Passivity and Female Workers in the Quebec Cotton Industry, 1880–1910

Gail C. Brandt

Introduction

'[W]omen do not go on strike and do not get drunk.' Appearing before the Royal Commission on the Relations of Labor and Capital in 1879, Mr John A. Rose, a cigar manufacturer from London, Ontario, gave this succinct summary of why he preferred to hire female workers. While acknowledging that they were paid substantially less than men, he claimed that he would still prefer to hire women even if they were to receive the same rates of pay as men. Not only were women much less partial to strong drink than male workers, but they were also cleaner and less 'abusive', and they did not join unions—the real source of the working man's problems, in Rose's opinion.[1]

This view of girls and women as a cheap, sober, and docile pool of labour was a pervasive one in late nineteenth- and early twentieth-century accounts. But if employers valued female workers, male labour leaders largely resented them for precisely the same ascribed attributes. The latter characterized female factory operatives as a form of unfair competition, especially for skilled male workers, and as a serious impediment to the establishment of an effective union movement. Union men frequently justified the exclusion of female workers from their ranks by claiming that they could not be organized; after all, as temporary workers they lacked a long-term commitment to paid employment and consequently did not 'possess that spirit of solidarity, characteristic of men in industry'.[2] Indeed, the exclusionary practices of the skilled crafts unions appear to have been motivated as much by prevailing gender stereotypes and biases as by rational economic concerns. In 1898 the Trades and Labour Congress officially declared itself in favour of 'the abolition of female labour in all branches of industrial life'.[3]

It would be misleading to suggest, however, that only men viewed female workers as obstacles to the betterment of the working man's situation. In her pioneering study of women and labour published in 1892, Jean Thomson Scott concluded that women did not remain long in the work force, and therefore were not interested in the benefit and pension schemes that organized labour was struggling to implement. 'Moreover,' she wrote, 'there does not exist that "class spirit" among women in employments that is necessary to organized progress; and men with reason complain that it is difficult to operate plans of any sort which require unselfish action among large bodies of women.' Scott did soften her harsh indictment of female workers somewhat by pointing out that where women and men performed the same work and were represented by unions demanding equal pay for equal work, the women were eventually forced out of their positions. Thus women knew 'in such cases that it is not to their individual advantage to belong to the unions'.[4]

With the development of women's history in the 1970s, historians began to challenge some of the conventional wisdom about the negative impact of women workers on the union movement. Nonetheless, most accounts continued to depict the demographic characteristics of the female industrial work force in the late nineteenth and early twentieth centuries as serious impediments to workplace solidarity. Female operatives, it has been stressed repeatedly, were young, single women who entered the labour force for only a few years before marriage. Once married, the vast majority traded paid employment for domestic duties in the home. Even historians who have challenged the notion of 'passive' female workers have stressed these characteristics in accounting for the low levels of female involvement in union activity. For example, in her comprehensive recent study of working women in Peterborough, Ontario, Joan Sangster suggests that the youth of the female workers was problematic for sustained workplace action in that city's woollen mills: 'Mere teenagers at the time, the women remember that they did not really know what was going on with the union. This may have been partly because of their youth and their understandable hesitation to become politically committed, especially to such a radical concept, when they were barely fifteen.'[5] Similarly, Joy Parr has observed that older, married women and widows employed in the knit goods industry in Paris, Ontario, 'were most conspicuous among the female union activists . . . as in New York and New England textile centres and the woven-goods districts of northern France, they had the most compelling and long-standing commitment to wage work.'[6]

Historians have also pointed to the sexual division of labour in the workplace to explain why women had less opportunity than men to develop a class-consciousness that would manifest itself in direct workplace action. The sex-segregated nature of work, they argue, meant that men and women seldom performed the same work or shared the same workspace. They portray female industrial workers as unskilled, and therefore as easily replaceable by hordes of similarly unskilled women seeking employment in the same few industries open to them. Female workers, it has been noted, were subject to stricter discipline than were men in factory settings, as employers imposed fines on women and children not only to punish shoddy work or damage to company property, but also to curtail activities, such as talking and laughing, that could help to build a sense of camaraderie and solidarity. The passage of protective legislation in the 1880s reinforced the division of the work force according to sex, since women were prohibited from working night shifts. As a result, in industries where men and women might do the same or similar work, women performed such work during the day, and men at night. Taking these various factors into account, authors have suggested that female workers were robbed of any effective control over the work process and denied the potential for collective action.[7]

Finally, historians have advanced ideological reasons to account for the absence of women from militant activities. An all-pervasive ideology that represented women as nurturing, unassertive, irrational, and subservient was not, they claim, conducive to either women or men viewing female workers as constituting a significant force in the battle between labour and capital. As part of their socialization through institutions such as the family, school, and church, female employees themselves must have internalized many of the values set out in the prescriptive literature of the day.[8] Following this line of argument, it would have been extremely difficult for them to engage in behaviour that could have been construed as 'unladylike', such as speaking up at predominantly male union meetings, or walking picket lines. In her analysis of the testimony presented by female workers before the Royal Commission on the Relations of Labor and Capital, Susan Mann Trofimenkoff has emphasized their reticence to testify, arguing that 'only when they muffled their own voices [by remaining anonymous], would they speak out. . . . Perhaps one has here an aspect of "female culture", the silence that is both imposed upon and accepted by women. That silence may be both the cause and the consequence of the economic dependency of women in the family and in the factory.'[9] Ruth Frager has argued that unions were inextricably bound up with male culture, and that the concepts of 'fraternity' and 'brotherhood' central to the union movement automatically defined women as outsiders.[10] Similarly, Mercedes Steedman has found that even in the needle trades, the language of unions rarely acknowledged the presence of women. 'The social prescriptions of masculine and feminine behaviour,' she concludes, 'further ensured that men and women would continue to play out their destinies—men as protectors of class and women as its caretakers.'[11]

Despite continued emphasis on the demographic, structural, and ideological impediments to activism among working women, a number of historical studies have demonstrated that various groups of female industrial workers in the past were far from acquiescent.[12] Increasingly, authors have acknowledged the importance of ethnic culture, as well as gender and class, in explaining the dynamics of working-class women's activism. They have also underscored the necessity of linking the public—women's paid employment—with the private—their reproductive and domestic roles—if we are to understand the parameters of women workers' activism.[13] Influenced by postmodern theory, historians of the 1990s have shown increasing sophistication in their treatment of the issues surrounding the development of female working-class consciousness. They have demonstrated the dangers of generalization by documenting how widely female workers in the same work setting varied in their responses to unions and militant activities such as work stoppages and strikes. By exploring the complexities of accommodation and resistance, they have raised a number of issues that merit further examination.[14]

To begin with, recent studies remind us of the importance of interpreting terms such as 'militancy' and 'activism' in the broadest possible terms, for female workers demonstrated their resistance to the exploitative aspects of industrial capitalism in manifold ways. In short, it now seems clear that there was a continuum of resistance ranging from the individual and informal (leaving one's job for another job or for marriage) to the collective and formal (participating in a work stoppage or joining a union). Women workers engaged in a variety of strategies to counteract managerial power and control. These included helping other women complete their tasks, counteracting 'speed ups' by controlling the pace of work through mutual consent, and using humour or ridicule to counter the harsh discipline of over-zealous foremen. In short, working-class women used both informal and formal networks, in the workplace and outside it, to exercise active agency in their own right.

My own research on women in the Quebec cotton industry from 1880 to 1950 has provided an opportunity to grapple with many of the theoretical issues regarding female factory workers and their workplace behaviour. In this paper I will explore the dimensions of workplace activism by female operatives in this industry from 1880 to 1910. Most of the following analysis is based on a study of primary and secondary sources, although I also interviewed nineteen women, born between 1895 and 1904, who began working in cotton mills located in Valleyfield and Magog before the end of the First World War. My central focus is the manifestation of collective resistance (labour disputes and union activity) rather than individual acts of defiance, although there is evidence that these occurred on a daily basis.

THE ROLE OF GIRLS AND WOMEN IN THE QUEBEC COTTON INDUSTRY

By the end of the nineteenth century, manufacturers located in Quebec were producing more than half the value of Canadian cotton goods and employed over 55 per cent of the nation's cotton workers.[15] Like its counterparts in other industrializing nations, the Quebec industry relied heavily on the labour of women and children. Statistics contained in the Census of Canada for 1891 indicate that 335 girls under the age of sixteen and 1,741 women were employed in Quebec cotton factories; together, they accounted for 55 per cent of the industry's work force. No doubt the number of girls was underrepresented, since it is well documented that manufacturers illegally employed underage children. In 1911, female workers made up 52 per cent of the industry's work force, and 80 per cent of them were under twenty-five years of age. In fact, adolescent and young adult women would continue to constitute the majority of Quebec cotton workers until the 1920s,[16] and overwhelmingly they were of French-Canadian origin.

Female workers were employed in the carding, spooling, spinning and weaving rooms, and as cloth inspectors, folders, and packagers. As in other industries, there was a clear sexual division of labour that allocated the most physically demanding work (handling cotton bales, operating heavy machinery), the most skilled work (mule spinning, loom fixing), and all supervisory positions to men. Women's work ranged from unskilled (doffing and packaging) to what was considered semi-skilled (spooling, spinning, and weaving). Most female workers spent their days in exclusively or predominantly same-sex workrooms, although those in the carding and weaving divisions were more likely than others to work alongside male employees.

Among the distinguishing features of cotton manufacturing establishments were their large size and high degree of horizontal and vertical integration; for example, the Montreal Cottons Company, established in Valleyfield in 1874, had eight buildings housing 200,000 spindles and 5,000 looms, and employed some 3,000 workers by 1907.[17] In Magog, a small town of 3,500 in the Eastern Townships, Dominion Cotton Mills' factory, dye facility, and print works provided work for approximately 1,000 workers. Dominion Cotton also owned vast tracts of land— some 3,000 acres—in and around the town. The company operated other mills in St-Grégoire-de-Montmorency, just outside Quebec City, and in the Montreal neighbourhoods of Hochelaga and St-Henri, which employed thousands more workers. The creations of the most powerful anglophone capitalists in the province, these monopolistic companies exercised considerable economic, social, and political influence on the communities in which they were located.

The companies' extensive public relations campaigns to the contrary, working conditions within the industry were notoriously bad. In the carding and spinning rooms, floating cotton fibres filled the air the workers breathed and covered them in fine white dust; in the weave rooms, the incessant reverberation of hundreds of clacking looms damaged workers' hearing, and in many areas of the plant, extreme high heat and humidity were constant. Even after the introduction of provincial legislation, work for women and children officially commenced at 7 a.m. and stopped at 6 p.m., with one hour for rest and refreshment at noon. Thus the normal work week at the end of the century was 60 hours for women and children; but management could, and often did, extend it up to 72 hours by securing special permission from a provincial factory inspector. In 1910, the Quebec government amended its factory legislation to reduce the workweek for girls, women, and youths in textile mills to 58 hours per week, with a further reduction, to 55 hours, in 1912. Nevertheless, these groups of workers routinely worked longer hours. The factory doors were opened and the machines turned on each day well before the official 7 a.m. starting time; most workers showed up at least a half hour in advance to clean their machines so that they could maximize their meagre earnings by not taking time out of the regular work day for this unproductive work. Similarly, it is well documented that workers continued to run their machines during the legislated one-hour lunch break, in order to increase their output.

The preponderance of women and children was a clear indication that cotton manufacturing was a low-wage industry. Nearly all were paid by the piece, a situation that contributed significantly to the physical and nervous strain of the work. Discipline was strict, and numerous reports confirmed that foremen verbally and physically abused the women and children under their supervision. The practice of fining women and children was also widespread, as a way to enforce discipline and penalize workers for work considered substandard.

The cotton companies liked to boast that they were equal-pay employers: that women and men were paid at the same rates for the same work. On average, however, women's wages were consistently lower than men's. The difference was due primarily to the sexual division of labour, for women and men seldom performed precisely the same work. The most skilled and highly remunerated occupations in the mill, such as mule spinning and loom fixing, were exclusively male preserves. In 1908, for example, mule spinners at the Hochelaga mill earned a daily average of $1.55, whereas ring spinners, who were nearly all women, took home an average of 88 cents a day.[18]

Although wages for female workers in cotton mills were low, they compared quite favourably with those paid to women in other industries. Certainly they were well above the wages paid to domestic servants, by far the largest group of employed women during this period. Thus hundreds of women continued to flock to the cotton factories in search of jobs. Most of them came initially from rural areas, and were recruited along with other family members by agents acting on behalf of the companies. This practice of recruiting entire families from the countryside lasted well into the 1920s, as company recruiters travelled the *rangs* of less prosperous agricultural regions looking for families with several adolescent children who could help fill the company's large labour requirements. In the 1880s girls and boys as young as ten years of age found work in the mills. As a result of negative publicity generated about the exploitation of children, the government of Quebec prohibited the employment of boys under 12 and girls under 14 in industrial establishments as part of its 1885 factory legislation. However, the law did not really take effect until 1888, when the first factory inspectors were appointed, and even then the practice of child labour continued. In 1907 the government increased the starting age to 14 for boys as well, and gave factory inspectors the right to demand an affidavit to verify proof-of-age documents, which were frequently falsified. Despite these measures, however, the inspection mechanisms were inadequate, and some parents were still sending 12- and 13-year-olds into the mills well into the third decade of the twentieth century. The vast majority of single young workers continued to live with their families and hand over nearly all their wages to their parents: in short, they were an indispensable part of the family wage economy.

To summarize, female cotton workers appear to have closely resembled the female industrial work force of this period in most ways: they entered the industry at a young age, and few worked once they were married. The industry considered them unskilled or semi-skilled. They were usually recruited as part of a family labour force and were significant contributors to the family's income. At a time when French Canadians had a reputation for being docile workers,[19] and in a society that stressed patriarchal authority and female submission as cardinal virtues, these adolescent women should have been powerless pawns in monopoly capital's game. Yet, as the evidence amply demonstrates, many refused to play that role.

FEMALE WORKERS' ACTIVISM

From the beginning of cotton manufacturing's rise as a major industry in Quebec, women figured prominently in labour disputes and work stoppages. One of the earliest recorded such incidents occurred at the Hochelaga mill in April 1880, when women weavers abandoned their looms to protest increases in work hours and in the quantities of cloth they were expected to produce. An angry confrontation ensued between a group of 100 female and 50 male strikers, during which the mill manager was knocked down in the mud. His response was to call in three Montreal detectives to arrest his assailants. He also threatened to have arrested anyone who tried to prevent the resumption of work. Defying this show of force, the striking women engaged a lawyer to draw up a list of their grievances, rather than follow the advice of their parish priest and the mayor, who were counselling an immediate return to work. Each striker also signed an agreement to pay a $10 fine if she returned to work before an acceptable settlement was reached.[20]

Over the next two decades there were at least eight other labour disputes in the Quebec cotton industry; in at least six of these disputes, female workers played a key role, with weavers the most frequent initiators of work stoppages.[21] One of these disputes, at the Merchants manufacturing mill in St-Henri in October 1891, was reported in *La Presse* under the banner headline 'Grève des Femmes'. According to the newspaper's account, the walk-out began when 207 'tisseuses' (female weavers) left their looms to protest the replacement of five of their foremen by workers from the United States. They were particularly incensed that a foreman by the name of Duplessis, who had worked for seven years at the mill, had been let go without cause. In fact, the weavers were convinced that he had been fired for being too lenient, and for not imposing sufficient fines. They further resented the hiring of one of the English-speaking manager's nephews to oversee the inspection department, as they found his discipline too harsh. As one of the most experienced female weavers explained:

> For us, M. Duplessis was a good foreman. We had already gone on strike on 1 July because our bosses were demanding time they weren't entitled to. They wanted to make us catch up for the time we lost on the Corpus Christi holiday by having us work on Saturday from 6.30 a.m. to 6.15 p.m., without even a minute for lunch.[22]

In her mind, the real objective of the strike was to have an unpopular supervisor named Lanton removed from his post. She equated his arrival with the use of an inferior grade of cotton that greatly reduced the weavers' output and resulted in more breaks in the cloth, and hence more fines. Experienced weavers who previously had been able to earn up to $15 per week were now claiming that their wages were reduced to $6.50 even though the work had doubled. For apprentices the situation was even more serious: reportedly, nearly all found their wages eaten up by fines.

Initially, the weavers carried their protests into the main streets of St-Henri, insisting that they would return to work only when their foremen were reinstated. Obviously unaware of female workers' key role in work stoppages in the previous decade, the reporter from La Presse offered the following commentary:

> This is the first time we have had occasion to report a strike by women. Women being more stubborn than men, it remains to be seen whether they will be able to keep a strike going longer than the bearded sex can.[23]

In fact, the weavers did attract others to their cause, including the twenty men who had continued working on the first day. One estimate set the number of participants in the four-day strike at 400, about three-quarters of them women, while another report referred to 800 strikers.[24] In response, the company told city officials, whom they considered too sympathetic to the strikers, that they would move the mill out of St-Henri. According to the ongoing coverage in La Presse, by the third day the female weavers had set aside their street demonstrations in favour of having 'les hommes'—the mayor and municipal councillors—resolve the dispute. On the evening of 8 October the strikers aired their grievances at a huge public meeting at the municipal hall. After considerable discussion, they decided to submit their demands in writing and have them presented to the company by a delegation consisting of the mayor, the parish priest, and a village doctor. Their principal demands included a reduction in the fine system, restriction of the work week to sixty hours, and amnesty for all the strikers. Surprisingly, the rehiring of M. Duplessis was not included in the list.

Reporters from both the Montreal Star and La Presse recorded in some detail the next morning's meeting of the strikers' representatives with the company officials. The company denied that it routinely demanded more than sixty hours a week, and cited evidence from the labour commission indicating that the Merchants mill had the lowest level of fines of all the province's mills. It also argued that the return on investment for its shareholders had never exceeded 1.5 per cent over eleven years of operation. The result of this conversation was that the curé went to the balcony of the factory to address the strikers assembled below. Promising that they would be treated justly, he advised them to return to work immediately. According to the newspaper report, the strikers accepted this recommendation and went back to work that afternoon. Thus the high-profile 'women's strike' came to an abrupt and inconclusive end.

Within two years, however, approximately 50 women at Dominion Cotton's Ste-Anne mill led a remarkably similar strike. Once again the ostensible cause was the replacement of a French-Canadian overseer by an English-speaking one from

Cornwall, Ontario. The protesters alleged that the new supervisor was excessively rigorous and unjust in his dealings, and imposed too many fines. As in the 1880 dispute, the women engaged a local lawyer to draw up a list of their grievances to present to company officials.[25]

Additional examples of female militancy occurred in 1898 and 1899, apparently with more favourable results for the workers. In the former instance, a group of weavers at Montreal Cottons in Valleyfield struck to protest management's decision to impose a half-day of overtime work. The company backed down and accepted the weavers' commitment to increase production during the regular hours.[26] In May 1899, seven or eight young women precipitated another work stoppage at the St-Henri mill, an action that cost them their jobs. However, the other 'girls' rallied to their cause and walked off the job, refusing to return unless the company awarded them a 10 per cent wage increase and reinstated all the strikers. No doubt remembering what had happened to the 'women's strike' in 1880, the strikers declared that they had no need of outside intervention; they were quite capable of handling their own difficulties. They appear to have been right, for the dispute was quickly settled when the two parties agreed on a 6.5 per cent increase.[27]

This tradition of workplace protests by female operatives extended well into the first decade of the twentieth century, the most dramatic illustration being the 'grève des jeunes filles' at Montreal Cottons in Valleyfield. The dispute initially erupted in early February with the decision by superintendent Louis Simpson to hire additional female 'learners' to work in the spooling department of a new mill, thereby reducing the amount of work available for experienced spoolers. The latter, 37 in number, walked off the job to protest this decision as well as the introduction of new machinery that they alleged had lowered their earnings to the point where they were unable to survive on their wages. The most notable aspects of this strike were the youth of the workers, their resolve, and the impact they had on other workers: later all 2,500 employees of the mill walked off the job. In response to this pressure, Simpson promised that the management would study the spoolers' grievances and institute satisfactory increases where justified.[28]

The peace was short-lived, however, for by the end of February the spoolers had walked out again to demonstrate their dissatisfaction with Simpson's proposed wage increases. One of the leaders, Florina Lalonde, was only 14, but had already worked in the Valleyfield mills for three years. Referring to Simpson's offer to provide an increase of two cents for every 100 pounds of cotton worked, she defiantly declared, 'We have refused that and we won't work under those conditions; none of the spoolers will, and we will be hard on anyone who has the nerve to turn up for work at those rates.' She and her companions declared that they would return to work only if they received an increase of ten cents per 100 pounds of yarn spooled. In response to their protest, Simpson closed the mills and locked out more than 2,000 other employees.

Simpson also sent a detailed account of his problems with the spoolers to Mgr Emard, the bishop of Valleyfield, in which he complained that the young women had been engaging in a work slowdown after returning to work at the beginning of the month. He asked Emard to use his influence to get the spoolers 'to do their best'.[29] He also reported on his confrontation with some of the spoolers when they walked off the job for the second time:

> I reached the mill office at 8:30 a.m., having already learned that there was trouble. I found the office full of girls. In the outside office were the four bad girls who have raised the whole trouble, and I was told that upon the person of Bertha Lecompte were found two bludgeons, which had evidently been cut of green wood the day before, and which she had brought into the mill in order to use to assault somebody.[30]

Simpson was incensed that the local chief of police refused to imprison the girls, but the police did load the leaders into a police van and drive them home.

Although the second walkout was roundly condemned by a few local craft union leaders and some members of the town's professional and commercial classes as irresponsible, other workers soon demonstrated their support by walking off the job. The strike/lockout lasted two weeks, but in the end the spoolers won a general increase of 10 per cent, and for some types of work the increase amounted to as much as 35 per cent.[31]

From 1900 to 1908 there were some forty industrial disputes in Quebec's cotton mills, half of which occurred between 1906 and 1908.[32] In 17 instances, groups of employees composed exclusively or mostly of men initiated work stoppages; in eight cases, classes of operatives composed entirely or mostly of women did so; and in 15 cases it is not possible to determine whether the strike began among male or female workers. Even when groups of male workers such as the mule spinners took the lead in work stoppages, they increasingly sought the support of female operatives in the carding and spinning departments. As ring spinning replaced mule spinning as the most common method, women workers' support was essential to bring production to a halt, since they constituted the vast majority of ring spinners. The large number of conflicts, the number of lost work days, and the resulting economic impact reflected the increased militancy of cotton workers of both sexes, a militancy that new industrial unions in the province sought to exploit and control. In fact, it has been suggested that the many strikes occurring from 1880 on, most of them involving large numbers of women, provided a powerful model for subsequent union organization and tactics.[33]

The first group to attempt to organize cotton workers on a large scale was the Chevaliers du Travail (Knights of Labor). In a letter addressed to Mgr Emard in March 1899, Louis Simpson complained that the Knights were once again attempting to set up locals in Valleyfield, as they had on three or four occasions in the previous decade. That they had not been successful, to date, Simpson credited to Emard's clergy. However, there is some evidence that the Knights did support the spoolers during their difficulties with the company less than a year later, in

February 1900. In August 1900 they succeeded in organizing nearly the entire work-force at the Montmorency Falls cotton mill, and they played the lead role in the ensuing strike over union recognition, which dragged on for some two months.[34]

As various studies of the Knights have demonstrated, this organization was unique in the North American union movement at the time, for it came to accept most industrial workers into its ranks, regardless of their skill level, race, or sex.[35] In fact, the Knights represented an appropriate form of unionism for the large cotton-mill work force, composed as it was of workers of both sexes and multiple skill levels. For a number of reasons that have been elaborated elsewhere,[36] the Knights were unable to realize their potential; nonetheless, they created a model of industrial unionism that other labour organizations working in the cotton indus-try later emulated.

The first such organization was initiated by Wilfrid Paquette in the summer of 1906. In response to a series of successful walkouts orchestrated by his movement in Montreal and Magog, over 3,000 textile workers had joined the new organiza-tion by the fall of 1906. Like the Knights, it actively recruited workers of both sexes and various skill levels. Officially named the Fédération des Ouvriers du Textile du Canada (FOTC) after 1 September 1906, it included some locals that restricted their membership to skilled male workers such as mule spinners, while in Valleyfield girls and women had their own local, 'Les Dames et Demoiselles de Valleyfield'; for the most part, however, female workers joined the same locals as men. In commu-nities where there were significant numbers of English-speaking workers, they too had their own locals.

According to a description of the 19 locals existing in 1907, women held execu-tive positions in five, in addition to those in the separate women's local in Valleyfield. In the mixed locals, however, the position was always that of vice-pres-ident and, unlike other executive positions, it was likely more honorific than instrumental.[37] Nonetheless, significant numbers of women showed up for union rallies, and on occasion they assumed prominent roles in labour disputes involv-ing the FOTC. In May 1909, for example, a female former employee of the Magog mill reportedly delivered an eloquent address to a large public assembly during the strike there.[38] During the 1906 strike at the Hochelaga mill, female workers turned up in large numbers at the local meeting hall, applauded their union leaders, and joined their union brothers in songs. Mlle Imelda Mary, identified as the 'live-wire' of the Ste-Anne mill, kept the audience entertained with her seemingly inex-haustible repertoire of songs.[39]

The numbers of female delegates at FOTC conventions, and the roles they played in these meetings, seem to have varied from minimal to substantial. At the December 1906 convention, participants voted unanimously to send a five-person delegation to Ottawa to impress upon the Minister of Finance, W.S. Fielding, the necessity to raise the tariff to protect the cotton industry: two of the delegates chosen to represent workers at mills in Montreal were Christine Cadet and Louise Rhéaume. Two other women were appointed to local committees established to make recommendations on salary scales.[40] At the third general convention of the FOTC, held in Valleyfield the following spring, women made up one-third of the delegates from the Montreal district, and they were seated on the stage along with the male union leaders. However, since there appear to have been no female delegates from the other four districts (Magog, Valleyfield, Montmorency, and Chambly), those from Montreal accounted for approximately one-quarter of all official representatives. Along with their union brothers, they unanimously approved a resolution to reduce the workweek for women and children to 55 hours. Many authors have argued that organized labour's campaign to restrict the hours of work performed by women, while making no demands for similar limits on men's hours, was motivated more by self-interest than by chivalry or humanitarianism. By restricting the time of day and number of hours that women could work, they made female workers less competitive.[41] Interestingly, earlier speeches given by FOTC president Wilfrid Paquette referred to the need to reduce the work week generally in the textile industry. At the convention where the resolution was approved limiting the hours explicitly for children and women, he declared his intention to fight for the 55-hour workweek 'pour tous'.[42] Given the excessively long hours prevalent in the industry and a sexual division of labour that meant there was little direct competition for jobs between men and women, it is not surprising that many women workers would have endorsed the resolution.

Like their union brothers, women who joined the FOTC could find themselves punished by mill management for their organizational involvement or for speaking out. According to one account, a widow, with a child, who had worked at a particular mill for six years was discharged for being a member of the executive committee of her local union.[43] Another Valleyfield worker, 16-year-old Delima Viau, testified before a royal commission in 1908 that she had been a member of the union from the time she entered the mill at 13. The number of spinning frames assigned to her was reduced from two to one following the May 1908 strike at the Valleyfield mill, and she was informed that this drastic blow to her livelihood was due to the fact that she agreed to appear before the commission.[44]

The opportunity for women to advance the cause of female workers through involvement in the FOTC was short-lived. The meteoric rise of the FOTC was paralleled by an equally rapid decline. Union solidarity evaporated as a result of internal divisions arising from charges of fiscal mismanagement and authoritarianism on Paquette's part. Some dissidents formed a rival organization, the Union Amicale, which gained support in the spring of 1908 when it opposed striking to protest a general 10 per cent wage reduction throughout the industry. The strike, intended to demonstrate the FOTC's opposition to the wage reduction, involved some 6,000 workers and succeeded in closing down the province's major mills for a month in most cases, but ultimately it failed. Given the depressed state of the cotton trade, mounting unemployment, bitter internal divisions, and a dramatic increase in union dues imposed by the FOTC in an effort to recoup its losses, union membership plummeted. Following another unsuccessful strike led by the FOTC in

May 1909, the organization had virtually disappeared by the end of that year.[45]

Union or no union, women workers, especially those with ability and experience, continued to exert some control over their working conditions. When they became fed up with their working conditions, or felt the need for a holiday, they might simply leave their machines for a day or so, counting on the foreman to take them back in order to keep up production. A detailed report submitted in August 1907 by the foreman of the card room at one of the Montreal Cotton Company mills contains several examples of individual and collective job actions that female workers took. Some, such as Orise Leduc, Yvonne Monpetit, and Antoinette Seven, left their jobs without permission and were seen shopping or attending local fairs. Others refused to run certain machines or certain types of yarns, and in one case, Pamelia Laberge persuaded all the female operatives in her workroom to stop work and threaten to walk out unless a particular worker was assigned to a specific set of machines. In several instances, the foreman noted that although he sent uncooperative workers home, he took them back the next day.[46]

For this period, oral history is of limited use in confirming the evidence about female workers' activism that can be pieced together from written sources. Few women who worked in Quebec's cotton mills prior to 1914 are still alive, and their memories are not always reliable. Nonetheless, four interviews I was able to conduct with workers from this era suggest that female workers used both individual and collective methods to exercise some control in the workplace. As 'Véronique', a twisting-machine operator in Valleyfield from 1908 until 1918, succinctly described the situation: 'we worked, but not too hard. The employees weren't dedicated, since they could have worked harder than they did.'[47] 'Agathe', who began working in the Magog print works in 1909, recalled playing an April Fool's trick on the straw boss, and said she and her work mates always kept an eye on the boss when they were not busy, so that he would not find them idle and increase their work load.[48]

Conclusion

The foregoing outline of various types of workplace solidarity and job action demonstrated by female operatives in the Quebec cotton industry between 1880 and 1910 clearly reveals their agency in combatting the exploitation they encountered, and challenges generalizations about the 'passivity' of female industrial workers in the late nineteenth and early twentieth centuries. Florina Lalonde, Bertha Lecompte, Orise Leduc, Delima Viau, and countless other cotton workers would certainly have had difficulty recognizing themselves in the following description of women workers in Quebec: 'The women were afraid to speak, and they were afraid to protest. They were afraid of drawing attention to themselves as they were made to feel that their presence in factories was somehow illegitimate.'[49] On the other hand, it would be equally inaccurate to suggest that all female cotton workers engaged in active resistance to their working conditions.

Nor should we assume that the degree of militancy manifested by the cotton workers was replicated in other industrial settings. In fact, in his comparative study of women workers in the Quebec shoe and boot industry with those employed in the cotton industry, Jacques Ferland has shown that it was not. In his estimation, the numbers of workers facing the same working conditions, and the extent to which their interests converged, directly affected their ability to resist the exploitative aspects of industrial work. The militancy of the young women in the cotton industry, he argues, can be attributed to the large numbers of them doing the same job, facing the same conditions and the same problems; in the boot and shoe industry, the sexual division of labour and the highly segmented work process denied women workers, who were largely confined to the more marginal jobs, the same opportunities to express solidarity.[50] This argument is persuasive, although other factors must also be taken into account. While it is true that there were hundreds of women toiling in the cotton mills, and that those working in the same departments might appear to have faced the same working conditions, in fact they did not. The machines used for carding, rooms, spinning, spooling, and weaving varied widely, as did the types of cotton yarns to be worked. As a result, there was a byzantine array of wage rates for what was ostensibly the same work. One of the ongoing grievances of workers was their lack of knowledge about actual wage rates and how they were set. An individual piece-worker's wage-earning capacity was also directly affected by the foreman's decisions to assign superior or inferior materials and machines, or to impose fines. Indeed, it was frequently who their direct supervisors were, and how they behaved, that sparked protests among female workers. If, as some have suggested, strict discipline and the fining system may have served to dampen militant activity, it could also incite women to take collective action. What gave them leverage during this period was their central role in the manufacturing process, and their ability to bring production to a halt when they refused to work.

Clearly the youth of the female work force in this industry did not preclude militant action. As Jacques Rouillard has also noted, at the turn of the century, strikes in the mills were mostly the work of young people.[51] Before the First World War, the concept of adolescence was not deeply rooted in working-class consciousness, and the family wage was still the *modus vivendi* for most working-class families, especially in Quebec. Financial necessity dictated that they send their teenagers into the factory in order to make ends meet. As I have argued elsewhere,[52] the life cycle of women cotton workers in the pre-1914 period was characterized by early entry into the workplace (often at 12 to 14 years of age) and a fairly late age at first marriage (normally around 23).[53] These circumstances meant that many had at least a decade of working experience, and the importance of their economic contributions to their families reinforced their perception of themselves as workers. The women I interviewed who began working before 1918 consistently expressed great pride in their roles as wage-earners. In this they differed significantly from teenagers of later decades, who had shorter connections with the workplace because they entered industry at a later age and married earlier.

The fact that young women lived in homes where there was usually more than one wage-earner made it possible for them to engage in occasional job actions that they could not have afforded to consider if they had been living on their own. Their family and kin networks in the workplace could provide solidarity and support in the case of labour disputes. In addition, the class, religious, and ethnic dynamics peculiar to the cotton industry at this time—exceedingly wealthy and powerful, non-resident, Protestant, anglophone company officials versus many of the poorest, least powerful francophone Catholic workers—created a context in which mill workers could usually count on considerable local support when they took job action.

In short, it was the complex interplay of several factors, including the nature of the work they performed, their work environment, their individual and family characteristics, and the community support they received, that enabled female workers in the Quebec cotton industry to assume an active role in combatting the exploitative features of industrial capitalism prior to the First World War.

NOTES

1. Greg Kealey, ed., *Canada Investigates Industrialism* (Toronto, 1973), 134–5.
2. H.A. Spencer, 'Minimum Wage Laws for Women', *Canadian Congress Journal* 4 (March 1925), 38.
3. Quoted in Margaret McCallum, 'Keeping Women in their Place: The Minimum Wage in Canada 1910–25', *Labour/Le Travail* 17 (Spring 1986), 37.
4. Jean Thomson Scott, *The Conditions of Female Labour in Ontario* (Toronto, 1892), 27.
5. Joan Sangster, *Earning Respect: The Lives of Working Women in Small-Town Ontario, 1920–1960* (Toronto, 1995), 185.
6. Joy Parr, *The Gender of Breadwinners: Women, Men and Change in Two Industrial Towns, 1880–1950* (Toronto, 1995), 100.
7. Wayne Roberts, *Honest Womanhood: Feminism, Feminity and Class Consciousness among Toronto Working Women, 1896–1914* (Toronto, 1977), 49; Patricia Hilden, 'Class and Gender: Conflicting Components of Women's Behaviour in the Textile Mills of Lille, Roubaix and Tourcoing, 1880–1914', *Historical Journal* 27, 2 (1984), 369.
8. For an interesting discussion of working-class women, religion, and the social construction of womanhood, see Lynne Marks, 'The "Hallelujah Lasses": Working-Class Women in the Salvation Army in English Canada, 1882–92', in *Gender Conflicts: New Essays in Women's History*, ed. Franca Iacovetta and Mariana Valverde (Toronto, 1993), 93–8.
9. Susan Trofimenkoff, 'One Hundred and Two Muffled Voices: Canada's Industrial Women in the 1880s', *Atlantis* 3, 1 (Fall 1977); reprinted in *Rethinking Canada: The Promise of Women's History*, 1st edn, ed. Veronica Strong-Boag and Anita Clair Fellman (Toronto, 1986), 82–94.
10. Ruth Frager, 'No Proper Deal: Women Workers and the Canadian Labour Movement, 1870–1940', in *Union Sisters: Women in the Labour Movement*, ed. Linda Briskin and Lynda Yanz (Toronto, 1983), 56.

11. Mercedes Steedman, *Angels of the Workplace: Women and the Construction of Gender Relations in the Canadian Clothing Industry, 1890–1940* (Toronto, 1997), 254–5.

12. See, for example, Evelyn Dumas, 'The Shmata Strikes', in *The Bitter Thirties in Quebec*, ed. and trans. Arnold Bennett (Montreal, 1975), 43–69; Jacques Ferland, '"In Search of the Unbound Prometheia": A Comparative Study of Women's Activism in Two Quebec Industries, 1869–1908', *Labour/Le Travail* 24 (Fall 1989), 11–44; Ruth Frager, 'Sewing Solidarity: The Eaton's Strike of 1912', *Canadian Woman Studies/Cahiers de la femme* 7, 3 (Fall) 1986, 96–8; Mary Horodyski, 'Women and the Winnipeg General Strike of 1919', *Manitoba History* 11 (Spring 1986), 28–37; Linda Kealey, 'No Special Protection, No Sympathy: Women's Activism in the Canadian Labour Revolt in 1919', in *Class, Community and the Labour Market: Wales and Canada, 1850–1930*, ed. Deain R. Hopkin and Gregory S. Kealey (St John's, 1989), 134–59; Michelle Lapointe, 'Le syndicat catholique des allumetières de Hull, 1919–1924', *Revue d'histoire de l'Amérique française* 32, 4 (March) 1979, 603–28; Catherine McLeod, 'Women in Production: The Toronto Dressmaker's Strike of 1931', in *Women at Work, Ontario 1850–1930*, ed. Janice Acton et al. (Toronto, 1974) 309–29; Star Rosenthal, 'Union Maids: Organized Women Workers in Vancouver, 1900–1915', *BC Studies* 41 (1979), 36–55.

13. Bettina Bradbury, *Working Families: Age, Gender, and Daily Survival in Industrializing Montreal* (Toronto, 1993); Ruth Frager, *Sweatshop Strife: Class, Ethnicity and Gender in the Jewish Labour Movement of Toronto, 1900–1939* (Toronto, 1992); Franca Iacovetta, *Such Hard-Working People: Italian Immigrants in Postwar Toronto* (Kingston and Montreal, 1992); Parr, *The Gender of Breadwinners*; Sangster, *Earning Respect.*

14. See especially Parr, *Gender of Breadwinners*, and Sangster, *Earning Respect.*

15. *Census of Canada*, 1901, vol. 3, 34–5, 86–7.

16. *Census of Canada*, 1891, vol. 3, Table I, 120; 1911, vol. 3, Table V, 216–17.

17. *Le Progrès de Valleyfield* (10 Oct. 1907), 3.

18. National Archives of Canada, Royal Commission respecting industrial disputes in the Cotton Factories of the Province of Quebec (1908), Table of Wages of Employees of Cotton Mills in the Province of Quebec from Information supplied by the Dominion Textile Company.

19. Jacques Rouillard, *Les Travailleurs du coton au Québec 1900–1915* (Montreal, 1974), 80–3.

20. Jacques Ferland, 'When the Cotton Mills "Girls" Struck for the First Time: A Study of Female Militancy in the Cotton and Shoe Factories of Quebec (1880–1910)', paper presented to the Canadian Historical Association, Winnipeg, 1986, 18–19.

21. Jacques Ferland, 'Syndicalisme "parcellaire" et syndicalisme "collectif": Une interprétation socio-technique des conflits dans deux industries québécoises, 1880–1914', *Labour/Le Travail* 19 (Spring 1987), 83.

22. 'M. Duplessis était pour nous un bon contremaître. Nous nous sommes déjà mises en grève le 1er juillet parce que nos patrons nous chargeaient un temps auquel ils n'avaient pas droit. Nos patrons ont voulu nous faire gagner le temps que nous avions perdu le jour de la Fête-Dieu en nous faisant travailler le samedi de 6.30 a.m. à 6.15 p.m., sans une minute pour le repas de midi'; *La Presse* (7 Oct. 1891).

23. 'C'est la première fois que nous avons l'occasion d'enregistrer une grève des femmes. Les femmes étant plus entêtées que les hommes, il reste à savoir si elles peuvent faire durer une grève plus longtemps que le sexe barbu'; *La Presse* (6 Oct. 1891).

24. The first number is reported in *La Presse* on 6 Oct.; the second in the same newspaper's account on 8 Oct. This discrepancy may be the result of additional workers' walking off the job by the third day of the strike.

25. *La Presse* (27 Sept. 1893).

26. *Canadian Journal of Fabrics* (August 1898), 247.

27. *La Presse* (9–10 May 1899).

28. *La Presse* (2–3 Feb. 1900).

29. Archives du diocèse de Valleyfield, Simpson-Emard Correspondence, Simpson to Emard, 10 Feb. 1900.

30. Ibid., Simpson to Emard, 24 Feb. 1900, 2–3.

31. *La Presse* (2 March 1900).

32. National Archives of Canada, RG 27, vol. 67, 'Table of Strikes and Lockouts in the Cotton Industry in the Province of Quebec from February 1900 to June 1908, inclusive'.

33. Ferland, 'When the Cotton Mill "Girls" Struck . . .', 14.

34. *Canadian Journal of Fabrics* (October 1900), 305–6.

35. See Douglas R. Kennedy, *The Knights of Labor in Canada* (London, Ont., 1930); Gregory S. Kealey and Bryan D. Palmer, *Dreaming of What Might Be: The Knights of Labor in Ontario, 1880–1900* (New York, 1982). The Knights' acceptance of Black workers did not extend to Asian workers.

36. Rouillard, *Les Travailleurs du coton*, 85–6.

37. *Le Fileur* 8 (June 1907), 75–86.

38. *La Presse* (5 May 1909).

39. *La Presse* (4 May 1906).

40. *Le Fileur* 3 (December 1906), 6–7.

41. See, for example, Alice Klein and Wayne Roberts, 'Besieged Innocence: The "Problem" and Problems of Working Women—Toronto, 1896–1914', in *Women at Work, Ontario*, 219–22; Veronica Strong-Boag, 'Working Women and the State: The Case of Canada, 1889–1945', *Atlantis* 6, 2 (1981), 1–9; Jane Ursel, *Private Lives, Public Policy: 100 Years of State Intervention in the Family* (Toronto, 1992), especially 77–100.

42. *Le Fileur* 7 (April 1907), 5.

43. Ibid., 4.

44. *La Presse* (8 Aug. 1908).

45. Rouillard, *Les Travailleurs du coton*, 99–103.

46. Archives du diocèse de Valleyfield, Simpson-Emard correspondence, 'Reports of Help in the cardroom, Montreal mill at Valleyfield'. The incidents reported in this document covered the period from 7 Aug. 1907 to 22 April 1908.

47. Valleyfield worker, 1908–18.

48. Magog worker, 1910–17.

49. The Clio Collective, *Quebec Women: A History* (Toronto, 1987), 163–4.

50. Ferland, 'When the Cotton Mills "Girls" Struck . . .', 22.

51. Rouillard, *Les Travailleurs du coton*, 82.

52. Gail Cuthbert Brandt, '"Weaving It Together": Life Cycle and the Industrial Experience of Female Cotton Workers in Quebec, 1910–1950', in *The Neglected Majority: Essays in Canadian Women's History*, vol. 2, ed. Alison Prentice and Susan Mann Trofimenkoff (Toronto, 1985), especially 163–6.

53. Of fourteen women I interviewed who were born between 1895 and 1904, nine began working in Valleyfield or Magog mills at age 14 or younger. Among those who married, the mean age at marriage was 22.9 years.

Standards versus Sisterhood

Dr Murray, President Kim, and the Introduction of Medical Education at Ewha Womans University, Seoul, 1947–1950

Ruth Compton Brouwer

This paper examines a brief missionary moment: the period in the late 1940s when veteran Canadian medical missionary Florence Murray (1894–1975) served under the administration of President Helen Kim (1899–1970) in the new medical department at Ewha Womans University in Seoul, now the largest women's university in the world. A one-line summary of this moment—a Westerner and an Asian woman disagreeing over institutional development in a newly decolonized country—might well lead readers to expect an orthodox postcolonial analysis in what follows, an analysis positing a lingering Western imperialist agenda challenged by a feisty, newly expressible nationalism. Although there are elements in the situation I describe that might lend themselves to such an interpretation, it does not seem to me to be the most useful one, and not only because the colonial power in this case was Japan rather than a Western nation.[1] My argument does take race consciousness and the colonial legacy into account, of course; but they are part of the context rather than the dominant explanatory themes in my account of the reasons why Dr Murray and President Kim took distinctive approaches to medical education at Ewha in the difficult post-war years when Korea was newly free of Japanese colonial rule. While my title—standards versus sisterhood—is itself an oversimplification, it nonetheless serves as a useful shorthand for the essential differences in educational values and goals that divided Murray and Kim and that lay behind the former's early departure from Ewha.

In a paper dealing with an earlier phase of Murray's long missionary career (it lasted until 1969), I suggested that her strong commitment to Western standards of professional medicine led her to reject the 'separate spheres' approach to missionary service favoured by an earlier generation of women missionaries.[2] The present paper argues that her dissatisfaction with Ewha in the immediate post-war period should also be understood as a product of that commitment. As president of Ewha, Kim maintained the segregated approach to Western-style female schooling introduced to Korea by the American Methodist women missionaries who had been her mentors, in the process carving out a role as Korea's foremost advocate of women's rights. Murray, by contrast, epitomized the modernizing and increasingly ecumenical trend in mainline Protestants' mission-sponsored institutional work, a trend that favoured a few strong and efficient institutions over numerous small facilities with distinct denominational and gender concerns. Although her professional responsibilities were more narrowly focused than Kim's, and her profile decidedly lower,[3] Murray was no less concerned than Kim with the need for sufficient influence and material resources to pursue her agenda. Finding these in short supply at Ewha, she left for the somewhat more hopeful professional environment of a larger—and largely male—medical institution.

Given my own cultural background and the unevenness of my documentary sources, I obviously cannot do equal justice to the concerns of these two women; the ordering of names in my title is meant to signal that fact. Nevertheless, with access to relevant secondary sources and some of Kim's writing, as well as contacts with Koreans who knew Kim personally or are currently studying her career,[4] it does seem feasible to try to take both women's perspectives into account. The paper will provide biographical background on Murray and Kim before reconstructing Murray's brief Ewha interval and presenting a context for it.

1 FLORENCE MURRAY

One of the six high-achieving children of a Presbyterian minister and his wife, a former schoolteacher, Florence Jessie Murray was raised in rural and village manses in Nova Scotia and Prince Edward Island before enrolling in Dalhousie University's medical school in the autumn of 1914.[5] Her years at Dalhousie and two subsequent years of North American practice coincided with a period when new standards of professionalism were being emphasized in medical colleges in the United States and Canada, standards associated with a scientific approach, laboratory-based research, and extensive clinical experience involving strict attention to antiseptic and aseptic techniques. In conjunction with Murray's stereotypically Presbyterian upbringing, which emphasized hard work and instilled a strong sense of duty, the nature of her medical training ensured that she went to Korea with high expectations about her own performance as a medical missionary, as well as high expectations of those whom she would mentor.

Inevitably, her first term (1921–7) in the Presbyterian Church in Canada's mission in northern Korea[6] was a difficult one as, arriving with predetermined conceptions of Asian peoples, she tried to introduce scientific Western medicine in a premodern society and within a mission that had previously viewed medical work mainly as an aid to securing conversions. In the years that followed, however, as she continued in the role of superintendent in the mission's general hospital in Hamhung, Murray became a more adaptable and effective administrator. Though her hospital was not associated with a medical college, she trained interns and other staff in the methods and standards of work that she valued. Having learned what was *not* possible in the short term, she took great satisfaction in small, incremental gains in the quality and growth of personnel and facilities. She clearly thrived on the leadership roles she exercised within and beyond the mission hospital, devel-

Dr Florence Murray and Dr Lee with newborn babies delivered at Hamhung, northern Korea, 1941. From "Medical Work in the Canadian Mission" by Florence J. Murray, M.D., The Korea Mission Field, May 1941. (Courtesy of Archives of The United Church of Canada/Victoria University, Toronto.)

oping what one relative remembered as 'the habit of command'.[7] Yet she also developed a rapport with northern Koreans within and beyond the mission community, and the strength of that rapport would be evident in moving reunions with Hamhung refugees in Seoul in the post-war years.[8] By the time she was sent back to Canada in June 1942, as part of an exchange of wartime internees between the Canadian and Japanese governments, Murray had overseen significant advances in the quality and scope of the mission's medical work. The hospital that she had taken over as a ramshackle ten-bed affair now had one hundred beds, a school of nursing, and some specialized medical departments.[9] In Canada from 1942 to 1947 she looked forward impatiently to the time when she could return to her field, and with that goal in view obtained further experience and additional training in the treatment of tuberculosis, Korea's biggest public-health problem. But with the north under communist control at the end of the war, further missionary work there was impossible. Hence Murray was asked by the Woman's Missionary Society of the United Church of Canada to undertake new work at Ewha in Seoul, in compliance with an urgent request for her services from Helen Kim.[10]

II HELEN KIM

Helen Kim was part of a family of first-generation Christians, baptized in 1905 by an American Methodist missionary. In adolescence she experienced a 'spiritual awakening' to which she attributed her subsequent commitment to 'humble service to the womanhood of my country'. Encouraged by their mother, Helen and her sisters attended school. Despite some opposition from her father, who wanted her to marry, Helen went on to college-level studies at Ewha, graduating in 1918.[11]

Established by an American Methodist missionary in 1886 as the first Western-style school for girls in Korea, Ewha had added a college department in 1910. With the aid of mentors there, Kim went to the United States for further study, obtaining a Ph.D. from Teacher's College, Columbia University, in 1931. It was the first doctoral degree awarded anywhere to a Korean woman. She began teaching at Ewha in 1918, becoming the first Korean president of the college in 1939 when its American staff prepared for withdrawal in the face of rising tensions between the United States and Japan. During the Second World War, despite pressure from local Japanese officials to take over all of its facilities for military purposes, Kim managed to maintain a tenuous existence for Ewha as a college, and in 1945 she presided over its institutional advance to university status.[12]

As well as serving as Ewha's president until 1961, Kim represented her country nationally and internationally on numerous government, volunteer, and religious bodies, becoming by far the best-known Korean woman abroad. Following her retirement as Ewha's president, she was executive-secretary of a year-long national evangelistic campaign. She also continued to collect honorary degrees at home and abroad, and to participate in such international organizations as UNESCO, the

Dr Helen Kim, the first Korean president of Ewha, Seoul. (Used by permission, Ewha Womans University.)

Red Cross, and the International Missionary Council.[13] Though her autobiography, *Grace Sufficient*, presents these achievements as signs of God's grace and guidance, it is clear that Kim was an unusually able and ambitious woman as well as a committed Christian. Notwithstanding her numerous other involvements, it is also clear that Ewha was her priority and her passion.

III EDUCATIONAL MODERNIZERS WITH DIFFERENT AGENDAS

With the end of the Second World War and thirty-five years of Japanese colonial rule, Kim undertook to rebuild and enlarge Ewha's skeletal facilities and staff. In 1945, with 900 students enrolled in its three colleges (Liberal Arts and Sciences, Music and Fine Arts, and Healing Arts), she looked to North America, particularly to the New-York-based Ewha Cooperating Board (ECB), for assistance. Made up mainly of American Methodists, the Board had also had United Church of Canada representation since 1929. During a trip to North America in 1946, Kim asked the United Church WMS whether three of its Korea missionaries could return to her country as Ewha faculty members. The request, reported and processed through the ECB, identified Florence Murray as the priority appointment for transport purposes as soon as the US military began permitting Western women to travel to Korea.[14] This priority reflected the fact that Kim had already made a commitment to begin training doctors at Ewha, with the first class of medical students due to enter in 1947 (pre-medical and nursing classes had already begun), and also the fact that more than half of the 173 students admitted to begin studying at Ewha as a university in 1947 had applied for pre-medical and pharmacy programs.[15]

Despite strong misgivings, Murray accepted the new appointment. In preparation, she visited nine small medical colleges in the United States and Canada and studied plans for the proposed new medical school at the University of British Columbia. She also investigated, or recommended to the ECB, initiatives for obtaining medical supplies from war surplus, the Red Cross, and the Rockefeller Foundation.[16] Arriving in Seoul in July 1947 with the two other Canadian appointees, the Revd Elda Daniels and nurse Ada Sandell, she quickly discovered that, as she had feared, war-ravaged Ewha was poorly positioned to begin medical training. She also learned—and this she had not anticipated—that she was to be only the *associate* dean in the medical department and the *assistant* superintendent in the teaching hospital, working in both cases with Korean male doctors who gave priority to their private practices.[17] As for the hospital itself, formerly the American Methodist mission's East Gate Maternity Hospital, it was located several miles from the Ewha campus, and its current ownership was before the courts.[18] In an early letter home she assured her family that she and Ada Sandell had been warmly welcomed by the hospital's superintendent and staff, but the physical conditions she went on to describe were dismal:

> The hospital is smaller than the one we had in Hamheung and not very well planned. The roofs all leak and the plaster is coming down in places. . . . The water does not go above the first floor and the operating room is on the second. The

sterilizer does not work. The lab was locked and no one knew where the key was to be found so I judge that department is not much used. . . . They have an x-ray apparatus which has never been set up and there does not seem to be a place for it, nor is there a room for an office for the supt. of nurses.[19]

Murray was even more dismayed by prospects in the 'medical school',[20] where 'the powers that be' had accepted fifty-nine students, 'at least twice as many as they should try to manage even if they had some equipment with which to start'.[21] With no funding commitment from North America, and no building or laboratory facilities for students beyond the first year, Murray urged Kim either to delay beginning medical training at Ewha, or to cooperate with Severance Union Hospital and Medical College, a larger ecumenical medical institution in Seoul dating back to the turn of the century.[22] She also recommended the latter course in an early report to the ECB in New York.[23]

But her arguments were unsuccessful. Kim would consider neither a postponement nor the possibility of coeducational training with Severance, maintaining that the latter institution would allow only 15 per cent of its student body to be female.[24] As for the ECB, it was at first inclined to accept Murray's advice. Since the 1920s, mainline Protestant mission bureaucrats, ecumenically minded laymen, and philanthropists like John D. Rockefeller, Jr, had all come to favour union institutions and coeducation as vehicles for making missionary institutional work more modern and efficient. The costs involved in establishing and maintaining medical work made the arguments for cooperation in that sphere especially compelling.[25] Moreover, Murray's report from Seoul was just one of several from Western medical authorities recommending that Severance be strengthened as a coeducational institution and advising against the establishment of a new medical program at Ewha. But when Kim and her supporters insisted that Korea was still far too backward in its views on women's roles to make medical coeducation workable for female students, their arguments carried the day. Indeed, an earlier board resolution strongly endorsing the position espoused by Murray was ordered deleted from the minutes.[26] As its deliberations revealed, the ECB was caught on the horns of a dilemma: it wanted to avoid supporting costly, inefficient, and 'old-fashioned' mission strategies, but it also wanted to avoid the decision-making style of an earlier era when home-base officials and missionaries had used their financial clout to impose North American solutions on indigenous Christian leaders.[27] As various crises developed at Ewha, including a disastrous fire at the teaching hospital early in 1949, followed by the resignation of the superintendent, the obstetrician's departure for the US, and the jailing of the medical head, Murray agreed to become temporary superintendent. The deanship of the medical school had fallen to her earlier. But these were not positions she was willing to retain. She continued teaching in the school on a part-time basis until 1950 in order to avoid penalizing the students 'for what is not their fault'[28] or adding to the burdens of Ewha's acting president in the absence of Helen Kim, who was once again out of the country on fund-raising and political assignments. But she was unwilling to remain permanently on the Ewha staff, especially in the face of needs and opportunities in other medical institutions.[29] After serving half-time on a committee to investigate internal difficulties at the new Seoul National University Hospital and, later, as the government-appointed adviser to its beleaguered superintendent, Murray joined the staff at Severance, teaching in the medical school and becoming assistant superintendent of the hospital and temporary head of pediatrics.[30]

Murray's twenty years in northern Korea, and to an even greater degree her activities during and following the Korean War (1950–3), make it clear that she *was* capable of adapting to sub-standard physical conditions in medical practice.[31] But when it came to training future doctors, she believed there was 'a minimum of basal necessities that must be attained or the work is not worth doing'. In the matter of clinical facilities, for instance, Ewha medical students had access to less than one hospital bed per student at a time when the Western standard for adequate clinical training was reportedly a minimum of ten beds per student.[32] Standards were further undermined by the university's unwillingness to allow any students, once admitted, to fail. Ewha's medical-training program—even its status as a university—was, she declared, premature.[33]

Given the cross-cultural context, it seems necessary to consider the extent to which Murray's criticisms of Ewha, and her decision to leave, may have reflected unease about working in a subordinate position to Koreans, as well as professional concerns. That adjusting to the new order of things at the end of the Second World War presented a challenge to returning missionaries is beyond doubt. The changes wrought by the war and the end of Japanese colonial rule ensured that in many mission-founded institutions Koreans would henceforth be in positions of leadership. In many cases, in fact, they had held such positions since the late 1930s, when increasing Japanese nationalism had forced Westerners out (even earlier where devolution was an active practice). In 1945, having got rid of the Japanese overlords who had made these 'leadership' roles difficult, often merely nominal, positions, they were not about to go back to the days when missionaries were in charge.

At the same time, Christian missionaries in Korea did not bear the stigma of direct association with the colonial system—quite the contrary in many cases.[34] After some initial hesitation, many Koreans in medical institutions evidently concluded that they could benefit from Western expertise, as well as financial and technical aid, in their work.[35] The willingness to accept Western medical mentorship was strongest, according to Murray, among an older generation of Korean Christian staff and weakest among Koreans trained under Japanese instructors, particularly during the war years. Unconvinced that they had anything to learn from missionaries offering current medical expertise from the West, the latter instead initially regarded the foreigners as a threat to their new-found autonomy.[36] In these circumstances, the challenge was how to make the new relationships work so that Korean supervisors could draw on their Western colleagues' expertise without losing face or sacrificing ultimate authority, and so that Westerners like

Murray could work in their new subordinate roles without abandoning the standards they regarded as essential to medical schools and hospitals worthy of those names.[37]

As Murray's letters describing her experiences at Seoul National University Hospital and, later, Severance, make clear, negotiating the new relationship was far from easy, and the fact that she had been invited to take on roles in these institutions by no means guaranteed that her presence or advice was universally welcomed.[38] Writing to the medical secretary of the New-York-based Cooperating Board for Christian Education in Chosun soon after her transfer to Severance, Murray explained that her position there was actually 'somewhat anomalous', notwithstanding the various roles nominally assigned to her on joining the institution. And since her appointment as assistant superintendent had not been publicly announced to the staff, she had 'no authority except personally with the superintendent himself'.[39] Clearly, then, if working in a subordinate relationship to Koreans had been a factor in Murray's decision to leave Ewha, in moving to Severance she had succeeded only in jumping from the frying pan into the fire.

In fact, however, the crucial issue for her at the time was not whether doctors in general and supervisory personnel in particular were Korean or Western—the era of the latter was clearly waning[40]—but whether the Korean personnel had Western training or experience, or at least a willingness to recognize that Western-style expertise could improve their country's medical care. From the early 1920s it had been something of a refrain with Murray that Korean doctors needed to go abroad to see what a 'real' hospital was like, since neither mission hospitals nor Japanese institutions *in* Korea could give them that exposure.[41] By 'abroad' in those days she had meant metropolitan Japan and China (where the Rockefeller-funded Peking Union Medical College was an internationally renowned institution) as well as the West. By the late 1940s she regarded the need for overseas experience as even more urgent: with all medical institutions in Korea having been under Japanese control during the war years, teaching standards and medical practice had deteriorated even further as the war effort had consumed vital human and physical resources. Hence the importance of assisting Koreans to obtain scholarships and placements for study abroad, along with measures to rehabilitate existing medical plants physically and technologically. Both steps were necessary if standards were to be raised.[42]

In pursuing these goals there was, quite simply, 'more to encourage' at Severance than at Ewha.[43] Physical conditions were still bleak, as at Ewha and indeed all hospitals, but the others were 'worse off as to the standards of their staffs', and many were 'torn asunder by political strife'.[44] At Severance the prospects for ongoing improvements in staffing and facilities were markedly greater, in part because of the support it could obtain from the Cooperating Board for Christian Education in Chosun, whose resources were significantly greater than those of the parallel but less broadly ecumenical ECB. Murray was in a position to make a significant personal difference in this regard, since she acted as a conduit to the Board in presenting Severance's needs and was viewed by Board officials as 'sane and judicious' in her recommendations. Without masking its many shortcomings, she urged generous support in the form of equipment and scholarships so that Severance could become a place in which the Board could take pride.[45]

Nevertheless, the fact remained that Murray had left a medical training program specifically for women in order to join one in which no women students would be enrolled until 1952, and then in the context of wartime needs.[46] This raises the question of her attitude towards the feminist goals that motivated Helen Kim and an earlier generation of women missionaries who had devoted their careers to work for women under what one scholar has called 'one of the most ideal types of patriarchy in the world'.[47] Addressing this question requires a brief look at Murray's early attitudes to women's roles and her view of gender-segregated medical work during her years in northern Korea.

Murray had been raised in a home where higher education was encouraged for daughters as well as sons, turning her own sights on medicine after learning that a career in the ministry was not an option for Presbyterian women.[48] An advocate of women's political rights in her student days,[49] in later years she was particularly likely to comment on the more mundane burdens and inequalities that women experienced in marriage, especially in Korea, but also in the West.[50] In her relationships with Korean women doctors she was supportive in personal and practical ways. Kim Hyo-Soon, the only female practitioner in her hospital in Hamhung in the inter-war years and a steadfast friend during the wartime interval when Murray was under house arrest, was in turn assisted by Murray when she came as a refugee to post-war Seoul, and the two remained lifelong friends. Lee Heung Joo, a young medical student at Ewha in the 1940s, initially regarded Murray as a stern and humourless teacher, but later came to know her as a positive and practical kind of mentor; today, in old age, Lee reveres her memory.[51] For many years Murray met monthly with women doctors in Seoul for discussion of medical matters, lending her own Western medical books and journals for their use.[52]

Such things suggest that Murray was not without a feminist consciousness and a personal sense of sisterhood. But in the end the professional ability of doctors was more important to her than their gender. She was simply not prepared to devote her efforts to a women-only institution if that appeared to be an inefficient way of producing the modern professionals that Korea needed or an approach likely to institutionalize second-rate standards for female practitioners (and their patients). That had been her position from the 1920s, when she had resisted the urging of some older women missionaries, including East Gate Maternity Hospital's Dr Rosetta Sherwood Hall (an early graduate of the Woman's Medical College of Pennsylvania), to abandon general medicine and concentrate on 'women's work for women'.[53] Trained herself in a coeducational institution that she had found personally congenial, she had neither sentimental nor professional reasons for wishing to confine her practice or her teaching to women. Indeed, after observing standards at East Gate shortly after her arrival in Korea and hearing that female medical missionaries were not held in high professional regard, she had been scathing in her criticism of the hospital and resolved to 'demonstrate to the missionary community that women doctors are not necessarily cantankerous and inefficient'.[54] As Nancy Cott has made clear, many professional women of Murray's generation in North America prized professional standards, and their professional identity, over the values and practices of an earlier generation of social or maternal feminists.[55] In this respect, Murray was a representative figure.

The concerns she expressed about the new medical training program at Ewha should thus, I believe, be taken at face value as statements about the minimum professional standards and facilities she thought essential for medical training worthy of the name, rather than as an indication of inflexibility or a smokescreen for racism and indifference to 'feminist' concerns.

IV KIM'S TENACITY

Helen Kim, meanwhile, was passionately committed to Ewha and the goal of educating women as part of a larger concern with women's rights in Korea. Here too, attention to the years preceding and following the three-year period under direct consideration in this paper is helpful in understanding her position in regard to medical training at Ewha.

During the Second World War, in order to maintain Ewha's tenuous existence as a college, Kim had co-operated with the Japanese in various ways in the demands they made on the institution, leading some Koreans to regard her as a collaborator.[56] During the Korean War, when Seoul was twice captured and controlled by communist troops, she again showed her tenacious commitment to Ewha, establishing a campus in exile in Pusan, the port city on the southeast coast to which Syngman Rhee's government had fled. Huts and ragged tent classrooms on a mountainside, pianos in 'music boxes' beside them where students could continue to practice—these symbolized her determination to carry on. As for the medical students, they carried on in a 'shack-style hospital' erected near the marketplace, 'adequate', she declared, under the circumstances, 'to give clinical service in all departments'.[57] In 1951 the first class of doctors graduated at this campus in exile.

After the Korean War, Kim would continue for many years to look to North America as a source of funds for Ewha's development. She had done the same in the immediate aftermath of the Second World War, the period to which I now return. In September 1946, at the request of the ECB's executive secretaries, Kim had started an English-language diary, periodically forwarding instalments to New York for circulation among Board members and former faculty to keep them informed of Ewha's needs and activities.[58] Given its purpose, the diary is not revealing in the way that a private document would be. But it does show what Kim wanted to convey to her supporters abroad in an effort to persuade them of the merits of her approach to women's education in Korea. Though the idea of the diary had not originated with her, it served her well strategically, especially at a time when North American missionary modernizers were advocating plans that were at odds with her own inclinations.

The modernizers' calls for some sort of federation of Seoul's three major institutions for Christian higher education—Ewha, Severance, and Chosun Christian College—to produce one first-class Christian university were especially significant in this regard.[59] In 1957 the latter two would unite to form Yonsei University, but Ewha remained apart. Kim participated from 1946 in deliberations of the Joint Committee for Cooperation of the Christian Institutions for Higher Education in Korea. Yet as her diary reveals, she and other alumnae took the position that 'nothing should be done that would jeopardize the unique contribution that Ewha has been making and still has to make in the pioneering movement of women's education . . . in Korea,'[60] a position that effectively meant insistence on ongoing autonomy. Political events such as the defeat of all the female candidates in the May 1948 election for the first National Assembly (Kim included) were cited in the diary as evidence of the persistent opposition to non-traditional roles for women and hence of the need for separate women's educational institutions.[61]

Since few Korean women had the necessary qualifications to teach in a university, Kim was eager to have staff as well as financial assistance from North America. Several American missionaries were already back on the campus when the three Canadian women arrived in July 1947. Kim's diary entries about their arrival speak of how welcome the Canadians were, especially within the College of Healing Arts, where Murray and nurse Ada Sandell were to serve.[62] Shortly thereafter, however, Kim observed that Murray seemed 'challenged' by 'the lack of facilities', tersely remarking, 'Who isn't?'[63]

Though she could scarcely afford to express stronger criticism, given the public nature of the diary, Kim's remark undoubtedly reflected frustration that Murray, who had spent the nightmarish war years safely in Canada, was focusing only on the obstacles to establishing medical training at Ewha. Moreover, having just arrived, she could not know of the efforts Kim had made in the previous year to obtain classroom and laboratory facilities.[64] Nor, given her focus on her own particular professional concerns, could she appreciate the fact that, as president, Kim was responsible for all of Ewha, not just its new medical program. Thus she had to cultivate connections *within* Korea, as well as internationally, to strengthen its local financial base and make it a source of national pride.[65] In view of the work that this involved, and under conditions of extreme physical hardship, Kim could scarcely be expected to see the problems facing the medical department in the same light that Murray did.

v Beyond Professional Differences: A Shared Christian Vision

Clearly, Florence Murray and Helen Kim had very different educational priorities. For Murray, there were minimum standards that had to be met if a medical training program was to be worth mounting. An inadequately trained doctor (especially one who thought she was adequately trained) was a far more serious matter than a badly trained pianist or home economist. For Kim, committed to separate education for Korean women as the only way to secure their advancement in a strongly patriarchal society and not herself a medical specialist, the quality of the medical training to be provided at Ewha was not a crucial issue. As had been the case right after the liberation, when she was seeking to raise Ewha from college to university status, what was important for Kim in 1947 in regard to medical education was making an immediate start[66] and thus signalling the new roles that women should be prepared, and allowed, to play in the newly liberated country. The signal rather than the substance was important. Arguably, her larger concern as university president was to produce graduates who could make a contribution to public life as wives of the educated élite and thus help vanquish the old assumption that respectable women did not participate in the public sphere.[67] Hence the importance of such richly visual and symbolic public ceremonies as the 1947 graduation day exercises celebrated in poetry by the Revd William Scott—the Canadian whose contributions to Ewha in the late 1940s Kim seems to have valued most.[68] Hence, too, the symbolic importance of carrying on during the Korean War at Ewha's Campus in Exile.

In the context of the time, the professional priorities of Murray and Kim were impossible to reconcile, especially since both were 'strong-minded women'[69] whose personalities in other respects were strikingly different. Nonetheless, they shared an overarching goal in their desire to see educated Korean Christians play a leading role in building a free, non-communist Korea.[70] Murray's departure from Ewha, therefore, did not mean a burning of bridges. She served for years on the Ewha Board, as did other missionaries of the United Church of Canada, which continued to assist Ewha financially.[71] Moreover, even as she had questioned Kim's judgement in the matter of establishing a medical training program at Ewha in the late 1940s, Murray had expressed pride in the remarkable contributions she was making to Korean public life.[72] And when Kim died in 1970, Murray readily acknowledged that she would have been 'a very remarkable woman for any country'.[73]

CONCLUSION

What are we to make of this brief moment in the history of missions, education, and medicine? From a present-day perspective, Murray's strong commitment to 'standards' may seem at best naive—at worst culturally arrogant and potentially harmful.[74] Yet it is important to remind ourselves that the practices and assumptions of scientific medicine that began in the West and that missionaries sought to transfer are ones that medical professionals in Korea and other Asian countries have decisively made their own, notwithstanding the continuing importance of indigenous medicine to large segments of Asian societies and our own current enthusiasm for elements of 'traditional' practice.[75] Indeed, in seeking to establish a medical-training program at Ewha, Kim was testifying to the value she placed on the ideals of Western medicine, even if her haste signified a lack of appreciation for what was involved in the implementation of those ideals.

As for Kim's approach to Korean women's education generally, the arguments for it seem in many ways to be incontestable. Coeducation has not become the norm in Korea that it is in the West. Ewha was still educating more than half of Korea's university women in the 1960s,[76] and its continued growth has, as noted, made it the largest women's university in the world. The loyalty of its graduates and the prestige that an Ewha degree carries in Korean society have become the stuff of legend. Lady Bird Johnson's praise for Ewha's women and for emeritus president Helen Kim during a 1966 visit to the campus need to be viewed in the context of Vietnam war politics (South Korea had become a valued US ally in 1965), but the very fact that such a visit was on the First Lady's agenda signified the importance that Ewha and Kim were deemed to hold in South Korea's public life.[77] As for Kim herself, years after her death she continued to be cited as a role model by successful Ewha faculty and graduates. Feminist scholars who have come to the fore at Ewha in the era of second-wave feminism regard her legacy of separate women's education as crucial to Korean women's advancement.[78]

And yet on the matter of professional training the verdict is less clear. In establishing a separate women's medical college in the 1940s, Kim was swimming against a very strong tide: the Union Mission Medical School for Women in Vellore, India, established in 1918, was forced to become coeducational in the 1940s to cope with the costs involved in state requirements for higher standards of medical training (the reluctant administrator in this case being an American woman), while in China the move to medical coeducation had begun in the 1920s.[79] Under the circumstances, Ewha's medical training program had an uphill struggle to establish its credibility. In the 1960s its graduates were still considered less desirable as residents and interns than those of Yonsei and Seoul National University. As with many other institutions, its more limited financial base had contributed to an emphasis on increasing student numbers rather than improving the quality in professional training.[80] Also relevant was the universal marriage ethos in Korean culture,[81] which shaped the nature and goals of education for women even in professional programs. Graduates typically married and became housewives, using their training for, at most, auxiliary roles. 'Modern education', writes Ai Ra Kim, herself a 1960s Ewha graduate, 'was geared to providing men with "better" housewives and (financial) supporters.'[82] In the 1990s Ewha was still known for its 'finishing school atmosphere'.[83] Explaining that this image clings to South Korean women's universities generally, Ji-moon Suh maintains that, as a result, women who seek to be fully accepted as professionals 'tend to choose coeducational schools over women's colleges'.[84] Clearly, in South Korea as in North America, the differences in educational philosophies that Murray and Kim represented are still unresolved, and likely to remain so.

In mapping those differences in this paper I have focused on geographic and colonial terrain seldom traversed in postcolonial scholarship. I have also, I hope, demonstrated that there can be fruitful ways of exploring relationships between missionaries and non-Westerners that go beyond the familiar themes of racism and resistance.

NOTES

I am happy to acknowledge the assistance of the following: Associated Medical Services, Inc., through the Hannah Institute for the History of Medicine, for funds that facilitated research for this paper; librarians, archivists, and translators in Korea and North America; Professors Patricia Dirks and Jean Mackenzie Leiper and five former Korea missionaries for useful comments on an earlier version of the paper; scholars at the Asian Center for Women's Studies and the Korean Womens Institute, Ewha, for sharing ideas and research material on Kim; and all those who provided personal reminiscences of Murray and Kim or insights into this era. I take sole responsibility for errors of fact or interpretation.

1. Within the last several years a few scholars, while themselves writing from a postcolonialist perspective, have nonetheless challenged some aspects of this new orthodoxy, including its tendency to ride roughshod over particular contexts of time and place; see, e.g., Dane Kennedy, 'Imperial History and Post-Colonial Theory', *Journal of Imperial and Commonwealth History* 24, 3 (September 1996), 345–63, and Nicholas Thomas, *Colonialism's Culture: Anthropology, Travel and Government* (Cambridge, 1994).

2. 'Beyond "Women's Work for Women": Dr. Florence Murray and the Practice and Teaching of Western Medicine in Korea, 1921–1942', in *Challenging Professions: Historical and Contemporary Perspectives on Women's Professional Work*, ed. Elizabeth Smyth et al. (Toronto, 1999).

3. Murray was recognized by the Danish and Korean governments for medical service in Korea and was awarded two honorary doctorates from Dalhousie University near the end of her career. Unlike Kim, however, she did not become a prominent public personality.

4. See the acknowledgements above.

5. Biographical information on Murray comes from her published memoir, *At the Foot of Dragon Hill* (New York, 1975); United Church/Victoria University Archives (UCA) biographical file; and Public Archives of Nova Scotia, Maritime Missionaries to Korea Collection,MG1, vol. 2276, file 1 (references hereafter are to PANS, MMKC, with relevant volume and file number). Information on the Murray family is available in United Church of Canada (UCC), *Record of Proceedings, Thirty-Second Annual Meeting of the Maritime Conference* 5–10 June 1956, 43, obituary of Robert Murray; and in Robert Murray Personal Notebooks (RMPN), vol. 8, 'Family Records', privately held.

6. Established in 1898 by Maritime Presbyterians, the mission became part of the United Church of Canada's overseas work in 1925. See UCA, William Scott, 'Canadians in Korea: A Brief Historical Sketch of Canadian Mission Work in Korea', 1975; A. Hamish Ion, *The Cross and the Rising Sun: The Canadian Protestant Missionary Movement in the Japanese Empire, 1872–1931* (Waterloo, 1990), and Ruth Compton Brouwer, 'Home Lessons, Foreign Tests: The Background and First Missionary Term of Florence Murray, Maritime Doctor in Korea', *Journal of the CHA 1995 Revue de la S.H.C.*, New Series, vol. 6, 103–28.

7. Telephone interview with Isabelle Johnston (Murray's niece), Toronto, 23 Feb. 1996. The phrase originated with Mrs Johnston's husband.

8. See, for instance, Dalhousie University Archives (DUA), MS-2/535, Robert Murray and Family Papers (MFP), A-18, Florence Murray to parents, 17 Aug. 1947, and ibid., A-19, 2 Jan. 1948.

9. *Dragon Hill*, Ch. 20; PANS, MMKC, vol. 2276, file 37, 'Report of the Interim Committee of the Korea Mission of the United Church of Canada', Aug. 1942, 11–12.

10. UCA, UCC, Woman's Missionary Society (WMS), Overseas Missions, Korea Correspondence, box 83, file 51a, Mrs Hugh Taylor to Murray, 16 May 1946 (hereafter, Korea Correspondence).

11. *Grace Sufficient: The Story of Helen Kim by Herself*, ed. J. Manning Potts (Nashville, 1964), Chs. I–II (quotations at 30).

12. Ibid., Chs. IV–VII; also Ewha Womans University Library (EWUL), Helen Kim Collection, Helen Kim, 'Personal History' (curriculum vitae).

13. Ibid.

14. Yale University Divinity School Library and Archives (YDL), RG 11A, United Board for Christian Higher Education in Asia (UBCHEA), box 148A, file 1961, ECB minutes of 18 May 1946.

15. EWUL, Kim Collection, Kim Diary, June 30 [1947].

16. UCA, UCC, WMS, Korea Correspondence, box 3, file 51a, Murray to Mrs. Hugh Taylor, 21 May and 18 Dec. 1946; box 2, file 25, Murray, 'Report on Medical Education', Sept. 1947; and box 83, file 51a, Murray to Thomas Hobbs, 28 Nov. 1946. See also DUA, MFP, Florence Murray, 'Return to Korea', unpublished ms., Ch. Two. Murray was revising this second volume of her memoirs at the time of her death in 1975.

17. Ibid., 12–13, 17, 20. Murray had understood that she was 'to be the dean and organize the school' (12).

18. Ibid., 16, 64–5.

19. DUA, MFP, A-18, Murray to family, 7 Aug. 1947.

20. The question of terminology is an interesting one in the two women's recollections of this era: Murray recalls that Kim spoke only of starting a new department 'like the English Department or the Music Department', thus downplaying the cost and scope of the undertaking; DUA, MFP, Murray, 'Return', 15. In her own memoir Kim has almost nothing to say about any aspect of Ewha's medical training program but refers to starting a 'College of Healing Arts' as one of three colleges in 1945; *Grace Sufficient*, 114.

21. DUA, MFP, A-18, Murray to family, 7 Aug. 1947.

22. UCA, UCC, WMS, Korea Correspondence, box, 2, file 25, Murray, 'Report', 3–4; DUA, MFP, A-18, Murray to parents, 17 Aug. 1947, and ibid., 'Return', 13–14. On Severance and the medical college's Canadian founder see Allen DeGray Clark, *Avison of Korea: The Life of Oliver Avison, M.D.* (Seoul [1979]).

23. YDL, UBCHEA, box 148A, file 1961, ECB executive committee meeting, 13 and 14 Dec. 1947. See also DUA, MFP, A-18, Murray to parents, 17 Aug. 1947.

24. DUA, MFP, Murray, 'Return', 14–15.

25. William Ernest Hocking, comp., *Re-Thinking Missions: A Laymen's Inquiry after One Hundred Years* (New York, 1932), especially 201–11, 267–8, 328–9; Jessie Gregory Lutz, *China and the Christian Colleges, 1850–1950* (Ithaca, 1971), especially 151, 156, 157–8.

26. YDL, UBCHEA, box 148A, file 1961, minutes of meeting of ECB executive committee, 13 and 14 Dec. 1947, 2–4, and of full board, 12 May 1948, 4.

27. See Edward W. Said, *Culture and Imperialism* (New York, 1993), 39–41, for a fascinating instance of the old-style approach in the late twentieth century and the frustration it caused for a leader of the Arab Protestant community in the Levant to which Said himself is attached by birth.

28. UCA, UCC, WMS, Korea Correspondence, box 3, file 51a, Murray, '1949 Annual Report', 1.

29. DUA, MFP, A-19, Murray to parents, 2 Jan. 1948.

30. DUA, MFP, A-20, Murray to Alexander and Esther, 27 July 1949; and 'Return', Ch. Five, and 72.

31. In March 1952, more than a year before the truce ending the war, Murray was back at Severance, where most of the plant had been destroyed; she was reportedly the first Western doctor to return; 'Story of the Years', *Missionary Monthly* (August 1961).

32. UCA, UCC, WMS, box 2, file 25, Murray, 'Report on Medical Education', Sept. 1947 (quote at 1–2); DUA, MFP, Murray, 'Return', 15.

33. DUA, MFP, A-19, Murray to Alex, 24 July 1948, and 'Return', 62. As Murray acknowledged, the practice of passing all students was not unique to Ewha.

34. Korean Christians had played a disproportionately large role in the Independence Movement of March 1919, with sympathetic and sometimes active support from missionaries; see Chong-Sik Lee, *The Politics of Korean Nationalism* (Berkeley, 1963), Part III, and, for Canadian missionaries' attitudes, Ion, *Cross*, 188–208. Christianity's positive association with Korean nationalism has undoubtedly been a factor in allowing it to become Korea's second-largest religion.

35. YDL, UBCHEA, RG11—181A-2576, College Files, Yonsei, Murray, Florence J.: Murray to Dr R. Morris Paty, 14 April 1949, 2; also DUA, MFP, A-19, Murray to parents, 8 March 1948.

36. Ibid., Murray to Alex, 24 July 1948, and A-20, Murray to Alex, 31 March 1949; also 'Return', 83–4.

37. This paragraph is based largely on Murray's private and official correspondence during the late forties and early fifties, and in particular that between Murray and officials of the Cooperating Board for Christian Education in Chosun, based in New York. The latter was one of several ecumenical boards that later united to form the United Board for Christian Higher Education in Asia (UBCHEA).

38. DUA, MFP, A-20, Murray to Alex, 31 March 1949; communication from Dr Helen Mackenzie, Balwyn, Australia, 20 Aug. 1997.

39. YDL, UBCHEA, file 181A-2576, Murray to Paty, 14 April 1949.

40. UCA, Scott, 'Canadians', 160, 171. Murray believed that there was still a place for new Western doctors in mission hospitals to provide needed specialties and to mentor Korean doctors with 'indifferent training', but she recognized that they would form only a minority of the medical staff; see YDL, UBCHEA, RG11-181A-2577, Yonsei, Murray, Florence J.: Murray to D.N. Forman, 24 April 1954.

41. See, e.g., PANS, MMKC, vol. 2276, file 3, Murray to 'Dear Folks', 2 Oct. 1922.

42. YDL, UBCHEA, Murray to Paty, 14 April 1949, and DUA, MFP, Murray, 'Return', Ch. Eight.

On Korea's hospitals after the war see also Albert E. Cowdrey, *United States Army in the Korean War: The Medics' War* (Washington, 1987), 38, 51, 53.

43. DUA, MFP, A-20, Murray to Alexander and Esther, 27 July 1949.

44. YDL, UBCHEA, Murray to Paty, 14 April 1949. See also DUA, MFP, Murray, 'Return', Ch. Five, regarding intense political strife at Seoul National University Hospital, which Murray attributed to communist subversion.

45. YDL, UBCHEA, RG11-181A-2576, Murray to Paty, 14 April 1949; quoted comment from attached note.

46. Ibid., RG11-181A-2577, Yonsei, Murray, Florence J: 'Severance Hospital' [1954],1. Severance's gender ratio was especially significant, since in 1954 its graduates comprised more than one-third of South Korea's total stock of doctors. It had agreed to open its doors to women students in 1947, but following Ewha's decision to offer separate medical education for women, it had evidently either not received, or not accepted, female applicants.

47. Chang Pilwha, 'The Rise of Women's Education Against the Korean Patriarchy', in *The Rise of Feminist Consciousness Against the Asian Patriarchy*, Asian Center for Women's Studies (Seoul, 1996), 5.

48. Murray, *Dragon Hill*, viii.

49. Interview with Dr Anna Murray Dike Musgrave, Clarkesburg, Ont., 25 June 1990.

50. See, e.g., PANS, MMKC, vol. 2276, file 6, letter to Alexander, 17 Feb. 1924; file 8, to Father, 24 Aug. 1925; and file 12, to 'Dear People', 5 Aug. 1929, espec. 2–3.

51. Regarding Dr Kim, see *Dragon Hill*, 232–3, and UCA, UCC, Florence Jessie Murray Papers, box 1, diaries, file 4, entries for 15 Feb. and 2 April, 1966, and file 8, entry for 19 Feb. 1970. Information about Dr Lee comes from her letter to the author, 20 Aug. 1997, and from letter of Dr Helen Mackenzie, 9 July 1997; also letter from Murray in *United Churchman*, 23 June 1965, 12.

52. UCA, UCC, WMS, Korea Correspondence, box 3, file 51a, '1949 Annual Report'; DUA, MFP, Murray, 'Return', 93; author's conversation with Dr Park Jung Jai, Seoul, 15 May 1997.

53. PANS, MMKC, vol. 2276, file 8, Murray to Father, 24 Aug. 1925.

54. Ibid., file 3, Murray to Father, 27 Dec. 1922. This concern is discussed more fully in Brouwer, 'Beyond "Women's Work for Women"'.

55. Nancy F. Cott, *The Grounding of Modern Feminism* (New Haven, 1987), Ch. Seven. See also Thomas Neville Bonner, *To the Ends of the Earth: Women's Search for Education in Medicine* (Cambridge, 1992), 166: 'Efforts to combine the new scientific and professional orientation of medicine with the older gender separation of the nineteenth century were doomed to failure.'

56. Kim, *Grace Sufficient*, Ch. VII, espec. 98. See also George Hicks, *The Comfort Women* (St Leonard's, Australia, 1995), 25, 27–8, 136.

57. Kim, *Grace Sufficient*, Ch. IX (quotations at 141).

58. EWUL, Kim Collection, Diary. Information about the diary's origins and purpose comes from a note by the executive secretaries, preceding the first entry (generally unpaged).

59. YDL, UBCHEA, box 148A, file 1961, Joint Meeting of Ewha Cooperating Board and Cooperating Board for Christian Higher Education in Chosun, 17 May 1946.

60. EWUL, Kim Collection, Diary, 21 July [1947].

61. Ibid., Diary sequence for 2–22 May and 23 May–3 June [1948].

62. Ibid., 28, 31 July [1947]. At this point Murray was the only Western woman doctor to have returned to Korea; see Rosetta Sherwood Hall, 'Foreign Medical Women in Korea', *Journal of the American Medical Women's Association* 5, 10 (Oct. 1950), 404–5.

63. EWUL, Kim Collection, Diary, 4 Aug. [1947].

64. Ibid., 1, 26 May 1947.

65. Ibid. See, for example, entries for 15 and 27–9 March, and 13 June 1947.

66. Kim, *Grace Sufficient*, 116–17; EWUL, Kim Collection, Diary, 5 Oct. 1946.

67. See, e.g., ibid., Dec. 1946, and segment for 22 Dec. 1947 to 21 Jan. 1948. In the latter segment Kim emphasized that Ewha graduates had played key roles in recent public functions held to welcome the United Nations Commission to Korea, notwithstanding the initial objections of their husbands. In former times, she stated, only dancing girls would have been present at such events.

68. Ibid., entries for 9, 11 June 1947. See also Scott, 'Canadians', 174–5, and 188–9. Though he was not on Ewha's staff, Scott worked closely with Kim on several important university committees during the early postwar period. Perhaps more important in terms of their mutual regard, he sympathized with her determination and with such educational gestures as piano lessons on a battered instrument on a Pusan hillside in wartime, in a way that the practical-minded Murray could not.

69. Interview with former Korea medical missionary Ian Robb, Halifax, 25 July 1994.

70. The view that President Kim and Dr Murray were animated by a shared Christian vision in their work for Korea is emphasized by Murray's former student Dr Lee Heung Joo and by Dr Yim Kil Chai, a former colleague, both of whom nevertheless strongly endorse Kim's educational strategy over Murray's; Lee to author, 18 March 1998, and Yim to author, 25 Aug. 1996.

71. EWUL, Kim Collection, box 11, Canadian Mission Materials, E.J.O. Fraser to Dr Kim, 11 April 1953; Marion L. Conrow, *Our Ewha, 1886-1956: A Historical Sketch* (Seoul, 1956), Preface. In 1956 Ewha even conferred an honorary degree on Ruth Taylor, WMS overseas missions secretary for the United Church, citing her commitment to 'women's rights' and 'Christian higher education in various Asian universities'; UCA biographical file for the Revd Hugh D. Taylor containing 'In Memoriam' to Ruth Taylor.

72. For instance, DUA, MFP, A-19, Murray to parents, 18 Jan. 1948, describing Kim's speech in Korean and English before a crowd of 200,000 to welcome the United Nations Commission.

73. UCA, UCC, Murray Papers, box 1, file 8, Diary, entry for 19 Feb. 1970.

74. Medical missionaries' confidence in the superiority of their 'product' over that of traditional practitioners has been a favourite target of postcolonial critics with an interest in discourse analysis; see, e.g., Luise White, "They Could Make Their Victims Dull": Genders and Genres, Fantasies and Cures in Colonial Southern Uganda', *American Historical Review* 100, 5 (Dec. 1995), 1379–1402.

75. See Soon Yong Yoon, 'A Legacy without Heirs: Korean Indigenous Medicine and Primary Health Care', *Social Science and Medicine*, 17,19 (1983), 1467–76, and, for an

interesting parallel, David Arnold 'The Rise of Western Medicine in India', *The Lancet* 347, 9034 (19 Oct. 1996), 1075. When Soon's article was being researched, South Korea's government still provided no support for research and training in indigenous medicine, and few medical schools integrated it into primary health care.

76. Kim, *Grace Sufficient*, 149.

77. Carter J. Eckert et al., *Korea Old and New: A History* (Seoul, 1990), 367; EWUL, Kim Collection, 'Mrs Lyndon B. Johnson' file, copy of Mrs Johnson's remarks, 1 Nov. 1966.

78. Lee Hie Sung, 'A Case Study on Achievement Motivation of Women Professors in a Women's University in Korea', in *Challenges for Women: Women's Studies in Korea*, ed. Chang Sei-wha, trans. Shin chang-kyun et al. (Seoul, 1986), 202, 210; Chang, 'Rise'; conversation with Professor Sohn Seung-Hee, Seoul, 24 May 1997.

79. Belle Choné Oliver, 'Vellore Christian Medical College', *Journal of the Christian Medical Association of India, Burma and Ceylon* XXI, 2 (1946), 49–51; Dorothy Clarke Wilson, *Dr. Ida: The Story of Dr. Ida Scudder of Vellore* (New York, 1959); Lutz, *China*, 157–8.

80. Interview with Dr Hugh Rose, former chief of staff, Wonju Union Christian Hospital, Korea, 5 June 1998; YDL, UBCHEA, RG11A, 148A-1964, 'Report on the Self-Study Survey of Ewha Womans University', 1961, 34; also UCA, UCC, Board of World Mission, UBCHEA Collection, box 4, file 68, containing 'Memo on Yonsei University', 1961, and box 6, containing 'An Appraisal of the Protestant Christian Effort in Higher Education in Asia: Korea', 1968. Both memos express concern lest Yonsei be tempted to follow the national trend towards increased student numbers and thus jeopardize its historic standing.

81. Laurel Kendall, *Getting Married in Korea: Of Gender, Morality and Modernity* (Berkeley, 1996).

82. Ai Ra Kim, *Women Struggling for a New Life* (Albany, 1996), 45, 46; see also Ko Hwang-kyung, 'Korean Women and Education', *Korea Journal*, 1 Feb. 1964, 10–13, and In-Ho Lee, 'Work, Education, and Women's Gains: the Korean Experience', in *The Politics of Women's Education: Perspectives from Asia, Africa, and Latin America*, ed. Jill Ker Conway and Susan C. Bourque (Ann Arbor, 1993), 77–104.

83. In-Ho Lee, 'Work', 87.

84. Ji-moon Suh, 'Commentary', *Asian Women* 3 (Winter 1996), 104.

PART FIVE

NATIVE PEOPLE

Ignored Voices

Nineteenth-Century French-Canadian Views of Iroquois–French Relations

José António Brandão

Iroquois–French relations played a vital role in shaping the social, political, economic, and military history of New France.[1] Nineteenth-century French-Canadian historians were keenly aware of the Iroquois's impact, and did not fail to examine both its effects and its causes. The works of four stand out: François-Xavier Garneau, Abbé Jean-Baptiste-Antoine Ferland, Abbé Étienne-Michel Faillon, and Benjamin Sulte.[2] Not only were they important writers in their time, but their works are still used today in studies of the history of New France. The same cannot be said of most of their contemporaries. For Garneau, Ferland, Faillon, and Sulte, Iroquois hostilities against New France were sparked by the desire for revenge, fuelled by cultural obligations, and the need to protect Iroquois territories. Despite the four historians' cultural biases, they grounded their interpretations of Franco–Iroquois relations firmly in the culture of the Iroquois and suggested reasons for Iroquois hostilities that modern scholars of the Iroquois have increasingly turned to in order to explain Iroquois warfare and the nature of Iroquois–French relations.

The views that Garneau, Ferland, Faillon, and Sulte held about Indians played a part in shaping their interpretations of Franco–Iroquois relations.[3] Garneau often portrayed Indians in rather idealized terms.[4] The views of the Catholic priests Faillon and Ferland were shaped by the dogmas of their religion. Believing that Indians were living in a 'barbaric' and 'graceless' state because they did not know God, they trusted that knowledge of God and European ways could make them both civilized and welcome members of God's Kingdom.[5] Sulte painted a clearly negative picture, writing that Indians were at 'the bottom of the ladder of humanity'.[6] In the end, though, these views were not always clearly reflected in their explanations of Franco–Iroquois relations. Garneau, for example, despite his 'noble savage' view, accounted for Iroquois warfare by stressing the Indians' 'barbarity', and Sulte, despite his low opinion of their place on the the the ladder of humanity, pointed to the shrewd policy of the Iroquois as the source of their hostilities towards New France.

Of greater significance to their interpretations was the nationalism of these historians. The role of the Iroquois in New France's history was subordinated to this broader ideological consideration. Faillon and Ferland were 'clerico-nationalists'. For them, the history of New France was the story of the growth of a French-Catholic people and the religious institutions that made that development possible.[7] More important, if for Ferland and especially Faillon the history of New France represented God's visible hand at work, then the Iroquois were God's tool:[8] the means through which God first tested the mettle of the colonists and then showed His mercy by ultimately saving them from the Iroquois peril. Garneau and Sulte, on the other hand, were 'secular nationalists'. For Garneau the history of New France was the story of a struggle towards a liberal and democratic society.[9] For Sulte it was the story of a pastoral people surviving in the face of materialistic forces and, at times, despite religious organizations.[10] If for Sulte the story of New France was one of long struggle to establish an agrarian paradise, the Iroquois served as both vivid examples of the hurdles to be overcome to reach that goal and of the calamities drawn upon the colony by materialist and mercantile efforts to exploit the fur trade at the expense of agricultural settlement. For Garneau the wars against the Iroquois show 'clearly the situation of our ancestors, the dangers to which they were continually exposed, the courage and steadfastness that they showed in these barbaric battles'.[11] In short, they were an obstacle that French Canadians had to overcome on the road towards creating a liberal democratic nation.

In Garneau's view, New France's problems with the Iroquois began when Samuel de Champlain, the colony's first governor, involved the French in long-standing Native hostilities; Champlain's battles with the Iroquois initiated nearly a hundred years of Iroquois wars against the colony.[12] But Garneau does not explain how or why that came about. His explanation of Franco–Iroquois relations is based on a rather simplistic and crude notion of the causes of Indian warfare. He recognized that Indians fought for many reasons: to gain right of passage through, or access to, hunting territories, to defend their lands, for revenge, for love of battle 'or pillage'.[13] Of all these reasons, however, it was love of battle that Garneau seems to have felt was the most significant cause of Native warfare. He ascribed to Indians a type of bloodlust, an almost physiological reaction at the prospect of fighting, which led to war.[14] This urge to fight is never stated to be the sole reason for hostilities against New France, but it seems to underlie and give added impetus to other causes.

Nor does Garneau blame Champlain for embroiling the French in wars with the Iroquois. Rather, he suggests that Champlain tried to bring peace to the warring tribes around the colony—they simply would not heed his advice.[15] The fact that after 1640, the Iroquois increased their attacks against the Hurons and Algonquins Garneau attributed to their anger at French settlement on their lands: they needed to avenge the French insult and, since they had a 'decided superiority' over those tribes, they attacked them rather than the French.[16] (Garneau's reasoning here implies that the Iroquois were too weak or cowardly to attack New France, the true source of their anger.) The Hurons could not resist the Iroquois who wanted to make but one people and one land with them.[17] Encouraged by their victories in the Great Lakes region, the Iroquois then turned in earnest against the French.[18] French military expeditions bought the colony some peace until the 1680s, when war again broke out. This war, Garneau concluded, was fostered by the English who used the Iroquois to try to gain sole control of the fur trade.[19] As the French–English commercial rivalry heated up towards the end of the century, the 'barbarity' of the Iroquois, 'who asked for nothing but to fight', made them 'blind instruments' of the competing European forces.[20]

Elements of Garneau's views can be found in the works of Faillon, Ferland, and Sulte. Champlain's role in provoking the wrath of the Iroquois is not the only assumption shared by the four. But the differences between Garneau and the others are more significant. Faillon, Ferland, and Sulte offer more complex interpretations of Franco–Iroquois relations.

The interpretations of Faillon and Ferland have much in common, though Ferland's is by far the more complete. Both Faillon and Ferland view Iroquois–French relations in the broader context of relations between the Iroquois and other Native groups before European settlement in Canada. The Iroquois had been fighting the Algonquins and their Huron allies before the advent of the French.[21] When Champlain arrived, he joined the Algonquin-Huron side, killed some Iroquois and, as a result, incurred the lasting hatred of the Iroquois.[22] Thus the wars against New France were not a new phenomenon, but rather the extension of existing hostilities to include the French.

Champlain's role is central to each historian's interpretation. For Faillon, Champlain's actions represented a type of 'original sin': as with Adam and Eve, the fault of one extended to—and must be atoned for—by all.[23] The penance for Champlain's sin was almost a century of Iroquois attacks against the whole colony. Ferland offers a less theological explanation. He devotes a good deal of space to explaining the roles played by revenge, clan obligations, and individual freedom in starting Iroquois wars.[24] Without stating it explicitly, he implies that it was these cultural factors, including the obligation to avenge deaths and attacks, that led to ongoing Iroquois incursions against New France. For Ferland, Champlain's error was unwittingly to have involved the French in the endless cycle of Native wars.

For both men the factors that explained both the early Iroquois wars against other Native peoples and their later extension to New France also helped to account for their persistence throughout the seventeenth century. Although Faillon does point out the motives behind specific Iroquois dealings with—and attacks against—the colony, and describes the destruction of the Hurons, he suggests no reasons for these actions;[25] the implicit assumption is that the overall motive for attacks against New France was revenge for Champlain's actions, while the destruction of the Hurons and other tribes merely continued timeless intertribal feuds.[26] For Ferland too, the motives for war remained constant throughout the century, and the most important of them was revenge.[27] He does, however, suggest that there might have been a greater overall purpose to these wars. Ferland thought that 'Iroquois policy' was aimed at 'surrounding their country with a vast wilderness, and to ceaselessly extend this circle of desolation by the destruction, or the dispersion, of nearby tribes'.[28] Unfortunately, if there was some other consideration behind this attempt to create space or a buffer zone between the Iroquois and their Indian neighbours, Ferland fails to explain what it might have been. In any case, once the Hurons were destroyed, the Iroquois turned their attention towards the French. Now they could exact revenge for Champlain's actions through renewed attacks against the colony.[29]

Sulte's interpretation of Iroquois motives in part resembles that of Faillon and Ferland. Like them, he stresses the longevity and ongoing nature of Native warfare before the arrival of the French.[30] He also attributes the early hostility of the Iroquois to Champlain's actions. But—unlike Faillon and Ferland, and much like Garneau—Sulte does not blame Champlain. According to Sulte, Champlain merely acted in self-defence.[31] Nor did revenge and ancient tribal hostilities account for all Iroquois hostilities throughout the century, in Sulte's view: by the 1630s new causes for war had developed. The Dutch were putting pressure on the Iroquois for furs, while the French were expanding their efforts in the fur trade.[32] Caught between ancient Native foes behaving like European monopolists and Europeans ready to overrun them, the Iroquois 'decided to employ diplomacy in order not to be closed in between these two influences and to exploit them to their advantage. From this plan, which was pursued with tenacity and a rare adroitness, was born the war against the Hurons and the French.'[33] The goal of Iroquois policy was two-pronged: 'to contain the Europeans [and] increase the power of the Iroquois.'[34] In their quest for furs to appease their European allies, the Iroquois 'annihilated the Hurons, who were a stumbling block, and enveloped in their vengeance the white men who supported their hereditary enemies'.[35] In short, French efforts to exploit the fur trade were the cause of Iroquois wars against the colony because they brought the French into conflict with Iroquois policy in general, and with their plans for the fur trade in particular.[36]

In the end, though, the often suggestive views of these early French-Canadian historians came to be largely ignored. In Quebec before 1930 the cadre of historians was small; they were preoccupied with contemporary Quebec society; and their research tended to focus on the period after 1763.[37] Iroquois–French relations in the seventeenth century rarely occupied centre stage. The exception was Lionel Groulx's retelling of the battle of the Long Sault, but even there the emphasis was on nation-building rather than Iroquois–French relations.[38]

The views of Faillon and the others were also ignored outside Quebec. Whether because they wrote in French or because the various 'nationalist' concerns that informed their work held little resonance outside Quebec, only a few nineteenth- and twentieth-century anglophone historians writing on Franco–Iroquois relations owe much of a debt to them. Like Garneau, Faillon, and Ferland, the American historian Ruben Gold Thwaites attributed Iroquois hostilities against the

French to Champlain's raids against the Five Nations.[39] By contrast, William Kingsford, in his multi-volume history of Canada, attached no significance to Champlain's raids, attributing Iroquois hostility simply to the desire to protect their land;[40] Ferland too had made this point. But these English writers were the exception. Most scholars accepted Francis Parkman's 'beaver wars' interpretation as the explanation for Iroquois wars in general, including those against New France.[41]

Francis Parkman was an American historian from Boston who chose as his life's work the history of the struggle between France and England for control of northeastern North America. Parkman wrote most of his major works in the last third of the nineteenth century. The military nature of the conflict between France and England, the differences between 'feudal' France and 'liberal' England, and the roles of Native people all played important roles in his histories.[42] While some Quebec historians appreciated Parkman's bringing the history of New France to a wider audience,[43] most resented his condescending tone, as well as the anti-Catholic bias that was deemed inherent in any work by a Protestant, and few—if any—cited his work approvingly.[44] That they rejected Parkman's work is no surprise, given that he wrote his history of New France as a cautionary tale suggesting what might have befallen America had liberty, Protestantism, and the Iroquois not put an end to the French-Catholic experiment.[45]

Yet if his interpretation of the causes of Iroquois warfare against the colony had little influence on nineteenth-century Quebec historiography, Parkman's work remains among the most widely read English-language histories of New France, and his views of the Iroquois and of their relations with the French have had a profound influence on the historiography of both peoples. Whether he was arguing that the Iroquois fought because of a 'bloodlust' or because they depended on European trade goods for survival, Parkman's work and the responses to it, positive or negative, continue to shape the debate on Iroquois–French relations.[46] His views are central to what has come to be known as the 'beaver wars' interpretation of Iroquois hostilities, in which Iroquois culture was changed by contact with Europeans and became dependent upon European material goods; having quickly depleted their fur supply in trading for the new goods, the Iroquois destroyed neighbouring tribes so that they could steal the beaver pelts they needed in order to maintain an uninterrupted flow of European trade goods. The Iroquois waged war against New France to gain control of the trade they needed in order to obtain European goods. By 1915, when Charles McIlwain embellished on Parkman's views by contending that lack of furs and necessity had driven the Iroquois to become middlemen in the fur trade, the 'beaver wars' interpretation had taken firm hold as the dominant explanation of French–Iroquois relations.[47] In 1930 Harold Innis used this explanation to account for Native participation in the fur trade, and in 1940 George Hunt used it as the basis for his explanation of Iroquois hostilities against various Native groups in the Great Lakes region.[48]

Like his French-Canadian contemporaries, Parkman had tried to find the roots of Iroquois aggression in their culture. At first he offered an explanation based on racial qualities specific to the Iroquois—a type of 'bloodlust'.[49] Although his negative view of Indians did not change, his understanding of the reasons for Iroquois aggression did: he came to believe that 'primitive' Iroquois culture had changed through contact with 'superior' European culture and the European-American economic system. While Garneau, Faillon, Ferland, and Sulte were often no more sympathetic than Parkman in their portrayal of the Iroquois, they saw less change in the latter's culture and were able to appreciate the enduring importance of certain cultural practices.

By the 1940s, when Quebec historians and specialists on the Iroquois again focused their attention on Iroquois warfare, the ideologies behind Garneau's, Ferland's, Faillon's, and Sulte's various interpretations had come into question. Modern students of Iroquois–French relations who read their works rejected both those ideologies and the interpretations to which they had given rise. Now historians seeking to explain Iroquois–French relations again turned to the 'beaver wars' interpretation. Parkman's whig version of history, with an element of economic and materialistic determinism grafted onto it, found fertile ground in a post-1940s North America enamoured with the progressive and economic schools of historical enquiry. The economic and 'scientific' view of history fitted especially well with the then current preoccupations of French-Canadian historians.[50]

A brief overview of the interpretations of French–Iroquois relations offered by post-war Quebec historians confirms the centrality of the economically deterministic 'beaver wars' view. For example, Léo-Paul Desrosiers argued that Iroquois need for furs drove them to steal pelts when their position as middlemen could not produce the required amount for trade with the English. Inevitably, the struggle for control of this lucrative trade led to war with New France.[51] Abbé Groulx by and large echoed Desrosiers' analysis.[52] Gustave Lanctot did not completely dismiss revenge and desire for land as motives for Iroquois hostility towards New France, but he subordinated them to the overarching economic goal of deriving profit from the fur trade.[53] For Marcel Trudel the Iroquois wars against New France were simply an extension of their wars against other Native peoples, sparked by the Iroquois's desire to become middlemen in the fur trade.[54] In short, these modern historians ignored the views of their nineteenth-century predecessors in favour of what appeared to be a more 'rational' and 'scientific' perspective on French–Iroquois relations.

Although Garneau, Faillon, Ferland and Sulte did attempt to shape the history of Iroquois–French wars to fit their respective nationalist agendas, at least they had consulted the documents of the seventeenth century. (Faillon's work was the most carefully documented, and much of it was based on original unpublished documents; the others relied more heavily on previously published work.) Their histories reflected the opinions of French authorities and the words of Iroquois combatants and negotiators—albeit in translation. Thus Garneau, Sulte, Faillon, and Ferland found the root causes of Iroquois wars in the nature and obligations of Iroquois culture. These nineteenth-century nationalists did not quite know what to make of references to wars of revenge and pride, to the role of clans in sustaining government and war, and to Iroquois self-interest in protecting themselves and their land. Nor were they able to reconcile their often negative assessment of Native cultures with the apparent coherency of Iroquois policy towards some groups—the French in particular. But, to be fair, understanding the Iroquois was not the focus of their work. It was the evolution of French-Canadian society that interested them.

Nonetheless, Garneau, Faillon, Ferland, and Sulte presented culturally rational explanations of Iroquois hostilities against other groups, Indian and French alike, and pointed to underlying causes of war that some modern writers are beginning to recognize. Today a growing body of literature offers explanations of Iroquois hostilities that often echo the views of these early writers. Like them, more recent historians ground their interpretations in Iroquois culture, and—unlike the 'beaver wars' school—they accept that Iroquois culture changed slowly; that traditional values and motives for war such as the need for captives and revenge were not completely, or even largely, replaced by the desire to gain access to furs; and that the main focus of Iroquois policy was to preserve their political and cultural independence.[55] These are all themes that were clearly articulated in the nineteenth-century works of Garneau, Faillon, Ferland, and Sulte. It is unfortunate that their suggestive work went so long ignored, and exerted so little influence on subsequent scholarship.

NOTES

At a conference to honour Ramsay Cook, a scholar with varied interests and expertise, it seemed appropriate to present a paper on a topic that would speak to several of Professor Cook's interests: Native history, French-Canadian nationalism, and intellectual history. This is a tall order for a short essay, but in reality, I did not really fashion this paper to cover those subject areas. Rather, when I had finished researching what major nineteenth-century French-Canadian historians had to say about Iroquois–French relations, this was the answer, with its various implications, that emerged. I would like to thank the editors, Marcel Martel and Michael Behiels; the session commentator, Cornelius Jaenen; the conference participants; and the anonymous readers at Oxford University Press for their helpful comments.

1. W.J. Eccles, *The Canadian Frontier, 1534–1760* (Albuquerque, 1978); Champigny au ministre, 14 Oct. 1698, Archives Nationales, Paris, Archives des Colonies, series C11 A, 16: 102–3 (hereafter AN, C11A).

2. François-Xavier Garneau, *Histoire du Canada* [1845–1852], 5th ed., rev., 2 vols (Paris, 1913-20); Abbé Jean-Baptiste-Antoine Ferland, *Cours d'histoire du Canada*, 2 vols (Quebec, 1861 and 1865); Abbé Étienne-Michel Faillon, *Histoire de la Colonie Française en Canada* [1534–1682], 3 vols (Villemarie, 1865–6); Benjamin Sulte, 'La guerre des Iroquois, 1600–1653', *Mémoires de la Société Royale du Canada*, 2nd series, vol. 3, sect. 1 (1897), 63–92.

3. For a more detailed discussion of the views of Garneau, Ferland, and Faillon on Indians see B.G. Trigger, *Natives and Newcomers: Canada's Heroic Age Reconsidered* (Montreal and Kingston, 1985), 29–32.

4. This was probably a consequence, as Serge Gagnon has observed, of Garneau's use of Natives as a tool to criticize contemporary French-Canadian society; Gagnon, *Quebec and its Historians: 1840 to 1920* (Montreal, 1982), 29.

5. Ferland, *Histoire du Canada*, 1, 96; Faillon, *Histoire*, 1: 298–301. See also Gagnon, *Quebec and its Historians*, 58–9.

6. Sulte, 'Guerre des Iroquois', 65.

7. Ferland, *Histoire du Canada* 1: iii–vi; Faillon, *Histoire*, 1: xii–xiii.

8. Gagnon, *Quebec and its Historians*, 52–3. Even Sulte did not rule out the work of providence; ibid., 76.

9. Garneau, *Histoire* 1: xlii–lii. See also Gagnon, *Quebec and its Historians*, 9–43.

10. Gagnon, *Quebec and its Historians*, 71, 86–8. Sulte, for example, was vehemently anti-Jesuit. He resented the Jesuit focus on mission activities because it detracted from parish work and drew the hatred of Natives upon the French; ibid., 78–82.

11. Garneau, *Histoire*, 1: 335.

12. Ibid., 76.

13. Ibid., 124.

14. Ibid., 123–4.

15. Ibid., 149.

16. Ibid., 158.

17. Ibid., 159. Like others who would come across this clearly stated goal of Iroquois policy, Garneau did not make anything of it.

18. Ibid., 169.

19. Ibid., 315.

20. Ibid., 319.

21. Ferland, *Histoire du Canada* 1: 146; Faillon, *Histoire*, 1: 136.

22. Ferland, *Histoire du Canada*, 1: 148; Faillon, *Histoire*, 1: 138.

23. Faillon, *Histoire* 1: 355. He even pointed out that the Mohawks warned the French not to get involved in their wars; ibid., 141.

24. Ferland, *Histoire du Canada* 1: 110, 133.

25. Faillon, *Histoire* 2: 28–9, 63, 111–13, 370, 391–2; 3: 13.

26. See his analysis of Iroquois peace efforts in 1641 and 1645; Faillon, *Histoire* 1: 361–7; 2: 34–42.

27. Ferland, *Histoire du Canada*, 1: 423–4.

28. Ibid., 387.

29. Ibid., 388–9.

30. Sulte, 'La guerre des Iroquois', 66–7.

31. Ibid., 67.

32. Ibid., 68. He does not suggest that the Iroquois had no furs, but that the best furs

were from *Haut Canada* and that the Hurons and Iroquets were trading these to the French.

33. Ibid., 69.

34. Ibid. Why the Iroquois wanted to contain the Europeans, and to what end they wanted to increase their power, is not made clear. Given the context, one can assume that it was to control the fur trade, but that is not obvious, nor can other motives be ruled out.

35. Ibid.

36. This is a central theme of Sulte's work and is part of his criticism of government and religious organizations of the colony. For him, the efforts at trade rather than agricultural development lay at the root of the colony's ills; ibid., 70, 83, 86–7, 89.

37. Ronald Rudin, *Making History in Twentieth-Century Quebec* (Toronto, 1997), 13–55.

38. For an interesting discussion of the historical controversy surrounding Dollard des Ormeaux and its implications see Patrice Groulx, *Pièges de la mémoire: Dollard des Ormeaux, les Amérindiens et nous* (Hull, 1998).

39. R.G. Thwaites, *France in America* [1905] (facsimile reprint, New York, 1968), 35–7. Thwaites was quite well connected to nineteenth-century French historians and clerics. He had relied heavily on them for information, advice and documents when compiling and editing his multi-volume *Jesuit Relations and Allied Documents*. See Luca Codignola, 'The Battle is Over: Campeau's *Monumenta* vs. Thwaite's *Jesuit Relations*, 1602–1650', *Native American Studies* 10, 2 (1996), 3–7.

40. William Kingsford, *The History of Canada*, 10 vols (Toronto, 1887–98), 1: 185.

41. See the various essays in Justin Winsor, ed., *Narrative and Critical History of America*, 8 vols (Boston, 1884–9), 1: 283, 285; 5: 2. Indeed, even Kingsford, in his explanation of Iroquois wars in the 1680s, came to adopt Parkman's thesis; Kingsford, *The History of Canada* 1: 473.

42. See the introduction by C.E. Heidenreich and J.A. Brandão to the recently republished editon of Parkman's *The Jesuits in North America in the Seventeeth Century* (Lincoln, 1997).

43. The most notable of these was Parkman's friend the Abbé Casgrain. However, even he was not averse to criticizing Parkman for what Casgrain thought were errors inspired by Protestant bias; H.R. Casgrain, *Parkman* (Quebec, 1872), 11, 65. See also Parkman's letters to Casgrain in Wilbur R. Jacobs, ed., *Letters of Francis Parkman*, 2 vols (Norman, 1960), 2: passim (hereafter, *Parkman Letters*).

44. See Parkman to Pierre Margry, 13 Jan. 1880, Jacobs, ed., *Parkman Letters*, 2: 137. Serge Gagnon has called Parkman 'the foreign writer most frequently criticized' by French Canadians in the nineteenth century (Gagnon, *Quebec and its Historians: 1840 to 1920*, 143, note 6.) Benjamin Sulte was particularly hostile to Parkman; ibid., 68, 99.

45. See W.J. Eccles, 'The History of New France According to Francis Parkman', *William and Mary Quarterly*, 3rd series, XVIII, 4 (April 1961), 163–75.

46. José António Brandão, *Your fyre shall burn no more: Iroquois Policy toward New France and its Native Allies to 1701* (Lincoln, 1997), 5–18.

47. Charles H. McIlwain, ed., *An Abridgement of the Indian Affairs contained in four folio volumes, transacted in the colony of New York, from the year 1678 to the year 1751* [1915]

(New York, 1968), xlii–xliv. See also W.B. Munro, *Crusaders of New France: A Chronicle of the Fleur-de-Lys in the Wilderness* (New Haven, 1918), 42; Louise Kellogg, *The French Régime in Wisconsin and in the Northwest* [1925] (New York, 1968), 222, 243.

48. Harold Innis, *The Fur Trade in Canada* [1930, revised 1956] (Toronto, 1970), 15–21; George Hunt, *The Wars of the Iroquois: A Study in Intertribal Trade Relations* (Madison, 1940).

49. Brandão, '*Your fyre shall burn no more*', 5–18.

50. See Rudin, *Making History in Twentieth-Century Quebec*, passim.

51. Léo-Paul Desrosiers, *Iroquoisie* (Montreal, 1947), 39, 109, 184, 185, 207, 209. He recognized that Champlain's actions initiated hostile relations with the Iroquois, but this was of minor consequence since the economic competition would inevitably lead to hostilities; ibid., 25, 185.

52. Lionel Groulx, *Histoire du Canada Français*, 2 vols [1950] (Montreal, 1976), 1: 125–31.

53. Gustave Lanctot, *A History of Canada [1534–1763]*, 3 vols (Toronto, 1963–5), 1: 170, 179–80.

54. Marcel Trudel, *The Beginnings of New France, 1524–1663* (Toronto, 1973), 57, 149, 217–24. More recent works on New France by Quebec historians have focused on social and economic history (often writ small), or community and institutional studies, and either don't deal with Iroquois–French relations at length or repeat some version of the economically deterministic 'beaver wars' thesis. See, for example, Louise Dechêne, *Habitants et marchands de Montréal au xviie siècle* (Montreal, 1974); François Rousseau, *La Croix et le scalpel: Histoire des Augustines et de l'Hôtel-Dieu de Québec, I: 1639–1892* (Montreal, 1989) The same reliance on the 'beaver wars' interpretation marks the theory-driven work of many Quebec social scientists. See, for example, Denys Dêlage, *Le Pays renversé: Amérindiens et Européens en Amérique du nord-est, 1600–1664* (Montreal, 1985) and Trigger, *Natives and Newcomers*. For an explanation of the views that shaped Trigger's work, see Peter Cook, 'Symbolic and Material Exchange in Intercultural Diplomacy: The French and the Haudenosaunee in the Early Eighteenth Century', in *New Faces of the Fur Trade: Selected Papers of the Seventh North American Fur Trade Conference . . . 1995*, ed. Jo-Ann Fiske et al. (East Lansing, 1998), 75–100. Cook, unfortunately, offers yet another 'model' for studying Iroquois–French relations.

55. See Brandão, *Your fyre shall burn no more*, passim; Lucien Campeau, SJ, *La Mission des Jésuites chez les Hurons, 1634–1650* (Montreal, 1987), 289–90, 345–9; W.J. Eccles, *France in America*, rev. edn (Markham, 1990), 46–7, 91, 95–6; Conrad Heidenreich, 'History of the St. Lawrence-Great Lakes Area to A.D. 1650', in *The Archaeology of Southern Ontario to A.D. 1650*, ed. Chris Ellis and Neal Ferris (Occasional Publications of the London Chapter, Ontario Archaeological Society, No. 5, 1990), 475–92; Dean Snow, *The Iroquois* (Cambridge, 1995), 109–11, 114–15, 127; Daniel K. Richter, 'War and Culture: The Iroquois Experience', *William and Mary Quarterly* 3rd ser., 40 (October 1983), 528–59; Richard White, *The Middle Ground: Indians, Empires, and Republics in the Great Lakes Region, 1650–1815* (New York, 1991); Roland Viau, *Enfants du Néant et mangeurs d'âmes: Guerre, culture et société en Iroquoisie ancienne* (Montreal, 1997).

The Indian Vote in
Saskatchewan Elections

James M. Pitsula

Native history has, since the Second World War, moved to the centre of the writing of Canadian history, a development that reflects the increasing prominence of Native peoples in Canadian life generally.[1] The entrenchment of treaty and Aboriginal rights in the Constitution, Supreme Court decisions bearing on land claims, expansion of self-government including the creation of Nunavut, battles over compensation for residential-school abuse, and numerous other issues have filled the headlines and entered the Canadian consciousness. John Ralston Saul's recent argument that Canada is based on a 'triangular reality'—the Aboriginal, the francophone, and the anglophone—would have been regarded as eccentric in the earlier part of this century, when the concept of the 'vanishing Indian' held sway.[2]

One sign of the resurgence of Native peoples in Canada's public life was the extension, in 1960, of the federal franchise to all Indians. Extension of the provincial franchise began with British Columbia in 1949 and ended with Quebec in 1969. Saskatchewan, the subject of this study, gave the vote to Indians in 1960.[3] Although forty years have passed since the extension of the full franchise, very little has been written about how Indian people have used their vote, and what has been written focuses mainly on the low participation rate and the presumed reasons for it. This essay seeks to throw light on that topic through an intensive examination of the Indian reserve vote in Saskatchewan elections from 1960 to 1995.

First, though, a quick review of the existing literature is in order. Roger Gibbins, in his study for the Royal Commission on Electoral Reform and Party Financing, made the useful point that since elections play an important symbolic role in reaffirming the connection between the individual citizen and the state, 'low rates of electoral participation are symptomatic of distress within the political process and/or political community. When particular groups stand apart in this way, a low rate of participation suggests a significant degree of alienation and disaffection.'[4] In other words, Indians' abstention from voting signified lack of integration with non-Native society.

David Bedford and Sidney Pobihushchy gave this idea a twist in their analysis of voting patterns in the Maritimes. They detected a decline in Indian voter participation in federal and provincial elections from the 1960s to the present, a decline they attributed to the process of 'decolonization', the affirmation of Aboriginal nationalism, and the recovery of Aboriginal traditions: 'We are proposing that this change in consciousness—from Canadians who are Indians, to members of the Maliseet or Micmac nations—is the most important reason for the decline in voter turnout.'[5]

Both Bedford/Pobihushchy and Gibbins correlated a low voting turnout with a weak identification with province and/or country and a high voting turnout with a strong identification. Tim Schouls, on the other hand, observed that some Aboriginal leaders want more Aboriginal representation in Parliament not in order to forge links of common citizenship between Native and non-Native Canadians, but rather to campaign for and facilitate Aboriginal self-government initiatives.[6] In other words, a high Aboriginal voter turnout may not indicate a strong affinity with province or country; it may reflect a strategy aimed at achieving a greater measure of self-government or sovereignty.

This paper attempts to look beyond the issue of voter turnout to compare Indian with non-Indian voting patterns in the province of Saskatchewan. Métis and urban Indian votes are ignored, not because they aren't important, but rather because they cannot be segregated from non-Indian votes. The only votes we know to be Indian are those cast in polls located within the boundaries of Indian reserves. The question is whether these votes form a recognizable and explicable pattern, and, if so, how it compares with that of the rest of the voting population.

However, before proceeding to quantitative analysis, historical context must be provided. In the 1960 Saskatchewan election, the first in which all Indians had the right to vote, two main parties vied for power: the Liberals and the Cooperative Commonwealth Federation (CCF). The latter was renamed the New Democratic Party (NDP) in 1967, six years after its federal counterpart had changed its name. There were serious ideological differences between the two parties, the CCF holding the left-of-centre ground and the Liberals the right-of-centre.

The CCF under Premier T.C. (Tommy) Douglas introduced the 1960 legislation extending the franchise.[7] This reform was considered 'the right thing to do', but it was not carried out before a serious study was undertaken to calculate how the Indian vote would affect the CCF's chances for re-election. The CCF assumed that most Indians would vote Liberal: first, because most Indian agents were federal Liberal appointees who could be counted on to guide reserve residents onto the 'correct' political path,[8] and, second, because most Saskatchewan Indians were nominally Roman Catholic and subject to anti-socialist propaganda from priests.[9] Thus the CCF government's study gave the Liberal Party 60 per cent of the Indian vote and only 30 per cent to themselves. Nevertheless, when these numbers were added to the poll results from the 1956 provincial election, the Liberals gained only one seat, the northern constituency of Athabasca.[10] Hence the CCF knew it could give the vote to Indians without, as a consequence, jeopardizing its hold on power.

Many Indians were deeply skeptical about voting in provincial elections. When news of the possible extension of the franchise filtered out in 1956, two northern Indians wrote Premier Douglas as follows: 'In fact the Indian people haven't got enough, not half enough education to become fully pledged citizens to do this Mr. Premier to send the northern Indians to the polls you might as well send a green Englishman to the trap line.... So Mr. Douglas I'm not going to sell my birth rights which the British Crown had given me just for me to vote and to drink the white man's Fire water.'[11] The reference to loss of 'birth rights' related to the provision in the Indian Act whereby 'enfranchised' Indians lost their status as Indians and became citizens of Canada with the same legal rights and responsibilities as other Canadians. Although Douglas promised that treaty rights would in no way be compromised by provincial voting rights, resistance to the franchise was strong.[12]

To mollify opposition, the Premier invited Indians to a conference held on 30 and 31 October 1958 at Fort Qu'Appelle, attended by 57 chiefs, along with 57 councillors and other leaders representing 57 of the 61 bands in the province.[13] The conference was designed to 'sell' Indians on the idea of voting, but the strategy backfired. The delegates were divided into small discussion groups, with those reputed to be most strongly opposed to the provincial franchise assigned to a group headed by Dr Morris Shumiatcher, a gifted lawyer who was one of the government's top advisers on Indian policy. Shumiatcher's job was to win the Indians over, but this he signally failed to do:

> The degree of understanding about the political and legal complexities of the vote, reflected by this group, was astonishing. Notwithstanding brilliant persuasion by Dr Shumiatcher to which this group was exposed for a day, they still failed to change their opinion. In fact when he started five of the group were in favor but when the day ended they were unanimously opposed! Significantly, the group asked Dr Shumiatcher to prepare their negative report.[14]

Douglas called a second Indian conference in October 1959. Once again delegates were asked to approve the provincial franchise and once again they refused. Frustrated and impatient, Douglas decided to move ahead even though it meant breaking his commitment not to proceed with the legislation 'without the approval and consent of the Indians'.[15] He knew that the decision would be unpopular with some Indian leaders, but he hoped that with the passage of time fears about the loss of treaty rights would be put to rest.[16] Clearly, granting the vote was a 'top-down decision' imposed on Indians, many of whom were hostile to the 'rights' being conferred upon them. Inevitably, the manner in which Saskatchewan Indians acquired the vote would influence their subsequent voting behaviour.

In general there was little to choose, initially, between the policies the CCF and the Liberals presented to the Indian electorate. Both were on the side of ending discrimination and integrating Indians into the larger society and economy. Woodrow Lloyd, who succeeded Douglas as CCF leader and premier in 1961, declared: 'There is a goal upon which most of us will readily agree. It is the steady integration of all minority groups into the mainstream of Canadian society.' To achieve this goal with respect to Indians, he called for removal of 'the artificial division in public services between them and all other Canadians'; in other words, he urged that responsibility for the delivery of services to Indians be transferred from the federal to the provincial government.[17] In the April 1964 general election the CCF was defeated by the Liberals under Ross Thatcher, who continued the integrationist policies of the previous government. He agreed with Lloyd that the provincial government should deliver services—including social welfare, health, education, natural resources, and agriculture—to Indians.[18] In addition, Thatcher launched an ambitious program designed to integrate Indian and Métis people into the economy. A provincial Indian and Métis Branch was established to place persons of Aboriginal ancestry in jobs, arrange for their training, provide housing, and give grants and loans to Aboriginal entrepreneurs.[19]

The CCF at first supported Thatcher's programs, but gradually began to question what he was doing. In 1964 the party initiated a policy review under the auspices of a Minorities Policy Committee. The name itself is significant. At this stage the CCF hierarchy evidently regarded Indians as just one among a number of ethnic minorities, rather than as First Nations with special status and entitlements. But the ground was shifting. One of the Committee members, CCF MLA Bill Berezowsky, set off a hot debate when he explicitly condemned integration and argued that a bloc of land should be set aside where Indians could forge their own separate destiny, beyond the reach of interfering non-Indians.[20]

Berezowsky's proposal drew the wrath of another member of the Minorities Committee, the economist Helen Buckley. She said that the 'national territory' Berezowsky had in mind was equivalent to a system of apartheid.[21] Despite these deep divisions, the Minorities Policy Committee eventually produced a report, which was submitted and approved by the CCF provincial convention in 1966. Although Buckley won out over Berezowsky, the policy statement did suggest a new sensitivity to some of the possible drawbacks of integration. The CCF declared that it stood for 'equality of opportunity'—but 'provision of equal opportunity does *not* [emphasis in original] mean forced assimilation; people of Indian ancestry must have a real choice whether or not to use programs and services and must be free to suggest alternative programs.' In addition, 'minorities must participate in the decisions which affect their lives,' and 'new opportunities must be seen, not as submerging the traditional Indian culture, but as a means to a more abundant life in which can be kept what is wanted from the past.' The CCF still favoured the transfer of responsibility for Indian affairs from the federal to the provincial level of government, but only if 'present rights and privileges' were preserved.[22]

The next step in the evolution of CCF policy was taken in reaction to the federal government's 1969 White Paper. Regarded as a catalyst in the development of the Aboriginal political movement in Canada, the White Paper recommended phasing out the separate legal category of 'status Indian', eliminating the federal Indian Affairs Department, transferring responsibility for delivering Indian services to the provinces, giving title to reserve lands to Indians rather than the Crown, and moving away from treaty obligations.[23] Premier Thatcher lauded the document as an 'excellent start'[24] to the reconstitution of Indian/non-Indian relations, but the NDP (as the Saskatchewan CCF was now known) was harshly critical. It faulted the federal government for failing to consult adequately with Indians, and it insisted that the government live up to its treaty obligations. The White Paper proposed that the 'treaties be reviewed to see how they can be equitably ended.'[25] The Saskatchewan NDP, by contrast, called on the federal government to negotiate 'an acceptable definition of the status and meaning of the original arrangements (treaties) and guarantees given to the Indian population'. The NDP added that it would be unthinkable for the federal government to transfer Indian affairs to the provinces without giving 'solid guarantees that the aboriginal and residual rights would be protected' and without 'general agreement across Canada on the part of the organizations which represent the Indian people'. It concluded by noting that 'the white man's legalistic definition of "equality" is not by itself an acceptable goal. Only out of procedures which recognize the historical rights of the Indian people can come workable decisions which will lead toward the establishment of mutual trust.'[26]

The Saskatchewan NDP had travelled a long distance since 1964, when its Indian policies had been virtually indistinguishable from those of the Thatcher Liberals. Woodrow Lloyd played a leading role in this transformation. He reconceptualized the philosophical basis of policy by posing a new question. Instead of asking 'what should an NDP government *do* for Indians?', he asked 'what relationship should the Government of Saskatchewan have with the Indian community?' As soon as this question was formulated, the door leading to Indian self-government could be opened. The shift in Lloyd's thinking can be detected in a memorandum he sent to the NDP party president in July 1969:

'Program' [referring to the NDP's Aboriginal program] needs defining. Admittedly it should include 'things' which a New Democratic Party government would undertake to do. Equally important, and indeed I think more important, is the necessity to define the kind of relationship we want to develop with members of the Indian community wherever such a community exists. This is turn involves some definition of the role for Indian people. It involves also a method of transferring certain essential authority to the Indians in their communities. Obviously if authority is to be meaningful there must at the same time be access to certain resources.[27]

Allan Blakeney, who succeeded Lloyd as leader in 1970, continued down the same path. Following a meeting with the executive of the Federation of Saskatchewan Indians in September 1970, he criticized the provincial Indian and Métis department, saying that it had become a rigid bureaucracy much like the federal Indian Affairs department. More significantly, he publicly disavowed the integration policy: 'Several years ago, a clear answer to discrimination was integration. That may now not be necessarily so.'[28]

As the provincial election of 23 June 1971 approached, NDP Indian policy became sharper and more focused. An internal election strategy document pointed out that 'the Indian culture is far from being destroyed, and any attempt to appeal for Indian votes on the basis of an invitation into the "mainstream" will be politely received, but not accepted.' It advised that the NDP promise to fight any plan by the federal government to break the treaties. Gone was the proposal the party had championed in the early 1960s to transfer Indian programs from the federal to the provincial level. Instead, the strategy document suggested the NDP take the line that the provincial Indian and Métis Department should be eliminated or greatly altered. The reason was obvious: 'The Liberals set up that department because they knew that the Federal Government was going to try to get out of its responsibilities to the Indians, and Thatcher wanted to be the first to help them to do it. We will insist that Ottawa live up to its obligations to the Indians, and keep the treaties.'[29]

The 1971 NDP platform, entitled 'New Deal for People', mirrored the strategy document. The party promised to overhaul drastically or even abolish the Indian and Métis Department, provide substantial grants to the central organizations of the Indian people and the Métis people, and ensure that Indian and Métis organizations were effectively involved in planning and implementing the programs that affected them. Grants were promised to enable Indians to make a thorough study of treaty rights, and funds were pledged for 'programs worked out in cooperation with Indian and Métis leaders, and where feasible and desired by them, administered by their organizations'. The NDP platform affirmed that 'the goals to be pursued must be those arrived at freely by the native people themselves, not those prescribed by an alien society "for their own good."'[30] Certainly this was not full-blown Aboriginal self-government, but it represented a step in that direction, and it was definitely not the integrationist policy to which the Liberals still subscribed.

Why had NDP policy evolved while Liberal policy had not? Part of the answer lies in the fact that NDP politicians were more aware of and sensitive to developments occurring within the Federation of Saskatchewan Indians (FSI) during the 1960s. Under the leadership of Walter Deiter[31] and David Ahenakew, the FSI emerged as a strong and effective organization. A key breakthrough was a federal government grant of $69,000 in 1967-8 (the provincial grant was only $10,000 per year), which enabled the Federation to hire a staff of six communication workers and to become, for the first time, a program-delivery organization, rather than a mere lobby group.[32] Neither Deiter nor Ahenakew could be described as a 'radical militant', but they were firm in their resolve to assert Indian rights to self-determination. 'I don't go along with the idea of Black Power or Red Power . . . they [Indian people] don't have any of these notions of revolution or wanting to control the whole world,' Deiter was quoted as saying; but he added that Indians might have to be tougher and more demanding in order to achieve their goals. Ahenakew, who had served for sixteen years in the Canadian army, also rejected a violent or militant approach. He spoke instead of a 'quiet revolution' in the relationship between Indians and non-Indians.[33]

Woodrow Lloyd and Allan Blakeney knew that the FSI had become disenchanted with the Thatcher government's integrationist policies and lack of support for the FSI. They also knew that the Indian vote was vital in certain constituencies.[34] It made sense from a pragmatic point of view to take advantage of Thatcher's rigidity and reposition the NDP to win Indian support. At the level of ideology and principle, this strategy conformed to the CCF tradition of 'humanity first' and siding with the disadvantaged.[35]

The federal NDP was also revising its Indian policy at about this time. Frank James Tester et al. note that the policy resolutions of the 1963 national NDP convention favoured integration: the repeal of the Indian Act, 'elimination of all government activities which place Indian people in a separate group', the introduction of self-government to reserves, the transfer of responsibility for Indian Affairs to provincial government, an aggressive program of educational integration, establishment of an Indian Court of Claims to hear disputes over lands or trusts, and establishment of an 'Economic and Social Development Board' for economic development and job creation. There was, however, an important caveat. The repeal of the Indian Act was to be accomplished at a pace 'commensurate with the needs and desires of Indian people', and responsibility would be transferred to the provinces only 'providing such transfers accord with the desires of the Indians'. Even as the national NDP put forward an integration program, they promised to heed the voices of Indian people. According to Tester et al., this commitment to consultation was the reason the NDP rethought its Indian policy more quickly than did the other national parties. When the Trudeau government introduced the 1969 White Paper, the initial reaction of Frank Howard, the federal NDP Indian Affairs critic, was positive; but the next day, after Indian leaders denounced the Paper, the NDP view 'suddenly chilled'. Tester et al. maintain that what made the sudden reversal and embracing of First Nations' self-determination possible was the federal NDP's strong belief in allowing First Nations to articulate their own needs, rather than imposing external solutions.[36]

The same might be said of the Saskatchewan NDP, but it was somewhat ahead of its federal counterpart in moving away from the integrationist approach. As we have seen, the party in Saskatchewan initiated a policy review in 1964, culminating in a report, approved by provincial convention in 1966, that modified the integration policy. The reaction to the White Paper confirmed and greatly reinforced a trend that was already under way. The provincial Liberals, dominated by the strong personality and firm convictions of Ross Thatcher, made no concessions to the changing times and the new terms of political discourse concerning Indian/non-Indian relations.

By 1971, then, the Saskatchewan NDP Indian policy diverged significantly from that of the Liberals, and it would be reasonable to expect this difference to have had an impact on the Indian vote in the provincial election held that year. Elections, however, are not just about policy, and they are not fought solely on the abstract plane of ideas. A fuller understanding of Indian voting patterns requires a descent from the heights of policy to the trench warfare of party politics.

Woodrow Lloyd's cardinal rule for attracting Indian votes was to make personal contact with Indian voters, and not just at election time. In fact, he said that election time was probably too late. He not only advised CCF candidates to this effect,[37] but also practised what he preached in the two reserves in his Biggar constituency. Prior to the 1960 election, he sent copies of the CCF newspaper to Lennox Wuttunee, Chief of Red Pheasant Reserve, and invited the reserve to send delegates to the Biggar constituency convention.[38] After the election Lloyd kept in contact, attending the Red Pheasant sports day and making sure that the chief had his mailing address and telephone number.[39] On behalf of his Indian constituents, Lloyd wrote provincial government ministers trying to hasten the building of grid roads and the extension of electric power to the reserves.[40] He repeatedly lobbied the federal minister of Indian Affairs on such matters as roads, housing, water supply, clearing and breaking of land for agriculture, and eligibility for social assistance.[41] In short, he did whatever he could to give practical help to reserve residents.[42]

Lloyd also tried to involve Indian people in the organizational structures of the party. At the local level, the annual Biggar constituency convention in 1969 featured presentations by two Indian university students, Valentine Nighttraveller and Rodney Soonias.[43] Attempts were made to encourage Indians to join constituency executives and committees. For example, it was suggested at a meeting of the provincial CCF Organization and Finance Committee in January 1967 'that constituencies with native population be continually reminded and urged to get Indian representation on their executive, zone committees, etc.',[44] and Lloyd expressed satisfaction that some of the delegates to the 1967 provincial convention were Indians.[45] Matthew Bellegarde, a treaty Indian, was not only elected to both the Provincial CCF Youth Executive and the Provincial Council, but also wrote a column for the *Commonwealth*, the party newspaper.[46]

Lloyd's good intentions and best efforts notwithstanding, significant numbers of Indians did not join party committees at either the provincial or the constituency level. Phil Thompson, an Indian from Alberta who was brought in to work on the 1967 campaign,[47] lamented the lack of communication between the CCF organization and the reserves: although there were Indian representatives on the Melville and Moosomin executives, he said, that was the extent of participation in that part of the province.[48]

It could be that the CCF rank and file did not fully share Lloyd's enthusiasm for welcoming Indians into the organization. Helen Shingoose, who served on the CCF Provincial Council, felt that she had been treated badly when she was not hired as a paid organizer: 'When it comes to being a paid organizer it's too good a job for an Indian. . . . I know I've been used as a cigar store display. The NDP party can say we have an Indian as councillor just for a big false front.'[49] Thora Wiggins, a prominent CCF activist from the Prince Albert area, confided to Lloyd: 'I needn't tell you that even among our own supporters there is often prejudice.'[50] Helen Buckley, who worked on the Minorities Policy Committee, had a similar complaint: 'It is my opinion that the CCF-NDP could care less about Indians. They like to think they have a committee "working on the problem", but they have no intention of using our document, of taking a stand and formulating a CCF-NDP policy for Indians, of taking the Thatcher government to task for the glaring inadequacies of its program, etc.'[51] The tepid response of Indians to the CCF's invitations to become involved and accept positions in the party were perhaps the result of these discriminatory attitudes.

The battle for Indian votes was at times fierce and rough. S. Dale Perkins, a CCF supporter from Balcarres, alleged that 'the [Thatcher] Government is availing themselves of every means to "get at" the Indian people for political purposes.' Perkins claimed that the Federation of Saskatchewan Indians had been 'conned' into setting up meetings on reserves for the benefit of Liberal politicians in return for provincial grants to the Federation.[52] Another sign that the line between programs for Indians and politicking was blurred came in a memo from Deputy Premier Dave Steuart to Thatcher in which Steuart stated that he was under pressure to appoint an Indian and Métis Community Development officer in the Indian Head-Fort Qu'Appelle-Melville-Balcarres areas: 'In view of the fact that the Indian population in this area could affect at least four of the provincial seats we now hold, I would recommend that we be given permission to add one employee and one vehicle to our establishment.' Thatcher scrawled on the memo: 'With a lack of enthusiasm, I agree. Can he produce[?]'[53]

Reports from the Meadow Lake constituency, which had a large Aboriginal population, provide more specific insights into the way campaigns were fought. In February 1967 CCF candidate Martin Semchuk worked the reserves with two Indian organizers, Chief Ed Laliberte and Sidney Fineday. The election had not yet been called:

Waterhen reserve both Ed and Sidney: Met with Chief Martell. Fred Martell and most of his relatives will vote Semchuk. Left instruction with Chief Martell that if the Libs hand out goodies such as liquor as in the last election people are to be advised to take all they can get and ask for more. After the election if they are asked why they didn't support the Liberal candidate they are to answer "we were too drunk."... Also held meeting at Canoe Narrows with Chief John Iron (formerly cons.) talked to a group of about 15 people indicated that we might have Ed Laliberte running as CCF candidate in Athabasca constituency. If this should develop many Indian and Metis people in the province could change from conservative [sic] to ccf. . . . Little Pine reservation. Talked with a very staunch ccf organizer Burton Batiste. Had a long talk re: ccf organizing on the reserve. His wife has been doing considerable work in this regard. She felt that there were a lot of people changing from Cons. to CCF because of the possible involvement of an Indian ccf candidate. Others were turning to the ccf because of the possible passing of Chief John (Dief). . . .[54]

This report hints at a number of aspects of Indian participation in provincial politics: the role of liquor in elections, the tendency for families to vote as blocs following the lead of the chiefs, the appeal of an Indian candidate to Indian voters, the involvement of Indian women in party politics, and the personal popularity of John Diefenbaker.[55]

The level of intensity increased several notches when the campaign was actually under way:

> ... Liberals are threatening the native people that they will be cut off welfare if they vote CCF; the Hudson Bay store manager at La Loche has threatened to cut off Indians' credit if they vote CCF or help the party in any way. Martin [Semchuk] says the 'liquor is flowing at Green Lake.' ... Martin just found out that in the 1964 election, the priest at La Loche (Father Matthew) went around house to house in the last days of the campaign and told his parishioners—'if the CCF get in again, they will take away your beads and smash your Holy pictures, etc.' Martin says he believes he will do it again this time.[56]

The CCF responded by circulating an election pamphlet in Meadow Lake that featured Premier Thatcher's infamous quote to the effect that Indians and Métis were 'breeding faster than rabbits'.[57]

It is evident that both the NDP and the Liberal Party fought hard to win as many Indian votes as possible. They employed a variety of methods ranging from strategic, long-range policies to electioneering tactics that descended to the grosser forms of bribery and intimidation. We now turn to the question of how Indians responded to these appeals, threats, and blandishments.

The study of Indian voting is complicated by the fact that it is impossible to identify the Indian vote when both Indians and non-Indians voted in the same poll. It is necessary, therefore, to confine the analysis to polls located entirely within reserve boundaries. In the 1960 election, there was only one such poll, and in 1964, only two—not enough to yield meaningful evidence. In 1967, by contrast, there were 27 polls within reserve boundaries (4,313 eligible voters); in 1971, 30 (5,881 eligible voters), and in subsequent provincial elections, at least 40 (see Figure 1).[58] This represented only a fraction of the Saskatchewan's 143 reserves, but is sufficient to give some indication of the Indian vote.

Reserve polls are, of course, rural polls. Thus it is appropriate, when comparing the Indian and non-Indian vote, to focus on the *rural* vote, defined by the Chief Electoral Officer for Saskatchewan, 1991, as including all constituencies except for Regina, Saskatoon, Moose Jaw, Prince Albert, Swift Current, Yorkton, and North Battleford. Otherwise, the extraneous variable of 'urbanness' is introduced, disturbing the comparisons between Indian and non-Indian voting patterns.[59]

Figure 1 compares the voting turnout among the rural population in Saskatchewan elections from 1967 to 1995 with the turnout of Indian reserve voters. It shows that the Indian voter participation rate is significantly lower than that of the rural population as a whole. In 1967, 79.31 per cent of all eligible rural voters cast a ballot, compared with 56.09 per cent of Indian voters. In 1971, the

Figure 1. Voter Turnout in Saskatchewan Provincial Elections, 1967-1995: Rural Population and Reserve Polls

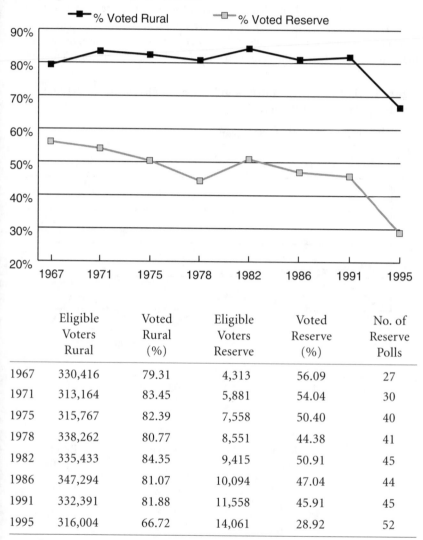

	Eligible Voters Rural	Voted Rural (%)	Eligible Voters Reserve	Voted Reserve (%)	No. of Reserve Polls
1967	330,416	79.31	4,313	56.09	27
1971	313,164	83.45	5,881	54.04	30
1975	315,767	82.39	7,558	50.40	40
1978	338,262	80.77	8,551	44.38	41
1982	335,433	84.35	9,415	50.91	45
1986	347,294	81.07	10,094	47.04	44
1991	332,391	81.88	11,558	45.91	45
1995	316,004	66.72	14,061	28.92	52

figures were 83.45 per cent and 54.04 per cent respectively.[60] In subsequent provincial elections there was a difference of roughly 30 to 35 percentage points between the rural voter participation rate and the Indian participation rate. There may be many reasons for this relative lack of interest in provincial elections, but it seems reasonable to conclude, following Roger Gibbins,[61] that a low rate of participation reflects a relatively weak attachment to the provincial political community.

Figures 2–4 compare the vote obtained by the various parties in rural Saskatchewan with the vote on the reserves. In the 1967 election the rural vote broke down as follows: Liberal, 46.17 per cent (reserve, 44.81 per cent); NDP, 42.54 per cent (reserve, 36.59 per cent); Progressive Conservative, 9.77 per cent (reserve, 18.60 per cent). These results show that CCF were correct in their supposition, prior to granting the vote to Indians in 1960, that the Liberals had an edge. The Liberal

Figure 2. NDP Vote in Saskatchewan Provincial Elections, 1967-1995: Rural Population and Reserve Polls

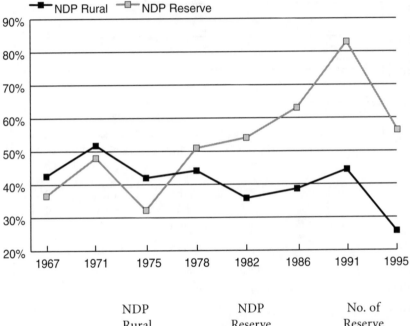

	NDP Rural (%)	NDP Reserve (%)	No. of Reserve Polls
1967	42.54	36.59	27
1971	51.80	47.99	30
1975	42.00	32.24	40
1978	44.14	51.01	41
1982	35.83	54.06	45
1986	38.61	63.04	44
1991	44.41	82.91	45
1995	25.84	56.27	52

reserve vote was almost as strong as the party's rural vote, while the NDP reserve vote trailed its rural vote by six percentage points. The Progressive Conservative reserve vote was surprisingly high, possibly because of the continuing influence and popularity of John Diefenbaker.

In 1971 there were some shifts in the rural vote: Liberals, 44.23 per cent (reserve, 50.69 per cent); NDP, 51.80 per cent (reserve, 47.99 per cent); and Progressive

Figure 3. Liberal Vote in Saskatchewan Provincial Elections, 1967-1995: Rural Population and Reserve Polls

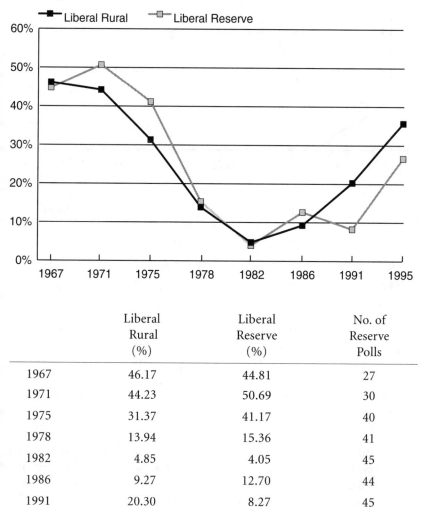

	Liberal Rural (%)	Liberal Reserve (%)	No. of Reserve Polls
1967	46.17	44.81	27
1971	44.23	50.69	30
1975	31.37	41.17	40
1978	13.94	15.36	41
1982	4.85	4.05	45
1986	9.27	12.70	44
1991	20.30	8.27	45
1995	35.68	26.56	52

Figure 4. Progressive Conservative Vote in Saskatchewan Provincial
Elections, 1967-1995: Rural Population and Reserve Polls

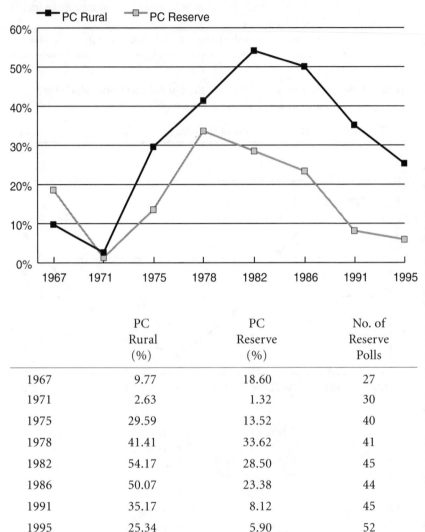

	PC Rural (%)	PC Reserve (%)	No. of Reserve Polls
1967	9.77	18.60	27
1971	2.63	1.32	30
1975	29.59	13.52	40
1978	41.41	33.62	41
1982	54.17	28.50	45
1986	50.07	23.38	44
1991	35.17	8.12	45
1995	25.34	5.90	52

Conservative, 2.63 per cent (reserve, 1.32 per cent). The vote became polarized
between the Liberals and the NDP as the Conservatives faded. Both the Liberals and
NDP showed gains in the Indian vote. The Liberals grew 5.88 percentage points and
the NDP, 11.4 percentage points. Why this movement towards the NDP occurred is
difficult to say. Although it may have been the result of organizational efforts in
particular constituencies, the fact that by 1971 the NDP was espousing a degree of

Figure 5. Reserve Vote in Saskatchewan Provincial Elections, 1967-1995

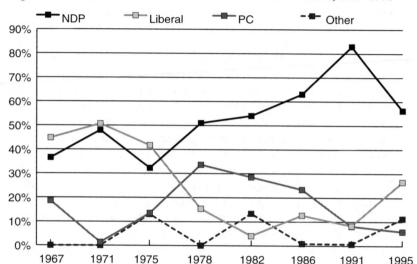

	NDP (%)	Liberal (%)	PC (%)	Other (%)	No. of Polls
1967	36.59	44.81	18.60	0.00	27
1971	47.99	50.69	1.32	0.00	30
1975	32.24	41.71	13.52	13.07	40
1978	51.01	15.36	33.62	0.00	41
1982	54.06	4.05	28.50	13.39	45
1986	63.04	12.70	23.38	0.88	44
1991	82.91	8.27	8.12	0.70	45
1995	56.27	26.56	5.90	11.26	52

Indian self-determination, while the Liberals adhered to the integration policy, probably increased the swing to the NDP.

Figure 5 shows that since 1975 the reserve vote has consistently favoured the NDP, sometimes by a very wide margin. In 1991, for example, 82.91 per cent of Indian voters supported the NDP. The reasons for this pattern are undoubtedly complex and varied, but the fact that the NDP has been in the forefront of advocating a measure of self-government for Indians is surely relevant. On the other hand, Figures 2–4 show that reserve voting patterns are very similar to general rural voting patterns. The graph lines for the Liberal rural vote and reserve vote are almost identical, while the lines for the NDP and Progressive Conservative parties are very similar. They move up and down in synchronized fashion. This suggests that Indian and non-Indian voters were, so to speak, marching to the same drummer and subject to the same swings in public opinion. As Figure 5 makes clear, parties other than the NDP, Liberals, and Conservatives have obtained scant support on the reserves. In 1975 Independents garnered 13.07 per cent of the vote. In 1982 the Aboriginal People's Party of Saskatchewan took 7.43 per cent, and together the Western Canada Concept Party and one Independent took 5.97 per cent. In 1995 four candidates endorsed by the United Aboriginal People's Party captured 11.26 per cent of the reserve vote. In all the other provincial elections the vote count for parties other than the mainstream parties was either zero or close to zero.

This paper has taken Saskatchewan as a case study to examine Indian voting behaviour. We have seen that both of the main contenders for power, the CCF/NDP and the Liberals, aggressively pursued the Indian vote after the extension of the franchise in 1960. Both parties initially favoured a policy of integrating Indians into the provincial mainstream, but the NDP broke with this policy in the late 1960s and moved in the direction of endorsing Indian self-government. The Thatcher Liberals adhered to the idea that the solution to Indian problems lay in integrating Indians as equal, undifferentiated citizens into the provincial economy and society. This difference in approach may explain the shift in Indian electoral support from the Liberals to the NDP in the late 1960s.

At the grassroots constituency level, the fight for Indian votes was intense. CCF leader Woodrow Lloyd emphasized personal contact and tried to introduce Indians into party structures, but with minimal success. Other variables included family bloc voting, the influence of Roman Catholic clergy, patronage, liquor, and the threat of losing welfare benefits. More research is needed in this area to understand the political culture of reserve communities and how it resembled or differed from that of non-Aboriginal communities.

The low voter turnout among Indians is striking evidence of disengagement from the provincial community. In addition, the overall trend since the 1960s has been for Indian voters to give their support to the party most identified with the policy of Indian self-government. On the other hand, the fact that fluctuations in the party preferences of those Indians who did vote closely matched those of non-Indians suggests a degree of integration into provincial party politics. Indian voters seem to have responded to the same influences and trends as other residents of Saskatchewan. This suggests that simple dichotomies are misleading and that a more subtle interpretation is needed. Indian voters in Saskatchewan were alienated from the provincial political process, but not completely alienated. When Indian votes are compiled and compared with non-Indian votes, similarities as well as differences emerge. Mainstream political parties were not indifferent to Indian voters, and Indian voters were not indifferent to the mainstream political parties. Traced over decades, voting patterns suggest shared political experience as well as separateness and disaffection.

NOTES

1. Bruce G. Trigger, 'The Historians' Indian: Native Americans in Canadian Historical Writing from Charlevoix to the Present', *Canadian Historical Review* LXVII, 3 (1986), 338.

2. John Ralston Saul, *Reflections of a Siamese Twin: Canada at the End of the Twentieth Century* (Toronto, 1997), 81; Daniel Francis, *The Imaginary Indian: The Image of the Indian in Canadian Culture* (Vancouver, 1992), 53–7.

3. Canada, *Royal Commission on Aboriginal People* 1 (1996), 299–300.

4. Roger Gibbins, 'Electoral Reform and Canada's Aboriginal Population: An Assessment of Aboriginal Electoral Districts', in *Aboriginal Peoples and Electoral Reform in Canada*, ed. Robert A. Milen (Toronto, 1991), 154.

5. David Bedford and Sidney Pobihushchy, 'On-Reserve Status Indian Voter Participation in the Maritimes', *Canadian Journal of Native Studies* XV, 2 (1995), 269.

6. Tim Schouls, 'Aboriginal Peoples and Electoral Reform in Canada: Differentiated Representation Versus Voter Equality', *Canadian Journal of Political Science* XXIX, 4 (December 1996), 739.

7. For a discussion of the extension to Indians of the right to vote in Saskatchewan provincial elections see James M. Pitsula, 'The Saskatchewan CCF Government and Treaty Indians, 1944–64', *Canadian Historical Review* 75 (1994), 21–52.

8. Saskatchewan Archives Board [hereafter SAB], T.C. Douglas Papers, R-33.7 I 291a, Committee on Indian Affairs, First Report, 19 Nov. 1956.

9. Ibid., R-33.1 XLV 864c (49) 3/6, Angus Mirasty and William B. Charles to T.C. Douglas, 9 April 1956.

10. Ibid., R-33.7 I 291a, Committee on Indian Affairs, First Report, 19 Nov. 1956.

11. Ibid., R-33.1 XLV 864c (49) 3/6, Angus Mirasty and William B. Charles to T.C. Douglas, 9 April 1956.

12. SAB, W.S. Lloyd Papers, R-61.1 I 34 (1), Provincial Conference of Saskatchewan Indian Chiefs and Councillors, Valley Centre, Fort Qu'Appelle, 30 and 31 Oct. 1958.

13. Ibid., R-61.3 E-27 17/21, G. Campbell to W.S. Lloyd, 3 Nov. 1968.

14. Ibid.

15. Ibid., R-61.1 I 34 (1), Provincial Conference of Saskatchewan Indian Chiefs and Councillors, Valley Centre, Fort Qu'Appelle, 30 and 31 Oct. 1958.

16. SAB, T.C. Douglas Papers, R-33.1 XLV 864e (49), T.C. Douglas to Dan Kennedy, 23 Feb. 1960

17. SAB, F. Meakes Papers, R-74.1 II 3, E.I. Wood to All Chiefs, 14 February 1964, attached Dominion-Provincial Conference—Excerpt from Premier's Statement, Nov. 1963.

18. SAB, J.R. Ross Barrie Papers, R-10 VII 48a, A Submission from the Government of Saskatchewan on the Administration of Indian Affairs, Aug. 1964; *Leader-Post* (Regina), 29 Oct. 1964.

19. James M. Pitsula, 'The Thatcher Government in Saskatchewan and Treaty Indians, 1964–1971: The Quiet Revolution', *Saskatchewan History* 48 (1996), pp. 5–9.

20. SAB, W.S. Lloyd Papers, R-61.8 XXI 125b 1/2, MLA Report on Indian and Métis Minority Policy, William J. Berezowsky, Jan. 1966.

21. Ibid., R-61.8 XXI 106k, CCF Minorities Policy Subcommittee to Members of the CCF Caucus, authored by Helen Buckley, 16 April 1966.

22. Ibid., R-61.8 XXI 106n 1/3, Cooperative Commonwealth Federation, Saskatchewan Section of the New Democratic Party, 1966 Provincial Convention, The Indian and Métis Minorities Policy Statement.

23. Statement of the Government of Canada on Indian Policy, 1969.

24. Leader-Post (Regina) (5 Aug. 1969). See also Pitsula, 'The Thatcher Government in Saskatchewan and Treaty Indians', 13–17.

25. Statement of the Government of Canada on Indian Policy, 1969, p. 11.

26. SAB, A.E. Blakeney Papers, R-1143 X 1c, Statement of the Saskatchewan New Democratic Party on the Recent Federal Government Policy that the Provinces Would Assume Responsibility for Indian Programs and Services, 30 July 1969.

27. SAB, W.S. Lloyd Papers, R-61.8 XXI 119b 2/2, W.S. Lloyd to Bev Currie, 16 July 1969.

28. Leader-Post (Regina) (30 Sept. 1970).

29. SAB, A.E. Blakeney Papers, R-800 III 25 16/38, Wylie Simmonds to Allan Blakeney, Ted Bowerman, Gerry Wilson, Norm Kennedy, Hal Tate, 28 May 1971.

30. Ibid., R-800 I 214 2/2, 'New Deal for People', New Democratic Party of Saskatchewan, Feb. 1971.

31. Patricia Ann Deiter, 'A Biography of Chief Walter P. Deiter', MA thesis, University of Regina, 1997.

32. Pitsula, 'The Thatcher Government in Saskatchewan and Treaty Indians', 12–15.

33. Ibid., 12–13.

34. SAB, W.S. Lloyd Papers, R-61.8 XXI 125f 4/4, W.S. Lloyd to All CCF MLAs and Candidates, 14 July 1966, 'You will know that there are a number of constituencies in which the Indian vote can be the decisive factor.'

35. Pitsula, 'The Saskatchewan CCF Government and Treaty Indians, 1944–64', Canadian Historical Review 75 (1994), 26.

36. Frank James Tester, Paule McNicoll and Jessie Forsyth, 'With an Ear to the Ground: The CCF/NDP and Aboriginal Policy in Canada, 1926–1993', unpublished paper.

37. SAB, W.S. Lloyd Papers, R-61.8 XXI 125f 4/4, W.S. Lloyd to All CCF MLAs and Candidates, 14 July 1966.

38. bid., R-61.3 G-2 40/42, W.S. Lloyd to Lennox Wuttunee, 16 May 1960.

39. Ibid., W.S. Lloyd to Lennox Wuttunee, 15 June 1960.

40. Ibid., R-61.3 G-2 42a, W.S. Lloyd to L.F. McIntosh, 14 Oct. 1960; R-61.3 G-2 42a, W.S. Lloyd to R. Brown, 14 Oct. 1960.

41. Ibid., R-61.8 XXI 144c, W.S. Lloyd to R. Tremblay, 30 June 1965; R-61.8 XVIII 81, W.S. Lloyd to A. Laing, 21 Oct. 1966.

42. Ibid., R-61.8 XVIII 81, W.S. Lloyd to Chief Nicotine and Chief Mosquito, 16 Feb. 1967.

43. Ibid., R-61.7 3b, Report of Annual Constituency Convention—Biggar, 19 April 1969.

44. Ibid., R-61.8 XXI 106l 2/2, CCF Organization and Finance Committee, Minutes, 7 Jan. 1967.

45. Ibid., R-61.8 XXI 115b, News Release—CCF Provincial Convention—25 Nov. 1967.

46. Ibid., R-61.7 3a, W.S. Lloyd to Chief George Batiste, 13 March 1968; R-61.8 XXI 108-20, W.S. Lloyd to John J. Morrow, 31 May 1968.

47. Ibid., R-61.8 XXI 106r, L.G. Benjamin to W.S. Lloyd and Strategy Committee, 29 Aug. 1967.

48. Ibid., Minutes, Joint Strategy-Publicity Meeting (CCF), 23 Sept. 1967.

49. Ibid., R-61.8 XXI 119b 2/2, Helen Shingoose to Fred, 12 March [no year given].

50. Ibid., R-61.4 XXI 445, Thora Wiggins to W.S. Lloyd, 24 Feb. 1964.

51. Ibid., R-61.8 XXI 106k, Helen Buckley to G.B. Mather, 18 Feb. 1966.

52. Ibid., R-61.8 XXI 125f 1/4, S. Dale Perkins to W.S. Lloyd, 11 May 1967.

53. SAB, J.R. Barrie Papers, R-10 VII 53d, D. Steuart to R. Thatcher 19 May 1967.

54. SAB, W.S. Lloyd Papers, R-61.8 XXI 108–20, Brief report on the work of Ed Laliberte and Sidney Fineday in Meadow Lake Constituency, 1–12 Feb. 1967.

55. Prime Minister John Diefenbaker championed the rights of Indians and other minorities who were outside the British Canadian mainstream. He extended the federal vote to status Indians in 1960 and appointed the first Indian senator. In addition, his strong support of the monarchy appealed to some Indians who saw an intimate connection between the Crown and the treaties; see Denis Smith, *Rogue Tory: The Life and Legend of John G. Diefenbaker* (Toronto, 1995), 191. It would be natural for the provincial Progressive Conservatives to try to exploit Diefenbaker's personal popularity. However, Martin Pederson, the provincial leader from 1959 to 1969, also made a deliberate effort to cultivate the Indian vote. (Comments made by Martin Pederson at a conference held in Saskatoon, 6–8 March 1997, in honour of the fortieth anniversary of Diefenbaker's accession to power as prime minister of Canada.)

56. SAB, W.S. Lloyd Papers, R-61.8 XXI 108–20, memo headed 'Martin Semchuck [*sic*]— Meadow Lake'.

57. Ibid., 'The Indian and Métis Problem: The Shame of Our Nation in Centennial Year', election pamphlet, 1967, authorized by the Meadow Lake CCF.

58. I would like to thank research assistant Constance Maguire for her extensive and careful work in gathering, tabulating, and graphing poll results. Results are taken from the reports of the Chief Electoral Officer for Saskatchewan.

59. The voter turnout in Saskatchewan elections for the entire electorate, both urban and rural, is very similar to that of the sub-category of rural voters. In 1967, for example, 77.45% of all eligible voters cast a ballot compared with 79.31% of all eligible rural voters; Report of the Chief Electoral Officer for Saskatchewan, 1967.

60. Enumeration of voters on reserves may not always be correct and complete. Some chiefs discourage enumeration, and on some occasions the band list is used as the voters list, which means that band members who do not live on the reserve are counted as eligible to vote.

61 Gibbins, 'Electoral Reform', 154.

Native Feminism versus Aboriginal Nationalism

The Native Women's Association of Canada's Quest for Gender Equality, 1983–1994

Michael D. Behiels

The Native Women's Association of Canada (NWAC) gained national prominence in 1992 for its militant feminist approach to constitutional reform. During the 1991–2 'Canada Round' of constitutional negotiations culminating in the referendum of 26 October 1992 on the Charlottetown Consensus Report, NWAC fought hard to ensure that the Canadian Charter of Rights and Freedoms would apply to all self-governing First Nations. Its leaders contended that the Assembly of First Nations (AFN), representing status Indian communities, was a male-dominated organization that could not be trusted to defend and promote the gender-equality rights of Native women. When the Canadian government rejected the NWAC's demand to be represented at the constitutional talks, its leaders sought redress through the courts. Although the Federal Court of Appeal granted a declaratory remedy calling on the Mulroney government to provide the NWAC with equitable funding and a seat at the negotiating table, the government refused to comply, on the grounds that negotiations were completed.

In fact, however, constitutional negotiations were ongoing as bureaucrats and lawyers worked feverishly to transform the complex Charlottetown deal into an acceptable legal text. A determined NWAC applied unsuccessfully to the Federal Court for an injunction to halt the referendum. After Canadians had rejected the Charlottetown deal, the Mulroney government appealed the Federal Court's initial declaratory remedy to the Supreme Court of Canada, and in October 1994 the latter overruled that decision.

First, how does one account for the conflict between the NWAC and the AFN over the question of gender-equality rights versus Aboriginal collective rights? Second, on what grounds did the Supreme Court overturn the initial favourable decision of the Federal Court of Appeal?

The conflict between the NWAC and the AFN had its origins in the bitter and prolonged struggle over gender rights for Native women, a struggle that predated the 1982 Charter but was intensified by its implementation. In the course of this battle, non-status Native women disseminated a Native feminist ideology that contested the patriarchal nature of the Aboriginal neo-nationalism fuelling the

AFN's drive for the inherent right to self-government. NWAC leaders galvanized a great many Native women into action and made Canadians aware of their gender-rights concerns.[1] The NWAC's achievement of the 1983 constitutional amendment, s. 35(4) of the Constitution Act, 1982, guaranteeing 'aboriginal and treaty rights equally to man and female persons', and the 1985 amendment deleting the Indian Act's offending sex-discrimination clause, whereby Indian women lost their Indian status and band membership if they married non-Indian men, constituted important but partial victories. Indeed, both amendments proved unacceptable to the vast majority of Native communities, which refused to implement them. The NWAC sought redress via an additional constitutional sexual-equality provision that would help to change the sexist attitudes of Indian men towards Indian women.[2]

By 1992, the severe limitation of their gender-equality victories, coupled with the AFN's refusal to take their concerns seriously, had radicalized the NWAC. Its leaders adopted a militant position during constitutional negotiations to ensure that gender equality and the inherent right to Aboriginal self-government would be achieved simultaneously or not at all.[3] They were determined to prevent the 'malestream' AFN and governments from constitutionalizing the entrenched 'patriarchy' of Canadian society and the Aboriginal communities.[4] In fact, a close analysis reveals that what the AFN was determined to entrench was not patriarchy, but the ideology of Aboriginal nationalism. Its primary goal was to ensure recognition of the sovereignty of First Nations through entrenchment of the inherent right of self-government. Following months of intensive lobbying, the prime minister and provincial premiers agreed to an unprecedented comprehensive Aboriginal constitutional package guaranteeing, among other things, that Aboriginal collective rights would take precedence over the Charter. Aboriginal collective rights trumped Native feminism and gender rights because collective rights were deeply rooted in Aboriginal traditions, culture, and history. Yet this setback has not dissuaded the NWAC's leaders from pursuing their goal of gender equality within the emerging self-governing Aboriginal communities.

1 THE NWAC AND THE IDEOLOGY OF ABORIGINAL NATIONALISM

The NWAC concentrated on the social and economic issues facing Native women.[5] For strategic purposes, its leaders preferred to let a more militant organization, the National Committee on Indian Rights for Indian Women (IRIW), grapple with the controversial issue of sexual discrimination in the Indian Act. Meanwhile, the NWAC sought to maintain close ties with the National Indian Brotherhood (NIB), the AFN's predecessor. This strategy proved difficult to sustain following the defeat of the Lavell and Bedard cases in the Supreme Court and the refusal of the NIB to support the reinstatement of Indian women who married non-Indian men. The NWAC championed the cause of Indian rights for Indian women and over the next decade led the fight for gender equality despite the NIB's criticism of it as a hotbed of 'white' feminists.[6]

The AFN's neo-nationalism, formulated in response to the Trudeau government's 1969 White Paper advocating integration, was fuelled by the negotiations culminating in the 1982 Constitution Act, and by four unsuccessful Aboriginal constitutional conferences that followed. The principle of unextinguished Aboriginal sovereignty, which lay at the heart of the AFN's neo-nationalism, made it impossible for the federal and provincial governments to accept an undefined inherent right to self-government.[7] Despite the emerging conflict between gender-equality rights and Aboriginal collective rights, the NWAC's leaders supported the basic tenets of Aboriginal nationalism. In its 1980 *Declaration of Principles and Beliefs*, the NWAC asserted that 'the aboriginal peoples of this land belong to sovereign nations that have the right of self-determination.' This principle of unextinguished sovereignty, embodied in treaties, agreements, and conventions, incorporated Aboriginal peoples' right to determine their own form of government and citizenship. On the basis of this declared sovereignty, the NWAC served notice that it intended 'to relate to Confederation as equal partners with the Federal and Provincial Orders of Government.'[8]

NWAC's support for this Aboriginal neo-nationalism did not lessen the rising tension between it and the AFN. Nor did the hard-won victory for the recognition of Aboriginal and treaty rights in s. 35 of the 1982 Constitution Act mend any fences. The AFN denounced the addition of the term 'existing' to s. 35 because it would limit self-government by entrenching the prevailing band structure, which was controlled by Ottawa.[9] The NWAC opposed s. 35 because it did not state that Aboriginal and treaty rights applied equally to male and female persons and because s. 25 guaranteed that the Charter could not abrogate or derogate from those rights.[10]

Throughout this debacle, the NWAC pursued its own constitutional agenda. Although they embraced the concepts of Aboriginal sovereignty and the inherent right of self-government, NWAC leaders had a different definition of Aboriginal nationalism and society. Their goal was to ensure that achievement of any form of self-government would entail simultaneous recognition of sexual equality as a 'collective aboriginal right.'[11] In its 1980 *Declaration of Principles and Beliefs*, the NWAC stated that 'it is the fundamental right of Native Women to have access and participation in any decision-making process, and full protection of the law without discrimination based on sex or marital status.'[12] AFN leaders vigorously rejected the NWAC's dualist strategy and emphasized the paradox of its supporting the inherent right of self-government and Aboriginal citizenship while insisting on the imposition of a foreign charter of rights.

With the failure of the four Aboriginal conferences and the recognition of Quebec as a distinct society in the Meech Lake Accord of May 1987, AFN leaders became increasingly critical of the Charter. Constitutional adviser Mary Ellen Turpel, a law professor at Dalhousie University, believed that

Although there is no culture or system of beliefs shared by all Aboriginal peoples, the paradigm of rights based conceptually on the prototype of right of individual ownership of property is antithetical to the widely-shared understanding of creation and stewardship responsibilities of First Nations Peoples for the land, for Mother Earth.[13]

Following the defeat of the Meech Lake Accord, Turpel joined the AFN as its senior constitutional adviser. She advanced a thesis of 'cultural differences' according to which the Charter's Anglo-European rights paradigm was incompatible with the Aboriginal nations' social, cultural, political, judicial, and spiritual world-view. Aboriginal peoples, Turpel maintained, based social interaction on the communitarian principles of the Four Directions. In those teachings, life is structured on and regulated by four responsibilities—trust, kindness, sharing, and strength— incompatible with a principle of individual rights that was first propounded in an effort to protect private property during the British industrial revolution. Aboriginal peoples could not expect any true redress of their colonial status through the legal application of ss. 25 and 35 of the Constitution Act, which

> in a strange way bolsters the idea that Aboriginal peoples are sovereign and distinct (but entrapped) nations. The only effective way for Aboriginal peoples to survive and thrive as autonomous and fundamentally incommensurable communities was to attain the recognition of their right of self-determination, not a limiting right of self-government, under international as opposed to Canadian law.[14]

In response to this catch-22 predicament, NWAC leaders adopted a strategy of trying to reconcile Native feminism with a more traditional Aboriginal nationalism. In order to conform to the differentiation and segregation imperatives of the ideology of Aboriginal nationalism, initially NWAC distanced itself both from the more radical pan-Canadian women's movement and from Canadian society in general. It did so by adopting as its central vision the traditional Indian motherhood concept based on different but equal roles for Aboriginal men and women, the central role of women in the family and the transmission of culture, and the rejection of Western notions of femaleness that degraded Aboriginal women. This traditional Indian motherhood concept dovetailed with Aboriginal nationalism's drive to preserve and promote all traditional aspects of Aboriginal cultures and languages.[15]

NWAC leaders believed that the concept of traditional Indian motherhood, shared by Amerindians, Inuit, and Métis, could serve as a unifying ideology. Their strategy was to lay the blame for sexual discrimination on the systemic discrimination inherent in the Indian Act imposed upon Native peoples by a male-dominated Canadian society—rather than on the male-dominated leadership of the AFN. The NWAC hoped that its very conservative definition of sexual equality would be less threatening to the tradition-oriented Native leaders and their constituents in non-industrial, non-urban communities. In return, traditional Native men and women would embrace the Charter within their self-governing communities. In sum, any effective rehabilitation of Native communities under self-government required the restoration of Native women's traditional status, which included equality with men. For the NWAC the traditional motherhood concept fostered unity and political activism not only among Native women but within the larger Aboriginal movement.[16]

II THE TRADITIONAL INDIAN MOTHERHOOD STRATEGY IN ACTION

In the wake of the 1982 Constitution, NWAC's dualist strategy proved to be more of a liability than an asset. It failed to persuade the AFN to support the entrenchment of sexual-equality rights. AFN leaders rejected any NWAC representation in the four Aboriginal constitutional conferences, insisting that sexual equality was a matter to be resolved within future self-governing Aboriginal nations. Nevertheless, working through a high-powered lobby group called the National Committee on Aboriginal Rights, NWAC leaders managed to persuade the prime minister and the premiers to pass an amendment (ss.4) to s. 35 stating that existing Aboriginal and treaty rights 'are guaranteed equally to male and female persons'.[17] To the NWAC's dismay, its victory was undermined when the AFN insisted that 'membership or citizenship matters were the prerogative of the First Nations and could not be dictated by the federal government.'[18] NWAC leaders hoped to overcome this setback with a second amendment, one that would ensure comprehensive reinstatement of non-status women into their respective communities at the same time as those communities acquired self-government.[19]

In a parallel campaign to rid the Indian Act of its sexual discrimination clause, the NWAC unsuccessfully lobbied Parliament's Subcommittee on Indian Women and the Indian Act as well as its Special Committee on Indian Self-Government (the Penner Committee). Both committees recommended that the Indian bands should have jurisdiction over band membership in order 'to ensure cultural, linguistic and ethnic survival' of First Nations peoples.[20] Ironically, NWAC leaders had a closer rapport with the outgoing Trudeau Liberal government than with the committees. On 18 June 1984, the government introduced Bill C-47, proposing to abolish the discriminatory aspects of the Indian Act and to reinstate those women and children who had lost their Indian status and band membership. After a two-year waiting period, all those who regained their status, including children of mixed marriages to the second generation ('one-quarter Indian blood'), would also be granted band membership.[21]

Fearing unilateral federal government legislation on Aboriginal self-government as well as the Indian Act issues, on 17 May 1984 the AFN pressured NWAC leaders into accepting the 'Edmonton Consensus', according to which the AFN agreed to support the elimination of the discrimination clause and allow 'the reinstatement in the general band list of all generations who lost status or were never registered', in return for the NWAC's acceptance of the bands' jurisdiction over membership.[22] Although for different reasons, and despite some disagreement over the terms of their compromise, both the AFN and the NWAC opposed Bill C-47. The AFN objected that the Bill undermined self-government by denying band jurisdiction over membership and reinstatement and by providing too few financial and land resources to integrate the reinstatees. The NWAC, for its part, objected that the 'one-quarter blood line' rule was too restrictive because it discriminated against grandchildren of reinstated Indian women while granting status to the grandchildren of Indian men. It also objected to the termination of legal status for non-Indian women.[23] Bill C-47 was passed in the House of Commons, but the AFN and the NWAC managed—with the help of Senator Charlie Watt, a former Inuit spokesperson—to delay the Bill long enough in the Senate to ensure its demise when Parliament was dissolved for the federal election in September 1984.[24]

The newly elected prime minister, Brian Mulroney, chose a Toronto MP, David Crombie, as his Minister of Indian Affairs and Northern Development. Crombie had barely six months to remove the discriminatory clause from the Indian Act before the Charter, including the equality provisions in s. 15(1), came into effect in April 1985. Showing his distaste for the Indian Act, he supported the Penner Committee's recommendation of self-governing powers for First Nations communities. In December 1984 Crombie told the Standing Committee on Aboriginal Affairs that discrimination was 'an Indian issue' rather than 'a women's issue', and had to be resolved on the basis of a compromise between the bands' collective interests and the women's equality interest. Discussing Bill C-31—his replacement for the lapsed C-47—before the Standing Committee in March 1985, Crombie stated that it represented a compromise based on three policy objectives: 'First of all, the removal of discrimination from the *Indian Act*; secondly, recognition of band control of membership; and thirdly, the restoration of rights to those who lost them.'[25]

Faithful to these objectives, Bill C-31 proposed deleting the discriminatory clause 12(1)(b); restoring legal status and membership to Indian women; restoring legal status but not band membership for first-generation children; denying legal status and band membership for second-generation children; and separating legal status and band membership questions, the federal government controlling the former and the band controlling the latter. For Crombie, Bill C-31 was a practical application of the concept of self-government because it gave bands control over membership and legalized their right to control residency.[26] Bill C-31 became law on 28 June 1985 and was made retroactive to 17 April, the date when certain Charter provisions came into force.

The NWAC had given Bill C-31 a mixed review before the Standing Committee. It approved the Bill's reinstatement of legal status and band membership for the women discriminated against by clause 12(1)(b), and the granting of jurisdiction over membership to the bands. On the other hand, the NWAC maintained that C-31 was weaker than C-47 because it gave paramountcy to Native collective rights over women's equality rights. NWAC's president, Marilyn Kane, expressed strong concern that the Bill included new forms of discrimination: it treated women and their children under the second-generation cut-off rule differently from men and their children; it created different categories of First Nations people by separating legal status and band membership; and it included no mechanism to allow reinstated women to participate in the creation of band membership codes.[27]

Most of the NWAC's concerns about Bill C-31 materialized during the implementation process undertaken by the Department of Indian Affairs and Northern Development (DIAND). Ottawa underestimated the number of women and children who would claim reinstatement by some 22,000. By 1991, DIAND was scrambling hard to add nearly 80,000 people to the status Indian rolls, an increase of 16 per cent.[28] The NWAC monitored the implementation process and appeared before the Standing Committee to express its concerns. The Committee issued a series of detailed recommendations, but the government ignored them.[29]

From the NWAC's perspective, Bill C-31 proved to be a monumental disaster, a political nightmare masquerading as a masterpiece.[30] The separation of legal status from band membership and the granting of band control over membership codes allowed band councils and chiefs to express their long-standing opposition to Bill C-31 by denying band membership to virtually all the reinstatees and their children. Indeed, by 1990 barely 2 per cent of the 80,000 Indian women and children concerned had obtained band membership—even though the federal government has spent $295 million and approved a further spending of $2.3 billion until 1994.[31] Separation of legal status from band membership created new forms of discrimination. Status Indian women and children who are refused band membership lose access to a range of political, economic, social, cultural, health, and psychological rewards and benefits associated with being full-fledged residents of their respective communities. Even those women and children who regain both legal status and band membership can be denied residency on the reserve if the band lacks sufficient financial and land resources.[32]

The NWAC denounced these more insidious forms of discrimination. The 1985 Indian Act divided the Indian population into 'full' Indians under 6(1) and 'half' Indians under 6(2); the latter had status but no right to band membership, residency, and all the benefits they entailed. It also discriminated between male and female illegitimate children.[33] Even the AFN agreed with the NWAC that 'Discrimination based on sex still exists within the Indian Act, although it now rests in section 6 rather than in section 12(1)(b).' Furthermore, on some reserves a new lower class of returning C-31 reinstatees was created that bore the brunt of criticism for these communities' deep-seated problems.[34] Despite the strong support of the Canadian Advisory Council on the Status of Women's National Action Committee,[35] and the Standing Committee on Aboriginal Affairs, nothing was done to remove the offending provisions of the new Indian Act. Contrary to the NWAC's aspirations, the reforms did little to improve the poor and often violent lives of Indian women and their families.[36] Instead, new forms of sexual discrimination contributed to rising social and political tensions and hostility on the reserves.

III The 'Aboriginal Constitutional Package' versus the Charter, 1991–1992.

During the three-year debate over the ill-fated 1987 Meech Lake Constitutional Accord, the NWAC remained preoccupied with the implementation of the amended

Indian Act. Following the demise of Meech in 1990, the Mulroney government created the Royal Commission on Aboriginal Peoples to examine all aspects of the thorny issue of self-government. It then initiated the Canada Round of mega-constitutional negotiations by putting forward its own set of constitutional proposals.[37] After their disastrous experience with Bill C-31, NWAC leaders were determined to participate in the Canada Round. Its new president, Sharon McIvor, and constitutional coordinator, Teressa Nahanee, adopted a radical feminist discourse and aggressive lobbying strategy. Their goal was to prevent entrench-ment of the patriarchal power structure created and perpetuated by the Indian Act.

Nahanee warned that if Native women did not speak out and act decisively, they would lose what little they had gained in the 1980s. She encouraged them to get involved in the constitutional debate so as 'to ensure that there is a feminist perspective to self-government, to Native justice, to Native child care, to education and social development'. The only way to bring an end to patriarchy in their communities was to ensure that all Aboriginal citizens had access to a compre-hensive charter of rights. In the absence of a separate Aboriginal charter, enforce-able in Canadian courts, the only option was to ensure that the Canadian Charter applied to all Aboriginal self-governing arrangements. Self-government alone would not solve the endemic problems of poverty, unemployment, violence, and suicide facing Aboriginal people, nor could it empower women at the community level.[38] What the NWAC hoped to promote was a 'matriarchy/equalitarian' social system based on kinship, equality, and caring human relations at the community and family levels.[39]

The NWAC lobbied vigorously to become a full participant in constitutional nego-tiations. When its leaders took their case to the Special Joint Committee on a Renewed Canada in February 1992, Gail Stacey-Moore argued that 'under sections 15, 28, and 35(4) of the *Constitution Act, 1982*, aboriginal women are entitled to substantive equality rights'—rights that could be achieved only by eliminating patri-archy in the governments and societies of Canada and Aboriginal peoples alike.[40] Nevertheless, the Special Committee, without explanation, did not recommend that the NWAC be granted direct participation in the constitutional renewal process.[41]

In mid-April 1992 the AFN published the report of the First Nations' Circle on the Constitution, entitled *To The Source*. A dramatic expression of the AFN's increasingly militant Aboriginal nationalism, it declared that First Nations peoples considered themselves to be inherently self-governing, sovereign nations that had never relinquished that status since the moment they had negotiated treaties with Euro-Canadian authorities as their equals. Furthermore, the Aboriginal peoples formed distinct societies with unique languages, cultures, judicial systems, and biochemistry. Although the report's authors admitted that the Canadian Charter was 'perhaps the single most contentious issue among Aboriginal people concern-ing self-government', they condemned it as an imperialistic and assimilationist instrument preventing Aboriginal communities from returning to their values and rebuilding the equality of men and women along traditional lines. They recommended that gender equality be formally recognized in an Aboriginal charter once self-government had been achieved.[42]

NWAC leaders were furious that *To the Source* deliberately rejected women's perspectives, and argued that women had been underrepresented at the hearings.[43] Fearing that the government would accept the AFN's position on the Charter, the NWAC had already met with Constitutional Affairs Minister Joe Clark on 16 March 1992. Rejecting its request for a seat at the table, Clark merely promised to keep the NWAC informed of all developments relating to the Charter. Insult was added to injury when the government announced a cut of 25 per cent in funding for all Aboriginal organizations.[44] Frustrated, NWAC leaders decided to take their case for direct representation and funding to the Federal Court, Trial Division, on 18 March 1992. Justice Walsh dismissed the NWAC's request for a prohibition order against the government granting any further funds to the Aboriginal organizations until the NWAC had been granted direct representation and funding. On 16 April the NWAC filed Notice of Appeal in the Federal Court of Appeal and on 11 June 1992 it was granted a hearing.[45]

In the interim, the NWAC monitored closely the Multilateral Meetings on the Constitution chaired by Clark between 12 March and 7 July 1992. While maintaining that the inherent right to self-government was an existing treaty and Aboriginal right under s. 35, the NWAC declared to the Special Joint Committee that 'Recognizing the inherent right to self-government does not mean recognizing and blessing the patriarchy created in our communities by a foreign government.'[46] The granting of self-government should be conditional on the application of the Canadian Charter to all Aboriginal governments; the non-extension of s. 33, the notwithstanding clause, to Aboriginal governments; and the inclusion of NWAC leaders as equals in negotiations to determine all aspects of Aboriginal self-government.[47]

The NWAC rejected the AFN's claim that the Charter was a foreign, white man's document. Pointing to the Charter of the United Nations and the Universal Declaration on Human Rights, it argued that fundamental rights and freedoms were universal legal, political, and constitutional rights that attached to human beings because they are human beings. Canada, as a signatory to these documents, had a responsibility to ensure that newly created Aboriginal governments were denied access to s. 33, the Charter's override ('notwithstanding') clause.[48] Nevertheless, in June the NWAC was informed that Ottawa was thinking seriously of allowing Aboriginal governments to use s. 33 to override fundamental Charter rights. Denouncing Ottawa for ignoring its obligations to uphold the Charter and the Constitution under s. 32 and for giving preference to the male Aboriginal voices, the NWAC pleaded with Clark to support an amended s. 35(4) reinforcing, yet again, Aboriginal women's gender-equality rights—an amendment that had the full support of the Inuit Women's Association of Canada, as well as the National Action Committee on the Status of Women (NAC).[49] By 3 July the NWAC learned that the AFN was winning the battle to have the matter of Aboriginal 'gender rights' put over to the next round of constitutional negotiations. Furious,

NWAC leaders fired off letters to Clark, the premiers and the leaders of the Aboriginal organizations demanding that they confirm their support for gender equality for Aboriginal women.[50]

On 10 July, the Status Report of nine premiers and four Aboriginal leaders involved in the Multilateral Meetings on the Constitution was leaked to the press, confirming the NWAC's worst fears.[51] The Status Report proposed a comprehensive and complex series of amendments and political accords. This was a most dramatic turn of events. Frozen out of the Meech Lake Accord, the four national Aboriginal leaders had now negotiated a comprehensive 'Aboriginal constitution' within the Canadian Constitution. They would go on to convince Prime Minister Mulroney and all ten premiers, including a very sceptical Robert Bourassa, to accept a modified version of the 'Aboriginal constitution' in the Charlottetown Consensus Report of 28 August.[52] This largely unexpected achievement was welcomed by many specialists in Aboriginal affairs, one of whom referred to it as 'a magnificent coup for the aboriginal leaders'.[53] Another declared that the Accord 'represented a major departure from our colonial history and set us on the path of restoring the mutual respect and partnership that was the foundation of our initial relationship'.[54]

This achievement surpassed by far anything that Quebec had ever achieved. The 'Aboriginal constitution' sanctioned an extraordinary degree of institutional and constitutional separateness, granting the Aboriginal peoples a unique relationship with the Canadian state.[55] The Consensus Report proposed recognition of the 'inherent right to self-government within Canada' and the creation of a third order of government with authority over a wide range of responsibilities formally assigned to federal and provincial governments. Given that s. 35(2) of the Constitution defined the Aboriginal peoples of Canada as including Inuit and Métis as well as Indian people, this third order of government would embrace approximately one million Aboriginal people, on and off the reserves. Finally, the Consensus Report proposed the addition to the Constitution of a 'Canada clause' requiring that the entire document be interpreted in a manner consistent with Aboriginal peoples' inherent right of self-government.

At the heart of this 'Aboriginal constitution' was the proposal that Aboriginal governments have access to the Charter's 'notwithstanding clause', s. 33, which would exempt them from other Charter obligations and thereby allow the adoption of traditional non-elected modes of Aboriginal governance.[56] To further emphasize the separate status of Aboriginal communities, they were to be granted separate representation in the House of Commons and in an elected Senate, where Aboriginal senators would exercise a veto in Aboriginal matters. Finally, there were to be four new First Ministers' conferences on Aboriginal constitutional matters, beginning in 1996, in which Aboriginal representatives would have a veto over any amendments directly affecting their peoples. In sum, the national and provincial governments had made a quantum leap from their 1987 rejection of the concept of the inherent right of self-government. By 1992 they had sanctioned, with virtually no public input, a comprehensive recognition of Aboriginal nationalism and a third order of government, laid out in a separate 'Aboriginal constitution'. Reflecting the significance of what had been achieved, the leader of the Native Council of Canada (NCC), Ron George, declared that 'the acceptance of these provisions represents an historic breakthrough that is comparable to the bringing down of the Berlin Wall.'[57]

The NWAC had lost the battle to the AFN. Beginning in July, its leaders used every tactic and strategy to derail the constitutional process. 'The inherent right to self-government will be a license to discriminate against Indian women,' declared Sharon McIvor in a press conference;[58] the 'Constitutional "deal" wipes out the 20-year struggle by Native women for sexual equality rights in Canada.'[59] Gail Stacey-Moore addressed letters of protest to Ovide Mercredi, national chief of the AFN, and Ron George, president of the NCC, with copies to all federal and provincial leaders, and women's organizations. Together, she wrote, AFN and NCC leaders and the Canadian government had to share the shame for their decision 'to postpone constitutional entrenchment of sexual equality rights for Native women'. Their refusal to accept the NWAC's amended version of s. 35(4) put at serious risk the minor gains made by the Native women reinstated under Bill C-31. Politicians failed to understand 'the impact of constitutional recognition of the inherent right to self-government upon aboriginal women'. AFN and NCC leaders had no excuse because they were well aware that, under US self-governance legislation, 'American tribal governments have chosen to discriminate against their women on the basis of sex.' Native women's rights remained in jeopardy as long as the NWAC did not have direct representation in the constitutional process. NWAC leaders were determined to pursue their case before the Federal Court of Appeal.[60]

In late July, Clark confirmed that the matter of gender equality was put over to a future conference on Aboriginal matters.[61] Following the Quebec government's decision to join the constitutional talks in August 1992, the first ministers and Aboriginal leaders held several meetings to hammer out an agreement entitled the Consensus Report on the Constitution.[62] On 20 August, just days before their final deal, the Federal Court of Appeal rendered a decision in *Native Women's Assn. of Canada v. Canada* in favour of NWAC. Justice Mahoney ruled that the federal government had violated the Charter rights—s. 2(b) freedom of expression rights and s. 28 gender rights—of Aboriginal women by denying the NWAC appropriate funding during the policy-making stage of constitutional negotiations. The federal government, Justice Mahoney ruled, 'has accorded the advocates of male-dominated aboriginal self-governments a preferred position in the exercise of expressive activity'.[63]

The NWAC's legal counsel, Mary Eberts, declared that it had achieved a break-through: 'this was the first time a Canadian court has ruled on the right of women to free speech in a political process and it has recognized that this right has been infringed by Canada.' The NWAC was pleased that Justice Mahoney considered the NWAC 'a bona fide, established and recognized national voice of and for aboriginal women'.[64] Hoping to influence the negotiations, the NWAC and the NAC held a meeting in Ottawa on 24 August, attended by 150 leaders of women's organizations from across Canada. The general consensus was that the proposed constitutional amendments threatened both equality rights and social programs. Pressed for time, the NWAC pleaded once again with Clark, Mulroney, and the premiers 'not to postpone our equality any longer', and to invite the NWAC to take its rightful place at the Constitutional table in Charlottetown on 27 August 1992.[65]

The plea fell on deaf ears. Aware that negotiations over the legal text were ongoing, NWAC leaders denounced the postponement of gender-equality rights.[66] They were especially concerned with the wording of the section in the proposed 'Canada clause' defining the right of the Aboriginal peoples 'to promote their languages, cultures and traditions and to ensure the integrity of their societies' through their third-order governments,[67] since there was nothing in that clause to prevent Aboriginal governments from passing gender-discrimination laws. A passing reference to gender equality in the 'Canada Clause' could not be used to constrain Aboriginal government power because of the non-derogation written into s. 25. In fact, that section enhanced Aboriginal governments' powers by shielding the exercise or protection of Aboriginal languages, cultures, or traditions from the Charter; in effect, it granted non-elected Aboriginal governments the authority to override the Charter's guarantee of democratic rights. Adding insult to injury, the proposed new s. 35.7 on gender equality was drafted so as to ensure that it could be overridden by the 'Canada clause' which gave paramountcy to Aboriginal governments. Finally, the NWAC was not made one of the parties to the 'Aboriginal Political Accord' under which the framework for implementing the inherent right of self-government would be negotiated. To the NWAC's dismay, its exclusion was to be entrenched in law.[68]

Indeed, the NWAC had been routed. It was shocked to learn that several substantive changes, including the deletion of s. 35(4)—the 1983 amendment guaranteeing gender equality—had been made to the Charlottetown deal during the referendum campaign. Sharon McIvor questioned the federal government's 'utter disrespect' for the judicial system and argued that the very integrity of the referendum process was violated because 'the Charlottetown agreement is no longer the basis of the referendum day vote.'[69] NWAC leaders moved quickly to obtain a series of injunctions from the Federal Court, Trial Division, to have the referendum halted. Their application, on 15 September 1992, for an injunction had been stalled by Mr Justice Pinard at the request of the AFN. On 16 October Mr Justice Barry Strayer of the Trial Division dismissed the NWAC's request for a series of injunctions, including the one to halt the referendum. Justice Strayer argued that there was no legal basis for the proposition that the government of Canada was obliged to invite the NWAC into the constitutional renewal process on the same basis as the other Aboriginal organizations. He chided NWAC for abusing the courts.[70]

The judicial approach had proven futile, and the referendum was fast approaching. The NWAC focused its limited resources on the 'no' campaign in hopes of defeating the Charlottetown deal. NWAC leaders were not to be disappointed. An informal pan-Canadian coalition of 'no' groups had emerged to defeat the constitutional deal. To the great surprise and dismay of the 'yes' forces led by Mulroney, some premiers, the Aboriginal leaders, and business interests, nearly 55 per cent of Canadians voted down the Charlottetown deal. In fact, 62 per cent of on-reserve voting status Indians rejected the Aboriginal package for a wide variety of reasons.[71] The NWAC leaders were pleased, to say the least, with the outcome of the referendum; however, it did not end their legal struggles.

IV THE NWAC, PATRIARCHY, AND THE SUPREME COURT, 1994

Much to NWAC's dismay, it found itself before the Supreme Court when, on 11 March 1993, the federal government was granted the right to appeal the Federal Court of Appeal's decision of 20 August 1992. The case was heard on 4 March 1994, and the Court rendered a unanimous decision in favour of the federal government on 27 October. The crux of the Supreme Court's decision, delivered by Hon. Mr Justice Sopinka, was that the NWAC had not provided substantiating evidence to prove its claim that Aboriginal women's freedom of expression right had been violated because the NWAC was not directly represented in the constitutional negotiations.[72]

In its factum, the federal government argued that the Federal Court of Appeal's decision was politically motivated, and it questioned the court's right to convert the proceedings from an application seeking an order of prohibition to one providing a declaratory judgement against the federal government.[73] Ottawa argued that the NWAC had not provided evidence to prove either that it alone represented Aboriginal women or that government funding of the Aboriginal 'parallel process' had 'restricted the freedom of expression of *all* Aboriginal Women, not just the Respondents'.[74] The NWAC's case, according to the government, was based on mere conjecture as to what might happen during the Multilateral Meetings on the Constitution, rather than on any actual violation of the law. The NWAC had provided no evidence to prove that its freedom of expression, s. 2(b), was in any way impaired by the federal government's actions in choosing its advisers or in deciding what groups to fund. The Charter did not impose a positive obligation on Ottawa to listen to or provide funding for all points of view.[75]

NWAC leaders, believing the federal government's case was vindictive, argued that the appeal should be dismissed as moot, since the constitutional negotiations were now defunct. On the Charter issues of freedom of expression, s. 2(b), and equality rights, s. 15(1), as well as the existing Aboriginal and treaty rights of Aboriginal peoples, s. 35(1) of the Constitution, the NWAC argued that 'if the Government chooses to fund and to offer a voice to anti-*Charter* male-led Aboriginal organisations, it is under a constitutional obligation to do so justly, equitably, and in accordance with the *Charter*: the Government must also fund and offer a voice to pro-*Charter* female Aboriginal organisations.'[76]

Drawing on feminist critiques of patriarchy, the NWAC maintained that governments had a positive obligation to promote women's expressive activity if women were ever to break the hegemony exercised by men over the political and legal systems since time immemorial. Indeed, even the Supreme Court had recognized that the achievement of real equality required the courts and the legislators to move beyond the Aristotelian concept of formal equality. The effect, if not the intention, of the federal government's granting direct funding and participation to the four Aboriginal organizations was to deny freedom of expression to the NWAC, a bona fide representative of an important constituency, Aboriginal women.[77]

Turning its attention to s. 15(1), the NWAC maintained that Aboriginal women comprised a 'discreet and insular minority' with recognized legal rights. The Courts ruled in several instances 'that under-inclusive legislation violates section 15(1) of the *Charter*, affirming the positive right to equal benefit of the law'.[78] Finally, the NWAC applied its traditional motherhood concept to s. 35(1) of the Charter, which recognized and affirmed 'the existing aboriginal and treaty rights of the aboriginal peoples of Canada'. Aboriginal women retained a historical, non-extinguished Aboriginal right to participate in decision-making processes affecting Aboriginal society. The federal government had a fiduciary responsibility, affirmed by the Supreme Court in 1984, to fund and include in its constitutional negotiations a women-led group representing women. While the government had stated that the four Aboriginal organizations represented men and women, it had never 'determined that they *actually* represented the views and interests of both women and men in any real sense'.[79] In sum, the Federal Court of Appeal was both procedurally and substantively correct in granting the NWAC a remedy in the form of a declaratory statement.

The Supreme Court decided in favour of the Canadian government. On procedural matters, the Court rejected the NWAC's argument that the appeal was moot, since the appellant revealed that there was an outstanding action against the Crown for $6 million, based on the Court of Appeal's decision.[80] Turning to substantive matters, Justice Sopinka had to determine whether the government of Canada violated the freedom of expression of Aboriginal women represented by NWAC, as guaranteed by s. 2(b) taken together with s. 28 of the Charter. He agreed with the Appeal Court that the ability to communicate constitutional views to the governments at the conferences was 'unquestionably an expressive activity within the scope of s. 2(b) of the Charter'. But, since there was no evidence to indicate that the government had acted consciously or unconsciously to limit freedom of expression, it was necessary for the NWAC to prove the discriminatory effect of the government's decisions on funding and participation. In order to support the NWAC's claim that the Charter requires the government of Canada to provide the NWAC with a particular 'forum for expression equal to that of the other Aboriginal organisations', according to Sopinka, it was necessary that s. 2(b) of the Charter entail a positive duty on the part of governments.[81]

The traditional interpretation was that the 'freedom of expression contained in s. 2(b) prohibits gags, but does not compel the distribution of megaphones'. Yet in *Haig v. Canada* ([1993] 2 S.C.R. 995) the Supreme Court ruled that in certain cases positive governmental action, of a non-discriminatory nature, *was* required on occasion to make a fundamental freedom meaningful.[82] In applying *Haig* to the NWAC's claim of a right to a platform equal to that of the other Aboriginal organizations, Justice Sopinka concluded that 'there was no evidence to support the contention that the funded groups were less representative of the viewpoint of women with respect to the constitution.'[83] In reviewing the extensive evidence submitted on the histories of the NWAC, the AFN, the NCC, and the ITC, he concurred with the AFN that none of the funded groups advocated 'male-dominated Aboriginal self-governments', and that these groups represented the views of Aboriginal women just as much as the NWAC did. Finally, the evidence revealed that the NWAC had had ample opportunity to express its views on the necessity of the Charter to the government, both directly and through the four Aboriginal organizations.[84]

Finally, Justice Sopinka addressed the s. 15 Charter argument that, considering *Haig*, was more appropriate to the NWAC's argument. He concluded that, as with ss. 2(b) and 28, there was no evidentiary basis for the argument that the Canadian government had violated the NWAC's equality rights under s. 15. He also concurred with the Court of Appeal that the Aboriginal people of Canada do not derive their right to participate in constitutional discussions from 'any existing Aboriginal or treaty right' protected under s. 35, and that therefore the gender-equality provisions of s. 35(4) did not apply. Despite these concurrences with the Federal Court of Appeal, Justice Sopinka set aside its declaratory remedy for lack of evidence.[85]

CONCLUSION

NWAC leaders were dismayed but not surprised by the Supreme Court's decision. They issued a terse, if hollow, statement declaring that NWAC remained the bone fide representative of Aboriginal women.[86] Clearly the court had not been convinced by the NWAC's history of its protracted struggle for gender equality under the Indian Act. The unrelenting opposition of the AFN, acquiesced in by the Canadian government, to any changes in the Indian Act before the inherent right to self-government was entrenched in the Constitution had not been sufficient to convince the court that the AFN's primary objective was to entrench Aboriginal patriarchy. Neither had the Court been moved by the blatantly discriminatory impact of Bill C-31.[87] NWAC leaders had failed to present solid evidence challenging the AFN's counter-arguments, evidence that could withstand the close legal scrutiny of what they perceived to be a male-dominated Supreme Court.

A comprehensive analysis of the desperate socio-economic and psychological conditions faced by most of the Native women on reserves—a situation that was aggravated by the decision of the vast majority of band councils to reject band membership for 98 per cent of the recently reinstated women and children— might have persuaded the Court of the NWAC's claim that the AFN was too patriarchal to defend and promote adequately the interests of Native women. By uncritically supporting the concept of the inherent right of self-government grounded in an unfettered pre-contact Aboriginal sovereignty and a modern

Aboriginal nationalism, the NWAC had undermined its campaign for the recognition of gender-equality rights. For its gender-equality campaign to have succeeded, its leaders would have had to develop a constructive critique of the powerful collectivist ideology of Aboriginal nationalism. In the absence of such a critique, the Court found no evidence to support the feminist 'patriarchy' argument that the NWAC alone, and not the male-dominated Aboriginal organizations, could truly have represented the interests of Aboriginal women at the constitutional bargaining table.

Indeed, the Supreme Court had accepted the AFN's argument that self-government must be achieved before Aboriginal communities could decide how and to what extent social, cultural, and spiritual values would influence their choice among forms of governance. Apparently the NWAC, in its uncritical support for Aboriginal nationalism and the goals of self-government and separate Aboriginal citizenship, had failed to understand that male Aboriginal leaders would not— indeed could not—accept any competing ideology. In fact, the NWAC ideology of Aboriginal feminism, championing an individualistic gender equality, was perceived by the large majority of on-reserve Indians, men and women alike, as totally foreign to their cultures, past and present.

For the NWAC to have been more successful in its campaign for gender equality, its leaders would have had to come to grips with an increasingly militant Aboriginal nationalism and its proponents' remarkable achievement of a separate 'Aboriginal Constitution'. Most Aboriginal women, especially those who had regained their Indian status under Bill C-31, considered themselves Canadian citizens. NWAC's experience with Bill C-31 should have convinced its leaders that their constituents stood to gain very little from the establishment of sovereign Aboriginal governments empowered to determine the scope and nature of a separate Aboriginal citizenship. By the time they realized the fundamental conflict between Aboriginal nationalism and their Native feminism, their failure to obtain a seat at the negotiating table made it impossible to counter the arguments of the AFN and its constitutional adviser, Mary Ellen Turpel. Fortunately for the NWAC and Native women generally, a majority of Canadian citizens, for a wide variety of reasons, ensured that the Charlottetown deal never did become part of the country's Constitution. Nor has the NWAC given up its fight. Since 1992, with diligence and dedication, it has continued to pursue a Charter education campaign with the goal of achieving the social, economic, and cultural reforms so essential to gender equality.

NOTES

The author would like to thank Professors Alan C. Cairns and Olive P. Dickason for their very helpful critiques of the original version of this paper. Any flaws that remain are those of the author.

1. Liliane E. Kronsenbrink-Gelissen, *Sexual Equality as an Aboriginal Right: The Native Women's Association of Canada and the Constitutional Process on Aboriginal Matters,*

1982–1987 (Saarbrücken/Fort Lauderdale, 1991); Sally Weaver, 'First Nations Women and Government Policy, 1970–1992: Discrimination and Conflict', in S. Burt, L. Doce, and L. Dorney, eds, *Changing Patterns: Women in Canada* (Toronto, 1993), Chapter 3.

2. Kronsenbrink-Gelissen, *Sexual Equality as an Aboriginal Right*, 212.

3. Liliane E. Kronsenbrink-Gelissen, 'The Canadian Constitution, the Charter, and Aboriginal Women's Rights: Conflicts and Dilemmas', *International Journal of Canadian Studies* 7/8 (Spring–Fall 1993), 207–24.

4. Joyce Green, 'Constitutionalising the Patriarchy: Aboriginal Women and Aboriginal Government', *Constitutional Forum Constitutionnel* 4, 4 (Summer 1993), 110–20.

5. NWAC, *A Voice of Many Nations: Native Women* (Ottawa, 1985), 1–5.

6. Krosenbrink-Gelissen, *Sexual Equality as an Aboriginal Right*, 88–9; Weaver, 'First Nations Women and Government Policy', 100–4.

7. Bryan Schwartz, *First Principles, Second Thoughts: Aboriginal Peoples, Constitutional Reform and Canadian Statecraft* (Montreal, 1986); Radha Jhappan, 'Inherency, Three Nations and Collective Rights: the Evolution of Aboriginal Constitutional Discourse from 1982 to the Charlottetown Accord', *International Journal of Canadian Studies* 7/8 (Spring–Fall 1993), 232–8.

8. NWAC, *Declaration of Principles and Beliefs* (Ottawa, 1985) reprinted in Krosenbrink-Gelissen, *Sexual Equality as an Aboriginal Right*, 144–5.

9. Douglas Sanders, 'Prior Claims: An Aboriginal People in the Constitution of Canada', in *Canda and the New Constitution: The Unfinished Agenda*, vol. 1, ed. Stanley M. Beck and Ivan Bernier (Montreal, 1983), 233.

10. Krosenbrink-Gelissen, *Sexual Equality as an Aboriginal Right*, 101–2, 109–10; for ss. 25 and 35(1) see Canada, Department of Justice, *A Consolidation of the Constitution Acts 1867 to 1982* (Ottawa, 1989).

11. Krosenbrink-Gelissen, *Sexual Equality as an Aboriginal Right*, 115. In fact, the NWAC was supposed to have access to the $105,000 grant assigned to the AFN by the Secretary of State for research on sexual-equality rights, but it received less than a quarter of the amount.

12. NWAC, *Declaration of Principles and Beliefs*.

13. Mary Ellen Turpel, 'Aboriginal Peoples and the Canadian *Charter*: Interpretive Monopolies, Cultural Differences', *Canadian Human Rights Yearbook, 1989–90* (Ottawa, 1990), 29.

14. Ibid., 39–45; quote at 39.

15. Krosenbrink-Gelissen, *Sexual Equality as an Aboriginal Right*, 127.

16. Ibid., 129–40.

17. Department of Justice, *A Consolidation of the Constitution Acts 1867–1982* (Ottawa, 1989).

18. Joan Holmes, *Bill C-31 Equality or Disparity? The Effects of the New Indian Act on Native Women* (Ottawa, 1987), 6.

19. NWAC, *Contemporary Issues: Information Kit* (Ottawa, 1984), 54.

20. House of Commons, Standing Committee on Indian Affairs and Northern Development, Report of the Subcommittee on Indian Women and the Indian Act, *Minutes of Proceedings and Evidence* no. 58 (20 Sept. 1982); House of Commons, *Report*

of the Special Committee on Indian Self-Government in Canada (Ottawa, 1983), 54.

21. House of Commons, Bill C-47: An Act to Amend the Indian Act (Ottawa, 1984).

22. Weaver, 'First Nations Women and Government Policy', 113–14.

23. AFN/NWAC, 'Press Statement on Bill C-47, 22/6/84'.

24. Krosenbrink-Gelissen, Sexual Equality as an Aboriginal Right, 164.

25. Standing Committee on Indian Affairs and Northern Development, Minutes of Proceedings and Evidence no. 3, 4 Dec. 1984, 7 and 12; and no. 12, March 1985, 7.

26. SCIAND, Minutes of Proceedings and Evidence no. 12, 7 March 1985, 13–14, 8.

27. NWAC, 'Presentation on Bill C-31', in SCIAND, Minutes of Proceedings and Evidence no. 28, 28 March 1985, 56–70.

28. DIAND's Indian Registration System, Ottawa, 3 June 1992 cited in Weaver, 'First Nations Women and Government Policy, 1970–1992', 122–3.

29. NWAC, 'Presentation on Bill C-31', in House of Commons, SCAAND, Minutes of Proceedings and Evidence no. 33, 23 Feb. 1988, 4–13; Cf. SCAAND, C-31: Fifth Report, House of Commons Standing Committee on Aboriginal Affairs and Northern Development, Minutes of Proceedings and Evidence, no. 46, 28 June 1988.

30. Cited in Krosenbrink-Gelissen, Sexual Equality as an Aboriginal Right, 208.

31. Weaver, 'First Nations Women and Government Policy', 139, n. 168.

32. DIAND, Summary Report: Impacts of the 1985 Amendments to the Indian Act (Bill C-31), 15, 26–50.

33. NWAC, 'Presentation on Bill C-31', 4–13. Holmes, Bill C-31 Equality or Disparity?, 36–7.

34. AFN et al., Correcting Historic Wrongs?, 1, 27, 31.

35. NAC, 'Presentation on Bill C-31', House of Commons, SCAAND, Minutes of Proceedings and Evidence, no. 35, 1 March 1988, 4–12.

36. NWAC, An Aboriginal Charter of Rights and Freedoms: A Discussion Paper (Ottawa, 1991); Linda M. Gerber, 'Multiple Jeopardy: A Socio-Economic Comparison of Men and Women among the Indian, Metis and Inuit Peoples of Canada', Canadian Ethnic Studies 22, 3 (1990), 69–84.

37. Peter Russell, Constitutional Odyssey: Can Canadians be a Sovereign People? (Toronto, 1992), 169–70.

38. Teressa Nahanee, Native Women and the Constitution of Canada (Ottawa, 1991), 1–7, 10–11.

39. Ibid., 9–10; NWAC, Matriarchy and the Canadian Charter (Ottawa, 1992), 1–7.

40. NWAC, 'Presentation to the Special Joint Committee of the Senate and of the House of Commons on a Renewed Canada', Minutes of Proceedings and Evidence, 61, 6 Feb. 1992, 46–7; known as the Beaudoin-Dobbie Committee.

41. 'Report of the Special Joint Committee of the Senate and of the House of Commons on a Renewed Canada', Minutes of Proceedings and Evidence, 66, 28 Feb. 1992.

42. First Nations Circle on the Constitution, To the Source: Commissioners' Report, Assembly of First Nations (Ottawa, 1992), 1, 4, 15–18, 37–8, 59–63, 78; quote at 61.

43. 'Press release, April 28, 1992', in NWAC, Native Women and the 1992 Constitution (Ottawa, 1992).

44. 'Notes of March 16 Meeting with Joe Clark', in NWAC, *Native Women and the 1992 Constitution*.

45. NWAC, 'Press Release, April 24, 1992', and 'Press Release, June 11, 1992', in NWAC, *Native Women and the 1992 Constitution*.

46. NWAC, 'Presentation to the Special Joint Committee on a Renewed Canada', 52.

47. Ibid., 57.

48. Ibid., 53–6. NWAC, *Statement on the Canada Package* (Ottawa, 1992), 8–13; Teressa Nahanee, 'Aboriginal Women and the Constitution', in NWAC, *Native Women and the 1992 Constitution*.

49. 'Memorandum to the Right Hon. Joe Clark, June 8, 1992'; 'Aboriginal Women Seek equality in Constitutional Talks, Press Release, June 9', in NWAC, *Native Women and the 1992 Constitution*.

50. 'Letter to the Right Hon. Joe Clark, July 3, 1992'; Memorandum to Premiers and Government Leaders of NWT and YT, July 8, 1992; 'Letters to Mr. Joe Clark, Mr. Ron George, and Mr. Ovide Mercredi, July 8, 1992', in NWAC, *Native Women the 1992 Constitution*.

51. MMC, 'Status Report of the Multilateral Meetings on the Constitution, Rolling Draft as at June 11, 1992—End of Day'; sections reprinted in *The Globe and Mail* (10 June 1992).

52. Consult the 'Consensus Report of the Constitution', Charlottetown, 28 Aug. 1992, Final Text; and the 'Draft Legal Text', 9 Oct. 1992, in *The Charlottetown Accord, the Referendum, and the Future of Canada*, ed. K. McRoberts and P. Monahan (Toronto, 1993), 279–361.

53. Radja Jhappan, 'Aboriginal Self-Government', *Canadian Forum* (October 1992), 15–16.

54. Brad Morse, 'Indigenous Peoples in Quebec and Canada', *Literary Review of Canada* I, 10 (October 1992), 12.

55. Alan C. Cairns 'The Charlottetown Accord: Multinational Canada v. Federalism', in *Constitutional Predicament. Canada after the Referendum of 1992*, ed. Curtis Cook (Montreal/Kingston, 1994), 40.

56. 'Draft Legal Text', s. 24.

57. Ron George, 'Saying NO to a Generation of Hope', *Network* 2, 8 (October 1992), 3.

58. Sharon McIvor and Judy Rebick, 'Native Women will be the Hardest Hit by the New Constitutional Deal', NWAC Press Conference, 15 July 1992, in NWAC, *Native Women and the 1992 Constitution*.

59. 'Press release, The Native Women's Association of Canada Rejects Constitutional "Deal"', July 10, 1992', in NWAC, *Native Women and the 1992 Constitution*.

60. 'Letter to Ron George, July 10, 1992'; 'Letter to Ovide Mercredi, July 10, 1992', in NWAC, *Native Women and the 1992 Constitution*.

61. 'Joe Clark to Ms. Gail Stacey-Moore, July 28, 1992', in NWAC, *Native Women and the 1992 Constitution*.

62. McRoberts and Monahan, eds, *The Charlottetown Accord . . .*, 279–314.

63. *Native Women's Assn. of Canada v. Canada* (C.A) [1992] 3 F.C. at 196 and 212.

64. 'Press Release. Trial Division Erred. Canada Violated Charter Rights of Aboriginal Women in Constitutional Process, August 24, 1992', in NWAC, *Native Women and the 1992 Constitution*.

65. 'Gail Stacey-Moore to the Right Hon. Joe Clark, August 24, 1992'; 'Gail Stacey-Moore to the Right Hon. Brian Mulroney, August 26, 1992', in NWAC, *Native Women and the 1992 Constitution.*

66. Gail Stacey-Moore, 'Press Statement on the occasion of the First Ministers' Conference, Charlottetown, P.E.I, August 27, 1992'; 'Press Release. Gender Equality Postponed to 1996', in NWAC, *Native Women and the 1992 Constitution.*

67. Draft Legal Text, 9 Oct. 1992, in *The Charlottetown Accord . . .*, 315.

68. NWAC, 'Examples of Impediments to the Equality of Aboriginal Women in the Self-Government Package', in NWAC, *Native Women and the 1992 Constitution.*

69. 'Press Release. The NWAC Says Latest Changes to Aboriginal Package are Shocking, October 8, 1992', in NWAC, *Native Women and the 1992 Constitution.*

70. 'Appellants' Memorandum of Fact and Law', in the Federal Court of Appeal in the matter of *The Referendum Act* between the NWAC and Her Majesty the Queen, 4 Nov. 1992. This document presents a comprehensive analysis of the NWAC's critique of the Charlottetown Consensus Report and the Draft Legal Text.

71. Radha Jhappan, 'Inherency, Three Nations and Collective Rights', 225.

72. *Native Women's Association of Canada v. Canada* (Ont.) (23253), 27 Oct. 1994.

73. 'Factum of the Appellant', in the Supreme Court of Canada (On Appeal from the Federal Court of Appeal) between *Her Majesty the Queen and Native Women's Association of Canada, Gail Stacey-Moore and Sharon McIvor*, No. 23253, 9–12, 15–22.

74. Ibid., 12–15; quote 12.

75. Ibid., 22–8.

76. 'Factum of the Respondents Gail Stacey-Moore and Sharon McIvor', in the Supreme Court of Canada (On Appeal from the Federal Court of Appeal) between *Her Majesty the Queen and Native Women's Association of Canada, Gail Stacey-Moore and Sharon McIvor*, No. 23253, 22–31; quote at 31.

77. Ibid., 32–5.

78. Ibid., 35.

79. Ibid., 38.

80. *Native Women's Association of Canada v. Canada* (Ont.) (23253), 27 Oct. 1994, 16–19.

81. Ibid., 20–3; quotes at 21 and 23.

82. Ibid., 23–7.

83. Ibid., 30.

84. Ibid., 30–7.

85. Ibid., 38–9.

86. NWAC, 'Press Release, October 27, 1994'.

87. 'Factum of the Respondents Gail Stacey-Moore and Sharon McIvor in the Supreme Court of Canada', 1–22.

Appendix A

Ramsay Cook: A Bibliography

Books

The Politics of John W. Dafoe and the Free Press. Toronto: University of Toronto Press, 1963. Reprinted 1971.

With John C. Ricker and John T. Saywell. *Canada: A Modern Study.* Toronto: Clarke, Irwin, 1964. New editions, 1971, 1977.

Canada and the French-Canadian Question. Toronto: Macmillan, 1966. Second edition, 1986.

Le sphinx parle français: Un Canadien anglais s'interroge sur le problème québécois. Translated by François Rinfret. Montréal: HMH, 1966.

Provincial Autonomy, Minority Rights and the Compact Theory, 1867–1921. Ottawa: Queen's Printer, 1969.

L'autonomie provinciale, les droits des minorités et la théorie du pacte, 1867–1921. Ottawa: Queen's Printer, 1969.

The Maple Leaf Forever: Essays on Nationalism and Politics in Canada. Toronto: Macmillan, 1971. Revised edition, 1977. Japanese edition, 1984. Second revised edition, 1986.

With Craig R. Brown. *Canada, 1896–1921: A Nation Transformed.* Toronto: McClelland and Stewart, 1974.

With John Ricker and John Saywell. *Le Canada: Étude moderne.* Toronto: Clarke, Irwin, 1981.

The Regenerators: Social Criticism in Late Victorian English Canada. Toronto: University of Toronto Press, 1985.

Canada, Québec and the Uses of Nationalism. Toronto: McClelland and Stewart, 1986. Japanese edition, 1994. New edition, 1995.

The Voyages of Jacques Cartier. Toronto: University of Toronto Press, 1993.

1492 and All That: Making a Garden out of a Wilderness. North York, Ont.: Robarts Centre for Canadian Studies, 1993.

Articles

'Church, Schools, and Politics in Manitoba, 1903–12'. *Canadian Historical Review* XXXIX, 1 (March 1958), 1–23.

'J.W. Dafoe at the Imperial Conference, 1923'. *Canadian Historical Review* XLI, 1 (March 1960), 19–40.

'John W. Dafoe: Conservative Progressive'. *Canadian Historical Association/Société historique du Canada, Report/Rapport* (1961), 75–85.

'A Canadian Account of the 1926 Imperial Conference'. *Journal of Commonwealth Political Studies* III (1965), 50–63.

'L'historien et le nationalisme'. *Cité libre* XV, 73 (January 1965), 5–14.

'Some French-Canadian Interpretations of the British Conquest: Une quatrième domi-nante de la pensée canadienne-française'. *Canadian Historical Association/Société his-torique du Canada, Report/Rapport* (1966), 70–83.

'French-Canadian Interpretations of Canadian History'. *Journal of Canadian Studies/Revue d'études canadiennes* 2, 2 (May 1967), 3–17.

'Canadian Historical Writing'. In *Scholarship in Canada, 1967: Achievement and Outlook*, edited by Robert H. Hubbard, 71–81. Toronto: University of Toronto Press, 1968.

'The Coming of the Quiet Revolution'. Introduction to *Approaches to Politics*, by Pierre Elliott Trudeau, translated by I.M. Owen, 7–18. Toronto: Oxford University Press, 1970.

'Stephen Leacock and the Age of Plutocracy, 1903–1921'. In *Character and Circumstance: Essays in Honour of Donald Grant Creighton*, edited by John Moir, 163–81. Toronto: Macmillan, 1970.

'The Uses of Literature in Cultural History'. *English Quarterly* IV, 3 (Fall 1971), 25–30.

'Canadian Freedom in Wartime, 1939–1945'. In *His Own Man: Essays in Honour of Arthur Reginald Marsden Lower*, edited by W.H. Heick and Roger Graham, 37–54. Montreal: McGill-Queen's University Press, 1974.

'History: The Invertebrate Social Science'. In *Perspectives on the Social Sciences in Canada*, edited by T.N. Guinsberg and G.L. Reuber, 129–49. Toronto: University of Toronto Press, 1974.

'Introduction' to *The Woman Suffrage Movement in Canada*, by Catherine L. Cleverdon. Second edition, vi–xxvi. Toronto: University of Toronto Press, 1974.

'Landscape Painting and National Feeling in Canada'. *Historical Reflections* 1, 2 (Winter 1974), 263–83.

'Francis Marion Beynon and the Crisis of Christian Reformism'. In *The West and the Nation: Essays in Honour of W.L. Morton*, edited by Carl Berger and Ramsay Cook, 187–208. Toronto: McClelland and Stewart, 1976.

'The Professor and the Prophet of Unrest'. *Transactions of the Royal Society of Canada/Mémoires de la Société royale du Canada* Fourth Series/Quatrième série, 13 (1975), 227–50.

'Cultural Nationalism in Canada: An Historical Perspective'. In *Canadian Cultural Nationalism: The Fourth Lester B. Pearson Conference on the Canadian-United States Relationship*, edited by Janice L. Murray, 15–44. New York: New York University Press, 1977.

'The Golden Age of Canadian Historical Writing'. *Historical Reflections* V, 1 (Summer 1977), 137–49.

'Henry George and the Progress of Canadian Poverty'. *Canadian Historical Association, Historical Papers/Communications historiques* (1977), 142–57.

'Nationalist Ideologies in Canada'. *Options* (1978), 81–98.

'"The Ragged Reformer": J.W. Bengough: The Caricaturist as Social Critic'. In *A Political Art: Essays and Images in Honour of George Woodcock*, edited by William H. New, 53–81. Vancouver: University of British Columbia Press, 1978.

'Neglected Pine Blasters'. *Canadian Literature* 81 (Summer 1979), 95–108.

'The Paradox of Quebec'. In *Entering the Eighties: Canada in Crisis*, edited by R. Kenneth Carty and W. Peter Ward, 46–59. Toronto: Oxford University Press, 1980.

'William Kurelek: A Prairie Boy's Visions'. *Journal of Ukrainian Studies* 5, 1 (Spring 1980), 33–48.

'The Social and Economic Frontier in North America'. In *The Frontier in History: North America and Southern Africa Compared*, edited by Howard Lamar and Leonard Thompson, 175–208. New Haven: Yale University Press, 1981.

'French Canada'. In *A Reader's Guide to Canadian History. 2: Confederation to the Present*, edited by Jack L. Granatstein and Paul Stevens, 249–76. Toronto: University of Toronto Press, 1982.

'Has the Quiet Revolution Finally Ended?' *Queen's Quarterly* (Summer 1983), 330–42.

'The Making of Canadian Working Class History'. *Historical Reflections/Réflexions historiques* 19, 1 (Spring 1983), 115–25.

'Quebec and the New Constitution'. *Annual Review of Canadian Studies* (Japan) 4 (1983), 110–29.

'Imagining a North American Garden: Some Parallels and Differences in Canadian and American Culture'. *Canadian Literature* 103 (Winter 1984), 10–26. Japanese translation, 1990.

'Spiritualism, Science of the Earthly Paradise'. *Canadian Historical Review* LXV, 1 (March 1984), 4–27.

'Au Diable avec le Goupillon et la Tuque: The Quiet Revolution and the New Nationalism'. *Zeitschrift der Gesellschaft fur Kanada-Studien* 5, 2, 9 (1985), 15–30.

'Alice in Meechland or the Concept of Quebec as a "Distinct Society"'. *Queen's Quarterly* 94, 4 (Winter 1987), 817–28. Reprinted in *Navigating Meech Lake: The 1987 Constitutional Accord*, edited by Clive Thomson. Kingston, Ont.: Institute of Intergovernmental Relations, Queen's University, 1988. Also reprinted in *The Meech Lake Primer: Conflicting Views of the 1987 Constitutional Accord*, edited by Michael D. Behiels. Ottawa: University of Ottawa Press, 1989.

'The Triumph and Trials of Materialism, 1900–1945'. In *The Illustrated History of Canada*, edited by Craig Brown, 375–466. Toronto: Lester and Orpen Dennys, 1987. Spanish edition, 1994.

'The Evolution of Nationalism in Quebec'. *British Journal of Canadian Studies* 4, 2 (1989), 306–17.

'Multiculturalism and Canadian History'. (In Japanese). In *Ethnicity and Multiculturalism in Canada*, edited by Ayabe, Tsuneo, 3–23. Tokyo: Tsoui Shobu, 1989.

'Remembrance of Things Past'. Introduction to *With WK in the Workshop: A Memoir of William Kurelek*, by Brian Dedora, 7–9. Stratford, Ont.: Aya Press/Mercury Press, 1989.

'Robertson Davies'. In *Conversations with Robertson Davies*, edited by J. Madison Davis, 125–35. Jackson: University Press of Mississippi, 1989.

'Triomphe et revers du matérialisme, 1900–1945'. In *Histoire générale du Canada*, edited by Craig Brown and Paul-André Linteau, 449–566. Montreal: Boréal, 1989.

'Ambiguous Heritage: Wesley College and the Social Gospel Re-considered'. *Manitoba History* 19 (Spring 1990), 2–11.

'Cabbages Not Kings: Towards an Ecological Interpretation of Early Canadian History'. *Journal of Canadian Studies* 25, 4 (Winter 1990–91), 5–16.

'"I never thought I could be as proud" . . . The Trudeau-Lévesque Debate'. In *Towards a Just Society: The Trudeau Years*, edited by Thomas S. Axworthy and Pierre Elliott Trudeau, 342–56. Markham, Ont.: Viking, 1990.

'"Je n'ai jamais pensé que je pourrais être aussi fier" . . .' Le débat Trudeau-Lévesque'. In *Les Années Trudeau: La recherche d'une société juste*, edited by Thomas S. Axworthy and Pierre Elliott Trudeau, 363–77. Montreal: Le Jour, 1990.

'Language Policy and the Glossophagic State'. In *Language and the State: The Law and Politics of Identity/Langue et État. Droit, politique et identité*, edited by David Schneiderman, 73–81. Cowansville, Que.: Éditions Y. Blais, 1991.

'Social, Economic and Political Relations between Ontario and Quebec during the Last Twenty Years'. In *Twenty Years of Quebec-Ontario Relations 1969–1989/Vingt ans de relations entre le Québec et l'Ontario (1969–1989)*, edited by Sylvie Arend and Gail Cuthbert Brandt, 37–40. Toronto: Éditions du Gref, Collège Glendon, Université York, 1991.

'Towards the Discovery of Canadian Cultural History'. In *Art and Architecture in Canada: A Bibliography and Guide to the Literature*, by Loren R. Lerner and Mary F. Williamson, xi–xvii. Toronto: University of Toronto Press, 1991.

'T. Phillips Thompson'. In *Dictionary of Literary Biography: Canadian Writers before 1890*, edited by W.H. New, 327–9. Detroit, London: Gale Research Co., 1990.

'William Allen Pringle'. *Dictionary of Canadian Biography*. Vol. XII, *1891–1900*, 864–8. Toronto: University of Toronto Press, 1990.

'George Weston Wrigley'. *Dictionary of Canadian Biography*. Vol. XIII, *1901–1910*, 1111–15. Toronto: University of Toronto Press, 1994.

'Goldwin Smith'. *Dictionary of Canadian Biography*. Vol. XIII, *1901–1910*, 968–74. Toronto: University of Toronto Press, 1994.

'Nation, Identity, Rights: Reflections on W.L. Morton's Canadian Identity'. *Journal of Canadian Studies/Revue d'études canadiennes* 29, 2 (Summer 1994), 5–18.

'Sauvaiges, Indians, Aboriginals, AmerIndians, Native People, First Nations'. In *Welfare States in Trouble: Historical Perspectives on Canada and Sweden*, edited by Jack L. Granatstein and Sune Akerman, 27–38. North York, Ont.: Swedish–Canadian Academic Foundation, 1994.

'Afterword'. In *Perpetual Motion*, by Graeme Gibson, 267–71. Toronto: New Canadian Library, 1997.

'A Quebec Doctor and His Bishop'. *The Beaver* 77, 3 (June/July 1997), 17–23.

'Salvation, Sociology and Secularism'. *Literary Review of Canada* 6, 1 (April 1997).

'Still Life in a Landscape'. In *Tim Zuck: Paintings and Drawings*, edited by Ramsay Cook, 31–8. Canmore, Alta: Altitude Publishing, 1997.

'Albert Laurendeau'. *Dictionary of Canadian Biography*. Vol. XIV, *1911–1920*, 608–10. Toronto: University of Toronto Press, 1998.

'Edward Joseph Kylie'. *Dictionary of Canadian Biography*. Vol. XIV, *1911–1920*, 565–6. Toronto: University of Toronto Press, 1998.

'The Outsider as Insider: Cornelius Krieghoff's Art of Describing'. In *Krieghoff: Images of Canada*, edited by Dennis Reid, 144–63. Vancouver: Douglas and McIntyre, 1999.

'Postscript—Kenneth W. McNaught: Untypical Professor'. In *Conscience and History: A Memoir*, by Kenneth McNaught. Toronto: University of Toronto Press, 1999), 195–7.

'L'observateur empathique: l'art de dépeindre de Cornelius Krieghoff'. In *Krieghoff: Images du Canada*, edited by Dennis Reid. Quebec: Éditions du Trécarré, forthcoming.

EDITED BOOKS

The Dafoe-Sifton Correspondence, 1919–1927. Altona, Man.: D.W. Friesen, 1966.

Confederation. Canadian Historical Readings, 3. Toronto: University of Toronto Press, 1967.

Politics of Discontent. Canadian Historical Readings, 4. Toronto: University of Toronto Press, 1967.

Constitutionalism and Nationalism in Lower Canada. Canadian Historical Readings, 5. Toronto: University of Toronto Press, 1969.

French-Canadian Nationalism: An Anthology. Toronto: Macmillan, 1969.

With Eleanor Cook. *The Craft of History*. Toronto: CBC Publications, 1973.

With Michael Behiels. *The Essential Laurendeau*. Vancouver: Copp Clark, 1976.

With Carl Berger. *The West and the Nation: Essays in Honour of W.L. Morton*. Toronto: McClelland and Stewart, 1976.

With Wendy Mitchinson. *The Proper Sphere: Woman's Place in Canadian Society*. Toronto: Oxford University Press, 1976.

Dictionary of Canadian Biography. Vol. XIII, *1901–1910*. Toronto: University of Toronto Press, 1994.

Tim Zuck: Paintings and Drawings. Canmore, Alta: Altitude Publishing, 1997.

Dictionary of Canadian Biography. Vol. XIV, *1911–1920*. Toronto: University of Toronto Press, 1998.

EXECUTIVE EDITOR, CANADIAN CENTENARY SERIES, 1983–1988

John H. Thompson, *Canada 1922–1939: Decades of Discord*. Toronto: McClelland and Stewart, 1985.

Jack L. Granatstein, *Canada 1957–1967: The Years of Uncertainty and Innovation*. Toronto: McClelland and Stewart, 1986.

Dale Miquelon, *New France 1701–1744: 'A Supplement to Europe'*. Toronto: McClelland and Stewart, 1987.

Morris Zaslow, *The Northward Expansion of Canada, 1914–1967*. Toronto: McClelland and Stewart, 1988.

Appendix B
Ph.D. Thesis Supervisions

UNIVERSITY OF TORONTO

1966 Paul Stevens, 'Laurier and the Liberal Party in Ontario, 1887–1911'.

1968 Joseph Levitt, 'The Social Program of the Nationalists of Quebec 1900–1914'.

1968 Paul E. Crunican, 'The Manitoba School Question and Canadian Federal Politics, 1890–1896: A Study in Church-State Relations'.

1969 Michiel Horn, 'The League for Social Reconstruction: Socialism and Nationalism in Canada, 1931–1945'.

1969 Peter Oliver, 'The Making of a Provincial Premier: Howard Ferguson and Ontario Politics: 1870–1923'.

1971 David Bercuson, 'Labour in Winnipeg: The Great War and the General Strike' (supervision with K.W. McNaught).

1972 Christopher Armstrong, 'The Politics of Federalism: Ontario's Relations with the Federal Government, 1896–1941'.

1972 Michael Bliss, '"A Living Profit": Studies in the Social History of Canadian Business, 1883–1911'.

1973 Arthur I. Silver, 'Quebec and the French-Speaking Minorities, 1864–1917'.

1974 Patricia Grace Dirks, 'The Origins of the Union Nationale'.

1974 Peter Rider, 'The Imperial Munitions Board and its Relationship to Government, Business, and Labour, 1914–1920'.

1974 Mary Vipond, 'National Consciousness in English-speaking Canada in the 1920's: Seven Studies'.

YORK UNIVERSITY

1973 Ann Davis, 'An Apprehended Vision: The Philosophy of the Group of Seven'.

1973 Howard D. Palmer, 'Nativism and Ethnic Tolerance in Alberta, 1920–1972'.

1975 Douglas Francis, 'Frank H. Underhill: Canadian Intellectual'.

1975 Phyllis M. Sherrin, 'The World, the Flesh and the Devil: The Crusade of Lionel Groulx, 1878–1967'.

1976 Gail Cuthbert Brandt, '"J'y suis, j'y reste": The French Canadians of Sudbury, 1883–1913' (supervision with Michael Katz).

1976 Matthew Robert Bray, 'The Canadian Patriotic Response to the Great War'.

1976 Thomas Donald Traves, 'Security and Enterprise: Canadian Manufacturers and the State, 1917–1931' (supervision with J.T. Saywell).

1977 Ralph Heintzman, 'The Struggle for Life: The French Daily Press of Montreal and the Problem of Economic Growth in the Age of Laurier, 1896–1911'.

1978 Michael D. Behiels, 'Prelude to Quebec's "Quiet Revolution": The Re-Emergence of Liberalism and the Rise of Neo-nationalism, 1940–1960'.

1979 James M. Pitsula, 'The Relief of Poverty in Toronto, 1880–1930'.

1982 Barry G. Ferguson, 'The New Political Economy and Canadian Liberal Democratic Thought: Queen's University, 1890–1925'.

1982 Brian J. Fraser, '"The Christianization of Our Civilization": Presbyterian Reformers and the Defence of a Protestant Canada, 1875–1914'.

1982 Leila Mitchell-McKee, 'Voluntary Youth Organizations in Toronto, 1880–1930'.

1987 Ruth Compton Brouwer, 'Canadian Women and the Foreign Missionary Movement: A Case Study of Presbyterian Women's Involvement at the Home Base and in Central India, 1876–1914'.

1987 Patrice Dutil, 'The Politics of Liberal Progressivism in Quebec: Godfroy Langlois and the Liberal Party, 1889–1914'.

1988 Franca Iacovetta, 'Working-Class Immigrants: Southern Italians in Post-War Toronto, 1946–1965'.

1991 John David Thomas, '"A Pure and Popular Character": Case Studies in the Development of the Methodist "Organizational" Church, 1884–1925'.

1992 Sylvie Beaudreau, 'Quebec and the Problem of French Canadian Emigration to the United States, 1840–1896'.

1992 Norman J. Knowles, 'Inventing the Loyalists: The Ontario Loyalist Tradition and the Creation of a Usable Past, 1784–1924'.

1994 José António Brandão, '"Your fyre shall burn no more": Iroquois Policy Towards New France and her Native Allies to 1701'.

1994 Marcel Martel, 'Les relations entre le Québec et les francophones de l'Ontario: de la survivance aux "dead ducks" (1937–1969)'.

1995 Chad Reimer, 'The Making of British Columbia History: Historical Writing and Institutions, 1784–1958'.

1996 Alvyn Austin, 'Pilgrims and Strangers: The China Inland Mission in Britain, Canada, the United States and China, 1865–1900'.

* Molly Ungar, 'The Last Ulysseans: Culture and Modernism in Montreal, 1930–1939'.

* Xavier Gélinas, 'La droite intellectuelle québécoise et la Révolution tranquille (1956–1966)'.

* In process.

Appendix C

Contributors

Michael D. Behiels, Professor of Canadian History, University of Ottawa. Among his publications are *Canada at the Crossroads*, with J. Keshen (Toronto, 1999), *Futures and Identities: Aboriginal People in Canada/Avenirs et identités: Les peuples autochtones au Canada* (Montreal, 1999), *Canada: Its Regions and People*, with K.S. Matthew (New Delhi, India, 1998), *Quebec and the Question of Immigration: From Ethnocentrism to Ethnopluralism, 1900–1985* (Ottawa, 1991), *The Meech Lake Primer: Conflicting Views of the 1987 Constitutional Accord* (Ottawa, 1989), *Prelude to Quebec's Quiet Revolution: Liberalism Versus Neo-Nationalism, 1945–1960* (Montreal and Kingston, 1985); and *The Essential Laurendeau*, with Ramsay Cook (Toronto, 1976).

José António Brandão, Assistant Professor of History, University of Western Michigan. Among his publications are *'Your fyre shall burn no more': Iroquois Policy Towards New France and its Native Allies to 1701* (Lincoln, 1997), 'Introduction' , with C.E. Heidenreich, to *The Jesuits in North America*, by Francis Parkman (Lincoln, 1997), and 'The Treaties of 1701: the Triumph of Iroquois Diplomacy', with W.A. Starna, *Ethnohistory* 43, 2 (Spring, 1996), 209–44.

Gail Cuthbert Brandt, Principal and Vice Chancellor, Renison College, University of Waterloo. A co-author of *Canadian Women: A History*, with Alison Prentice, Paula Bourne, Beth Light, Wendy Mitchinson, and Naomi Black 2nd edn (Toronto, 1996) and *Canadian Women: A Reader*, with Wendy Mitchinson, Paula Bourne, Alison Prentice, Beth Light, and Naomi Black (Toronto, 1996), she has also published articles in such journals as *The Canadian Historical Review*, *Social History/Histoire sociale*, and *The Journal of the Canadian Historical Association/Revue de la Société historique du Canada*.

Ruth Compton Brouwer, Associate Professor of Canadian History, King's College University of Western Ontario. Among her publications are *New Women for God: Canadian Presbyterian Women and India Missions, 1876–1914* (Toronto, 1990); 'A Disgrace to "Christian Canada": Protestant Foreign Missionary Concerns about the Treatment of South Asians in Canada, 1907–1940', in *A Nation of Immigrants: Women, Workers, and Communities in Canada*, edited by Franca Iacovetta (Toronto, 1998); and 'Books for Africans: Margaret Wrong and the Gendering of African Writing, 1929–1963', *International Journal of African Historical Studies* 31, 1 (1998), 53–71.

Ann Davis, Director, Nickle Arts Museum, University of Calgary. Among her publications are *The Logic of Ecstasy: Canadian Mystical Painting, 1920–1940* (Toronto, 1992) and *Somewhere Waiting: The Life and Art of Christiane Pflug* (Toronto, 1991), winner of the UBC Prize for Canadian Biography.

Patrice A. Dutil, founder and first editor of the *Literary Review of Canada*; Director of Research, Institute of Public Administration of Canada. Among his publications are *L'Avocat du diable: Godfroy Langlois et la politique du libéralisme progressiste à l'époque de Laurier* (Montreal, 1996), and *Devil's Advocate: Godfroy Langlois and the Politics of Liberal Progressivism in Laurier's Quebec* (Montreal, 1994).

R. Douglas Francis, Professor of Canadian History, University of Calgary. The author of *Images of the West: Responses to the Canadian Prairies* (Saskatoon, 1989) and *Frank H. Underhill: Intellectual Provocateur* (Toronto, 1986), he is also co-author of *Origins: Canadian History to Confederation*, with Richard Jones and Donald B. Smith 3rd edn (Toronto, 1996), and *Destinies: Canadian History Since Confederation*, with R. Jones and D.B. Smith 4th edn (Toronto, 2000), and co-editor of *The Regions and People of Canada: A Historical Approach*, with Kazuo Kimuara (Tokyo, 1993).

Brian J. Fraser, St Andrew's Hall and Vancouver School of Theology, University of British Columbia. Among his publications are *Church, College and Clergy: A History of Theological Education at Knox College, Toronto, 1844–1994* (Montreal and Kingston, 1995), and *The Social Uplifters: Presbyterian Progressives and the Social Gospel in Canada, 1875–1915* (Waterloo, 1988).

Michiel Horn, Professor of Canadian History, Glendon College, York University. Among his publications are *Academic Freedom in Canada: A History* (Toronto, 1999), *Becoming Canadian: Memoirs of an Invisible Immigrant* (Toronto, 1997), *The Great Depression of the 1930s in Canada* (Ottawa, 1984), and *The League for Social Reconstruction. Intellectual Origins of the Democratic Left in Canada, 1930–1942* (Toronto, 1980).

Norman Knowles, Professor of History, St Mary's College, Calgary. Among his publications are *Inventing the Loyalists: the Ontario Loyalist Tradition and the Creation of Usable Pasts* (Toronto, 1997), 'The Rector and the Deaconess: Women, the Church and Sexual Harassment in Early Twentieth-Century English Canada, A Case Study', *Journal of Canadian Studies* 31 (Summer 1996), 97–114, and 'A Selective Dependence: Vancouver's Japanese Community and Church of England Missions, 1903–1942', *Journal of the Canadian Church Historical Society* XXXVIII (April 1996), 53–76.

Marcel Martel, Assistant Professor of History, York University. Among his publications are *French Canada: An Account of its Creation and Break-Up, 1850–1967* (Ottawa, 1998), *Le Canada français: Récit de sa formulation et de son éclatement, 1850–1967* (Ottawa, 1998), *Le deuil d'un pays imaginé: Rêves, luttes et déroute du Canada français: Les relations entre le Québec et la francophonie canadienne, 1867–1975* (Ottawa, 1997).

James Pitsula, Professor of Canadian History, University of Regina. The co-author, with Ken Rasmussen, of *Privatizing a Province: The New Right in Saskatchewan* (Vancouver, 1990), and author of 'The Social and Economic Impact of Saskatchewan Crown Corporations', in *Public Enterprise in an Era of Change*, edited by John Allan (Regina, 1998), 'The Thatcher Government in Saskatchewan and the Revival of Métis Nationalism, 1964–1977', *Great Plains Quarterly* 17, 3/4 (1997), '"Educational Paternalism Versus Autonomy": Contradictions in the Relationship between the Saskatchewan Government and the Federation of Saskatchewan Indians, 1958–1964', *Prairie Forum* 22, 1 (1997), 'The Thatcher Government in Saskatchewan and Treaty Indians, 1964–1971: The Quiet Revolution', *Saskatchewan History* 48, 1 (1996), he is also the editor of *New Perspectives on the Canadian Constitutional Debate* (Regina, 1997).

Peter E. Rider, Atlantic Provinces Historian and Curator, Canadian Museum of Civilization. He edited and contributed to a newly released CD-ROM entitled

Balancing the Scales: Canada's East Coast Fisheries (St John's, 1999). Other works include '"A Blot Upon the Fair Fame of Our Island": The Scandal at the Charlottetown Lunatic Asylum, 1874', *Island Magazine* 39 (Spring 1996), 3–9, and 'Canadian Toys: Historical Research and Museum Interpretations', with David R. Gray, in *Childhood - Playtime?*, edited by Michael H. Faber, 66–81 (Cologne, 1994).

Phyllis M. Senese, Assistant Professor of Canadian History, University of Victoria. Among her publications are 'Antisemitic Dreyfusards: Antisemitism and the Growth of Rights Consciousness in Western Europe and North America', in *Religious Conscience, the State, and the Law* , edited by John McLaren and Harold Coward (New York, 1999) and various articles in journals including *Canadian Historical Review, Journal of the University of Ottawa*, and *B.C. History*.

Mary Vipond, Professor of Canadian History, Concordia University. Among her publications are *Listening In: The First Decade of Canadian Broadcasting, 1922–1932* (Montreal, 1992) and *The Mass Media in Canada* (Toronto, 1989; rev. edn, 1992).